The Battle of the Ayatollahs in Iran

The Battle of the Ayatollahs in Iran

The United States, Foreign Policy, and Political Rivalry since 1979

Alex Vatanka

I.B. TAURIS
LONDON • NEW YORK • OXFORD • NEW DELHI • SYDNEY

I.B. TAURIS
Bloomsbury Publishing Plc
50 Bedford Square, London, WC1B 3DP, UK
1385 Broadway, New York, NY 10018, USA
29 Earlsfort Terrace, Dublin 2, Ireland

BLOOMSBURY, I.B. TAURIS and the I.B. Tauris logo are trademarks of
Bloomsbury Publishing Plc

First published in Great Britain 2021

Copyright © Alex Vatanka, 2021

Alex Vatanka has asserted his right under the Copyright, Designs and Patents Act, 1988, to be identified as Author of this work.

For legal purposes the Acknowledgments on p. xi constitute an extension of this copyright page.

Cover design by Alice Marwick
Cover images: [left] Khamenei © Stringer/Getty Images; [right] Rafsanjani © Iranian Supreme Leader Press Office/Handout/Anadolu Agency/Getty Images

All rights reserved. No part of this publication may be reproduced or transmitted in any form or by any means, electronic or mechanical, including photocopying, recording, or any information storage or retrieval system, without prior permission in writing from the publishers.

Bloomsbury Publishing Plc does not have any control over, or responsibility for, any third-party websites referred to or in this book. All internet addresses given in this book were correct at the time of going to press. The author and publisher regret any inconvenience caused if addresses have changed or sites have ceased to exist, but can accept no responsibility for any such changes.

A catalogue record for this book is available from the British Library.

A catalog record for this book is available from the Library of Congress.

ISBN: HB: 978-1-8386-0154-6
PB: 978-1-8386-0155-3
ePDF: 978-0-7556-0006-9
eBook: 978-0-7556-0005-2

Typeset by Newgen KnowledgeWorks Pvt. Ltd., Chennai, India

To find out more about our authors and books visit www.bloomsbury.com and sign up for our newsletters.

Alex Vatanka is a senior fellow and the director of the Iran Program at the Middle East Institute in Washington, DC. He specializes in Middle Eastern regional security affairs with a particular focus on Iran. He was formerly a senior analyst at Jane's Information Group in London. Born in Tehran, he holds a BA in Politics (Sheffield University, UK), and an MA in International Relations (Essex University, UK), and is fluent in Persian and Danish.

His first book was *Iran and Pakistan: Security, Diplomacy, and American Influence* (2015). He has also written chapters for a number of books, including *Authoritarianism Goes Global* (2016), *Handbook on Contemporary Pakistan* (2017), *Russia in the Middle East* (2018), *Winning the Battle, Losing the War: Addressing the Drivers Fueling Armed Non-state Actors and Extremist Groups* (2020), and *Global, Regional and Local Dynamics in the Yemen Crisis* (2020). Follow him @AlexVatanka.

This book is dedicated to my wife, Heidi; my children, Martin and Kathrin; my parents; and my sister, Buyuk, Shaheen, and Sharareh.

Contents

List of Illustrations	x
Acknowledgments	xi
Note to the Reader	xii
Prologue	xiii
1 (1978–9)—Khamenei and Rafsanjani: Waiting for Khomeini to Return from Paris	1
2 (1979–80)—Bloodletting between the Reds and Islamists to Seizing the US Embassy	17
3 (1980–1)—The Second Purge: Chaos at Home and War Abroad	33
4 (1981–5)—Rafsanjani and Khamenei Sharpen Knives for Each Other	49
5 (1985–9)—The Beginning of the End of Khomeini	61
6 (1989–93)—Khamenei: The Second Supreme Leader	81
7 (1993–7)—Dithering in Tehran as the Cold War Ends	99
8 (1997–2005)—The Era of Reformist Hope: Rafsanjani under Fire; Khamenei Hits Back	129
9 (2005–13)—The Election of Mahmoud Ahmadinejad	151
10 (2013–Present)—The Coming of President Hassan Rouhani	173
Epilogue	197
Notes	205
Select Bibliography	229
Index	231

Illustrations

Maps

1	Iran	127
2	Iran and its neighbors	127

Figures

1	The Shah of Iran and Henry Kissinger	119
2	Ayatollah Khomeini in exile in Paris in 1978	120
3	Iranian women as militant Islamism's first victims	121
4	Israel, the first foreign target of Khomeinists	121
5	Rafsanjani, the Speaker of Majles (parliament), President Khamenei, and Prime Minister Mir Hossein Mousavi (standing next to Khamenei)	122
6	Rafsanjani and Ahmad Khomeini as gatekeepers to the old ayatollah	122
7	Rafsanjani and Khamenei	123
8	Mohammad Khatami	124
9	Mahmoud Ahmadinejad	124
10	US Secretary of State John Kerry meets with Iranian Foreign Minister Javad Zarif in Vienna	125
11	Rouhani, Putin, and Xi	125
12	Khamenei and the Revolutionary Guards	126

Acknowledgments

To the outside world, the policy-making process in Tehran is a maze of peculiar concepts and baffling practices. The idea behind writing this book was to put human faces on this labyrinth as the trajectory of Iranian foreign policy is retraced from that momentous year of 1979. That the Islamic Republic's foreign policy is a whirlwind of sorts meant that writing this book was oftentimes a contest of catching up with events and forever emerging new revelations. As in any book project, I benefited greatly from the support of a long list of individuals. Colleagues at my intellectual home, the Middle East Institute (MEI) in Washington, DC, deserve particular appreciation. Paul Salem, Gerald Feierstein, Kate Seelye, and many other colleagues at MEI provided institutional and intellectual support. I also like to thank the MEI board and Chairman Richard A. Clarke, for keeping the flag flying as MEI celebrates its 75th anniversary in 2021. Ross Harrison's review of the draft manuscript and suggestions were invaluable as is his friendship. Glen Howard, Michael Ryan, and other friends at Jamestown Foundation always stood by ready whenever I came asking for counsel. Over the course of the research and writing of this book, I benefited greatly from the help of many research assistants, young talented and probing men and women who aided me in this effort. They all have my sincerest thanks. At Bloomsbury, I am thankful to Dr. Sophie Rudland as my senior editor who guided me through the publication process at every turn. I also like to thank Smith Richardson Foundation for their continued support for my work. Finally, I thank my family and the many friends who encouraged me from the moment I put pen to paper for this book.

Alexandria, Virginia

Note to the Reader

This book is a work of nonfiction. All events and individuals that you will read about in the following pages are based on real-life personalities and historic events. The book consults declassified government documents, personal memoirs, and hundreds of hours of primary and secondary interviews with former officials and participants in the events described. The research for this book also draws on the wealth of historical data available online in various formats, including archival audio, television footage, and Persian-language journalistic investigations conducted outside of Iran by the large Iranian community of researchers. The recounting of the political lives of Ali Khamenei and Akbar Hashemi Rafsanjani is only one way to unpack the evolution of the Islamic Republic, but it is arguably one of the most compelling approaches.

Prologue

At about six o'clock in the afternoon of January 8, 2017, the body of an 82-year-old man was found floating in a swimming pool in Saad Abad Palace in upscale north Tehran. The sprawling complex had once belonged to the late Shah of Iran. The dead man in the pool, Iran's former president Akbar Hashemi Rafsanjani, had been one of the principal architects of a popular rebellion that toppled the Shah's rule down exactly thirty-eight years earlier. By late evening that day, Tehran was inundated with rumors that Rafsanjani had been drowned in an act of political assassination. Few were willing to believe the official explanation that he had had a heart attack and subsequently expired in the water.

For about half of Iran's 82 million people, who had been born after the Islamists took over in 1979, Rafsanjani was a larger-than-life figure whose demise could surely not come in such an inconspicuous manner. In a country with a lively social media scene with millions of daily users, thanks not least to suffocating rules governing the press, different popular versions of what had transpired in that pool soon went viral on platforms such as Facebook, Twitter, Telegram, and Instagram. The rumor mill has been in full swing ever since. Months later, Rafsanjani's family claimed that his body had at the time of death contained ten times more radioactive elements than normal. This only further fueled speculation and Rafsanjani's final moments are an ongoing riddle.

Rumors aside, Rafsanjani's hard-line rivals inside the Iranian regime had long openly shown their antipathy toward him. He was fiercely independent and as president put Iran on a more pragmatic, less ideological foreign policy after the deadly Iran–Iraq war. They feared the old man's wily ways and believed he sought to engineer further big political changes in Iran. Once an uncontested Islamist, he had by the end of his life morphed into the godfather of the so-called moderate faction inside the regime. This is a powerful network that ostensibly includes Iran's current president, Hassan Rouhani.

At the other end of the spectrum, the hardliners, clustered mostly around Supreme Leader Ayatollah Ali Khamenei, had over the previous decade come to consider Rafsanjani as a compromiser, a *noufoozi* (secret agent) of the West. Rafsanjani had openly argued for cutting deals with the West—and the United States in particular, which the hard-line faction in Tehran viewed as opening the floodgates to Iran's transformation. Such transformation, the hardliners have always dreaded, can only come at their expense. Hence, they had—at least on paper—a strong motive to silence Rafsanjani.

§

No two other men than Khamenei and Rafsanjani have shaped Iran as much since the world's first modern-day theocracy, the Islamic Republic, was born in 1979. Known in Iran as the twin pillars of the revolution, the origins of the Khamenei–Rafsanjani friendship, collaboration, and the subsequent fallout and rivalry is to this day shrouded in much mystery. What is clear, though, is that the turbulent path of the Khamenei–Rafsanjani relationship not only shaped the course of the Islamic Republic at home but was a significant contributing factor in the many twists and turns of Tehran's interactions with the outside world.

They began as like-minded revolutionaries, but over the years, life, events, and a quest to hang on to maximum power gradually separated them to a point where each man personified distinct worldviews. By the end of his life, Rafsanjani had become the torchbearer of political moderation in both domestic and foreign policy realms even though his critics until the end painted him as an unscrupulous con artist. On the other hand, Khamenei has by design or accident changed into the patron of the most reactionary of interest groups inside the regime.

Khamenei is today the supreme leader of Iran, a role that his followers dubiously claim make him God's representative on earth and the cardinal guide for the Shia Muslim faithful that seek to be on the righteous path. The vanguard of the theocratic system, Khamenei likes to portray himself as a no-nonsense Islamist revolutionary that strives to bring about Godly inspired utopia on earth. But his decades-long track record as the captain of the regime is peppered with the choices of a mortal; fluke turn of events; a knack for micro-management but—to be fair—also responsiveness to the call of compromise when it has knocked on his door. He was a surprise choice to ascend to the pinnacle of power in 1989, but his dexterity to navigate the maze and cutthroat politicking of the regime while maintaining an upper hand is nothing short of an extraordinary feat.

Rafsanjani was commonly branded as the Islamic Republic's prototype of Niccolo Machiavelli. To his enemies, he was the "red eminence," a disapproving reference to Cardinal Richelieu, Louis XIII's unscrupulous cleric-turned-prime minister. What is beyond doubt, however, is that no other politician in the history of the Islamic Republic tasted both the fruits of victory and the agonies of defeat as much as Rafsanjani. He was a militant Islamist trailblazer that in his youth truly believed in building a society around the tenets of Islam. Over the course of his life, though, he came very close to publicly admitting that the separation of religion from everyday governance has undeniable virtues in that sanctities are shielded from the sins of politics. He was hardly alone in finding his name besmirched only because he opposed the direction of the revolution he had helped set in motion.

Rafsanjani was no saint. Instead, he was a nimble mover and shaker par excellence. As it turned out, that was a view of him that formed outside of Iran at a time when at home he was generally seen as another die-hard revolutionary. Charlie Allen, one of the CIA's most renowned intelligence officers, came to this conclusion early on. In 1985, Allen was a senior CIA operative asked to increase intelligence gathering on Iran. Rafsanjani's cachet inside the regime was hard to avoid and Allen felt a combination of pragmatism and opportunism made the Iranian politician worthy of America's attention. Allen was not the first, nor the last, American official to hold such a view of *Shah Akbar [King Akbar]*, a backhanded praise of his capacity to be a kingpin for so long.

In his thirty-eight years as a top figure in the regime, Rafsanjani managed to put together a vast and entrenched network of political and economic interest groups that looked to him for patronage. In that sense, the spirit and the network Rafsanjani left behind is very much alive. Reform, the Rafsanjanites have for some time concluded, is not a luxury of choice but a necessity to prevent the Iranian people from rising up against their Islamist rulers. On the other hand, the circle of hardliners around Khamenei is deeply skeptical about what they fear to be a reform process that will be unstoppable once it is initiated. This is the principal struggle in Tehran today as the two main factions inside the Islamic Republic—the Khameneites and the Rafsanjanites—vie to charter the future course of the regime.

A Popular Revolution Seized by the Most Rigid of Men

It was a hot summer evening in June 1981. I was 6 years old and watching television in my family's fourth-floor apartment in Yousef-Abad, a middle-class neighborhood just north of downtown Tehran. With the towering Alborz Mountains in the background, a huge blast suddenly rattled the windows. A couple of miles away, a bomb had exploded inside the headquarters of the Islamic Republican Party, at the time Iran's top Islamist faction. Within hours it became clear that about eighty top government officials and members of the Majles, Iran's parliament, had been killed.[1] It remains the deadliest single act of political violence in modern Iranian history. To a 6-year-old, the blast and the grisly pictures of the dead that hit the press in the following days were a numbing experience.

The country's long-ruling monarch, the Shah, had been toppled in February 1979. A 76-year-old Shia Muslim cleric by the name of Ayatollah Ruhollah Khomeini and his followers were busy seizing control of the country. In those pivotal months of the revolution, an array of anti-Shah factions found themselves bogged down in a bloody struggle for power. Assassinations, bombings, mob rule, and a thorough state of confusion had conquered this ancient land. The turmoil that was unleashed has not stopped since and the country of Iran still endures the aftershocks of 1979. It might sound like a cliché but try and argue that point with the Iranian public, a majority of whom today tend to hold one of the two following views: that the revolution of 1979 was fundamentally a national blunder, if not a tragedy, or that it was a grand grassroots-level struggle for freedom and justice that was brazenly stolen by a small group of Islamist extremists.

Within a few years, I left the chaos behind and immigrated to Europe. Since 1979, waves of Iranians have left the country, producing one of the modern world's largest Diasporas of about five million spread in all corners of the world. The Iranians, a people with limited history of emigration prior to 1979, can now rival the likes of the Lebanese, the Armenians, the Germans, or the Irish in the dash to leave their homeland for a better life. The ironies of the revolution of 1979 are many and giving birth to seismic emigration by Iranians is just one of the paradoxes that was born out of it.

The promises of the Iranian revolution were about building a freer society with political representation and economic justice. For those Iranians who actively took part in this iconic struggle—some historians still call it the last great popular revolution of our age—it was never meant to be one of repression at home and international isolation and the pursuit of militant Islamist adventurism abroad. And yet, this is exactly what happened. All these years later, a plurality of Iranians clearly lament how the country ended up here and yet most are still unsure about what precisely happened.

The small inner circle of militant clerics around Khomeini that hijacked the course of the revolution had a different vision in mind all along. What is also certain is that the ideology this group ultimately settled on was enormously shaped by political expediency of the immediate postrevolutionary period as opposed to a predetermined ideological course of action. Take anti-Americanism that became a mainstay of Khomeinism. It was at first meant to strip the rival political left of one of its ideological props before it became a runaway tenet of Khomeinism.[2]

That was one of many examples to come. For the die-hard minority around Khomeini the mission of the revolution turned out to be poorly defined and soon squabbling among them began. It turned out that instituting an "Islamic government" on earth is a road full of untested ideas. It was a novel concept as no such political experiment had ever been attempted before in Iran or anywhere else. The lack of clarity about what "Islam" and what "government" should respectively represent soon enough split even the minority victorious faction around Khomeini. Nor was this divide in vision limited to the handling of domestic affairs. In approaching the outside world, the Khomeinists often clashed. From Tehran's tortured dealings with Western countries to the necessity of exporting Khomeinism to outside of Iran's borders, the post-1979 Iran's foreign policy has been anything but uncontested.

The intention of this book is to tell that story—to be the fly on the wall while following in the footsteps of the inner members of the Khomeini group as they turned on each other and how this all shaped Iran's foreign policy. This is the history of militant ayatollahs and their followers who morphed from being brothers-in-arms in 1979 to being today's archnemesis. It's a tale of hunger for power, pride, and betrayal of each other, of the revolution, and of Iran's national interests. In this rivalry, the Iranian people were not just spectators but bore the brunt of the many pains this meandering contest has caused and continues to do so. And yet, as you will read in the pages of this book, this outcome was hardly the only available path to the Islamist revolutionaries of Iran.

When historians look at the evolution of the Islamic Republic, a boastful militant theocracy, there is a tendency to want to find the roots behind its actions in the religious ideological creed of the regime. Dogma has no doubt shaped much of this regime's behavior, but it fails to explain a considerable amount and some of the more critical turns and twists in Tehran's relations with the outside world. The case of the Islamic Republic is not that of a unitary rational actor. Another way to explain the actions of the Islamist ruling class, at home and abroad, is to look at it from the angle of rivalries among top political bosses. Many of the fights have been personal and petty, almost trivial, and puzzling that purported learned men of the cloth should succumb to such earthly transgressions. In other moments, the disputes among the ayatollahs were not just about policy preferences but life and death. All of it combined has greatly shaped Iran's foreign policy.

Meanwhile, as the Islamic Republic turned 40 in 2019, and as Iran's Supreme Leader Ayatollah Ali Khamenei reached the age of 80, it is no exaggeration to say that Iran is again at a pivotal juncture. This book is a chronicle of the power struggle inside the Iranian Islamist system. It is particularly centered on what this struggle meant in the process to make foreign policy. It starts in 1979 as those early years are foundational to why Iran has come to this point today. This is true in terms of both political realities inside of Iran, impacting its own people, and Tehran's relations with the outside world. This book is not, however, a catchall account.

§

The main focus of this book is on the foreign policy track record of the Islamic Republic where American–Iranian relations take precedence. Tehran's behavior since 1979 has been a constant irritant to the West and many of Iran's immediate neighbors such as the Arab states of the Persian Gulf and Israel. Be it related to Iran's nuclear program, Tehran's regional ambitions, or its desire to build anti-American alliances with countries further afield, the determination of Iran's Islamist rulers to challenge the international and regional status quo and expand Tehran's global influence is the subject of much debate and controversy.

What is also beyond doubt is the reality of shifting and competing ideas about Iran's role in the world and vested interests around this debate within the Islamic Republic. This is true both across the system's central institutions of power and among the ranks of its key personalities. In regard to the question of relations with the West, and the United States in particular, while part of the Islamist authorities speak of the need for a process of détente, others maintain that abandoning the hostility toward the West will only weaken the fabric of the Islamic Republic as a political model and hence its staying power.

A competition for ideas is healthy in any society. That said, in the Islamic Republic, the institutional policy-making process is deliberately set up to be obscure and counterintuitive. The elected offices, such as the presidency and the Majles (parliament), are frequently left out or strong-armed into submission by unelected powers, chief among them the Office of the Supreme Leader, and at the hands of the generals in the Islamic Revolution Guards Corps (IRGC). Hence, while the definition of mandate is constitutionally defined, and the republican component of the system should give voters at election time a chance to chart new policy paths, hard power flows ambiguously and the narrow self-interests of unelected agencies in the state overwhelmingly prevail. This competition between factions, and the hijacking of Iran's regional policy in recent years by the Revolutionary Guards, has meant that save for only a few events, Iran has tacked toward a hard-edged, antagonistic foreign policy.

This cryptic contest for ideas and interests is very much impervious not only to the Iranian public but also to the outside eyes. From Washington to Berlin and from Jerusalem to Beijing and beyond, the game of tracking policy making in Tehran is fraught with guesswork. Nonetheless, and thanks to the onset of mass information age in the 1990s, and the emergence of a host of online news and resources in Iran and in the large Iranian Diaspora, there is today more information available to Iran-watchers than ever before. Academics as well as the general audience should not ignore the many thousands of personal interviews, written memoirs, or oral histories available by individuals who at one point or another were participants or close-up witnesses when important events transpired in Tehran. For sure, media in Iran is not free. According to Reporters without Borders, Iran ranks 165 out of 180 countries for press freedom.[3] Even so, there is today an unparalleled pool of data rich in oftentimes unexplored Persian-language material. In a way, the media inside Iran operating under the watchful eyes of the Islamist rulers are forced to not fall too behind their secular rivals in the Diaspora, a fact that results in greater information generation and access.

This enhanced accessibility comes at an opportune moment. Iran's Supreme Leader Ayatollah Ali Khamenei, born in 1939, has already signaled that the end of his reign could happen at any day. The question of succession is already openly discussed among Iranian officials. The moment of power transition in Tehran will have much potential to become a vicious affair. What has been true since 1979, and continues to be true, is that the battle to steer Iranian foreign policy is intimately tied to the domestic political jockeying for power in Tehran. This is a battle that goes as far back as the November 1979 hostage crisis at the US embassy in Tehran and the dispute among the revolutionaries about the wisdom behind such an action.

Meanwhile, the fight to decide Iranian foreign policy intensified after the coming of the Rouhani presidency in August 2013. Rouhani's government and the generals from the Revolutionary Guards have repeatedly engaged in a war of words about who in the Islamic Republic best defends and promotes the country's international interests. This is just another item on a long list of foreign policy-related disputes taking place in the history of the Islamic Republic.

Finally, as with any country, the study of the foreign policy making process in Tehran has to pay far closer attention to where principal Iranian actors come from in terms of personal and political backgrounds, experiences, and factional affiliations and where they want to go from here as we aim to decipher Iran's present and likely future foreign policy calculations. In that regard, this book has two main protagonists. The first is Supreme Leader Ayatollah Ali Khamenei. The second is his late comrade-turned-nemesis, Ayatollah Akbar Hashemi Rafsanjani. The pair were not only present at every critical moment in the evolution of the Islamic Republic; their personal rivalry ended up greatly shaping modern-day Iran. Newly accessible sources of information allow the analyst to better evaluate the relationship between Khamenei and Rafsanjani, and the impact this relationship has had on Iranian foreign policy.

§

This book makes the case that the relationship between Rafsanjani and Khamenei gives us a unique lens through which to view the evolution of Iran's foreign policy from the 1979 revolution to the present. In the pages that follow, the reader will see some of the color and detail of the relationship between these two Iranian titans, but it will also be apparent how this relationship has shaped Iranian foreign policy. The main argument that will inform the rest of the book is that Iran's foreign policy was heavily shaped by how these two men defined their own parochial, political interests, and how these petty interests intersected, defined, and in many cases overshadowed Iran's national interest. And it will depict how the rivalry between these two pivotal figures played out on the regional and international stage.

The book is divided into ten chapters, each organized chronologically around key decisive moments in post-1979 Iranian history. The first chapter reminds the reader of the mercurial rise of Ayatollah Khomeini and his promises that lay the ground for the Islamic Republic. This chapter also traces the roots of the earliest relations between Khamenei and Rafsanjani: how Rafsanjani was the lead in this duet to begin with but Khamenei was always hot on his heels. Chapters 2 and 3 reevaluate the bloody consolidation of power at the hands of Khomeinists and how political pluralism is an early victim of the new order. Chapters 4 and 5 highlight how in the midst of frantic domestic and foreign policy decision-making in Tehran in the 1980s, Khamenei and Rafsanjani were largely united in rejecting the most reckless of policy options on the table in Tehran.

Chapter 6 draws attention to the vital role that Rafsanjani played in Khamenei becoming supreme leader at the death of Khomeini in 1989 and what motivated him to do so. While Khomeini lived, he hailed the Rafsanjani–Khamenei partnership as indispensable to the survival of the Islamic Republic. In Chapter 7, the reader will see how this once mutually advantageous division of power soon began to unravel. The rivalry between the two ayatollahs that intensified throughout the 1990s was very much an earthly affair in every sense of the word. Even the grand title of "ayatollah" that the two protagonists each adopted for themselves was trickery: neither man had secured the coveted rank through merit and traditional Shia Islamic learning but by force.

Chapter 8 is about the rise of the political reformist movement. The reformers around President Mohammad Khatami promised rebirth in domestic and foreign policy. They wanted to break up the grip of the Khameneists and the Rafsanjanites on power but fell embarrassingly short. They ended up giving Khamenei more enthusiasm to reinforce his control in all fields and a reason to go after Rafsanjani. Chapter 9 is about the presidency of Mahmoud Ahmadinejad. He was a mid-ranking right-wing populist that Khamenei banked on to neutralize the prospect of Rafsanjani returning to the presidential palace. Khamenei's scheme worked but it came at a steep cost for Iran's national interests. Chapter 10 deals with the presidency of Hassan Rouhani (2013–21), arguably the final parting shot of the Rafsanjani network against Khamenei's increasingly one-man rule.

§

Less than a year before his death, in January 2017, Rafsanjani was unceremoniously cast aside by Khamenei. His attempt to run for another presidential term was blocked by a regime organ (Guardian Council) under the control of his old partner. The official reason for his disqualification was his old age, a travesty of a pretense given that the upper echelons of power in Tehran are packed with octogenarians. "Who decided you are qualified to judge others," Rafsanjani whined at the other regime elders. The main target of his condemnation, Khamenei, did not even bother to respond.

Taking Khamenei under his wings was a decision that Rafsanjani came to deeply regret by the end of his life although he never said so openly. By the time Rafsanjani died, he had come to witness Khamenei's amassing powers no less than what the Shah had managed to accumulate during his nearly four-decade reign. His largely uncompromising personal style—and a taste for micro-management combined with his paranoia about internal and foreign plots against him—led Khamenei to become a quintessential tone-deaf despot. He managed not only to rally a majority of the Iranians against himself—as is plainly obvious due to the steady rise in protests in the streets—but his harsh Islamist model has turned the public off religion unlike anything before. Iranians are not just leaving Iran in droves: they are leaving Islam in droves too in an act of ultimate defiance. No wonder that some forty years after the militant Khomeinists took over the reins of power, whispers of dissent are growing louder even among clerics in Iran's most religious centers such as Qom and Mashhad.

Before his death, Rafsanjani lamented the state of affairs in Iran. Still, there can be no doubt that much of his resentment was down to him having being outsmarted. While it was a personal defeat for Rafsanjani, Khamenei's steady power grab since his ascent in 1989 was to fundamentally shape today's Iran where bitter domestic dissent and a turbulent foreign policy have become the new normal. It is no exaggeration to say Khamenei has put the country on a collision course on multiple fronts. It is equally true that despite over thirty years in power, he has shunned every opportunity to change course. And yet, Khamenei's worldview did not emerge in a vacuum, and international context matters plenty. As he approaches the twilight of his life, Khamenei shows no sign of introspection and is determined to confront his detractors at home and abroad. For him, it's all or nothing.

Questions of how Iran's foreign policy will evolve going forward is outside the purview of this book. Nonetheless, the story of the two men and the impact the relationship has had on Iran's foreign policy did not end with the death of Rafsanjani. And it will not end with the death of Khamenei. The relationship, and the legacy it has left behind, epitomizes the factional fight inside the Islamic Republic about Iran's place in the world. The echoes of the Rafsanjani–Khamenei clash will carry on into the future or at least as long as the Islamic Republic survives.

1

(1978–9)—Khamenei and Rafsanjani: Waiting for Khomeini to Return from Paris

Either we are doing something wrong or all the protesters are crazy.
But there is so many of them.
Can so many be crazy?

(Shah of Iran, May 8, 1978)

At around noon on January 16, 1979, Mohammad Reza Pahlavi, the King of Kings and the Shah of Iran, boarded his blue and white 707-Boeing jetliner, *the Shahbaz* or the fabled hawk. At the time, he was one of only five absolute monarchs left in the world. "I am going on vacation because I am feeling tired," he disingenuously told reporters. But as the cancer-stricken Shah suspected, it became the flight that took him to eternal exile.

Washington's staunchest ally in the Middle East since 1941, a man who had cemented his position as a pro-American bastion in the heart of this troubled part of the world and worked closely with eight American presidents from Franklin D. Roosevelt to Jimmy Carter, had in a mere four months—martial law had been declared on September 8, 1978—witnessed his imperial rule crumble in front of his eyes.

At home, the Shah faced a revolutionary motley crew that comprised a rainbow coalition subscribing to a diverse lineup of political creeds. The one and only fundamental point they converged around was the intention to fight for the Shah's fall to the bitter end. Few had anticipated the toppling of the Shah's kingship to unfold so rapidly. Fewer still had any idea what was to come after the Shah.

§

In Neauphle-le-Château, a sleepy suburb on the outskirts of Paris, a small circle of die-hard supporters lived and worked around Ayatollah Ruhollah Khomeini. The 79-year-old Shia cleric with his black turban—which signified his claimed descent from Prophet Mohammad—had by now become the undisputed spearhead against the Shah. He was about to become Iran's next leader. The group in Paris, a patchwork of men in Shia clerical garbs and Western-educated radicals in suits, tracked events in amazement as the Shah's aircraft hours later landed in Aswan, Egypt.

As he stepped off *Shahbaz* and was greeted by his good friend, the Egyptian president Anwar Sadat, the Shah might have still harbored some faint hope that his foreign excursion was to be temporary. But that hope would last only until the dark clouds hanging over Tehran had blown away. After all, he had been here before. Back in August 1953, when a popular prime minister, Mohammad Mossadeq, broke off with him, the Shah had been forced to flee the country for Europe. His return to Iran was made possible only after the British and American intelligence services concocted a swift counterstroke that led to Mossadeq's downfall and the Shah's return to his throne.

Fast forward to January 1979. This latest popular anti-Shah movement was hardly a spur-of-the-moment event. A few months earlier, in October, the Shah had himself piloted a helicopter flight over Tehran to see for himself the enormous size of one of the many demonstrations against him, an experience that left him both flabbergasted and indignant. Now, with his departure for Egypt, the revolutionaries in Paris sensed a historic opportunity to keep him in exile forever.

And yet they were woefully unprepared. No one in Paris had expected the Shah's regime to fall like a house of cards in a matter of months. Since Khomeini had arrived in Neauphle-le-Château in October 1978—from exile in Iraq where Saddam Hussein had kicked him out on the urging of the Shah—his followers had painstakingly deliberated about various options for the long war against the Shah's formidable American-supplied military. In rooms rented in a Bed & Breakfast not far from Khomeini's residence, many days and nights were consumed by weighing the most effective tactics in a dogged campaign of armed resistance that everyone believed was about to come.

The Iranian revolutionaries had long anticipated the need to launch an armed battle against the Shah's regime. They looked to learn from the experiences of the Algerian anticolonial resistance against the French in the 1950s or the mistakes of the Brazilian revolutionaries against the military junta there in the 1960s and 1970s. Often following instructions from Arab leftist radicals, such as the Palestinian Liberation Organization (PLO), armed cells across cities in Iran had been organized for the long battle. Such interaction with Arab radicals was the genesis of the anti-Israel posture that the Iranian state would later adopt when the pro-Israel Shah was removed.

For these Iranian would-be revolutionaries, training was provided on how to go underground, how to communicate with the resistance leadership in exile, and how to wage a propaganda campaign against the Shah. This was, after all, the generation of revolutionary militancy around the world. The Iranians activists, like the German Red Army, the Italian Red Brigades, or the PLO, were too deeply gripped by promises of cutting down the prevailing political order.

Among these Iranian revolutionaries, the weight of the culture of the militant international left was not only visible in the approach to organizing an underground movement. Inside the Paris circle there was a deep sense of pride in living meagerly while aspiring for lofty goals. When food was served at Khomeini's makeshift Paris dwelling, the chief overseer at the home—Haj Mehdi Araqi, a man who had only recently been released after thirteen years in the Shah's prison—made a point of handing out only bowls of rice. This was not due to lack of money.

At this point, many of the wealthy back in Tehran were banking on Khomeini's rise. He was receiving millions of dollars' worth in donations. He had become the seductive bandwagon to the unsuspecting masses. And yet, the same masses barely fathomed the man or his mission.

Khomeini's Sudden End of Exile

For all of its cerebrations, the sudden fall of the Shah put the Paris group in a limbo. As soon as the 59-year-old king left Tehran, the paramount question became when Khomeini should go back to the country he had been exiled from since 1964. The Shah had shortly prior to his departure installed a long-time political opponent, Shapour Bakhtiar, a secular nationalist and French-educated advocate of constitutional monarchy, to lead an emergency government and defuse the revolution by meeting some of the demands. Bakhtiar pledged his loyalty to the Shah despite much ill will between them. Back in 1934, Shah's father, Reza Khan, had executed Bakhtiar's father. But with the Islamist threat looming, the two sons now had reasons for a sober compromise.

Still, Bakhtiar had an impossible task and he knew it. He lasted a mere thirty-seven days in office. He told his cabinet the best they could hope for was to steer the direction of the revolution. But, he said, there was little chance of stopping it. Bakhtiar's vision of horror was one in which an Islamist dictatorship followed the monarchy. Later, even while hounded by the Khomeinists in exile in Europe, Bakhtiar would cut deals with just about anybody—including Saddam Hussein in Iraq—to prevent an Islamist autocracy to take root in Iran. Mossad's top analyst on Iran in January 1979, Yossi Alpher, remembers the day he was asked to opine on Bakhtiar's request that Mossad assassinate Khomeini. Alpher turned to his boss, Yitzhak Hofi, and said "We don't know enough about Khomeini for me to make a sound judgement."[1] Alpher was not alone, and Bakhtiar had also been turned down by the CIA, the British MI6, and the French intelligence.

Bakhtiar's condition for taking the job had been for the Shah to leave Iran until the political temperature had dropped. He had hoped this step would placate the revolutionaries. Instead, the Shah's departure blindsided the military, the monarch's purported bulwark and at the time the world's fifth largest armed force. The US-backed military hierarchy still had plenty of power to act, but its attitude was at this point at best one of bewilderment and paralysis.

Both the speed of the revolutionary upsurge and the Shah's abandonment of the country had caught them like deer in headlights. The US president, Jimmy Carter, had gambled he might be able to turn the tide. In mid-January, he dispatched and closely handled a secret mission by a four-star general to Tehran to mobilize the wavering Iranian military leaders. In Tehran, US air force General Robert E. Huyser, a man with full access to the top brass, soon found out that faltering Iranian leaders was only half of the problem.

The US embassy, particularly ambassador William Sullivan, had months earlier assessed the Shah's rule was lost. One of the few areas of agreement between Bakhtiar and the Shah's generals was fury at Sullivan's sense of inevitability that Khomeini would ultimately prevail. Zbigniew Brzezinski, Carter's hawkish National Security

Advisor, later concluded "[intra-US government] procrastination and bureaucratic sabotage prevented the US-sponsored military coup that might have saved Iran from Khomeini."[2]

A few weeks after Huyser's unsuccessful trip to Tehran, Iran's military leadership decided to do the unthinkable. On February 11 at 10:30 a.m., prime minister Bakhtiar got a call from General Abbas Qarabaghi, the joint chief of staff and the chief military organizer to tame the revolutionaries. A frantic Bakhtiar asked, "General, what is happening? Where are you?" The response was the last nail in the coffin of the monarchy. "Your excellency, Prime Minister. The *Artesh* [the armed forces] has just declared its neutrality." The game was all but over. Bakhtiar, lamenting what he saw as the military's cowardice, insisted that Khomeini's takeover of Iran could have been prevented if the Shah's top generals had not cut and run.[3]

Qarabaghi and his colleagues in the military in turn blamed the indecisive and often contradictory actions of Jimmy Carter's administration. The prevailing view in Tehran was that the Americans wanted to rid themselves of the Shah, a fatalistic opinion that even the beleaguered monarch deep down invariably subscribed to. As he put it in May 1980 to Katharine Graham of the *Washington Post* during an interview at Cairo's Koubbeh Palace, the Shah had come to believe Washington wanted him out. The Americans, he had come to believe, wanted to impose an Islamist system in Iran as a safer vanguard against Soviet communism.

§

In the camp of the opposition to the Shah, the question of the timing of his return hounded Khomeini's key advisors in Paris, including a US-educated academic-cum-revolutionary by the name of Ebrahim Yazdi. He had since 1972 been Khomeini's main representative in the United States. He had serious reservations about Khomeini's quick return to Tehran and what it might mean for the prospects of the Paris group. Mohsen Sazegara, another young US-educated anti-Shah idealist who a few weeks earlier had traveled from the United States to join the Paris group, recalls a conversation he had with Yazdi a few days after the Shah had left Tehran for Egypt.

Walking from Khomeini's rented house back to the B&B, Yazdi listened to the 23-year-old Sazegara as he made a passionate case for a rapid return to Iran. "Why shouldn't Khomeini go back now," implored the young man. "He will be welcomed by millions in the streets of Tehran and that display alone will bring down the Bakhtiar government and with it the Shah's Peacock Throne." For Yazdi, however, revolutionary speed was only part of the equation.

In Paris, Yazdi had over the course of the preceding months become a key gatekeeper to Khomeini. He was notably key in overseeing the hundreds of interviews Khomeini gave to the international press. He had been intent on making sure the old cleric did not stray from message. For Yazdi, a permanent US resident, tutoring Khomeini about the do's and don'ts in his messaging to the Western audience was hugely sensitive. The West's posture toward the anti-Shah coalition was deemed as one of the decisive factors that could secure victory. Much labor was devoted to portray Khomeini as a humble and good-hearted religious man who was spearheading a sacred grassroots movement and was no ideological apostle as such.

Meanwhile, in Paris, Yazdi had no doubt come to enjoy his role as Khomeini's right-hand man. He turned to Sazegara, and in a moment of wit and political shrewdness foretold what was in fact to unfold in the ensuing weeks and months. "If Khomeini goes back to Tehran now a few big *mullahs* (clerics) there will come to shape his agenda and the revolution will be ours no more," he said. To dampen the urge for hasty return to Tehran, Yazdi had instead proposed an alternative four-point strategy.

He wanted Khomeini to first establish a "Council of Revolution" while still in Paris. The makeup of the council was to be kept a secret and its main job was to select a provisional government in Tehran. That government was then first to end the mayhem in the country where large-scale popular protests had rocked the nation for months. In Yazdi's view, once these three conditions had been met, Khomeini could return to Tehran.

It was a robust plan with an inbuilt mechanism to hinder the hijacking of the revolution by any one single interest group. In fact, the trajectory of the Iranian Revolution of 1979 might have been markedly different had Yazdi's plan taken hold. The trouble for Yazdi was that Khomeini himself was inclined for a quick return. He had sought to cut a deal with Bakhtiar but increasingly felt the Shah's compromise prime minister was wittingly stalling and that a grand bargain with the Shah's appointees was impossible. In the end, of Yazdi's four-point strategy, Khomeini only carried out one of the points. While still in Paris, he ordered the establishment of the Council of Revolution. In the coming months, the membership and agenda of this council were a closely guarded secret. It would end up greatly shaping Iranian history.

§

Once Khomeini had made up his mind, the logistics around his return had to be planned. An Air France flight was chartered, leaving Paris around midnight for a prime 9:00 a.m. arrival in Tehran on February 1. There was a scramble to secure a seat on the 747 flight, but Yazdi, Sazegara, and the other interceders in the Paris group were determined to keep carpetbaggers at bay. Only about 30 carefully selected activists made the half-full flight. Accompanying them were 120 foreign journalists. The stringent selection process was meant to assure submission to Khomeini's vision. The international press was allowed to tag along only to broadcast the imminent victory of the revolution.

Among Khomeini's exclusive band of activists who accompanied him on that historic flight, most were soon to clutch power in Tehran but only fleetingly. There was the 46-year-old French-educated Abol-hassan Bani-Sadr who subsequently became the first president of the post-Shah regime. The 48-year-old Ebrahim Yazdi and the 43-year-old Sadeq Ghotbzadeh, another US-educated anti-Shah activist, each ended up briefly holding tenures as foreign minister. Another, the French-educated Hassan Habibi, was tasked to write the first post-Shah constitution of the country, a hybrid of Western and Islamic concepts that in the decades since has survived as an aching point of contention. Friction defined this inner circle, often leaving Khomeini exacerbated.[4]

The young Sazegara, who had abandoned physics studies at Illinois Institute of Technology to join Khomeini and dabbled in guerilla tactics, became a cofounder of the Islamic Revolution Guards Corps (IRGC), an organization that later became a balefire of anti-Americanism. Unbeknownst to the activists that boarded the flight to Tehran, most would quickly fall out of favor with Khomeini. Within three years, Khomeini had Bani Sadr flee back to Paris; Ghotbzadeh was executed for allegedly plotting to assassinate Khomeini; and Yazdi found himself loitering on the political margins for the remainder of his life.

These men—as there was not a single woman in the core Paris circle—were initially in Khomeini's loyalist circle as they had passed the old man's most basic of tests: they had all declared themselves to be "Muslim." But even this most common of proclamations was soon hotly contested. It became a badge of honor one could earn only through unequivocal faithfulness to Khomeini's particular vision. That was tough, mainly as the political order to come was a chaotic case of work-in-progress and as Khomeini began to divulge the severe side of his vision.

In the days following the flight, the predication Yazdi made in Paris and his worst fears about a few mullahs in Tehran hijacking the revolution came true. Iran's future kingmakers were in fact not on the flight from Paris but waiting impatiently in Tehran. The handful clerical members of the Khomeini-appointed Council of Revolution commandeered the revolution to unchartered pastures few in the rainbow anti-Shah coalition could have foreseen. Between Khomeini's arrival on February 1 and the official end of the Shah's regime on February 11, this small circle staged a coup within the revolution.

§

One of the very few certainties at the time of the flight from Paris was that Khomeini's fourteen-year exile was about to end. Other than that, there was plenty of trepidation. For the large crowds that had come out to welcome Khomeini at the airport the occasion was euphoric but not because of any articulations about the political order he had promised. In truth, on that clear but cold February morning, Khomeini's own sense of what was about to come after the Shah was at best cursory. Thanks to advice from the likes of Yazdi and other non-clerics in his entourage, Khomeini had expressed ideas that were loosely interpreted to be a call for a democratic system. "We will have a democracy like they have here in France," Khomeini promised.

Even the godless Iranian communists would have freedom of speech. Some communists in fact welcomed Khomeini's arrival with big banners. Vladimir Lenin would have been horrified by such adornment of a clergyman by people who claimed to subscribe to his creed. Khomeini's use of simple Persian to pledge an era of socioeconomic justice, from free-of-charge utility services to each family receiving a monthly share of the country's enormous oil wealth, mesmerized the masses. Iran had throughout the 1970s experienced a massive economic boom but many had been left on the sidelines. They wanted a share of the country's wealth. In Khomeini they saw a Robin Hood figure.

Through his populist slogans, the old cleric had veered the public's attention toward incontrovertible worldly matters. Khomeini frequently hinted that his own return journey from Paris was to take him back to the seminaries in the holy Shia Muslim city of Qom that sits about 80 miles south of the capital, Tehran. He reassured that he was not a man of politics but a man of religion. What had not been revealed fully at this time was that he deemed politics and religion to be inseparable. In Washington, there were plenty who looked on suspiciously. The Iran desk at the CIA was more than skeptical about Khomeini's claim that he had no desire to hold power himself. The slogans of his supporters spoke for itself. One famous banner had "God," the "Koran" written on it with an image of Khomeini in what looked to represent a holy trinity. This sort of careless adulation by the anti-Shah camp was a carte blanche to Khomeinists who soon insisted on all power.

The American analysts, who at one point had erroneously described him as a simple cleric and not a terribly deep thinker, saw Khomeini as at least to be prone to be manipulated by those around him.[5] Another CIA assessment, from just three years later, put it differently: "A new [post-Shah] regime in Tehran would obviously be greatly influenced by his [Khomeini's] beliefs."[6] While charges of incompetence leveled against the CIA for missing the signs of a revolution in Iran are broadly legitimate, the agency's predictions about what was about to come after the Shah's fall turned out to be on target. America's premier intelligence analysts predicted that the "most significant implication for the US of a regime change under the influence of Khomeini is likely to be instability in Iran itself." Khomeini, the agency warned, would be "unlikely to be able to contain the revolutionary impetus he has helped to spark." This tallied with the fears of the Paris group. As Yazdi had foreseen, on Khomeini's return his key lieutenants who had stayed back in Tehran had very different ideas than what the core Paris group had pictured about the future of Iran.

Two Young Clerics Waiting for Khomeini in Tehran

Among Khomeini's Tehran-based coterie, two younger clerics eagerly awaited the old man's return. They would end up shaping the post-Shah Iran more than anyone else, including Khomeini himself. Their names were Akbar Hashemi Rafsanjani and Ali Khamenei. In the ranks of senior Shia clerical class, they were youthful and miniscule figures in terms of theological scholarship. Neither had in fact finished their seminary studies by the time the revolution erupted. Nor would they ever again engage in serious theological studies. And yet both men compensated for the lack of clerical status by possessing insatiable political ambition.

They had first met briefly during a lecture in a seminary in Qom in 1959.[7] The lecturer was Ayatollah Mohammad Damad, a senior theological figure that had come to embrace the call to fight the Shah's regime. This was the age of the rise of Islamist militancy in Iran. A few years earlier, in 1953, the secular and pro-US Shah had been briefly deposed from power by a nationalist opposition and was only to be reinstated to his throne thanks to a joint British-American coup. Once back in power, the then 34-year-old Shah set out to build a formidable security apparatus that henceforth could secure his rule. The Shah was above all fixated on the threat posed by the "reds," the antimonarchy communist and other leftist forces. He was never oblivious to the "black" threat, the subversive efforts of radical Islamist clerics. He calculated, though, he could either co-opt the dissident religious forces or at least pit them against the reds.

This turned out to be a fatal miscalculation. In the decade between the events of 1953 until 1963, the clerical class in Iran endured a process of radicalization. The traditional clergy wanted to stay loyal to the court and extract concessions from the Shah but only through negotiations. It found itself increasingly under assault from a new breed of die-hard clerics that longed for an armed revolution. Still, the clerical class as a whole stayed more or less deferential to Grand Ayatollah Boroujerdi. He was the foremost religious authority in Iran at the time and frowned upon the idea of clerics turning militants.

Boroujerdi's death in March 1961 left a vacuum at the top end of the religious hierarchy. A relatively junior ayatollah by the name of Ruhollah Khomeini soon emerged as the darling of the radical clergy. The grand ayatollah's death coincided with the coming of the Kennedy administration in Washington. The young American president saw in the Shah a "Third World" dictator who was nevertheless needed in the fight against Soviet communism. The Kennedy administration, however, nudged him to pursue political reform at home. This the Shah did albeit reluctantly.[8]

It was not until 1963, when the Shah launched his "White Revolution"—an effort to end feudalism in Iran and a comprehensive reform package that undercut the political and financial interests of the clergy—that Khomeini openly collided with the king. This was the Shah's signature venture aimed to modernize the country and render any revolution from the streets unnecessary. Khomeini was scathing in his opposition. His unprecedented personal attacks on the monarch had him first land in jail and exiled in Iraq by November 1964.[9] His young aficionados back in Iran, such as Rafsanjani and Khamenei, would during Khomeini's fourteen-year exile remain loyal to him. It was the former that had all the access.

In 1959, when Rafsanjani and Khamenei first met in Qom, the former was not only already a seminarian but owned the neighboring house to Khomeini in that city. Khamenei, on the other hand, was the impoverished religious student that was only visiting Qom from his hometown of Mashhad. Khamenei was drawn to Qom, a major seat of learning in Shia Islam, not so much because of its religious stature per se but because of the city's restless political mood. In contrast, and despite the best efforts of Khamenei and his fellow radicals in his hometown, Mashhad never produced the same rebellious spirit as was found in Qom. In his memoirs, Rafsanjani claimed the reason why he first noticed Khamenei was due to his youthfulness in the crowd the first time they met, a quality they shared.[10] While living in different cities, a partnership if not a friendship soon began. Their contrasting family backgrounds, however, were not the only reason that set them apart.

Rafsanjani was a merchant at heart and as a political voice he was a man who never let his religious creed blind him about the dangers of Iran falling into the abyss as the rest of the world moved on. Decades later, as Khamenei continued to glorify militant resistance against the United States, Rafsanjani raised objections. "Look at [Nazi] Germany and [Imperial] Japan," he said in a speech only a few months before he died in January 2017. "What did militarizing their foreign policy get them [during Second World War]? And look what they have become today after they opted to focus on strengthening their economies instead," he observed. Despite the nickname his critics would later bestow on him (*King Akbar*), he was more of a wheeler-dealer and a patron for an old boys' network than a self-styled high priest like his mentor, Ayatollah Khomeini.

The "high priest" is the sort of title that is far more apt describing Khamenei's self-perception. From a young age, he oozed an exterior confidence that made others notice and yet he has throughout his life perpetually wrestled with a sense of inadequacy in his environment. Operating in a clerical field where the art of oratory can quickly make or break a career, Khamenei possessed a sharp tongue, an assured tone, and delivered his remarks with much energy and conviction. Many saw his self-confidence as a puzzle, and nor has it always been deep, but it was a key driver behind his political rise. The two young men had chosen to follow the teachings of Khomeini, whose core network was still relatively small but rapidly growing in the ranks of the clergy. In 1970, Rafsanjani and Khamenei traveled together to Najaf, the Iraqi Shia holy city, to visit Khomeini. The Iraqi authorities had in 1964 given him a sanctuary as a favor to the Shah who had hoped life in exile in Iraq would be the last he saw of Khomeini. For Rafsanjani and Khamenei, that trip to Najaf was an opportunity to become more familiar with each other. After that, Khamenei had temporarily moved to Qom to be closer to the devotees of Khomeini.

§

By the time of the revolution in February 1979, Rafsanjani and Khamenei had been friends for twenty years. Their life stories shared similarities but this was by no means a relationship of equals to begin with. Both men came from outside of Tehran, Iran's bustling capital that is the nerve center of the country and from where political A-list figures have historically emerged. They had both engaged in anti-Shah activism, collecting numerous arrests and prison terms over the years.

Rafsanjani, older by five years and born in 1934, hailed from the county of Rafsanjan that sits on the edges of *Dasht-e Loot*, Iran's large salt desert. The region is a world capital in the production of pistachios, the Rafsanjani family's source of wealth. Thanks to his trademark smooth face, due to an inability to grow facial hair, Rafsanjani looked younger than Khamenei whose jet-black bushy beard, thick-rimmed glasses, and a fondness for smoking pipes made him look more like a Marxist Latin American guerilla commander than a Shia Muslim clergyman. Unlike Rafsanjani, who wore a white turban, Khamenei claimed descent from Prophet Mohammad and hence wore a black turban just like Khomeini. It would be a detail that mattered when it came to the question of succeeding Khomeini.

While Rafsanjani was by nature jovial, Khamenei was an ascetic. His openness to humor was strictly self-regulated. A cellmate from prison days during the Shah period, a leftist by the name of Houshang Asadi, portrays Khamenei as deeply religious who laughed at jokes until they became lewd.[11] Few would have faulted Khamenei had he chosen Marxist militancy as his calling. In his hometown of Mashhad, Iran's holiest city and the burial ground of the eighth *imam* (leader) of the Shia Muslims, he had grown up in an impoverished family in a poor part of the city. His father, an ethnic Azerbaijani who spoke Persian with a deep accent, was a simple traditional cleric, born in Najaf in Iraq, which had for centuries been a stamping ground for Iranian clerics who came to study in the vicinity of Shia holy sites.

In Khamenei's words, life was not easy during his childhood. "We were eight kids from two mothers. My father had three kids from his wife—all girls. When the first wife died, a second wife gave him five kids: four boys and a girl." Khamenei was the second child of his father's second wife. The elder Khamenei would often see his children go to bed on empty stomachs. Nuts, raisins, and milk were often the only items on the dinner menu, or at least this is what Khamenei claims in his memoirs. But lack of money did not stop this poor family from being learned. Whipping by his father was common if he failed to do well in his studies. Khamenei was also deeply proud in his mother being literate and a lover of poetry such as the works of fourteenth-century Persian poet Hafez, a passion she would pass on to her son.

Years later as supreme leader, organizing gatherings for poetry recital would become a favorite pastime. "Our people are poetic by nature," he would say.[12] To this day, he adores political poems that laud his leadership and is equally quick to show his contempt for any dissent expressed by poets invited to his annual "nights of poetry."[13] As a seminarian, wearing a turban from the age of 13, Khamenei was still enthusiastic about sports such as football (soccer) and volleyball. From this self-depiction, an image is given to a spiritual-minded soul whose penniless earthly existence was no barrier to the pursuit of greater quests in life. Among the life stories of Islamist clerics, such purported humbleness is common. It is meant to absolve them from the sins they would go on to commit in pursuing political goals.

The young Ali Khamenei was later in life forced to occasionally accept handouts from his well-to-do friend, Akbar. Immediately before the revolution, Rafsanjani rented a two-story building in Tehran's Nayeb-Saltaneh neighborhood to escape prying by the Shah's intelligence service, the SAVAK. The Rafsanjanis lived on the first floor and let Khamenei and his family live on the second floor.[14] The oldest children from both families were almost of the same age and playmates. The families were close and the fathers were Islamist leaders-in-waiting.

Many from Khamenei's destitute social class had in the post–Second World War years turned their backs on Allah and joined the then Iran's many different types of leftist groups operating in Iran. There were the legions of Iranian youth that looked to Soviet Union for inspiration and others looked to Mao's China and a host of other leftist specimens in between. Khamenei, however, only flickeringly probed the beliefs of the godless. While he looked down on the traditional nonpolitical clergy, which he derided as "Mullahs of the Court," and found Marxism to carry too many taboos, he was early on besotted by the ideals of the then nascent militant Islam.

Sayyid Qutb, the Egyptian intellectual viewed by many as the mastermind of Sunni militancy, was an early idol for the young Ali. Khamenei had before the Iranian revolution translated three of Qutb's works from Arabic into Persian. In 1967, when he was 28 years old, Khamenei translated Qutb's *al-Mustaqbal li-hadhā al-dīn* (The Future of This Religion). In it, Qutb called for "the political supremacy of Islam, which will lead to the future submission of all humanity to Islamic ideology, and calls upon all Muslims to fight against the imperialist powers."[15] Qutb was not just an Islamist ideologue but a man who had come to harbor profound dislike of the American way of life as a result of his living in the United States in the 1950s.[16] That he early on became Khamenei's window into "America" and Israel was always destined to be a bad omen.

The anti-Americanism espoused by the communists in the anti-Shah movement also no doubt shaped Khamenei's opinions on the United States, the West, and Israel. Khamenei maintains that one of the first times he got into trouble with the SAVAK was when he spoke about the depiction of Jews in the Koran. "Why do you speak against the Jews and Israel," he claimed that SAVAK had warned.[17]

Still, Khamenei, a pipe smoker and a music enthusiast in his youth, was positively representative of a new breed of Iranian Shia clerics. The second son in the household, Khamenei had also from a young age been attracted to Russian literature and what it had to offer on questions about human nature and societal trials and tribulations. He read the likes of Mikhail Sholokhov, a favorite author of Josef Stalin, and Aleksey Tolstoy, and later in his life proudly stressed that he had been an enthusiast of avant-garde novelists. Meanwhile, as he aged, he was more smitten by the knack of rough craftsmanship as practiced by the Soviets.

In fact, Khamenei's infatuation with all things Russian has long fueled speculation that Moscow has a baffling sway over a man who eventually became the Iranian supreme leader. The rumor mill in Tehran has long churned out gossip at Khamenei having been recruited by the KGB in the 1960s and that he had attended the Patrice Lumumba Peoples' Friendship University in Moscow, an institution well-known for educating a host of future leaders for the so-called developing world.[18] An Iranian political dissident wrote an entire book on the subject of Khamenei's ties to the Soviets.[19] In his official biography, Khamenei makes no mention of having ever visited or studied in the Soviet Union.[20]

Back in Mashhad before the Iranian revolution of 1979, congregating with friends at his humble family home to chat about the radical left's critique of the economic order was one of his favorite pastimes. But Khamenei, the son of a common *mullah*, never mustered the courage to abandon the mosque and the family calling. He banked on radical Islam as the ousting force of the old order and as his shot at a political career.

On February 1, 1979, as Khamenei waited in the VIP lounge of the Mehr-Abad Airport to be among the first ones to welcome Khomeini, an anxious looking Khamenei was quashed in the middle of the large crowd of clerics. The 39-year-old, too junior to be in the front of the line, stood there with an intense glaze aimed at the entrance and counting the seconds for Khomeini to walk through the glass door. He was eager to let the old man know about his existence and offer his allegiance. Still, Khamenei's foremost ticket to be part of the inner circle of Khomeini was his old friend, Akbar Rafsanjani. Rafsanjani was not squashed in the crowd. He stood in the prized first line with the rest of the top revolutionary brass.

A Popular Revolution Seized by Islamists

At the time of his return to Tehran, Khomeini was very mindful that associating with his iconic image was in huge demand. As he disembarked from the aircraft, he opted to hold the hand of the French pilot as he walked down the airstairs. In Tehran, after all, the pilot was a nonentity and was soon to fly back to Paris and therefore the perfect escort.[21] On the other hand, Khomeini's close lieutenants that were on the flight were all thirsty for recognition. He, however, was not about to give anyone a freebie. Thus, Khomeini's penchant for methodically seeking to distribute power among his closest disciples was revealed before he had even set foot back in Iran. This stayed as Khomeini's most differentiating trait for the remainder of his life. And this model of operation was not lost on the man, Ali Khamenei, who subsequently succeeded Khomeini a decade later.

From Mehr-Abad Airport Khomeini was driven to *Behesht-e Zahra* (Zahra's Paradise), Tehran's enormous cemetery in the southern outskirts of the city. Sitting in the midst of the gravestones, he gave a speech that both immortalized Khomeini as the father of the revolution and also provided an early insight into the man's megalomania. The regime that he was about to raise would come to institutionalize it. He had deliberately opted to come here to pay respect to those killed in toppling the Shah's regime. It was his homage to the masses. His 29-minute-long speech was dotted with egalitarian rallying cries.

Khomeini's core line of attack was on the Shah's absolute power. "Did the people vote for your father, or you or your [rubber-stamp] parliament?" he asked again and again in reference to the Shah. "Every generation," he demanded, "should be able to choose the political system it wants." This was indeed a mighty articulation but one that Khomeini and his followers forgot all about once they held the reins of power. As Khomeini was championing democratic values, large banners in the crowd held up by his supporters had already sanctified him as the "leader." In those early hours after his return from Paris, it was still a token title and had yet to embody the vast powers that were soon to be institutionalized in that one function. In a sense, this bestowing of the leadership title to Khomeini was the first nail in the coffin of the democratic aspirations of the Iranian people before even the dust of the revolution had settled.

Khomeini mostly stuck to vague notions of the need for socioeconomic fairness in society. He spoke about justice for every Iranian and landed plenty of punches at Shah's cherished secular and free-market economic model. As early as the 1950s, the Shia clergy in Iran had adopted slogans of social justice in order to compete with socialist and communist propaganda aimed at the working class.[22] In his speech that day, there were only a handful of moments when Khomeini hinted at his primal wish to see the Iranian society radically transformed. It was about far more than just economics. "There are more liquor stores in this country than book shops," he bemoaned, betraying his cloaked plans for sweeping change and his ultimate goal to instill a radical Islamist rule over the nation.

Soon the sale of alcohol was banned, music was forbidden, and women were forced to wear the veil, just to mention a few of the oppressive new orders of the Islamists. When women held mass protests in the streets against compulsory veil, Khomeini's armed loyalists confronted them with the slogan "Ya rousari, ya tousari." (Either the veil or [being hit by] the baton.) Forced veil was first introduced among female civilian staff in military institutions.

The man who instituted the new policy was none other than Hassan Rouhani. At the time, the future Iranian president was the deputy of Ali Khamenei who was a member of the Council of Revolution and sat on the committee on armed forces. The mandatory veil would go on to become one of the most symbolic faces of Khomeinist dictatorship. Khamenei never wavered on the question but Rafsanjani—sensing how loathed of a policy it was—in time came close to denounce it.[23]

If under the Shah the Iranians longed for political rights, under Khomeini they not only failed to obtain that privilege but also lost their social freedoms. At this point, the theocracy that Khomeini was about to erect was an entirely novel idea and with no forerunner in human history. It took Western scholars years to figure out the basics of what Khomeini was striving to do in the name of Islam.

That first symbolically important speech was somber and Khomeini's voice was animated only once when he warned the last Shah-appointed government of prime minister Bakhtiar. In a fit of anger, he hollered: "I will punch this government in the mouth." As to make sure the point was not lost on anyone, he continued: "*I* will choose the government." Catching his miscue, he repeated the same line but added "with people's backing." This lip service to the importance of the consent of the people was pure tactical politics. While no one in Iran would ever have the opportunity to cast a vote for him as a leader, Khomeini was already the larger-than-life patriarch and arbiter of power.

Khomeini's First Provisional Government

In the next few days, the course of Khomeini's gradual separation from the Paris group was irreversibly set in motion. After his speech at *Behesht-e Zahra* cemetery, Khomeini and his closest cohorts settled in a primary school by the name of *Refah*. The Paris group had coordinated closely with Khomeini's top Tehran-based supporters to have him stay at the school. It was not in the north of the city, where the upper class lived, or in the south of the city, home to the working class and the poor.[24] Here, in the following ten days, Khomeini began to openly reveal his intentions about the future. Rafsanjani would years later say, "[What took place at] Refah school became the 'identity card' of the Islamic Republic."[25] Gone were the democratic tokenisms expressed to Western journalists in Paris, and it was here Iran's draconian Islamization process eagerly began. Khomeini's utterings about "Islam" began to sound alien to the average Iranian but he began the political transformation cautiously.

At Refah school, while still holding no official role as such, Khomeini on February 11 proceeded to appoint Mehdi Bazargan, an elderly moderate Islamist and long-time Shah opponent, as interim prime minister and told Bakhtiar to step down. Bakhtiar, whom the Shah had banked on as the neutralizer of the revolution, was forced underground and soon after fled the country for France. As Khomeini put it, a country cannot simultaneously have two prime ministers. The unelected prime minister of the already departed Shah was replaced by another unelected prime minister. One prime minister had been put in place by the crown, the other by the turban.

Back in Paris, Khomeini had on January 10 established the Council of Revolution whose existence at this time was still kept a secret. Khomeini had handpicked the core members of the body, which included Rafsanjani and four other clerics. After the Shah's fall, the council's membership expanded to include a number of key personalities from the Paris group such as Yazdi and Bani Sadr. The new prime minister, Bazargan, was one of the most senior of its members.

On the day of inauguration, Khomeini's decree to appoint Bazargan was read out by his acolyte, the 44-year-old Rafsanjani. Sitting in front of dark green curtains and next to Khomeini himself, the handful of minutes Rafsanjani took to read out aloud the formation of the provincial government under Bazargan placed the younger cleric on the political map like nothing before it. Bazargan, a veteran politician and almost 30 years his senior, sat there in his suit and a Western necktie looking somewhat bemused at Rafsanjani's function. This was not a haphazard event. Before Khomeini had been exiled to Iraq, Rafsanjani had been a devout student and an astute financial organizer for Khomeini in his fourteen-year banishment from Iran by the Shah. Rafsanjani had also been instrumental in acting as a courier for the old man's ideas. From Khomeini's exile in Najaf in Iraq, Rafsanjani took back the elder cleric's burgeoning ideas behind the necessity of establishing Islamic rule in Iran. This was the pre-Internet age and the simple job of distributing pamphlets and Khomeini's speeches recorded on cassettes inside Iran was a radical thing to do, and Rafsanjani had been a top logistician. Not to be forgotten is that Rafsanjani had become a close confidant of Ahmad Khomeini, the only surviving son who performed the role of a chief of staff to his father. Thus, Rafsanjani had the old man's full confidence and kept it until Khomeini's death in 1989.

§

Bazargan's premiership would not last until the end of the year 1979. Initially, he refused to have clerics in his cabinet. Later, as he sought to placate Khomeini's partisans, he let some key loyalists closest to Khomeini to enter his government. It was to no avail. Much of what the provincial government sought to do was undermined or outright opposed by the Council of Revolution, which refused to disband and remained packed with radical clerics. Bazargan and his other Western tie-wearing associates were soon out of the door. The Bazargan cabinet's blameless neckties soon after became synonymous with servitude to the West, the preferred villain of the Khomeini faction. To this day, male Iranian officials are easily spotted thanks to the credo ban on them to wear ties.

Meanwhile, Rafsanjani's persistent appearance next to Khomeini offered him the public's attention. In the minds of the Iranian people, he was quickly placed at the top echelon of the new regime. Perceptions are powerful and no one else in Khomeini's inner circle appreciated or cultivated this image of inseparability from the old ayatollah. This was Rafsanjani's most fateful achievement. It paved the way for him to eventually snatch the title of *Akbar Shah* (King Akbar).

§

While Rafsanjani became a household name after the Shah's departure, his stature had been building up throughout the 1970s. Fariborz Ghadar, a 31-year-old Harvard-educated head of Iran's export promotion center in the twilight years of the Shah, recalls the day a cleric walked into his office and demanded state financial support for pistachio exports. "I told him that there is no need as pistachios are exporting just fine without state support," Ghadar recalled telling the cleric, who was not much older than himself. "Listen, young man," the self-assured junior cleric said, "state support will help with sales in the German market."

Ghadar would not budge and the irked cleric stood up and said "very well" and left. The following day Ghadar got a phone call from the Shah's court. He was asked to give the cleric what he wanted and not to worry about the costs. The court, Ghadar was told, will find the money. That Rafsanjani was known to SAVAK was well known. It is the extent to which the Shah sought to placate him as a top Islamist agitator operator that is far less known and remains an unmapped subject. Rafsanjani had in fact for years played the role of the go-between between the Shah's court and the Khomeini clique.

At Khomeini's temporary headquarters at Refah School, Rafsanjani quickly morphed into one of the three principal gatekeepers to the old man. The other two men were 60-year-old Morteza Motahari and 51-year-old Mohammad Beheshti. They were clerics too but older than Rafsanjani and with much greater conventional religious credentials. They too happen to have been pupils of Khomeini before the Shah had him exiled. Anti-cleric forces assassinated Motahari only a few months after Khomeini's return, in March of 1979. Beheshti was killed in another bombing in 1981. But in those early weeks of the revolution, these three men carried the principal weight in the Khomeini inner circle.

Ali Khamenei, Iran's future supreme leader, was at this point barely standing out. He did have a background in opposition politics. SAVAK had once banished him to Baluchistan, Iran's far-flung province on the border with Pakistan. While his talent as a posed speaker soon put him in the public eye, he still had to fight for recognition among his clerical peers. His place in the backseat in those early days has haunted Khamenei ever since. At times, he has engaged in outright fabrications to free himself from his small start. In Khamenei's official biography, for example, one reads today that he had been in the initial membership of the Council of Revolution that Khomeini had appointed in Paris.[26] This was not the case.

Khamenei only joined the council as part of the second batch of members, which was added once the revolution had triumphed.[27] On the other hand, in today's Tehran where adjusting historical facts to suit one's political agenda is a pastime for officials, some pro-Khamenei sources omit Rafsanjani's name entirely from the first Council of Revolution. In fact, it was Rafsanjani who recommended Khamenei's name to Khomeini who had no idea about the 39-year-old from Mashhad. It is perhaps a testament to Rafsanjani's restraint—and certainly his survival instincts—that he would never until he died publicly call out Khamenei for such falsehoods.[28]

The Quick Demise of the Paris Group

After ten days at the Refah primary school, which proved too small for the flourishing bureaucracy that Khomeini's clerical inner circle put up to forward their ambitious agenda, the team moved to a new headquarters. This too was a high school, Alavi, and it was here that within forty-eight hours after Bakhtiar had gone underground before fleeing to France that Khomeinists began to settle scores with the old guard of the Shah. The use of force was in their DNA. The Islamists had engaged in political violence and assassinations of top personalities since they had emerged as a political bloc. It all began with a bang in 1946 when an Islamist fanatic assassinated Ahmad Kasravi, a celebrated secular historian who had questioned clerical dogma and religious grip on life in Iran. In the following decades, a number of officials, including two prime ministers of the Shah, were murdered in the name of Islam.

These same people, clustered around a pseudo-religious order called the "Fedayeen Islam" (*Devotees of Islam*), had now risen to the summit of power. Khamenei, in particular, would again and again proclaim his admiration for the group's violent tactics and its firebrand founder, Navab Safavi.[29] Years later, when he had become supreme leader, Khamenei called Navab, not Khomeini, the one who sparked the revolutionary zeal inside him.[30]

On the rooftop of the school, a number of senior military men from the Shah's regime were summarily executed. The following day, Tehran's newspapers carried photos of rows of dead senior officers. The killings were senseless and merely an act of revenge. Some of Khomeini's own supporters questioned the urgency to execute since the Shah's armed forces had essentially stayed neutral in the revolution. The bloody events at Alavi were a harbinger to an epic power struggle to come unlike anything the nation had ever experienced before. Across the country over the next weeks, months, and years, scores were killed for ties to the old monarchy. One thing the killings did achieve, though, was to firmly reinforce the herald of a new age.

The sight of corpses in a Tehran morgue would not have been the Paris group's first choice to broadcast to the world. In the early tumultuous days of this new age, the members of Khomeini's Paris group no longer had the same access and sway over him. The likes of Yazdi and Sazegara would soon find themselves needing permission in order to see Khomeini. The pendulum had shifted in favor of the Tehran-based clerics, majority of whom had been earlier pupils of Khomeini in his seminary in Qom before his forced exile by the Shah in 1964.

Unlike the Paris group, most of whom were Western-educated and sensitive to the international optics of the revolution, the Tehran circle was singularly captivated by the quest for maximum power as soon as possible. The sensibilities of the Western world— as they would illustrate time and again in the following decades—was of little concern to them. And, unlike the vast majority in the anti-Shah coalition, they had a close-knit network in place. It proved to be an exceedingly well-organized machine for political maneuvers. Meanwhile, the shell-shocked monarchist remnants of the Shah's regime and an assortment of leftist groups squabbled among themselves and often to death.

2

(1979–80)—Bloodletting between the Reds and Islamists to Seizing the US Embassy

With people's revolutionary rage, the king will be ousted and a democratic state, Islamic Republic will be established.[1]
(A statement by Khomeini while in exile in Paris, November 1978)

Don't listen to those who speak of democracy. They are all against Islam. They want to take the nation away from its mission. We will break all the poison pens of those who speak of democracy, nationalism and such things.[2]
(A statement by Khomeini while in power in Tehran, March 1979)

The months that followed the Shah's departure was the most chaotic political period in contemporary Iranian history. Many top political figures from different camps were assassinated, including some of Khomeini's top lieutenants. The thinning at the top gave added momentum to the rise of not only the youngish Rafsanjani but also Khamenei. Meanwhile, among Khomeini's closest associates, the Paris and the Tehran factions were quickly at loggerheads inside the Council of Revolution. But rivalries existed even within the two main factions. Khomeini had agreed to the establishment of the body in Paris. He had come to accept that an organized network was required inside Iran not only to consult him about realities on the ground while he was in exile but also to disseminate his wishes.

Rivalries Inside the Council of Revolution

Unsurprisingly, the council's first-tier membership comprised five men and all clerics personally close to Khomeini. They were Mohammad Bahonar, Mohammad Beheshti, Morteza Motahhari, Abdul-Karim Mousavi-Ardebili, and Akbar Hashemi Rafsanjani. The first three men ended up killed in the political violence that engulfed the country. The five original members were also asked by Khomeini to recommend new potential additions to the council. While the revolution was still raging on, the role of the body was to act as Khomeini's troubleshooting squad. After that, though, the council was meant to kick in as the temporary governing body for the country. A five-man committee was not going to cut it. Khamenei's idea to expand was an opportunity for Rafsanjani who was looking to strengthen his hand and could use allies. In particular, he was looking for ways to go around his rival in the body, Mohammad Beheshti.

Some viewed Beheshti as the nucleus of the clerical faction in the council. He was 51 at the time of the revolution. Tall and with a knack for wearing upmarket clerical garb, he came from the central city of Esfahan known both for its sixteenth- and seventeenth-century architectural wonders and its people's religiosity and entrepreneurial spirit. From the beginning until today, the city of Esfahan has produced a disproportionate number to fill the ranks of officials in the Islamic Republic.

Thanks to his managerial skills, the Shia religious leadership had in the 1960s sent Beheshti to Hamburg. This would not have been possible without the Shah's consent. Here, between 1965 and 1971, he headed one of the largest mosques in Europe that a group of Iranian businessmen had sponsored. His years in Germany made Beheshti familiar with Western ways, a trait most of his clerical peers who had no exposure to the outside world deeply lacked. This reality would soon make him into a suitable go-between for the United States and the more rugged elements among Khomeini's cohorts. However, he was not the only one that eyeballed the Americans. Rafsanjani and Beheshti had both emerged as Khomeini's top lieutenants in those fourteen years—from 1964 to 1978—he spent in Najaf. Shah's attempts to mollify Khomeini's inner circle was not limited only to Rafsanjani. Amazingly, the Shah's court had at one point made Beheshti into a principal advisor in the production for new religious textbooks for the country's schools. Shah's failure to co-opt these clerics was therefore not due to a lack of trying.

If Rafsanjani was Khomeini's plain-speaking fixer on the ground that dutifully collected financial contributions for the cause, Beheshti was the urbane Islamist militant intellectual. Khomeini thought of Rafsanjani as a reliable disciple. During his many arrests by the Shah's security services, he had been tight-lipped and proved he was loyal to Khomeini personally and was not just an ardent Islamist revolutionary. Khomeini deep down might have had reservations about Beheshti as a possible rival to himself in ways Rafsanjani could never be. Beheshti's systematic elimination of the opponents of the Khomeini camp was instructive even for his purported comrades-in-arms. Notably, as the head of the judicial branch, Beheshti turned this arm of the government into the judge, jury, and executioner. It was a legacy that has long outlasted him.

Rafsanjani was therefore not acting benevolently when he recommended to Khomeini that the young Ali Khamenei be added to the Council of Revolution. He was after allies in the council. "Who is he," Khomeini is said to have asked. "He has influence in [city of] Mashhad," Rafsanjani replies. "Salam be Mashhad-e bidar shode" (Hello to the awakened Mashhad), the old man exclaimed.[3] The city, Iran's second largest, had been mostly quiet during the revolutionary mayhem. Rafsanjani's pitch was that Khamenei could turn Mashhad around.[4] This is how Khamenei joined the council. Khomeini, however, would never again want to visit Mashhad.

Rafsanjani's clashes with Beheshti later on became common knowledge. Rafsanjani complained: "Mr. Beheshti acts unilaterally. He shuts down newspapers and claims it is the [Revolution] Council's collective decision when the rest of us were not consulted."[5]

Despite such tensions between Rafsanjani and Beheshti, they still shared one common interest: to institutionalize the idea of a clerical "Supreme Leader" and have Khomeini hold that office. To achieve this goal was tantamount to checkmating the non-Islamist and moderate clerical components in the revolution.

An Unelected Supreme Leader

Khomeini's track record in advocating for a strict religious rule was decades old. But he had prior to the revolution downplayed his ideas around a "government of pure Islam." Not even his Islamist supporters adopted the chant of "[demanding a] Islamic Republic" until about a few months before the fall of the Shah. Khomeini knew that the secular leftists and nationalists who were in the anti-Shah camp were disinclined to follow him if his theocratic designs took a front seat. He let his ideas dally without forcing the issue until the time was ripe.[6] While the Khomeini-appointed provincial Bazargan government set out to administer the bedazzled country, a select group of men set out to draft the post-Shah constitution that would shape the political order to come. Bazargan was nervous. As early as 1978, when he sent an emissary to Najaf, he had asked Khomeini to hold back from asking for an "Islamic Republic" until it was clearer what it entailed.

In order to exert maximum pressure on the outcome at this critical juncture, Khomeini's closest lieutenants—including Beheshti, Rafsanjani, and Khamenei—created a parallel track to the Council of Revolution. The name of the new entity was the Islamic Republican Party (IRP). It was founded on February 17, 1979, one week after the victory of the revolution. By April, the IRP created a parallel armed wing called the Islamic Revolution Guards Corps (IRGC). In the West, they were soon to be known as the Revolutionary Guards.

The IRP openly began to argue for "Islamization" of society in which Islamic values, commands, and laws govern all social relations.[7] This party alone would soon become the arbiters of what is "Islamic." The party's daily newspaper, *Jomhuri-ye Eslami* (Islamic Republic), became its public mouthpiece. The Khomeini clique now had a political branch and with a media machinery behind to propagate the message. They did, however, need to maintain an armed muscle to protect all their achievements, and hence the formation of the IRGC. Its singular mission was to keep the clerics in power against all other rivals.

At this point, in Tehran alone hundreds of armed groups, or "committees" as they were locally known, were roaming the streets. Many of these groups were banded together under the IRGC flag. Khomeini quickly put Rafsanjani and Khamenei in charge to jointly share the task of exercising supervision of this new body. This was to make sure the spirited young recruits of the IRGC stayed as clerical tools.[8] One lesson that Khomeinists had learned from the way the Shah's military abandoned him in his hour of need was to establish a military entity to defend the regime even when the conscripted soldiers might not.

Khomeini's advanced age was a significant factor in creating a sense of urgency. As part of this effort, the core goal of the IRP quickly became the establishment of a function for a "supreme leader," and with Khomeini in mind for this position. Even as Beheshti became IRP's first party leader, Rafsanjani later always took credit for having convinced a reluctant Khomeini to bless the party's creation. At first, Khomeini had spurned the idea of his clerical disciples forming a party. Even he could anticipate that plain politicking risked sullying the image of the clergy. But the argument for the necessity to have an organized machinery to prevent losing out to relentless leftist forces had eventually persuaded Khomeini.

§

In the process to draft the constitution, as it had done throughout the revolution, the Khomeini camp was willing to first embrace and then monopolize leftist terminologies.[9] It was a masterstroke of sorts. The Islamization of Marxist concepts had begun industriously by Ali Shariati, a sociologist seen by many as the ideological father of the leftist Islamists involved in the Iranian revolution of 1979. Like Ali Khamenei, Shariati came from the outskirts of Mashhad and also from a family of clerics. He was a few years older than his namesake but had unlike him broken free from the chains of traditionalism. Shariati was one of the many thousands of young Iranians that the Shah's government had sent abroad to equip themselves with the best Western education had to offer.

Shariati, however, had come back from Sorbonne in Paris armed with a passion to topple the Shah. But he was hardly a follower of Khomeini. In fact, contemptuous of the clergy, Shariati had a turbulent relationship with Khomeini's supporters. Khomeini had sought to ban Shariati from preaching at Tehran's leading Islamist center, the *Ershad*.[10] But the Khomeini circle recognized that Shariati's marrying up of Marxist-inspired socioeconomic rallying cries with his cultural and religious nativism had had big draw among the idealistic young and the poor, two key demographic groups in the manufacturing of any revolution. In Shariati's vocabulary, the proletariat had become the *mostazafeen* (downtrodden) and imperialism was labeled *estekbaar* ("world arrogance," meaning the West and specifically the United States). Khomeinists happily adopted such phrases as they had lifted militant vernacular from the likes of Sayyid Qutb and other Islamists.

At only 43, Shariati died in 1977 in England and did not live to see the fruits of his agitations. While he had in his writings argued for "religious guidance" in government, the Khomeinists linked it up to Khomeini's own ideas and took the concept to mean clerical control. Back in 1905-6, during Iran's Constitutional Revolution—which happened to have been the first popular rebellion in all of Asia that demanded a more democratic system—the clergy had asked for a seat—albeit an important one—at the political table. The clergy had then wanted a council made up of top religious figures that had a veto right over all national laws. The supposed aim was to make all legislation compatible with the basic tenets of Islam but not to become an instigator of legislation as such. After 1979, the Khomeinists insisted on not only a seat at the political table but also predominance.

This is how a new and hitherto novice notion of the rule of the "Supreme Leader," or "Rahbar," was introduced to a largely unsuspecting Iranian population. Nothing like it had been devised before in Shia Islam's 1,400 years of history. In fact, right from the 1905–6 Constitutional Revolution until 1979, and until the present day, a schism has existed inside the Shia clerical class about the role of religion and clergymen in government. Many Shia clerics did then and continue to reject the theological basis for the concept of political or even religious "guardianship by the Islamic jurist" or "Velayat-e Faqih."[11] Ezzatollah Sahabi, a prominent anti-Shah activist, raised the alarm about the dawn of new autocracy. The concept of "supreme leader," he said, is "betraying the people whose main aim in the revolution was freedom [to choose]."[12]

If the constitution of 1905–6 was a compromise between the secular and religious forces, the former aspiring for a Western-style constitutional monarchy with the latter just simply not wanting to be left behind the modernizing mood of the time, the constitution of 1979 represented a putsch.[13] Auxiliary mechanisms were soon enough arranged to give Khomeinists unbeatable command. An ingenious but wholly despotic creation was the Council of Guardians. An unelected body of twelve men appointed by the supreme leader, the council was supposed to have "responsibility for supervising the elections of president, the parliament (the Majles), and general referendums." There was initially no mention of it having the power to approve candidates or be able to reject legislation by the Majles.

The Council of Guardians became a filtering system that no undesired candidate or policy could beat. Khomeini welcomed it. "With this [constitution], the political order will remain Islamic permanently."[14] To this day, the existence of the Council of Guardians is one of the most obvious structural hindrances in the path of political reform in Iran. Rafsanjani, who at first strongly defended the body's role, was in 2013 told by the Council of Guardians that he was unfit to hold high office again.

§

At the time of the revolution in 1979, both the Paris and the Tehran factions in Khomeini's circle understood that blindsiding the United States entirely as the deliberations about the future political governance continued was not a good idea. The Khomeinists were at this point—the spring of 1979—still in regular contact with the US embassy. Ebrahim Yazdi, who was briefly foreign minister in this period (April–November), assured the US embassy that once "this procedure [drafting of the post-Shah constitution] was completed, the Council of Revolution and the Revolutionary Committees would be dissolved" and the country can go back to normality.[15]

Yazdi was not the only one in regular contact with the Americans. Rafsanjani's younger brother Mohammad—who was studying in California at the time—acted as a messenger for his brother and his American interlocutors. Back in 1975, Rafsanjani had traveled via France to see his brother in America. He had arranged to meet his brother, Mohammad, in Houston, Texas, where Yazdi at the time was a practicing physician. In Houston, Rafsanjani bought a car and opted to drive across the United States for ten days to his California destination. He wanted to familiarize himself with the American way of life. He is said to have concluded that the best system of a government is a fusion of the capitalist and the socialist models. But, unlike the unfavorable impressions left on the Egyptian Sayyid Qutb when he traveled in the United States in the 1950s, Rafsanjani was by no means abhorred by his American journey.

But in 1979 it was Beheshti who was viewed in Washington as their best hope in the new regime against the vehemently anti-American leftists and ultra-rightist clerics.[16] The Carter administration assessed Beheshti as the de facto No. 2 in the new regime. Such thinking was not without merit. Given Khomeini's advanced age at the time, at 77 years, Beheshti was the most obvious standby successor.

The Khomeini camp was in full swing. The old man had authorized a provincial government but kept the Council of Revolution intact as a counterweight. The two engaged in a bitter rivalry but the clerics in the council—such as Beheshti, Rafsanjani, and Khamenei—were closest to Khomeini and hence had de facto upper hand in imposing their will. As Prime Minister Bazargan put it himself, his government was "like a knife with no blade."

By March 1979, a referendum was held about Iran's political future. The choice was simple. As Khomeini put it, "Not the 'Republic of Iran,' nor the 'Democratic Republic of Iran,' nor the 'Democratic Islamic Republic of Iran,' just the 'Islamic Republic of Iran.'"[17] Those revolutionaries who insisted to include the word "democratic" in the title of the new regime were warned not to question God's will. Moderates, such as Bazargan, threatened to walk away but it was to no avail.

The choice was no easier for the average Iranian voter. At the day of the referendum, two ballots were available. The red ballot was for those opposed; the green ballot for those in favor. With Khomeini's allies mostly in possession of the looted arms, on the day of the referendum the average voter was met with zealous gaze of the Khomeinists who only wanted to see green ballots being cast. In July, Bazargan sought for a last time to neutralize Khomeini's closest allies by co-opting them. Among others, he brought both Rafsanjani and Khamenei into his cabinet but this only served to whet their appetite for more power grab.

Eliminating Clerical Opponents of the Supreme Leader

The concept of "Supreme Leadership" was never going to be left unopposed. Three groups had provided the leadership, ideological defense of, and financial backing for the revolution: the young—mostly leftist—intelligentsia, the militant clerics, and the younger generation from Iran's mercantile class in the *Bazaar*. Early on in the drafting of the new constitution, many on the political left but also secular nationalist forces had threatened to split from the revolution, seeing Khomeini as forcing his will down people's throats. Their grumbles did not dissuade the Khomeini faction. Opposition from within the revolutionary clergy, however, was a different matter.

§

Among the foremost clerical opponents of the "Supreme Leadership," two men stood out. One was Grand Ayatollah Kazem Shariatmadari and the other was Ayatollah Mahmoud Taleghani. Both feared Khomeini's radical agenda. The former was essentially a traditionalist and deeply suspicious of Khomeini's fusion of Shia Islam with militancy. In the West, that class of clerics has become known as "quietists" and is best exemplified by Ayatollah Ali Sistani, who in post-Saddam Iraq became the top religious authority in that country.

In late May 1979, Shariatmadari called for nation-wide marches for "democracy, freedom of expression, and freedom of press." As violence loomed, he called off the marches. The Khomeini people never forgot, or forgave, and Shariatmadari would in due time be defrocked and publicly humiliated despite his senior religious standing. The irony was that back in 1963, Shariatmadari had personally mediated to have Shah spare Khomeini's life and have him exiled instead.

Taleghani too was outspokenly against the new constitutional arrangement but his grassroots support base was among the left in the Islamist camp that later on converged under the Mujahedeen-e Khalq (MEK) or *People's Warriors*. And yet, in their common opposition to absolute clerical rule as the Khomeini faction was pushing for, Shariatmadari and Taleghani represented the clerical strand that wanted to go back to the basic ideas as set out in the 1905–6 constitution. The emphasis was on "people power" and elevating the roles of elected offices, such as city councils, and warning against excessive centralization of power in the hands of the senior clerics.

Taleghani's left-of-center sermons in particular drew big crowd in Tehran, the all-important element to keep the revolution alive. At the time, of Iran's roughly 40 million population some 50 per cent lived in rural areas. And yet, only 2 per cent of the 2,483 recorded demonstrations against the Shah's regime took place in the countryside. This was a revolution led by the big cities, Tehran in particular, and big-city clerics like Taleghani yielded much influence. They had the pulse of the urbanites, and that was a precious commodity, a reality that even Khomeini understood. A long-time anti-Shah activist, Taleghani had spent eight years in prison, at one point sharing a cell with Rafsanjani.[18] While incarcerated, he had also interacted with different kinds of leftist oppositionists. Once out, he said he preferred the company of ordinary folks over his fellow clerics. He would stay in Tehran and not live in Qom, the hub of clerical life. His popular appeal was so great Khomeini made him the leader of the Friday Prayer in Tehran. Giving Taleghani such a public platform was a risky step. Still, a first attempt to co-opt rivals was the usual modus operandi of the Khomeini circle. In the case of Taleghani, he was not drawn any closer to the Khomeini's inner circle. In his Friday sermons from this uppermost of podiums—a total of five before he died—Taleghani kept his deference toward Khomeini but his implicit attacks continued and it stung.

"Someone selfish but clever will seek to impose his will on us (religious dictatorship). Don't listen to pledges of free water, bread and some such."[19] This was precisely what Khomeini had promised earlier in a speech. At one point, Khomeini loyalists from the then nascent Revolutionary Guards, the armed wing of the radical rightist clerics, kidnapped two of Taleghani's sons and kept them for three days. Disgusted with the state of politics in Tehran, Taleghani left the city for seclusion on the Caspian Sea.[20]

Khomeini convinced him to return to Tehran. This was mostly due to the fact that Taleghani was never sure if the old man was himself that determined for religious rule or even aware of what the likes of Beheshti, Rafsanjani, and Khamenei were attempting to implement in his name. For sure, Taleghani had his reservations about Khomeini's younger underlings like Rafsanjani who he would at times dismiss as someone unable to drop his overlord bearings despite the victory of this purported revolution by the proletariat class. Not only was Taleghani against what he called religious dictatorship but he also urged for elected councils made by representatives of the people to be given political primacy. Khomeini's inner circle was aghast, viewing such calls as a de facto decapitation of the power of the militant clerics.[21] Behind his back, they denounced him as the "Red Ayatollah." Still, Taleghani had become a hero for many and the counter to Khomeini's forced Islamization of society and governance.

§

Taleghani's opposition to Khomeini's plans to become an absolute supreme leader resulted in his suspicious death. The night he died, the neighborhood where Taleghani lived had suddenly plunged into darkness. Not only electricity but the phone line went dead too. A few days earlier, Mehdi Olumi, Taleghani's personal bodyguard, had been assaulted by an unknown group and left with a broken leg. With his personal bodyguard out, Taleghani was alone.

Michael Metrinko was the US embassy's top liaison with the revolutionary clerics. A few days after Taleghani's death, he got a call from one of the sons of Taleghani.[22] Metrinko was asked to see the family. Taleghani had just prior to his death told Beheshti, Rafsanjani, and Khamenei that he could not support the creation of the role of a supreme leader. After his death, when the family asked Beheshti for an autopsy, they were told they will "all need autopsies" if they persisted. The last meeting Taleghani had the night he died was with a Soviet delegation headed by Moscow's ambassador to Tehran, Vladimir M. Vinogradov.[23] In his obituary in the *New York Times*, Taleghani was recalled as a "moderate second only to Ayatollah Ruhollah Khomeini in power in Iran."[24] But was that enough of a motive to have him liquidated?

Until today, the exact cause of his death is unsettled. Many, including his family members, refuse to believe he died of a heart attack as was announced at the time.[25] The Khomeini circle saw Taleghani's opposition to the idea of a supreme leader as a real obstacle to achieving their goals.[26] The Soviets clearly had an interest in guiding the trajectory of the Iranian revolution. To turn Iran from a pro-American bastion to an anti-American renegade nation amounted to a geopolitical coup. Still, whether they viewed Taleghani as a weak link in their plans for Iran—not to mention by opting to do so conspicuously by poisoning him as some have suggested—remains unknown.[27]

The anti-Khomeini crowd, however, quickly suspected foul play. "Beheshti, Beheshti, you killed Taleghani," his supporters chanted as Taleghani's body was buried. Callous action shortly after by men close to Khomeini reinforced the doubters. Remarkably, the studio of the state television that was airing a program to mourn Taleghani's death was raided, presumably to put a quick end to the aggrandizement of this charismatic rival of Khomeini that was seen to pose a threat even in death.[28] Metrinko—the US diplomat who knew the Taleghani family—ended up arranging for visas for them to go to the United States. As he remembers it, this was not a controversial decision. This was in mid-September 1979. These would be some of the last American visas issued in Tehran. Within a few weeks, on November 4, the US embassy was attacked by a group of radical Islamists who claimed to be followers of Khomeini.

Seizing the American Embassy in Tehran

From the vantage point of Washington, Taleghani's death on September 10 had left Shariatmadari as the revered figure that had any chance to stop Khomeini's march toward absolute religious dictatorship. The United States had sent messages to Shariatmadari as soon as it determined the Shah's reign was about to come to an end. The initial instincts of the Jimmy Carter administration had been to keep the Khomeini faction at arm's length. In the dying days of the Shah, Beheshti had sought to meet the US ambassador in Tehran, William Sullivan. On January 12, the embassy turned down the request as Carter did not want to bargain with Khomeini while the Shah was still in Tehran. But the following day approval was provided. Washington wanted to know how Khomeini viewed the Iranian military. This was the one institution America had over the previous decades invested most in to deter any Soviet designs on Iran.

Cyrus Vance, the US secretary of state, had at one point viewed Khomeini as the best safeguard against a communist takeover in Tehran. He even raised the possibility of close cooperation between the new regime in Tehran and Washington. Given events that would follow, Vance appears on the face of it to have been clueless about the worldview of the Khomeini circle. And yet Vance was going by messages he was receiving from the old cleric's key deputies. In Paris, Yazdi had told an American embassy emissary "Khomeini would be open to US investment but would be [generally] antagonistic toward the US." But he would be even more antagonistic to the "atheist" and "anti-religious Soviets." In the rough Cold War setting, being the second most hated superpower was not such a bad deal. Nor had the Khomeinists at first shown an interest in an open confrontation with the United States.

§

When on February 15, 1979, a group of radical leftist gunmen stormed the American embassy, it was an armed rescue squad dispatched by Khomeini that ended the brief siege. "You are our brothers. Don't worry," Khomeini's militiamen told the terrified US diplomats and military officers. The American ambassador told reporters that very same day: "We telephoned the Khomeini group and they came and saved us in a nick of time."[29] Among those rescued were US air force Lieutenant General Philip Gast and twenty-six other US military officers. Ebrahim Yazdi and Ayatollah Mohammad Beheshti had saved the day. Both men viewed this as an opportunity to secure a pat on the back from the Americans.

In the next few months, Prime Minister Bazargan repeatedly reaffirmed that Iran intended to have good relations with Washington. When he was attacked for being soft on the Americans by the far left or the Khomeinists, Bazargan defended himself by saying Khomeini had himself sanctioned talks with the United States. Bazargan repeatedly asked for US military and commercial supplies and on at least one occasion asked for intelligence from Washington. Economic ties, including Iranian purchases of American goods, continued, albeit on a much smaller scale than the days of the Shah. This was anathema to many Khomeinists, including Khamenei. "The [Bazargan] government saw no reason in having animosity toward the US, which they saw as a strong and rich country that really did not bother us," he complained.[30]

Khamenei claims he had threatened to resign from the defense committee in the Bazargan government in protest that the US military was still present in Iran months after the Shah's fall. The anti-Americanism of the Khomeinists on the public level was unfathomable to many in the interim government. "Why don't you people quit chanting 'Death to America,'" Bazargan asked them. Khamenei says he responded angrily. What is known is that behind the scenes the Khomeinists kept lines of communication open to the United States. Another key Khomeini ally, and future deputy supreme leader, who met US officials was Ayatollah Hossein-Ali Montazeri. He had been friendly and expressed his "great admiration for [President] Carter" and hope for expansion of relations.[31] Montazeri met American officials as late as one week before the storming of the US embassy.

On November 4, another group of pro-Khomeini militiamen returned to the US embassy but this time not as the rescuers but as the assailants. They seized the compound. It was growing competition for power in Tehran that paved the way for this event. Between the February 15 attack on the embassy and its seizure on November 4, the Khomeini circle kept musing American offers. In July 1979, Beheshti had met with the CIA's top Middle East man, Bob Ames, who visited Tehran from the agency's regional station in Beirut.[32] Ames had come to offer Iran's new Islamist rulers a new dialogue and to launch strategic intelligence cooperation. The trip had been fully coordinated with the White House and the Department of State. Beheshti was seen as more able to deliver than Yazdi or Bazargan. Above all, as US ambassador Sullivan later wrote in his memoirs, Beheshti had during his eight years in Hamburg come to acquire a "deep distrust of the Soviets and the East German Communists who handled the Communist Tudeh Party of Iran."[33]

For Iran's Islamists, the idea of open channels to Washington was then not yet the manufactured taboo that it later became. As early as the 1950s, Abol-Qasem Kashani, the most prominent clerical political voice in Iran at the time and a mentor to Khomeini, had secretly reached out to the US embassy asking for American support. In a letter to president Eisenhower he applauded the United States for "not being a colonialist power" and promised in exchange of American support to help keep the Soviets out of the Middle East.[34] As such, the Khomeini circle spent much of the fateful months of 1979 calculating how the United States could be useful to them in the effort to checkmate local rivals such as leftist and secular nationalist political forces.

Events on the ground soon took the revolution into an entirely different direction. The last months leading up to the seizure of the US embassy in Tehran on November 4 witnessed a torrent of fateful events. In June, the first draft of the new Iranian constitution was unveiled. It did not yet speak of a "supreme leader" with infinite powers but the writing was on the wall. It was bound to animate the leftists and other factions that had backed the revolution. On September 10, Taleghani suddenly died. For the religious-minded among the urban youth, he had been the principal clerical voice. The Islamist camp was soon forever ruptured between the rightist (the Khomeini faction) and the leftist Islamists. Among the latter, the MEK would be the most prominent. The universities, one of the main bastions of radical politics, were reopened on September 23, providing militant students seats of operation. Some of

Iran's most prominent future political personalities, including a 22-year-old Mahmoud Ahmadinejad, began their careers in the campuses at this time. Violent political rivalry among the various factions again returned. In the midst of this chaos, on October 22 the deposed Shah was admitted to the United States for cancer treatment. Khomeini was enraged and convinced Washington was plotting to undermine the consolidation of power by the militant clerics.

Prime Minister Bazargan had on November 1 traveled to Algeria to ostensibly take part in celebrating Algeria's Revolution Day. In Algeria, Bazargan met president Carter's national security advisor, Zbigniew Brzezinski. Back in Tehran, that infamous handshake in Algeria was seized as purported evidence of an American-orchestrated plot being underway to sideline Khomeini or even return the Shah back to power. Only three days later, militants who called themselves "Followers of the Imam [Khomeini]" stormed the US embassy and would keep fifty-two US diplomats as hostages for the next 444 days. The following day the Bazargan government washed its hands of the entire affair and resigned. In his resignation letter, Bazargan like many others before him deplored radical clerical takeover of Iran. His criticism of the Khomeinists only thickened with time. "What have you done [since coming to power], besides bringing death and destruction, packing the prisons, and the cemeteries in every city, creating long queues, shortages, high prices, unemployment, poverty, homelessness and a dark future?"[35]

For Bazargan, Khomeini's success in plowing through his rivals came down to one quality, and that was determination. Khomeini, Bazargan said, is a "bulldozer that crushes rocks, roots and stones in his path; I am a delicate passenger car."[36] Bazargan also said taking the US embassy equaled the capture of a lion. Khomeini's response was the sort of classic swagger that today defines the Islamic Republic. He said it would "be a petty to call [US president] Carter a lion." He then added, "At the same time as a lion roars, he produces another substance from its other end."[37] This was Khomeini's coarse way to call the American president a paper tiger.

Much has been written about whether Khomeini had prior knowledge about the plan to seize the embassy. What is beyond doubt is that he with eyes wide open blessed the continuation of the hostage crisis even as evidence piled up that the incident was costing Iran dearly on all levels. For him consolidation of his grip on power on the home front mattered the most, and the crisis with Washington had its distinct advantages for the Khomeinists.

At the time, three distinct benefits stood out. First, the hostage-taking crisis predictably led to resignation and later marginalization of the "liberal" or moderate Islamists around Bazargan. Second, the United States was suddenly put on the defensive and forced to reckon with Khomeini as the Shah's only true successor. Third, the bulk of the radical leftist youth were initially supportive of the takeover of the embassy, allowing Khomeini to peel off support from rival revolutionary factions. Khomeini's top lieutenants set out to manipulate the situation to the fullest extent. Narrow political gains triumphed over advancing the national interest. No one had a clue about the damage this action would for years incur on Iran. One of the student leaders said the idea had been to seize the embassy for no more than 48 hours but it was to last 444 days.

A Sudden Phone Call in Mecca

Not long before midnight on November 4, Rafsanjani and Khamenei were together in Mecca, Saudi Arabia, to perform the Muslim pilgrimage. A call came in from Tehran that the US embassy had been taken. Khamenei writes in his memoirs that his first question was, who had done it? Were the hostage-takers communists as had been the case in February? As Khamenei put it, the two men "found the news both exciting and frightening because we did not know which faction had done this."[38] Nothing suggests either man had had prior knowledge about the plan and still chose to be in faraway Mecca.

Both men quickly found out that the key clerical ringleader in that affair was a man by the name of Mohammad Mousavi Khoeiniha. He had a reputation as a radical and someone the CIA later assessed to be both close to Ayatollah Khomeini's son, Ahmad, and also open to Tehran moving closer to the Soviets in its coming foreign policy. This was for sure a different tune than was associated with Rafsanjani. Few months earlier, in March 1979, Rafsanjani had delivered a highly anti-Soviet speech at the funeral of Ayatollah Mottahari, Khomeini's right-hand man, who had been assassinated by a leftist-Islamist cell (*Furqan*). That anti-Soviet speech had been duly noted by the Western embassies.

Rafsanjani and Khamenei decided to back the seizure of the US embassy once they found out supporters of Khomeini were behind the act. The following day, the main headline in the IRP's newspaper hailed the event as the "Second Revolution." Once back from Mecca, the duet defended the embassy seizure. The phrase "Second Revolution" soon came to mean a blanket purge of Khomeini's opponents. The US embassy takeover was initially as much, if not more, about turning the tables against Bazargan and the other moderates—or "liberals" as they were disparagingly named—than drubbing the United States. The liberals, Khamenei said in a speech shortly after, believe "the embassy takeover would destroy the revolution—[that] Iran would be defeated and America would devour Iran."

To this day, Khamenei defends this "glorious" action. He is unmoved by the damage it did to Iran's standing in the world, not to mention the spiral of antipathy it set in motion with the United States. Khamenei wrote later that he supported the decision as soon as he found out "Muslim followers of Khomeini, and not leftists had done it."[39] It was a different story with Rafsanjani. The first time Rafsanjani called the seizure a mistake was in 1989, the year Khomeini died. Each man was reinterpreting the event in the pursuit of new political sights each had picked. What neither admitted was that the seized documents from the US embassy became pretext to neutralize anyone deemed an opponent. In one case, Abbas Amir Entezam, who was the deputy prime minister under Bazargan, was sent to a revolutionary court for having had communications with the US embassy. In reality, it was his opposition to the idea of Khomeini becoming a "supreme leader" that had him chastised and shortly after landed him a lengthy prison term.[40]

The hostage-takers released the US documents very selectively. Khomeinists in contact with the Americans were spared. Most importantly, Ayatollah Beheshti, the man the Carter administration for a while had viewed as a potential broker with Khomeini, was never exposed. Michael Metrinko, the US political officer at the embassy, had a front-row seat as the Khomeini camp increasingly wrapped itself in the mantel of anti-Americanism. A fluent Persian speaker who had lived in Iran's big cities as well as its smaller villages, he preferred the street-level view against the removed bureaucracy of the embassy compound. With years of schmoozing with an assortment of Iranian interlocutors, Metrinko often found himself at meals in the homes of top revolutionary families, whom he quickly realized often did not like each other very much.

Ali Khamenei might have been surprised that members of his own family knew Metrinko. This was not a subject that the political officer would bring up when the two men met while Metrinko was later taken as one of the US hostages. Still, dining with the family of Iran's future leader was a freak coincidence as the Khamenei family was at this point not a priority for the Americans in Tehran. Instead, Metrinko recalls how he had in March 1979 visited Beheshti in his house. Together with colleagues, such as John Limbert and John Stemple from the embassy, they had come to gauge the prospects of US–Iran relations under the new regime. At Beheshti's house, they were served cold tea. This was in Iranian cultural terms a deliberate affront. Unlike others at the embassy who were enthusiastic about Beheshti, Metrinko was sure this right-hand man of Khomeini had no particular proclivity toward the United States. His only motive behind meeting the US diplomats was to find out more about the American agenda in post-Shah Iran. Metrinko's instincts proved to be correct.

§

Following the embassy's seizure, Henry Precht, the officer at the Iran Desk at the State Department, picked up the phone and called Beheshti. "Is there a way you can help us free the diplomats?" Beheshti replied that he was about to go to a meeting at the Revolutionary Council. He promised to call back but never did.[41] It is at this point that in Tehran the taboo of dealing with Americans is fervidly born. Precht had a good inkling about the anguish found in the Khomeini camp. He had himself met Beheshti a week earlier, on October 27, in Tehran. Beheshti had asked Washington for two things: show its support for the revolution by refusing to provide sanctuary to the Shah and by "overcoming delays in shipments of military and commercial spare parts needed by Iran." The United States had not delivered on either point.

The fixation of the anti-Shah revolutionaries with the United States was not groundless even though it was vastly panic-struck. Nor was it only rooted in the events of the pro-Shah US-instigated coup of 1953. The revolutionaries were not imagining American machinations. Washington had been ready to move against them but had come short in terms of good options. Washington had been in touch with various Iranian anti-Shah factions, including the Khomeini camp. These secret efforts, although contradictory and ultimately self-defeating efforts as Brzezinski admitted, only fueled Iranian fears. These factions, even though some were loath to see the United States leave Iran, were at the same time apprehensive about the Americans favoring one faction over another. That was clearly the Khomeini camp's fear about an American collusion with the liberals.

Future Supreme Leader Ali Khamenei's ex post facto memory aside, the reality is that he was himself at the time a proponent of Iran continuing to tap into American expertise and supply of goods and services. In one instance as a Khomeini's representative on military matters in the Council of Revolution, he had vehemently argued for retaining recently procured US-made F-14s that others in the body viewed as costly examples of the Shah's extravaganza.[42] Khamenei's attitude was intrinsically a practical one, a trait that later in his career was not as salient. Nor could anyone in Tehran be oblivious to the fact that Iran was at the heart of a Soviet–American Cold War struggle. To keep both Moscow and Washington at bay but still have lines of communication open to them was more or less a consensus in Tehran. That was before the US embassy was taken. That event, of course, changed everything.

§

The Iranian revolution was a matchless affair in the twentieth century. No other nation in the Islamic World has witnessed anything similar to it before or after. Not even the gush of Arab popular rebellions that began with Tunisia in December 2010 produced such a transformative outcome as in Iran in 1979. Some see it not as a revolution but as a counterrevolution to the modernizing efforts of the Shah and his father before him that had for the previous fifty years pulled Iran in a direction many opposed, albeit for different reasons. The Shah and his rule had certainly been guilty of causing a deep schism in Iranian society.

The revolutionaries wanted an end to the Shah's autocratic system but most were horrified by the chaos that followed. In the midst of that pandemonium, the Khomeinists proved to be enormously organized and conniving. On each and every important turn, they managed to leave their anti-Shah partners-turned-rivals in the dust. No social class regretted taking part in the revolution as much as the urban middle class. They were the biggest victims of it. Educated, with jobs and access to social and cultural freedoms, they had joined the anti-Shah bandwagon and were politically totally naïve and unprepared for the world Khomeini came to represent. What followed truly shocked them.

By the end of 1979, the core Khomeini faction had achieved two specific accomplishments that since then have secured the grip of Khomeinists on power. First, they created the "Office of the Supreme Leader." To manipulate a popular movement aspiring for democracy morph into a theocracy was a spell of ingenuity by the Khomeinists. It came after a hard-fought battle. Even in the Khomeinist-dominated Assembly of Experts, the body that was charged to draft and pass the unorthodox constitution, about a dozen of its seventy-three members voted against the new constitution and a "supreme leader."[43]

The second marking of the auspicious foresight of the radical clergy was the creation of the Revolutionary Guards, which Khomeini ordered in March 1979. This marriage of convenience between the Khomeini camp with restless young armed men looking for a mission in life had two aspects to it. It gave the new Islamist regime immediate muscle on the street level where ultimately political destinies were decided. The Revolutionary Guards soon became a state-within-a-state with its own distinct agenda. This fledging theocracy backed by Revolutionary Guards represented a new political order. Hundreds of thousands of vacancies had to be filled.

From government ministers to teachers and from military officers to local village heads and preachers, Khomeinist purges opened up opportunities for many among the poor and other underprivileged social groups. As a rule, loyalty to the system was more important than being the best person for the job. The Iranian revolution was also overwhelmingly a young man's struggle. By the end of 1979, Rafsanjani and Khamenei, both still in their early 40s, were among top-tier deputies of Khomeini. That Rafsanjani was initially the bigger player of the two cannot be denied. In the memoirs of Anthony Parsons, the British ambassador who was among the most important foreign personalities in Tehran at the time of the fall of the Shah, Khamenei's name does not appear once. Rafsanjani, though, is mentioned by Parsons and in a case of clear flattery referred to as an "ayatollah" even though he hardly yet acquired that rank.[44]

For Rafsanjani, the ever merchant, closeness to sources of money was tantamount to power. As early as July 1979, Rafsanjani had unsuccessfully angled to become oil minister, the richest government ministry. A Khomeinist newspaper suddenly began to publish documents that claimed the sitting oil minister, Ali Akbar Moinfar, had been a SAVAK asset in the 1960s.[45] The character assassination against Moinfar failed on that occasion and probably for the best for Rafsanjani. He would soon acquire far more power than one single government ministry alone could ever provide. Khamenei, though, was always infatuated with military affairs and raw power. His first main role as Khomeini's representative involved the defense portfolio. In that capacity, he proved faster, and more determined in the long run, to cultivate the young men from the Revolutionary Guards. That became his ace card, and it was how he finally in time was to outflank Rafsanjani.

3

(1980–1)—The Second Purge: Chaos at Home and War Abroad

Our garden is lonely, our garden is lonely
All day long from behind the door comes the sound of shattering and explosions
All our neighbors plant bombs and machineguns in their gardens instead of flowers
All our neighbors cover their tiled ponds, which become unwitting secret storehouses of gunpowder
And the children along our street have filled their schoolbags with small bombs.
Our garden is confused.

(Forough Farrokhzad, Iranian poet)

On January 18, 1980, within a few short weeks after the seizing of the US embassy in Tehran, Khomeini had a heart attack.[1] The 78-year-old was hospitalized as an anxious public looked to see if he would survive. He had no successor designate. The transitional government led by prime minister Mehdi Bazargan had on November 5 resigned in protest against Khomeini's endorsement of seizing the US embassy. Khomeini's death at that moment very likely would have upended the power consolidation that his closest disciples had carried out in the previous eleven months.

Fearing such a scenario for months, the Khomeini camp had relentlessly hounded anyone deemed as rivals. The Khomeini-appointed Council of the Revolution was still operating and in the hands of Beheshti, Rafsanjani, Khamenei, and other loyalists of the old man. They were as powerful as ever. The Khomeinists were acutely conscious of one single powerful fact: that their fate was still entirely resting on the Khomeini's cult-like following. With him dead, the tables could have quickly turned against the militant clerics. Time was of the essence. On the bright side, the bulk of Iran's secular intellectual elite, the class that had heartily helped bring down the Shah, were proving feckless in the face of the militant Islamist onslaught. It is at this point, almost a decade before Khomeini actually dies, that jockeying for power inside the Islamic Republic sharpens decisively. Narrow factional interests soon dominated the political discourse and promises of "democracy" and advancing the "national interest" withered further in the background.

Rafsanjani and Khamenei Go after an Elected President

On January 25, 1980, as Khomeini lay in his hospital bed, Iran held its first presidential elections. The new controversial constitution—where a "Supreme Leader" was enshrined—had been rammed through eight weeks earlier. In the presidential elections, the winner with almost 11 million (76%) of the votes was Abol-Hassan Bani Sadr. The son of an ayatollah himself, he was a family acquaintance of Khomeini and had lived in Paris since the mid-1960s and was there when the senior cleric arrived in late 1978. He was one of the handpicked ones to accompany Khomeini on the flight back from Paris. His opponents said he was arrogant and uncharitably likened him in appearance to Groucho Marx. As a lofty intellectual idealist, he was quickly overwhelmed by the pitfalls of power.

Even though he himself came from a priestly family, Bani Sadr was against clerical control. His alliance with Khomeini was to be brief and one of the most acrimonious Iran would ever experience. To start his presidency, Bani Sadr went to the hospital bed of Khomeini. In front of television cameras, he kissed the old ayatollah's hand just as the Shah would have his prime ministers kiss his ring. Khomeini had not himself endorsed a single candidate for the elections. But since the IRP's candidate, Hassan Habibi, only got 3 percent of the vote, Khomeini's close circle had no option but to accept Bani Sadr. To his supporters, he had three main qualities: honesty, openness, and economic expertise (a PhD in economics). He wanted to, as he said, "normalize" the state but his idea of normal was hardly without its detractors. In the course of his polemical term in office that lasted a year and a half, Bani Sadr fought Khomeini's clique on two basic fronts.

First, he wanted to break up the revolutionary courts and disband the armed gangs that roamed the neighborhoods, and sought to have the Council of Revolution's arbitrary powers curtailed. This put him on a collision course against the IRP whose top leadership occupied the council's upper echelons. Second, Bani Sadr wanted to confront the predatory ways of the Revolutionary Guards. Once president Bani Sadr had focused on moving to have the American hostages released, calling the affair damaging to Iran's national interests, the Khomeinists denounced him as someone who would take Iran back to the US sphere of control if he were not stopped.[2] This was politics of pure convenience. Ironically, it later emerged that Beheshti had himself admitted that if the members of the Revolutionary Council had known of the plan to seize the US embassy, they would not have approved.

In March 1980,[3] a few months after the first presidential elections, Iran held two rounds of parliamentary elections. This was Bani Sadr's second big test against the IRP, and this time he lost. The IRP secured 31 percent of the seats; Bani Sadr and his allies managed to secure 12 percent of the seats of the parliament's then 270 seats.[4] Not only was the IRP still organizationally formidable but it had done really well, shoring up support among the rural population, a segment of society that had become mobilized and politicized as never before and would remain its key source of support for years to come. Among the Khomeinists running on the IRP's list of candidates, both Rafsanjani and Khamenei were elected as members of the *Majles* (parliament). Khamenei had come fifth in Tehran; Rafsanjani came fourteenth. To his dismay, Khamenei could still only play second fiddle. Thanks to his closeness to Khomeini, Rafsanjani won a majority of the votes in the chamber to become Speaker of the parliament. On his watch over the next eight years, this became one of the most powerful positions in Iran.

The Khomeinists set out to frustrate Bani Sadr at every turn. At one point, the Bani Sadr–appointed governor of the Central Bank was prevented from attending an IMF meeting in Washington, DC, seemingly out of fears of Bani Sadr petitioning the Americans for help. They would not even let Bani Sadr nominate his own prime minister. Bani Sadr, in the hope that he could undercut Khomeini's IRP darlings, offered the job of prime minister to Ahmad, Khomeini's only remaining son. This luring tactic was met by Khomeini's stiff disapproval. Instead, the IRP forced Bani Sadr to accept Mohammad Ali Rajai as his prime minister. Rajai had come to the IRP from Bazargan's camp from which he had split as he had supported the seizing of the US embassy. Bani Sadr found Rajai to be nothing but a simple low-social-class boor who had been imposed on him to choke his agenda. Still, while Bani Sadr taunted the party leaders of the IRP as "Stalinists," he nonetheless had to put up with them.

§

In retrospect, while creeping despotic tendencies were all too easy to spot by now, in the history of the Islamic Republic, this first post-Shah parliament turned out to be the most free and lively. It was the first freely elected parliament since 1952 and the chaos inside the chamber showed it. The early postrevolution mayhem from the streets reached the chamber where physical altercations were not uncommon. The parliament was certainly in no state to hold any dispassionate debates about the new regime's foreign policy. This meant the course of foreign policy was in the hands of few key men, each very much driven by domestic goals first. As Speaker of the parliament, Rafsanjani's firm hand prevented total paralysis in the legislature, but he was not comfortable to play the role of a hatchet man in public. In the campaign against Bani Sadr, that role went to Khamenei who soon went out of his way to portray the president as public enemy number 1.

Bani Sadr, with a doctorate from Sorbonne in Paris, was constantly painted as a closet bourgeoisie. Khomeinists said he was full of idealism but with no gusto to go after sweeping revamping of Iran's economic system and bringing about wealth redistribution as demanded by the poor supporters of the revolution. In hindsight, Bani Sadr was too quick to dismiss such charges. Instead, as his first big presidential initiative he turned to end the hostage crisis. He was adamant that the continuation of hostilities with the United States was undermining Iranian national interests. Washington agreed and was eager to put an end to this historic anomaly in Iranian–American relations. Well into the hostage crisis, the Americans believed "the establishment of a new security relationship with the USA is not an improbable development."[5] For the United States, anger at the seizure of its embassy in Tehran was no good reason to lose sight of imperative strategic logic to stay in Iran. "A restored US presence in Iran would not just be turning back the clock, it would represent a qualitative strategic gain for the US that would impede even prevent, implementation over time of regional policies designed to extend Soviet interests and influence," a CIA memorandum concluded.[6]

Through the mediation of the United Nations, Bani Sadr sought to find a resolution. He briefly thought he had reached one. Khomeinists had other ideas. Mansour Farhang witnessed this slugfest firsthand. An Iranian by birth, he had left the Shah's Iran for America in the 1960s and was a US citizen by the time of the revolution. A romantic with no clue about Khomeini's master plan, Farhang gave up his US citizenship to become a member of the new Iranian government's delegation at the United Nations. As he recalls, his enthusiasm rested on his belief that this was the world's first genuinely popular revolution. It did not take long for Farhang to drop his idealization of Khomeini.

Farhang found himself in a helicopter ride from Tehran to the city of Qom where Khomeini was staying at the time. Farhang was traveling with Ayatollah Montazeri, a close ally of Khomeini who was later appointed—albeit temporarily—as his successor. "This [hostage-taking] situation is really huge stain on Iran," Farhang remembers saying. The unpretentious Montazeri nodded in approval and was yet taken back by Farhang's naiveté. Khomeini "has developed a taste for the infamy" that comes with the crisis, Montazeri remarked. Khomeini had come to see much value in the anti-American platform at home. He also saw it as a way to make a name for himself in the Islamic and developing world where adopting a mantle of anti-Americanism in the 1970s still yielded ample street credibility.

In Qom, it was Farhang's job to sell the idea of a resolution to Khomeini. Fourteen of Khomeini's closest devotees were in the room. Farhang was told not to bore him with details and give him only the gist of his proposal. Farhang did so and was delighted to hear Khomeini's acceptance. But it turned out to be a misunderstanding. Khomeini had been under the impression president Carter would apologize to Iran as part of an arrangement, something that Washington had not agreed to do. On March 11, 1980, after seventeen days in Tehran, the UN delegation finally left empty handed. Farhang never quite figured out whether Khomeini himself wanted to drag out the hostage crisis as a step toward political consolidation on the home front or whether the likes of Beheshti, Rafsanjani, or Khamenei talked him into it. Farhang was soon after on the run and back in the United States. One of his American students asked him how he could have trusted Khomeini, a man who wants to ban music. "Well, Plato did not like music either," he had replied. It was a cop out of an answer, and Farhang admits so much today.

§

Back in Washington in spring 1980, the Carter administration revisited earlier plans for a military rescue operation. Gary Sick, a staff member in the National Security Council, remembers that the prevalent thinking in Washington at the time was that the Soviets were the hidden hand behind the protracting of the crisis. It was, as he puts it today, an assessment that was "hugely over-stated." If anything, the Khomeinists were becoming comfortable with the role of hostage-takers. On April 14, 1980, Ali Khamenei became the most senior official to visit the US hostages.[7] In his televised conversation with one of the seized US diplomats, the 36-year-old John Limbert, Khamenei had a pleasant manner but an unequivocal demand: the Shah has to return to Iran to face a trial. The fact that the ailing Shah was by now back in Egypt as a guest of president Anwar Sadat and outside of US reach was immaterial. Washington had earlier asked the Shah to leave American soil.

Ten days after Khamenei's visit of the hostages, on April 24, 1980, the Carter administration launched Operation Eagle Claw. It was to be a doomed rescue attempt carried out by the US Army, the Delta Force, and the CIA. Eight US personnel perished in a nighttime collision between two US aircraft in the Iranian desert hundreds of miles away from the besieged US embassy in downtown Tehran. The operation overnight became the latest political football in Tehran and another pretext to undercut Bani Sadr. The Khomeinists spread rumors that the US aircraft had all too easily entered Iranian airspace. This was meant as a suggestion that someone inside was collaborating with the Americans. Bani Sadr was an easy prey. Not only had he advocated an end to the hostage crisis but had fought tooth and nail to stop the mass purge of the military officer class. The Khomeinists still did not trust the Shah-era armed forces since they had had decades-long and deep relationship with the US military. Fearing a Trojan horse, thousands of senior officers were being purged or imprisoned or simply fleeing the country.

After Operation Eagle Claw, the fifty-two remaining US hostages were dispersed at different locations. The Iranians were not the only ones becoming more vigilant. Soviet satellites had failed to detect the US incursion deep into Iran. An additional reconnaissance satellite was launched to plug the glaring gap that prevented the Soviets from picking up the raid on their radar and sensor systems.[8] The Soviet–American cat and mouse was a reminder that the Iran hostage crisis unfolded at the height of the Cold War. Western press carried reports about how Moscow was air-dropping weapons and supplies to Kurdish, Azerbaijani, and other dissident Iranian ethnic or pro-Soviet elements that were interpreted in the White House as a likely prelude to a Soviet invasion of Iran. After all, the Soviets had only a few months earlier invaded Afghanistan under the pretext of supporting the local Afghan communist government in Kabul.

While no fan of Khomeini, president Carter nonetheless warned Moscow against such a move. Carter even considered using nuclear weapons in the defense of Iran.[9] The Americans also knew that Moscow was urging the Khomeinists to demand tough concessions—including financial compensation—from the United States as part of any end to the hostage crisis.[10] The Soviets were not the only ones who viewed the US–Iran crisis as advantageous from their vantage point, a stance they hold to this day. The undeterred Khomeinists remained preoccupied with the question of domestic political supremacy. After all, they still relied on techniques of mass mobilization to generate public support. They worked hard to paint the United States the boogeyman responsible for all of Iran's troubles. Washington could see the United States was a secondary goal; the continuation of seizing the embassy was to force the pace of the revolution and its direction.[11]

Bani Sadr's Open Split with Khomeini

Another reality dawning on Washington was the stubbornness of Khomeini once he had made up his mind. The CIA bemoaned the fact that it did not have an asset close enough to Khomeini to provide insights into his calculations. Nor did the CIA know much about the pecking order inside Khomeini's entourage.[12] But there was an upper hierarchy and it was fast shrinking. Khomeini could not avoid knowing about the foul rivalry between president Bani Sadr and the rightist clerics in the Majles. Each camp constantly sought to goad him. Khomeini, at first, urged peace and set out to distribute power. "Don't bite each other like snakes and scorpions," he told the rivaling factions. After Bani Sadr became president, Khomeini—with appointing powers vested in him as the supreme leader—had installed Ayatollah Beheshti as the head of the judiciary. This was a powerful organ that then as now persecutes political dissenters. With Rafsanjani as Speaker of the parliament, the Khomeinists hence controlled both the legislative and the judicial branches.

Egged on by his younger clerical aides, Khomeini soon started having doubts about Bani Sadr. He was told, not asked, by the unelected supreme leader what sorts of policies to pursue, who to appoint to his cabinet, and, above all, to work for the ill-defined and constantly shifting "Islam" over the lucid "melliyat" (the national interest). This rupture between the elected president versus the unelected supreme leader has never since been corrected and is at the heart of modern Iran's political paralysis.

In a sense, Bani Sadr became the leading opposition figure in the Islamic Republic. With his hands tied and much of the state machinery outside of his control, he too turned to tactics of mass mobilization. He held big rallies and claimed Khomeini had duped him. "Two days before he came to Paris, I prepared a list of 19 points on which we wanted him to make his positions clear." Khomeini, Bani Sadr claimed, had pledged limited political role for the clergy, support extensive political rights for women and religious and ethnic minorities. "He seemed to be, if not a revolutionary then at least a man of progressive views." When Bani Sadr confronted Khomeini's sudden opposition to let women run for the presidency, and reminded him that in Paris he had said this was possible, Khomeini simply replies: "Yes, I said many things in Paris. But I do not consider myself bound by them." He now said only parties and media outlets that acted "correctly" would be permitted.[13] Regardless of Bani Sadr's motivations, his efforts proved to be a case of too little too late.

By mid-1980, Khomeini's words no longer commanded the same unquestioning obedience among the public as a year earlier. Bani Sadr used his newspaper—*Enqelab Eslami (Islamic Revolution)*—to attack Khomeini and the IRP. His denunciations in public were so comprehensive that IRP deputies in the parliament sponsored a motion to impeach him for revealing state secrets. Bani Sadr turned to the regular armed forces for support against the Khomeinists. He rightly saw the Revolutionary Guards as the armed insurance policy of his rightist clerical rivals. Still, his many efforts for the year and a half he was president to defang the Guards came to naught. As Rajai had been imposed on him as prime minister, Bani Sadr—who as president was the commander-in-chief—was forced to accept Mohsen Rezai as the head of the Revolutionary Guards.

Bani Sadr could not stand the rugged 27-year-old Rezai who came from a family of shepherds and with no formal military background. Rezai responded in kind. This was largely because he felt secure with militant clerics, top among them Rafsanjani and Khamenei, protecting him. The latter was Khomeini's personal representative on military matters inside the Revolutionary Council. Unsurprisingly, Khamenei was a champion of the Revolutionary Guards over the interests of the regular conscripted armed forces, the *Artesh*. Rafsanjani too, from the podium of the Speaker of the parliament and as Khomeini's top aide, provided his own backing to Rezai and the Revolutionary Guards against the increasingly cornered president Bani Sadr.

§

As Khomeinists consolidated power in Tehran, they looked to expand their message internationally. This effort to export the "revolution" made neighboring states anxious. On this subject as well, Rafsanjani and Khamenei started as like-minded but in time parted ways. The first prominent international figure to visit the Khomeini's entourage in Tehran was the head of the PLO, Yasser Arafat. In one of its first foreign policy decision, the first post-Shah government had cut diplomatic ties with Israel. Arafat was treated loyally and handed the keys of the de facto Israeli embassy in Tehran. The remnants of the old guard did not like it a bit. Behrooz Sarshar, a senior officer who was in charge of the military band that played at the arrival of foreign dignitaries, was helpless when his uniformed group refused to play for Arafat. The role played by Arab militants, Islamists, but also leftists in bringing down the Shah's regime was still fresh in the minds of many Iranians and resented.[14]

The new leadership in Tehran was not just anti-American, anti-Israel, and pro-Palestinian but it was anti-status quo across the board. Close personal ties between Arab and Iranian militants dated back to the reign of the Shah. Mostafa Chamran, the first defense minister of the Islamic Republic, and many other opposition activists from that generation were first exposed to doctrines of irregular warfare in war-torn Lebanon and in Hafez Al Assad's Syria in the 1970s. This list of Iranians included many that later became prominent commanders in the Revolutionary Guards such as Yahya Safavi (IRGC's top boss from 1997 to 2007).[15]

There were few regional countries that escaped Khomeini's curse. He denounced leaders in Egypt, Jordan, Pakistan, and Turkey as either flawed or illegitimate lackeys of the United States. His harshest attacks, however, were reserved for Iran's immediate Arab neighbors. Furthermore, Khomeini swiftly added the sectarian layer to Tehran's quest for geopolitical influence. As a man who had lived over a decade in involuntary exile in Najaf, Iraq, during the era of Saddam Hussein, Khomeini was quick to turn against his old—albeit reluctant—host by inciting Iraq's Shia majority to rise against the Sunni Baathist strongman.

Unlike the Shah, Khomeini promptly framed the struggle against Saddam in Islamist revolutionary terms with tailored messages aimed at mobilizing the Iraqi Shia masses. It was often far from subtle. On April 19, 1980, the title of Iran's biggest daily, *Kayhan*, was "Imam [Khomeini] invites the Iraqi military to rebel [against Saddam]."[16] This was a first for Iranian foreign policy. Tehran had never before exploited a sectarian message as a way to mobilize receptive minority Shia in Arab countries.

Iraq, thanks to its geographic proximity and as a large Shia-majority Arab country, represented a tempting target for Khomeini. His notion of "Islamic Government" was to be a transnational, enshrined in the constitution of the Islamic Republic. "We are at war against the infidels ... I ask all Islamic nations, all Muslims, to join the holy war," Khomeini urged. "We must strive to export our revolution throughout the world and must abandon all ideas of not doing so."[17] Shia communities outside of Iran's borders were principal intended audiences for Khomeinists.

In Baghdad, Saddam Hussein was growing agitated. Ominous signs were evident by the summer of 1979. A cleric by the name of Mahmoud Doaei, Khomeini's envoy to Baghdad, was told by Saddam that Iraq would attack Iran unless Tehran stopped its incitement of the Iraqi Shia. Doaei came back to Tehran and warned Khomeini but he called it a bluff.[18] A terrified Doaei asked to be excused from going back to Baghdad, a wish Khomeini granted and likely saved his life.

Saddam Invades Iran

An anxious Saddam Hussein had for months been weighing his options. Khomeini was hell-bent in undermining his rule, but Baghdad did not know if the new political reality in Tehran was to be a lasting one. Would the exiled Shah ultimately return, backed by the United States, as had been the case in 1953? The answer to that critical question came on July 27, 1980. That was the day the Shah passed away at the Maadi Military Hospital in Cairo after a long battle with cancer. He was only 60.

Certain that the old Iranian order was gone for good, Saddam's air force attacked Tehran at noon on September 22, 1980. Three Iraqi Soviet-supplied MiGs attacked Tehran's main airport. Within two hours, the Iranian air force retaliated by dispatching sorties of US-made F-4s to hit targets inside Iraq. The following day, Iraq launched a land invasion of Iran along a 650 km front. Within a few months, the Iraqis would come to occupy large swaths of Iran's western border regions.

Iran's initial defense was chaotic at best. The Khomeinists had since the victory of the revolution purged the officer class. For example, Iran's US-equipped and -trained air force, the ace of the country's military prowess, was so distrusted that some of the Khomeinists at first believed the Iraqi attack at the airport in Tehran was an anti-Khomeini coup led by the Iranian air force.[19] In Tehran, policy planning to wage the war very quickly fell victim to factional squabbling. Bani Sadr, the beleaguered president, had for months been blocked at every turn by the IRP. He turned his attention to the war effort. As president and commander-in-chief of the armed forces, he sought to rebrand himself as the savior of the nation. It was yet another uphill battle.

The national address on radio to inform the public about the start of the war was delivered not by Bani Sadr—the titular commander-in-chief—but by Khamenei who was Khomeini's emissary on military affairs.[20] Khamenei and Bani Sadr began to seek to outdo each other by donning military uniforms.[21] It was a spectacle with one civilian economist and a junior cleric—whose only military qualification was his enthusiasm for the subject—pandering to public opinion. But as Bani Sadr more and more frequently showed up in military fatigue on the battlefront, he essentially neglected the politics of Tehran. Saddam's invasion was mostly a blessing for the radical clergy. As with the US embassy takeover, it acted as a major distraction for the public and an opportunity for further power grab. For the ordinary Iranian and almost all political strands of the time, the war became a case of country before politics or ideology.

The notable exception was Khomeini's camp. They regarded the anti-Saddam war as an event to proliferate Khomeini's ideas about "Islamic Government," a mission they flaunted as borderless. In its most exorbitant vocalization it was a messianic narrative. Earliest slogans of the war—such as "War, War Until Victory" (against Iraq)—soon shifted to an open-ended agenda of promising a global revolution. "War, War until the Removal of Intrigue from the Whole World" or "The Road to Jerusalem Goes through Karbala [the holy Shia city in Iraq]"[22] became the favored alternative chants of the martyrdom-hungry foot soldiers of Ayatollah Khomeini.

The fanaticism pouring out of Tehran was quickly turning not only the Arab World but most of the international community against Iran. But the fervor was the most evident inside Iran, even within the ranks of regime. When Bani Sadr chastised the Revolutionary Guards' boss, Mohsen Rezai, for cavalier tactics that led to senseless casualties in the war with Iraq he was told not to worry. Those killed had become "shahid" or "martyr." The militant clergy and their accomplices from the Guards had turned the defense of the motherland into defense of Islam. The trouble was this meant the war was to be an endless one given the breadth of Islamic lands and the many conflicts where Tehran could choose to implant itself. As it turned out, this is exactly what happened. Short on military expertise but full of religious and ideological zeal, Khomeinists would drag Iran through a war that ultimately lasted eight years (1980–8) and cost countless billions of dollars of damages. Some 260,000 Iranian military forces and tens of thousands of civilians would die.

Khomeini Decides to Talk to Washington

In the summer of 1980, with the Shah dead, the cost–benefit calculation about whether to continue to keep the US diplomats hostage in Tehran suddenly changed. Ayatollah Khoeiniha, the key clerical ringleader in the embassy seizure, put it this way: "We had reaped all the fruits of our undertaking. We defeated the attempts by the liberals [Bazargan and Bani Sadr] to take control of the machinery of the state. The tree of revolution has grown and gained in strength."[23]

On September 12, 1980, Khomeini asked for an end to the crisis. On September 14, Rafsanjani launched the motion in parliament. Together with the other Khomeinists, they attempted to twist how the crisis had unfolded in the first place. The blame, they said, lay with Bazargan and the provincial government. According to this sudden U-turn, only three to eleven of the US diplomats could be said to be spies (out of fifty-two). The Khomeinists, the same people who had called the seizure of the US embassy the "Second Revolution," were looking for the exit door. It was unashamed politics of convenience. For Khomeini, there was no longer a Shah to demand back. He decided he did not after all need an apology from Washington. Instead, he asked for the United States not to intervene in Iranian internal affairs, to unblock Iranian assets in the United States, and to cancel American financial claims against Iran that had come about following rupture in relations. Tellingly, Khomeini did not order the president, Bani Sadr, but the parliament to pursue the matter of ending the hostage crisis. This in fact meant Rafsanjani was charged with the job since he—as the powerful

Speaker of the parliament—was the inevitable channel for talks with the United States. Given president Bani Sadr's declining image in Khomeini's eyes, this turn of events was hardly coincidental. Nor was Rafsanjani a surprise choice. He had in the previous months been the one man in Tehran foreign interlocutors sought out the most.

In the case of the Europeans, they appealed to his mercantile soft spots. At the time of the revolution, the West European states constituted Iran's top trading partners. The Europeans saw this as leverage. Numerous initiatives were organized by the Europeans to broker an end to the hostage crisis. What was interesting is that the Europeans primarily targeted Rafsanjani. The nine members of the European Community (EC) of the time were so insistent that Rafsanjani repeatedly lost his cool with them. "Our foreign policy after the revolution has been based on not allowing our country to be enslaved by the superpowers. [Hence] we tried to upgrade our economic relations with the EC but now we understand you do not want to act independently of the US."[24] The Europeans were at the time aware that Rafsanjani, as part of a small group that years later came to be condemned by the hard-liners in Tehran as the "compromisers," was already in direct contact with the Americans.

In two alleged secret meetings in Madrid in the summer of 1980, the presidential campaign manager of Ronald Reagan, William Casey, met with Hassan Karroubi. He was living in Germany at the time but had been a top courier for Khomeini when he was in exile in Iraq.[25] He also happened to be the brother of Mehdi Karroubi, at the time a key figure among the Khomeinists. Hassan Karroubi met Casey at Ritz Hotel in July 1980.[26] The meeting had been brokered through the services of a few dubious brokers from each side. Casey put his offer on the table. If Khomeini kept the captive US diplomats until after the US presidential elections then a Reagan administration would look favorably at resuming US arms sales to Iran.

American accounts speak of Karroubi reportedly returning in August with a positive answer from Khomeini. According to this line of argument, a final deal was struck in Paris in October 1980. Iranian sources either have nothing to say about these meetings in summer 1980 or describe Hassan Karroubi's efforts to cut deals with Reagan's team to have been rejected in Tehran.[27] What is known is that Reagan had become the Republican presidential nominee on July 17, 1980. This was a time when the American intelligence community was disillusioned with president Carter. Reagan's running mate was George H. Bush, a former head of the CIA. Bush's alleged role as a facilitator between the Reagan campaign and the Iranians has never been verifiably confirmed. What is known beyond doubt is that the US intelligence community was in contact with elements among the revolutionary political class even as the Khomeinists were holding on to the US hostages. In one of the more remarkable instances, the CIA decided to actively back one of the presidential candidates in Iran's 1980 elections (Ahmad Madani, a former admiral in the Iranian navy) with $500,000 in the hope that his election would end the hostage crisis. Madani had come second to Bani Sadr.[28]

In the end, the US diplomats would be held until after the US presidential elections of November 4, 1980, to undermine Jimmy Carter's reelection chances. The hostages were released five minutes after Reagan had been sworn in as president on January 20, 1981.[29] They had been kept for 444 days, at an astonishing diplomatic and economic cost for Iran, including the loss of access to $12 billion of Iranian assets in the United States, international isolation, and a weakening of Iran that invited Iraq's invasion. It was also an affair that led to the consolidation of power by the Khomeinists.[30] As a CIA assessment put it, "during the 14 months of the crisis, a small core group of 40–50 followers maintained strict discipline among themselves and over the larger group of politically 'unsophisticated provincials' they recruited for the occupation."[31]

The Hot Summer of 1981

By late spring of 1981, Bani Sadr was calling for a popular rebellion against the clerics. He was hardly the first or the last Khomeini supporter to do so. People like Ebrahim Yazdi had also come to the conclusion that Beheshti, Rafsanjani, Khamenei, and others were predatory forces. As one Iranian political writer put it at the time, the actions of the IRP demonstrate that the "monster of fascism has been let out of the bottle."[32] In a jab at Khomeini, Bani Sadr perceptively warned any regime that declares itself "sacred" will quickly resort to "batons" to keep the population in line.[33] About a year earlier, he had kissed Khomeini's hand to accept the role of the president. He was now lashing out against the same man for hindering him from what he saw to be his rightful place as the top elected official in the land.

§

Bani Sadr was on the battlefield when news broke on June 10, 1981, that Khomeini had removed him as commander-in-chief. Khomeini had also three days earlier given the green light for the closing down of Bani Sadr's newspaper, his only remaining pulpit. His presidency was in shackles as the IRP-dominated parliament prevented him on most of his appointments and legislative efforts.

On June 21, IRP formally set in motion the procedure to impeach Bani Sadr. The president, fearing for his life, did not appear in the parliament to put up a defense. Rafsanjani and Khamenei were instrumental in his marginalization. From his seat as the Speaker of the parliament, Rafsanjani looked on as Khamenei read out a scathing attack on Bani Sadr's record. This was the one public speech that ended Bani Sadr's political life in the Islamic Republic for good. Khamenei read out that his opposition to Bani Sadr was not part of a personal vendetta or even about politics. It was much more than that. "This [motion to impeach Bani Sadr] is heavenly ordered" and is also a public demand," he claimed. He continued to read out the indictment against the president, which had no doubt been carefully put together by Khomeini's inner circle. President Bani Sadr was rebuked for undercutting his own prime minster, the IRP-backed Rajai, who had been forced on him. He was also said to be opposed to the Revolutionary Guards, disobedient toward Khomeini, and for having moved to align himself with the IRP's arch rivals, the MEK.[34] Rafsanjani watched with a glee on his face as Khamenei delivered the IRP's final blow to Bani Sadr.

Another young Khomeinist, who as a parliamentarian spoke against Bani Sadr and called him a "seditionist," was no other than a Hassan Rouhani who three decades later became president himself.[35] The Khomeinists had failed in preventing Bani Sadr from becoming president but succeeded in making it the shortest presidency in the Islamic Republic to date. At the time of his swearing in as president, most in the parliament had welcomed him with shouts of "Allah Akbar." Eighteen months later, they were now shouting "Death to Bani Sadr." Only a handful of the 217-member parliament opted to abstain or stayed away on the day of the vote. The Speaker of the parliament, Rafsanjani, could not have been more pleased.

The following day, Supreme Leader Khomeini dismissed Bani Sadr as president and ordered his arrest for treason. The persecuted president went into hiding. Bani Sadr's fall was a major blow not only to any moderate remaining but also to the radical militant left that had come to see Bani Sadr as their only chance for any resemblance of representation in this post-Shah Iran. With the realization that Khomeini's power consolidation was becoming harder to reverse by the day, anti-Khomeini elements resorted to a campaign of violence, which the other side was more than happy to reciprocate. Men and women who often had fought alongside against the Shah were now locked in a vicious spiral of violence and death.

On June 27, five days after Bani Sadr's impeachment, an attempt was made to assassinate Khamenei. A bomb had been placed in a tape recorder in front of Khamenei when he was to speak in a mosque. The group behind it, *Furqan*, was a militant anti-clerical group. The same group had unsuccessfully tried to kill Rafsanjani back in May of 1979. His supporters portrayed Khamenei's survival as a miracle. His right hand would be paralyzed for good. The incident hardly diminished his quest for political stardom. Like the Shah before him, who considered the three failed assassination attempts on his life as a sign of divine protection, Khamenei too spoke of his survival as preordained. "I knew right away [after surviving the assassination] God expects me to serve and I became ready. But I had no idea what mission God had in mind for me," Khamenei told his supporters.[36]

Much worse was to come. A day after the assassination attempt on Khamenei, the headquarters of the IRP was blown up in a bombing that killed over a hundred top Khomeinists including Ayatollah Beheshti, four cabinet ministers, and twenty-seven members of the parliament. The Khomeinists to this day blame the MEK for the bombing. The leader of the Islamist–Marxist group, Massoud Rajavi, had claimed to have seventy thousand supporters ready to fight to end Khomeini's supreme leadership. And yet, as is the case with almost all major political episodes in Iran since 1979, there is simply too many unknown variables to be able to confidently pinpoint the identity of those behind the bombing.

Bani Sadr, who was then still in hiding, has always maintained that this most deadly bombing in Iranian history was part of an internal struggle inside the ranks of the IRP. Bani Sadr alleges that his sources inside the *Artesh*, the regular Iranian military, had told him that the bombing was too sophisticated for the MEK. The ceiling of the large meeting hall had instantaneously crumpled. Only Artesh, the Revolutionary Guards, or a foreign power could have carried out such a complex bombing. And according to Bani Sadr, the Revolutionary Guards could not have done so without Khomeini's order. To corroborate his claim, Bani Sadr points out that a number of people closest to Khomeini, including his son Ahmad and Rafsanjani, had left the hall moments before the bomb exploded.[37]

In this narrative of events, as far as Khomeini's motive is concerned, it was the elimination of Beheshti. He was seen by some as a person who had what it took to one day stand up to Khomeini: he was both ambitious and enjoyed a political support base as a more refined cleric. Khomeini had not forgotten the seized US cables from the embassy that spoke favorably of Beheshti as compared to some of the other Khomeinists like Rafsanjani and Khomeini himself. Still, on the question of eliminating Beheshti, was it really crunch time for Khomeini as Bani Sadr and many others have since claimed? There is no irrefutable evidence either way. Rafsanjani and Khamenei have had to contend with much public suspicion about the roles they might have played in these sinister incidents in those early years. But that did not stop them from pushing ahead.

§

Meanwhile, shortly after the eruption of the violence in the summer of 1981, Rajavi and Bani Sadr made a political pact. They chose to continue the struggle from exile. On July 28, they fled Iran for Paris in a Boeing 707 air force tanker piloted by Colonel Behzad Moezzi, a MEK member that had long remained undetected in the Iranian air force.[38] In Paris, Bani Sadr and Rajavi created the National Council of Resistance. The months that followed once again brought Iran to the brink of total civil war. On August 30, Bani Sadr's bête noire—his former prime minister Mohammad-Ali Rajai who had succeeded him as president after a hurriedly held election on July 24 where he was said to have received 91 percent of the vote—was killed in another bombing. He died alongside his prime minister, Mohammad Bahonar. This bombing too, just five weeks into Rajai's presidency, remains shrouded in mystery—although Khomeinists blamed this one also on the MEK.[39]

What is true is that this double killing of Rajai and Bahonar was a blessing in disguise for Rafsanjani and Khamenei. Assassinations were thinning the top rank around Khomeini, paving the way for the rise of those who did not succumb to the violence or falling out with Khomeini. "The regime will soon be running short of experienced and well-known figures," a British diplomatic cable read. "It is not at all clear where they will find a new President who commands respect, without leaving a gap elsewhere." The same cable concluded: "Khamenei himself looks at present the most likely candidate."[40]

On October 2, 1981, at the time when the clerical–Revolutionary Guards alliance was edging closer to arresting or annihilating the militant leftists of the MEK, Khamenei was elected as the third president of the Islamic Republic. After a five-week hiatus from public life where he recovered from the assassination attempt on his life, he ran and was said to have secured 97 percent of the vote. Khamenei had just earlier been installed as secretary general of the Islamic Republican Party (IRP). It was a quick turnaround in the fortunes of the 41-year-old cleric who at the time could only work 3–4 hours a day as he recovered from his injuries.[41]

The other three presidential candidates ran only as a token gesture to competitive elections. All publicly endorsed Khamenei before election day. The wounded Khomeini camp no longer bothered even to pretend to hold free elections. Forty-one candidates had registered to contest the elections but Khomeini only approved four to run. For

Bani Sadr, who still in exile considered himself as Iran's legitimately elected president, Khamenei was still only a secondary actor. In an earlier interview from Paris on August 25, he had mentioned five men whose death would end the Islamic Republic. Rajai and Bahonar were on that list, and they died five days after the interview was published. Rafsanjani was on the five-man list too, but there was no mention of Khamenei.[42] Bani Sadr clearly considered Khamenei as a mere vassal of Rafsanjani as he goaded Khomeini toward all-out subjugation of rival factions. Rafsanjani called Khamenei's election as president a divine moment and a vindication of Khomeini's policies. But to Khamenei himself his election surely lacked popular legitimacy. This sense of lacking a popular mandate would haunt him for the remainder of his political life. In the meantime, the bloody purge endured. It reached all the way to Khomeini's small circle. Famously, Ayatollah Hassan Lahouti, a companion of Khomeini who was in Paris with him and the first cleric tasked to oversee what became the Revolutionary Guards, died mysteriously a few hours after arriving at Evin Prison. Lahouti, whose sons were married to the two daughters of Rafsanjani, had become critical of the power monopolizing of the Khomeinists. Rafsanjani told his daughters and sons-in-laws to drop the matter, which they choose to do by keeping silent for the next twenty-five years. In Khamenei's family, it was one his sisters, Badri, that most famously defected. She fled to Saddam's Iraq to join the MEK opposition based there. She told the *Sunday Times* of London that the Khomeinists were "spreading the word of God by force" and executing thousands in "the name of Islam."

§

In a span of a short few months, the Islamic Republic's first elected president had fled the country. Bani Sadr, the man who had flown back with Khomeini full of hope only two years earlier, was back in permanent exile in France. Two bomb explosions in the space of two months wiped out many of Khomeini's key supporters. From early 1979 until the end of 1981, key senior clerics such as Morteza Motahhari, Mahmoud Taleghani, Mohammad Beheshti, and Mohammad Bahonar had died. Among the main clerical survivors Rafsanjani and Khamenei stood out. No doubt the events of the year 1981 set the stage for the country to move furthest away possible from political democracy. The violent events of 1981 not only set in motion a process that led to the consolidation of the world's first modern-day theocracy but also speeded up the already transpiring Iranian retrenchment from the world.

The Iranian revolution was both a highly xenophobic affair and the birth of one of the most convoluted political systems the world had ever witnessed. Khomeini oiled these efforts from his tribune. "O God, you know that it is not our purpose to acquire position and power, but rather to deliver the oppressed from the hands of the unjust." This claim to divine rule, regardless of whether the Khomeinists believe it or not, was no obstacle to subsequent admissions by key figures that mistakes had been made in those earliest years of the revolution. This has perhaps been best epitomized in the attitude of the militants who seized the US embassy on that momentous day of November 4, 1979. Most of the hostage-takers have since expressed remorse.[43] Later on in his life, Rafsanjani referred to those hostage-takers as "extremists." "They occupied the American embassy [in Tehran] and at times they even started clashes in the universities. We had to manage the [country] under those circumstances," he said later.⁴⁴

Was this a case of genuine remorse or simply years later admitting to a deeply costly blunder? Supporters of Rafsanjani loved him for distancing himself from the hostage crisis and anti-Americanism as he grew older. His rivals vilified him as a master fabricator who was rewriting history because of winds of change.

Khamenei, the man who says he was altogether unaware of the operation and was with Rafsanjani on pilgrimage in Saudi Arabia when the US embassy was overtaken, has since politically had no choice but to embrace the event as an epic revolutionary gesture. The incident eventually became a *cause célèbre* for the most right-wing elements in the Islamic Republic, the crowd that Khamenei invariably had to choose as his political travel companions. Meanwhile, back in late 1981, Khamenei was now president. Rafsanjani was still in his position as the powerful Speaker of the parliament and Khomeini's second most trusted advisor after Ahmad Khomeini, the only surviving son of the ailing supreme leader. A total breakdown in leadership had been averted but the period of intense trial and error would continue as the Khomeinists looked to preserve the system they had fought tooth and nail to consolidate.

4

(1981–5)—Rafsanjani and Khamenei Sharpen Knives for Each Other

Assuming that the United States offers a 100 percent Islamic-humanitarian plan, we do not believe that they will act in the interests of peace and our interests. If America and Israel say "La ilaha ill Allah [There is no deity but Allah]," we do not accept it; Because they want to deceive us. Those who talk about peace want to bring the region to war.

(Khomeini)[1]

Rafsanjani called Khamenei's election as president a "vote for Imam [Khomeini], the clergy and the Majles." In truth, it was a defeat of sorts for Khomeini since he had maintained that clerics should not dominate the political system, which they undoubtedly did. But Rafsanjani never for a second thought of himself as Khamenei's subordinate. He was not. For the next eight years, Rafsanjani remained Khomeini's top council. Rafsanjani made sure that his office as Speaker of the Majles retained its central role as the political clearinghouse of the system.

In those same eight years, as Rafsanjani consolidated his position as the backstage kingmaker, Khamenei endured repeated painful political setbacks, and sometimes outright humiliation, as the occupier of the bootless presidential palace. It is this period in his political career that made Khamenei yearn for more power. But at this point, well before Iran's 1989 constitutional revision that abolished the function of the prime minister, the presidency was limited. The Office of the Supreme Leader and the person of Khomeini remained sacrosanct but the senior ayatollah stayed out of everyday governance. He, after all, did not need to prove anything to anyone. From 1981 to 1989, the job of governing—in terms of not only domestic policies but also how to tackle the outside world—was mostly left to the prime minister and the parliament commanded by Rafsanjani. But as has always been true for the Islamic Republic, policy decisions were rarely only a product of institutional calculations. The role and interests of key personalities were pivotal in shaping events.

On paper, Khamenei was henceforth to be somewhat sidelined in being in the symbolic role of a president. In reality, he was not ready to forego his chance to carve out a power base for himself. Be it in relations to Iran's war effort against Iraq, the question of the exporting of the revolution, or Tehran's soon-to-be-revealed secret dealings with Israel and the United States that eventually erupted as the Iran–Contra

Affair, Khamenei was nearly always an accessory in the decision-making process. Years later, after he became supreme leader, Khamenei twisted the facts about his tenure as president.

> I was elected to the presidency twice. I [had] rejected it both times. The first time I had just left the hospital [after the assassination attempt on his life], but friends insisted that no one else could do the job. So, I had no alternative. And the second time, the Imam [Khomeini] told me that it was imperative that I agree to become a candidate. I went to the Imam and told him that I could not accept. He said: "It is obligatory."[2]

Did Khomeini really view Khamenei as vital or irreplaceable for the regime? History has something to say about this that belies the narrative later told by Khamenei.

§

Rafsanjani wrote in his memoir that it was him, and not Khomeini, who had pushed for Khamenei to accept to run for the presidency.[3] "I convinced him," Rafsanjani wrote describing a meeting from a few weeks before the October 1981 presidential elections. Rafsanjani's precise motivations are unclear, but hazarding a guess is not difficult. A few years later, in 1989, Rafsanjani again advocated for Khamenei and this time for him to become Khomeini's successor as supreme leader. These efforts by Rafsanjani were hardly altruistic.

On both occasions he had believed his advocacy of Khamenei's rise would result in him having an underling that would act as an accessory to his big plans for himself and for Iran. But in doing so, Rafsanjani badly underestimated Khamenei's appetite for power and his tenacity, attributes that were soon put on full display. That said, Khamenei's bittersweet eight-year presidency very early on began as a disappointment. The Majles rejected his first choice for prime minister, the 36-year-old US-educated Ali Akbar Velayati, who went on to become Iran's longest serving foreign minister.[4] For his prime minister, Khamenei was forced to put forward Mir Hossein Mousavi who secured the votes in the parliament. The 39-year-old Mousavi was a relative of Khamenei and born in the latter's paternal hometown of Khameneh in the northwest of Iran. Mousavi had been a prominent non-clerical figure within the IRP and made a name for himself as chief editor of the IRP's official mouthpiece, the *Islamic Republic*. The newspaper had hammered Bani Sadr as "pro-American" and soft on "imperialism."

The anti–Bani Sadr campaign solidified Mousavi's position at the left flank within the IRP. This faction was not just anti-American—as it was under the sway of the international left—but stood for otherwise socialist dogma such as the redistribution of economic wealth. Khamenei, who was close to the traditional merchant class in the Bazaar, did not have much time for Mousavi's economic agenda of nationalization. But he soon found out that his constitutional power to nominate a prime minister did not amount to dictating policy to him. The spat between Khamenei and Mousavi was also personal. Despite their kinship, Mousavi refused to accept Khamenei as his superior, a reality the latter had foreseen. Khamenei, the son of an impoverished common cleric who had had no real choice other than a career as a cleric like his father, very likely also envied the life of his younger cousin. Mousavi, the son of a tea merchant from Tabriz, had moved to Tehran long before the revolution and studied architecture at one of the city's top universities. It is not hard to see why Khamenei might have resented Mousavi's opportunities in life that he himself never had. In the next few years Mousavi refused to be bossed about, leaving Khamenei more bitter. When the same Mousavi emerged as a key opposition leader in 2009, Khamenei had not forgotten and what he likely remembered as his cousin's betrayal all those years earlier.

For prime minister Mousavi in the 1980s, his boss could only be Khomeini himself. Over the course of his two terms, Mousavi repeatedly went over the head of president Khamenei and straight to the supreme leader. Khomeini liked Mousavi and took his side on more than one occasion when the Khamenei–Mousavi rivalry spilled into the open. When president Khamenei did not want to reappoint Mousavi as his prime minister in his second term, he asked for Khomeini's blessing. "Do as you wish. I only express my opinion as a citizen. I say to appoint anyone else [than Mousavi] is a betrayal of Islam."[5] Perhaps it was due to Khomeini's proclivity to prefer younger non-clerical figures over clerics who he did not want to exclusively dominate the state apparatus in this nascent Islamist polity. But Khomeini was also guarding his unique political spot. When Khamenei in a speech suggested the Office of the Supreme Leader not having "absolute" authority, Khomeini wrote him a harsh open letter and questioned whether the president understood the constitution. Khamenei famously wept and told confidants that Khomeini had "finished" him. That turned out to be a false premonition and Khomeini's doggedness a lesson for Khamenei for when he himself captured the supreme leadership.

Khamenei and Rafsanjani Each Court Followers

Rafsanjani was careful in how he played his cards as Khamenei and Mousavi battled it out. It is at this point where Rafsanjani emerges as part of the so-called pragmatic faction within the system. For him, it was a label that conveyed his common sense to everyday problems at home or in foreign affairs. For his foes, that same label implied opportunism and unscrupulousness. It is from this point onward that observers in the West began to favorably view Rafsanjani as a sort of a middle-of-the-road Islamist.

On the home front, he was neither with the "traditionalists," the circle Khamenei was closest to, nor with Mousavi's "radical" faction. Rafsanjani played it safe and, above all, stayed very close to Khomeini. As Speaker of the Majles who controlled the legislative process and the policy debate, he became synonymous with intrigue, cutting corners, displaying partiality, and downright petty politics. When during a parliamentary debate hard-liners physically attacked Mehdi Bazargan—the man whose premiership Rafsanjani had himself once announced to the nation—the Speaker did nothing.[6] On another occasion, newspaper photos showed him with a big smile on his face as Rafsanjani witnessed from the Speaker's rostrum another rival being knocked about by right-wing deputies.[7] The victim in that episode was none other than Ali Akbar Moinfar, the earlier oil minster whose job Rafsanjani once had unsuccessfully sought out. Such behavior raised suspicion and such incidents would go to shape public opinion about him.

§

By this point in early 1982, notwithstanding their internal differences the Khomeinists had removed main opponents from the scene. Bani Sadr and the MEK leadership had fled to Paris. The communists from the Tudeh party were keeping a low profile, joining the Khomeinists or opting for life in the rapidly growing Iranian Diaspora. That was the fate of the majority of those who subscribed to any of the secularist persuasions. As the nation was engulfed in the war with Saddam's Iraq, the Khomeinists turned on each other. Still, it was never an all-out war. In this competition for influence, the military stood out as a prize. Since a foiled attempt by members of the air force in July 1980 to stage a coup against the Khomeinists—which included the plan to bomb Khomeini's house in north Tehran—the various factions in the Khomeini camp had vied to cultivate supporters in the ranks of the armed forces. Different factions had supporters inside the Revolutionary Guards and the regular Ground Forces (*Artesh*). The one branch of the armed forces up for grabs was the air force. American intelligence from the time—based on information from defectors and human sources still in active duty—spoke of how Khamenei and Rafsanjani each sought to recruit supporters among air force personnel. The Shah, himself a pilot, had put the development of Iran's air force at the heart of his military and regional plans. Under close cooperation with the United States, Iran had prior to 1979 come to possess a first-rate air force with over five hundred of the most advanced combat aircraft.

For the Islamists, the air force was a double-edged sword: it was both an ace in the war against Saddam and also the most pro-American element in the armed forces. Most of the Iranian pilots had been trained in the United States and whether they could be loyal to the Khomeinists was an open question. One US assessment read: "the clerical regime distrusts the Air Force more than the Army or Navy, in part because it was the Shah's favorite service and because most pilots are well-educated." The Khomeinists were not imagining things. The CIA estimated that "85 percent of Air Force officers [are] opposed to the Khomeini regime." The Khomeinists did not even think that Iran's air force leadership would attack US forces because the pro-US sentiment was so strong. In June 1981, and again in May 1983, air force officers were arrested for conspiring to bomb Khomeini's home. Hundreds of air force personnel were either arrested or dismissed from the service.

Rivalry between president Khamenei and Speaker Rafsanjani was also a factor. Each wanted to expand their influence and attract followers within the air force. "Khamenei is pushing for increased benefits for the officer corps, while Rafsanjani emphasizes benefits for enlisted men and non-commissioned officers," one US report observed based on information from Iranian intelligence assets.[8] The same competition for recruits was occurring inside the Foreign Ministry. Some leading figures from both the ranks of the military and the political bureaucracy—people that ended up as long-time steady hands in the regime such as Ali Akbar Velayati, Hassan Rouhani, Javad Zarif, or top commanders of the Revolutionary Guards such as Mohsen Rezai and

Yahya Safavi—managed to stay close to both men. That fungibility explains the shelf life of their careers.

§

There was, however, one notable general difference between the kind of cadre Rafsanjani and Khamenei each courted. Rafsanjani mostly wooed young men from the middle class that had attended university. A surprising number of them had studied in the United States or in Europe during the days of the Shah. These young men, mostly in their early 20s when they began their government careers, would stay loyal to Rafsanjani until the end of his life. They were soon dubbed the "technocrats," a term they cherished as it implied a go-getter attitude. This so-called technocratic camp became Rafsanjani's brain trust and administrative muscle. Many of his closest associates were from his home province of Kerman. Many would in time emerge as leading industrialists of the country, adventurously straddling the public and private spheres. Rafsanjani promoted their careers inside the regime apparatus.

Later when he became president, Rafsanjani tapped into this pool to fill the ranks of his cabinet. This group saw its distinguishing trait to be its focus on economic policy, which they believed was the regime's redeemer. They quickly became a de facto club. Membership in it was exclusive and it would come to ooze of nepotism, which forever gave ammunition to both foreign and local detractors. When the American *Forbes* magazine ran a headline story in 2003 about "Iran's Millionaire Mullahs," it chose Rafsanjani's face to put on the cover. Two years later, in 2005, a diminutive man by the name of Mahmoud Ahmadinejad ran on a platform of anti-elitism to secure a shock victory against Rafsanjani.

To begin with Khamenei did not have such a clear-cut base as Rafsanjani. As he was from early on enraptured by military matters, and preferred raw power over immediate monetary riches, he was drawn to the armed forces. With time, some of the young commanders from the Revolutionary Guards gathered around him. They hailed predominantly from poor urban or rural backgrounds. The revolution of 1979 was a chance at power and access to money, a fortune they owed to Khomeini's bias for loyalty over competence. A good example was Qassem Soleimani, the infamous commander who in time would rise to lead Iran's proxy forces in the Middle East. He had no formal military background and came from the humblest of backgrounds where before the revolution he had to abandon middle school to work as a construction worker to support his family.

Over time, Rafsanjani and Khamenei came to spearhead two very different political networks. Both the "technocrats" and the Revolutionary Guards were forged in the chaos that immediately followed the revolution, but each took a different lesson from that period and the Iran–Iraq War that followed. At the ministries in Tehran, the technocrats learned firsthand how revolutionary fanaticism—cutting off trade with the outside world, for example—could lead to international isolation and harm the national interest. The Revolutionary Guards, meanwhile, found that same fanaticism indispensable for mobilizing a small yet determined base to advance its interests, first on the battlefield against Iraq's Saddam Hussein and later against opponents on the home front. It is a squabble that is still in full swing all these years later.

Hezbollah in Lebanon and the Export of the Revolution

By 1982, Iran's war effort against Iraq had turned the tide. "Iraq has essentially lost the war with Iran. Baghdad's main concern now is to prevent an Iranian invasion. There is little the Iraqis can do, alone or in combination with other Arabs, to reverse the military situation," Washington concluded.[9] The Khomeinists quickly made it clear they had no intention to settle for peace and gave Saddam and his Persian Gulf Arab backers little leeway. In spring of 1982, president Khamenei said that Khomeini should be supreme leader both of Iran and Iraq and that "Khomeini is not limited to international borders."[10] Khamenei made this statement in late May 1982 when Iranian forces finally liberated Khorram-shahr, the last city that had been under Iraqi occupation.

Instead of looking for favorable terms to end the bloody war, the Islamist ideologues in Tehran soon doubled-down on exporting Khomeini's revolution. Events in the region no doubt incited the most brazen figures in Tehran. Two weeks after Khorram-shahr's liberation, in June 1982, Israel invaded Lebanon as a response to attacks by the Palestinian Liberation Organization (PLO). The Lebanese civil war had raged since 1975 but the Israeli invasion helped further divide the country along sectarian and ideological lines. Among Lebanon's Shia community, the more militant began to abandon Amal, the hitherto main political-military platform for the Shia here, and joined the newly Iran-sponsored organization that called itself Hezbollah or the Party of God.

Immediately after Israel's invasion, hundreds of Revolutionary Guards arrived in Lebanon, although it is to this day not clear on whose orders. Hezbollah would go on to become the Islamic Republic's most daring, enduring, and arguably most successful ideological venture put in operation in another country. And yet, the Khomeinists were fretful at first. By some accounts, president Khamenei, as the titular head of the Defense Council, had approved the mission to Lebanon without Khomeini's approval.[11] Khomeini was not comfortable with it and told the military leadership "you are responsible if anyone [Iranian] is hurt."[12] Rafsanjani claimed later not to have had prior knowledge about the deployment of the Revolutionary Guards to Lebanon, an implausible stance that by implication meant he was to be absolved for Tehran's controversial intervention in Lebanon.

Rafsanjani's own account is that he was prior to the revolution of 1979 the principal advocate of the Palestinians in Iran. This included translating, producing, and distributing anti-Israel material he had brought back from the Arab World. In the early stages of the Lebanese civil war, Rafsanjani had travelled to Lebanon to meet Islamists, some of whom were training with the PLO. On his return, the Shah had him arrested.[13] Still, and while he might have called his youngest son Yasser after the PLO boss, once in power Rafsanjani was never the loudest advocate of the Palestinians. In time, it would be Khamenei that tapped into the "Palestine" question as his catapult to stardom in the Islamic World. Given Khomeini's opposition to large-scale Iranian military presence in Lebanon in the early 1980s—which invariably risked head-on collision with the Israeli military—the dispatched Revolutionary Guards were quickly brought back home. Instead, the collective Iranian leadership—including Khomeini, Rafsanjani,

Khamenei, and the top brass of the Revolutionary Guards—opted to go for the kill on Saddam Hussein. In July 1982, Iranian forces crossed into Iraqi territory. Tehran now held the military upper hand, but its ultimate goal was still imprecise at best.

Saddam was asking for peace and to this day Tehran's refusal to talk peace with Baghdad is a riddle. Islamist ideological zeal, and hatred for Saddam's secular Baathist regime, is most convincing but still does not entirely explain Iranian actions at this point in time. Nor did the slogan that "liberation of Jerusalem is through Baghdad" make sense. The quick Iranian withdrawal in Lebanon clearly demonstrated they preferred to fight Israel via proxy groups, such as Hezbollah, and not in a conventional military confrontation. Senior Revolutionary Guards' commanders who most forcefully pushed for the continuation of the war at the time still do not have a good answer.

The best rationale they can offer is that the war needed to go on until the moment Iran had a clear military and diplomatic advantage over Iraq. A decisive military push into Iraq itself was supposed to provide that advantage in order for Tehran to secure advantageous terms at the peace talks that invariably would happen. Both Rafsanjani and Khamenei were in favor of this approach. Their thinking was to capture Iraqi territory first and then settle for peace terms. It never worked out that way.

The Costs of a Revolutionary Foreign Policy

By 1982, Iran had helped bring about the birth of the anti-Saddam Badr Corps in Iraq and Hezbollah in Lebanon, both comprised of Shia Islamist activists that embraced Khomeini's doctrine of sweeping political change backed by arms. Both groups remain to this day the most successful Shia militant proxies aligned with Tehran. Throughout the 1980s, Iranian-inspired political radicalism and occasional acts of violence were witnessed in Bahrain, Kuwait, Pakistan, and Saudi Arabia. And yet, from early on there were murmurs of discomfort in Tehran about exporting the revolution. In Khomeini's inner circle there were those that could not avoid seeing a direct link between its radial actions and Iran's international isolation. The foreign ministry, as had been the case with the military, had been purged from any remnants of the Shah's professional cadre. Contempt for the outside world led to amateurish and harmful decisions. When Foreign Minister Velayati was asked how he, as a trained pediatric doctor, had become foreign minister, he had cavalierly uttered that "From the Islamic Republic's perspective, leaders of other countries are at the level of children and therefore a pediatric specialist is best suited for the job."[14] Meanwhile, the Khomeinists spearheaded a campaign of violence and assassinations—from Europe to Turkey to Pakistan and the Philippines— against opponents.

In February 1983, an institute was established to train new diplomats but the challenge was not one of training personnel but about the direction for Iran to go on the diplomatic stage. By early 1984, Tehran intensified its diplomatic efforts—focused on the Third World—to overcome international isolation. Khomeini publicly expressed regret. "I can count our friends on the fingers of one hand." This was somewhat counterintuitive. It had been Khomeini who had immediately after the revolution assaulted the idea of ties with the outside world. "Let them erect a wall around Iran and confine us inside. We prefer this to the doors being open and plunderers pouring in," he had said.[15] And yet the conflicting priorities remained alive in Tehran. There were efforts to expand trade and diplomatic ties. On the other hand, the pursuit of the proselytizing and spreading Islamic revolution was the preferred vocation of others. At this point, Rafsanjani was on the same page as Khamenei.

In a landmark speech by Khomeini on October 28, 1984, he again urged stepped-up diplomatic efforts. "Some people are up to mischief, asking why we should have relations with other governments." He called it a "fresh and very dangerous plot." As always, Rafsanjani gave it an Islamic veneer. "In the early days of Islam, Prophet Mohammad had sent ambassadors to all parts of the world to establish proper relations." He was adamant: "Lack of ties with other governments is contrary to Islamic precepts." In February 1985, the Majles passed a law charging the Foreign Ministry to be in lead to run diplomatic relations but also investing it with revolutionary mission. It was designed to strike a compromise between the contending viewpoints within the regime. Rafsanjani had seen the motion through the parliamentary pipeline and president Khamenei did his part to disseminate the new foreign policy emphasis. He told a crowd on February 21, 1985, "The open-door policy, which was emphatically recommended by the imam [Khomeini] a few months ago and [has also been explained] … is the firm policy of the Islamic Republic."

Such public pressuring was meant to press the most radicals that were inside the broader Khomeini and who still renounced routine diplomacy in favor of ties to revolutionary groups in other countries that Iran could nurture. Their view was that a return to normal diplomacy was a betrayal of a core calling of the 1979 revolution, namely the idea of shattering the existing regional and global orders. And yet, the pains of isolation in the midst of the war with Iraq expedited efforts aimed at normalization of Iranian foreign policy. The need for extensive diplomatic ties—even with states that did not share Iran's vision—was even defended by prime minister Mousavi and his many anti-Western cohorts found among the Islamist left. Reconciling the new recommended foreign policy path with old habits was bound to be an awkward process, which showed itself even as these deliberations were ongoing.

In December 1984, Hezbollah hijacked a Kuwait Airways flight en route to Karachi. The aircraft was forced to land in Tehran where majority of the hostages were eventually released after six days. Two Americans were killed by the hijackers. While Tehran officially condemned the act of hijacking, the Iranians refused to extradite the hijackers to the United States. Iran and the Reagan administration—which charged Iran to encourage "extreme behavior"—quarreled over the quality of the Iranian rescue operation, but the heart of the matter was the Iranian leaders were still not singing from the same sheet. Mousavi, the most leftist among the top Khomeinists, blamed "aggressive policies" of the United States in the Middle East to be at fault.[16] Rafsanjani saw an opportunity for a transactional moment and offered the four hijackers in return for Bani Sadr and other Iranian opposition figures in exile, a bid that US Department of State spokesperson described as "sick."[17]

Still, the soul-searching moment in Tehran was evident and reverberating around the Middle East as well. Saudi Arabia sent its foreign minister—Faisal Al Saud—to Tehran in May 1985 to suss out the atmosphere there. He met Speaker Rafsanjani, president Khamenei, and prime minister Mousavi. All three told Faisal a different version of the same message: that Iran under Khomeini was not an expansionist power, that the United States and Israel were the common enemy of Iran and the Arabs, and that Muslim unity was the solution of the problems of the Middle East.[18] In the case of the Saudis, this was still at best a half-baked Iranian charm offensive that was bound to be stillborn. The Khomeinists had from day one viewed the House of Saud with much scorn, judging them to be no more than a group of oil-rich pleasure-seekers acting as Washington's puppet. Rafsanjani is today remembered as a man who, unlike Khomeini or Khamenei, could reach across the aisle and meet the anxious Arabs of the Persian Gulf halfway. He could, and he did, but not until the early 1990s. In the mid-1980s, Rafsanjani was among those who was not still sure whether to court Riyadh or look for ways to bring down the House of Saud.

In those wild years of Iranian foreign policy in the 1980s, sensing an opportunity, the occasion of the Hajj (Islamic pilgrimage to Mecca) had on a few times been tapped by saber-rattlers in Khomeini's entourage to incite the Saudi population. A key figure in such Iranian efforts was none other than Mohammad Mousavi Khoeiniha, the same figure who had been the most senior cleric behind the siege of the US embassy in Tehran in November 1979. While a cleric, his aversion toward the United States and her regional allies was distinctly of a Soviet flavor. As head of Iran's Hajj organization, dealing with pilgrims going to Mecca, Khoeini-ha was held responsible for gunrunning into Saudi Arabia when unsuspected Iranian pilgrims had weapons put in their luggage. The Saudis were not pleased and warned the Iranians not to Islamicize Hajj and keep it as a religious occasion. Khoeini-ha was ultimately removed from his post, a move where Rafsanjani's intervention might have been instrumental, but that is merely a supposition given ongoing secrecy around the topic.

In fact, to this day there is uncertainty about the extent of Rafsanjani's anti-Saudi efforts in the 1980s. What is beyond doubt is that by 1988 the two countries broke diplomatic ties after hundreds of Iranian pilgrims clashed with Saudi security forces in Mecca in July 1987. With four hundred dead, including 270 Iranians, relations had hit a new rock bottom and Khomeini all but closed any prospect for reversal. "We might get over Saddam; we might get over Jerusalem [the question of Israel]; we might get over America's crimes, but we will never forgive the House of Saud." Riyadh, meanwhile, went back to bankrolling Saddam's war effort against the Iranians. Tehran's lack of prioritizing its foreign policy objectives was keeping the Islamic Republic's adversaries united. This was true nowhere else as much as among the Sunni Arab oil sheikhdoms of the Persian Gulf.

"Islamic Republic": A Contradiction in Terms

The contradictions in Iran's foreign policy were difficult to hide. This was an undisputed outcome of a contradiction that is even found in the official name of the country: "the Islamic Republic of Iran." Should it be an "Islamic," and by extension a "revolutionary" state, or act more like a "republic" where it gives priority to the narrow national interests of the Iranian people over the pursuit of adventurist and open-ended insurgent agenda hell-bent on restructuring the international power structure? The rulers in Tehran, with Khomeini at the top, sought to skip over this dichotomy and proceeded to assure the Iranian people that normality was just around the corner. "When the president of the republic [Ali Khamenei] visits several countries, and so does the prime minister [Mir Hossein Mousavi] and [foreign minister] Dr. Velayati—as it is proper they should [do so]—then everyone understands that Iran has relations with the world," Khomeini said in October 1984.

This was said a few weeks after Khamenei's first tour of a number of Arab capitals, including a visit to Damascus to be hosted by the anti-US and pro-Soviet Hafez Al Assad. This was the first time a president of the Islamic Republic had made an overseas trip since the revolution. What Khomeini did not say was that even the handful of allies Tehran had, such as Assad, were telling Tehran to scale back on the revolutionary bombast.[19] Damascus was backing Iran in the war against Saddam's Iraq, but the Syrians were also becoming increasingly fearful that refusal to start peace with Baghdad might force the United States or the Soviet Union to intervene in the region. The Iran–Iraq war was by now entering uncharted territory. It was no longer limited to the trenches on the Iran–Iraq land border. In March 1984, Iraq attacked Iranian oil tankers and facilities in the Persian Gulf, an event that was to be the prelude to the Tanker Wars and shortly after drew both the United States and the Soviets more directly into the region.

Besides the occasional reference to foreign policy in his dwindling public appearances, the ailing Khomeini by and large did not insert himself into the daily handling of Tehran's relations with the world. The four key official voices in this realm at the time were Rafsanjani, Khamenei, Mousavi, and Foreign Minister Velayati. Their foreign efforts, not always carried out in unison, were only part of the problem. The true conundrum boiled down to the regime's basic failure to relinquish earlier efforts to become the leading agitator force in the Middle East. For example, in June 1985, Rafsanjani called taking of American hostages by pro-Iran militant groups in Lebanon an act of "terrorism," a significant admission by the standards of Khomeinists. Rafsanjani then the following month visited China and Japan where the same message of Iran's return to "normality" was conveyed.

As Rafsanjani and Khamenei were trying to rehabilitate Iran's international image, senior Revolutionary Guards' commander Mohsen Rafiqdoost was in Lebanon and Syria in mid-1985 to plan a common strategy not only against Saddam but also against the Camp David Accords and Arab peace talks with Israel. That month, Iran and Libya's Qaddafi formed the "Army of Jerusalem" to liberate the Palestinians from Israel, as they put it.[20] It was a case of the Islamic Republic wanting to have its cake and eat it too. The matter about the identity of the Islamic Republic was plainly still in play.

Foreign policy is oftentimes a product and an extension of domestic political realities. In the case of Tehran, Washington's hesitance to put Iran down as a net loss in the tally of Cold War rivalry only confounded the Iranian deliberations. "The Iranian revolution has brought about the first revolutionary state in modern times to be founded on rigidly Islamic principles. Unlike our experience with a variety of Marxist revolutions, we have little precedence to by in assessing the likely course of behavior of the Islamic Republic," one top CIA report assessed.[21] Washington, with an eye firmly on Soviet intentions, was not ready to throw in the towel on the question of Iran. This American "let's wait and see" stance was feeding into an already rancorous fight in Tehran over how to deal with the outside world. It soon erupted as a schism that pitted Khomeini against his designated successor-in-waiting.

5

(1985–9)—The Beginning of the End of Khomeini

I think that the Rushdie affair was planned by the United States and by Zionism to deliver a blow against Iran. The position taken by the late Imam [Khomeini] in the Rushdie affair, which was a political masterpiece, exactly reversed the plot hatched by the Americans and the Zionists.
             (Mohammad Ardeshir Larijani, Iranian deputy foreign minister)[1]

One senior figure that shielded the die-hard supporters of exporting the revolution was Hossein Ali Montazeri. The 63-year-old Montazeri was one of Khomeini's closest associates. The 83-year-old leader of the revolution called him "the fruit of his life," a description both men would in time come to deeply lament.[2] Montazeri was also close to both Rafsanjani and Khamenei. Both had studied under him.[3] His rise and fall were very much tied to the political maneuverings of the two young clerics years his junior.

On July 17, 1985, the Assembly of Experts unanimously elected Montazeri as deputy (*Qaaem-Maqaam*) of the leader of the revolution and successor designate. This was not, of course, by coincidence. Nor was it due to Montazeri's clerical rank. There were more senior clerics available at the time. Khomeini's son, Ahmad, and Rafsanjani first introduced the idea and subsequently studiously labored for this designation. Rafsanjani had been the first to refer to Montazeri as "Grand Ayatollah," the highest rank in Twelver Shia Islam. Why curry such a favor? It would put Montazeri on par with Khomeini and thereby oil the machinery for the succession process.

Ahmad Khomeini and Rafsanjani had a plan they deemed foolproof. They essentially needed someone as a lame duck figure to succeed Khomeini who by now had a severe heart condition. To have the supreme leadership rest in the hands of a singular man also meant they would triumph over those within the system who were pushing for a "Council of Leaders." The notion of "Supreme Leadership," as conceived by Khomeini in 1979, was entirely a political doctrine and was by the mid-1980s still open to sweeping religious critique. Many Shia clerics viewed the idea, and many still do so to this day, as nothing but heretical. At one point, Rafsanjani and Khamenei had disagreed over this point. Rafsanjani, who was closer to Montazeri, felt the continuation of the one-man leadership formula was the way forward. Khamenei had expressed support for a three- to five-man council, but this would have effectively diluted Montazeri's powers and hence Rafsanjani's influence in the post-Khomeini era that everyone at the time saw as imminent.

Personal relations might have been a driver behind the process, but it was only part of it. Montazeri was seen as mostly besotted by seminary life and bound to shun day-to-day politics if he ever took over from Khomeini. Montazeri had quickly abandoned Tehran after the revolution for quasi-seminary life in Qom. He had also time and again urged Khomeini to join him in Qom. Khomeini had himself made the pledge that he would settle in Qom for a life of teaching of the scriptures over the politics of Tehran. That pledge was never fulfilled. He would stay in Tehran until the end of his life. Perhaps he enjoyed the limelight in the capital. Alternatively, his closest advisors needed him in Tehran as cover as they perpetually contemplated how to hang on to power after Khomeini's death.

Montazeri was undeterred. He had chosen Qom and asked the much junior Ali Khamenei to succeed him as the Tehran Friday prayer leader. It had been a golden opportunity for Khamenei. Choosing to distance himself from Tehran was in the end a fatal decision for Montazeri's position. Montazeri adopted positions while in Qom that belied the agenda of those very same people who had propelled him to become Khomeini's successor-in-waiting. Above all, Montazeri was in the mid-1980s still a hawk on the question of foreign policy. He had shortly after the revolution helped his son, Mohammad, establish the Office for Islamic Liberation Movements (OILM), an organization whose key mission was to provide financial and military support to revolutionaries in other countries with a particular emphasis on the Middle East.

Montazeri's association with foreign revolutionaries was reflective of his provincial grasp of the outside world and his obliviousness to the threatening message such Iranian activities were sending to ruling political classes in neighboring states.[4] In February 1985, he told leaders from a number of Muslim states that certain Muslim countries have become "subservient to the major powers of the West and the East." By mostly residing in the seminary city of Qom, Montazeri was removed from the day-to-day difficulties of running the state. He was hence still blissfully ignorant of the damages the scorched earth foreign policy of the revolution had inflicted on Iran in just a few years.

Bleeding Badly in the War with Iraq

On the home front, the war with Iraq remained a central test for the Khomeinists. The Iraqi military was rebounding. In the "War of the Cities," Iranian population centers were hit by an array of aerial raids and missiles that Iraq had access to from France, Soviet Union, and many other suppliers in between. It was Iran that was isolated. Khomeini's stubborn stance that "Saddam has to go," as he was painted as an enemy of Islam, was increasingly met by skepticism even at home. In one episode, in an explicit defiance of Khomeini, Grand Ayatollah Qomi Tabatabaei said in Islam war is only justified in self-defense and Saddam had repeatedly asked for a ceasefire. There were only a handful of grand ayatollahs in Iran at the time. They either stayed out of politics or openly opposed Khomeini.

Rafsanjani, meanwhile, as the de facto head of the war effort, had to look for ways to replenish the rapidly dwindling Iranian military inventory. His efforts, evident as early as 1984, to convince Khomeini to declare victory and end the war, came to nothing. For Khomeini, compromise over the war was compromising the revolution he had led. Khomeini had set an impossible litmus test for his followers and the widening gap between intentions and abilities had become embarrassing. By 1984, for example, the Iranian air force no longer had effective offensive operational capabilities. Nor could it provide effective air support to Iranian ground forces. Iran's air force went from about four hundred aircraft in 1979 to about sixty-five to eighty by 1984. There was a shortage of spare parts, and restrictions on the sale of US-made parts afflicted the war effort badly. Iran had to turn to Libya, Syria, and North Korea for supply, but these mostly failed to deliver. Iran's suspicions of Moscow, meanwhile, meant that Iran would not ask the Soviets for aircraft.

Furthermore, by 1985, Iran was solidly broke. Foreign investors were reluctant to lend it money. The Islamic Republic was still a perilous riddle to investors. Prime minister Mousavi complained that he was not able to organize an "Islamic economy," because there are no examples of it anywhere in the world. Iran also faced a historic brain drain. Some of the country's best and brightest were leaving in droves. In one case, Tehran had to restrict foreign travel by physicians or have them leave behind loved ones to ensure their return. Efforts to turn the emigration tide failed. Rafsanjani urged Iranian exiles to return. "Return to Iran," he urged his wary compatriots. "We have great plans to build the country and we need you."[5] Needless to say it was a cry that fell on deaf ears.

Iran's very few partners in the region, such as Syria and Libya, were also not that much better off. A glance at Iran's foreign policy partners at the time would also have revealed another stark reality. A few years into the Islamic Republic and the vast majority of Iran's military collaborators had one thing or two things in common: they all had one form or another of leftist dictatorial bent (North Korea, Syria, Libya, China) and long anti-American track records. Otherwise, they shared very little and there was certainly no strategic or value framework that bound them together. This was the international coalition of anti-American mavericks.

Khomeini's aversion toward the United States had by implication put the Iranian theocracy in the same camp as the Godless leftists on the global stage. During the eight-year war with Iraq, a total of nineteen countries supplied military equipment to Iran. China, North Korea, the Soviet Union, Libya, and Syria topped the list.[6] Heavy equipment, such as armored vehicles, and surface-to-surface missiles comprised most such sales. It amounted to a critical juncture for the Iranian military as it began a slow but sure transition away from historic Western military partners. It was to herald a new era. From the Swedish military training mission that arrived in Iran in 1910 to Tehran's first purchase of a Junker F-13 aircraft from Germany in 1923 and the dispatch of Iranian cadets to France for training that same year, Europe and later the United States had long formed the spine of Iran's armed forces.

After 1979, the military assistance the anti-US states provided was not insignificant. For example, it was supplies and subsequent reverse engineering of Soviet-origin missiles from these states that would later make Iran into a top Middle Eastern missile power. And yet, during the bulk of the Iran–Iraq war, the Iranian armed forces were still a US-made military thanks to the legacy of the Shah's pro-American era. Only the United States had the urgent spare parts for Iran's fighting machine. Since there were no diplomatic relations between Tehran and Washington, procurement of US hardware was near an impossibility. To publicly pursue US military parts was politically infeasible even though everyone in Tehran could see lack of parts was hurting the war campaign. Most famously, Ali Khamenei had in mid-1979 put up a fight against those in the provincial government who had wanted to return the Shah-procured F-4 and F-14 aircrafts back to the United States. Khamenei had defended the purchases as a military requisite for the nation's defense.

Tehran, faced with dwindling oil income and a number of military setbacks in the war, also had to increasingly grapple with growing domestic disquiet. The old organized opposition inside Iran was all but dead, but economic hardship mobilized the working class. Strikes hit a number of cities with more frequency. A new entity, the *Solidarity Committee of Iranian Workers*, is said to have been modeled after the successful Polish *Solidarity* movement but it lacked political weight. A combination of growing economic strains and emerging political opposition trends was necessitating discernable change of course. And nothing could turn things around as ending the war with Iraq once and for all. Khomeini still put on a good show. "At times calamity becomes a blessing. It is under pressure that the spirit soar to the higher world," he said. Rafsanjani, above all, wanted to end a war that had morphed into a sacred mission which only Khomeini had the sufficient authority to end while he was still alive. Once again, Western states, including the United States, started to put their hopes in the so-called moderate-wing of the Islamic Republic. In Tehran, the hunt for the much-needed US military parts hence became the spur of the moment.

The Origins of the Iran–Contra Affair

An uncommon dinner party was held in an imposing brick house in Washington in 1985. The host was the Iraqi ambassador, Nizar Hamdoon, who had taken up his post in late 1983. Iraq had broken diplomatic relations with the United States in 1967 in protest against Washington's pro-Israel policies. Now, five years into the Iran–Iraq war, Saddam's ambassador was pitching a new line to a select small group of US government official and influential Jewish-American figures. Hamdoon kept a copy of a map he was handing out. It showed "Iranian forces advancing through Iraq, through Jordan and Israel—and the target was Jerusalem."[7]

Baghdad evidently deemed the Islamist fervor in Tehran invariably leading to Iran's permanent rupture with the West, which was by now highly uneasy about the rise of militant Islam in the Middle East. Among the US officials at the dinner was Howard Teicher, the director of Near East and South Asian Affairs at the National Security Council. In an unlikely twist, it was soon to be Tehran, and not Baghdad, that became Teicher's port of call. Iraq was, after all, already a Soviet client but Iran had not yet become one.

Washington was at this time primarily concerned about Soviet intentions toward Iran and the likely resurgence of the communists in the Tudeh Party. The party had warned that "it will come out from under [Khomeini's] robe when the time is right and get control of the government in 48 hours." Remnants of the Shah's regime, which comprised the bulk of the human intelligence assets available to the Americans at this time, by all accounts had a good reason to exaggerate the threat of communist takeover in Iran. An American intervention at this time was the only conceivable way for them to regain power. Dire warnings about a communist face-off in Tehran often reached Bill Casey, the head of the CIA. "It is hard to believe that the axis of Tehran-Damascus-Tripoli-Aden is not linked to Moscow," concluded a memo prepared for Casey.[8] The same exiled Iranian sources were telling the Americans that Rafsanjani was taking a soft position on the Tudeh Party. There were suggestions that Moscow had found a way to intimidate Rafsanjani although there was nothing specific to such reports. These Iranian dissident accounts about Rafsanjani were tailored to achieve one goal: to make Washington give up on him as the man who held the keys to the normalization of US–Iran relations.[9]

To top it off, over the years Iranian exiles presented Khomeini to Westerners as a fanatic who paid little attention to conventional national security calculations that states usually perform when executing policy. "We do not worship Iran, we worship Allah. For patriotism is another name for paganism. I say let this land [Iran] burn. I say let this land go up in smoke, provided Islam emerges triumphant in the rest of the world." There is no evidence that Khomeini ever uttered these words but anti-Khomeini Iranian opposition in exile presented him as such.[10] For America's Cold War warriors fixated on containing the Soviet Union, Khomeini was an unrestrained international Islamist and hence a potential dangerous weak link that Moscow could manipulate for its ambitions in the Middle East.

The Soviets had deployed large number of military forces on the Iranian border in the north. Soviets forces in Afghanistan had also increasingly deployed along the Iran–Afghan border. The United States in particular feared that one scenario in which the Soviets could move into Iran militarily was if a leftist takeover of power happened in Tehran. In such a scenario, the Soviets could opt to move in to uphold such a regime as they had done in Afghanistan in late 1979 when a leftist government in Kabul called for a Soviet intervention. Such American calculations and fears of a system collapse in Tehran were happening at a time when power succession from Khomeini to his successor was universally reckoned to be a hazardous, and mercurial, process. By 1985, Khomeini ordered all government offices to remove his photo, fueling rampant belief that he was on his deathbed.

There were at this point some 2,500 to 3,000 Soviet economic advisors in Iran, working on some fifty economic and technical projects. The number of Soviets had been 4,000 under the Shah but then some 50,000 Americans worked and lived in Iran as well. Not only did the American presence disappear from Iran after 1979, a presence that had functioned as a counter to Moscow, but Tehran was still a prime target for Soviet espionage. The Soviets had some 100 to 200 military advisors and another 440 accredited diplomats, attaches, journalists, and trade representatives deployed across Iran. The United States had a distinct absenteeism problem in Iran.

From a US perspective, efforts by Khomeini's son, Ahmad, and Rafsanjani to arrange for a smooth succession to Khomeini was meant to solidify their consolidation on power. But while the American assessment judged that the core of Khomeini's base, the lower urban and rural classes, was by this point an integral part of the state machinery and largely content, the same was not true for the old merchant class in the Bazaar. This group, which had been instrumental in helping Khomeini rise to power, was by now deeply worried about the leftist policies of prime minister Mousavi. Efforts to redistribute wealth, impose stricter control over foreign trade, increase taxes, or launch land reform made Mousavi into an antihero of sorts for many in merchant circles. Everyone, including the Americans, could see that a power struggle was brewing. This was hence a moment for the United States to revisit the idea of détente with Tehran. Both to stunt Soviet efforts and turn the United States into a player in the process in the post-Khomeini period were on the horizon. Some key officials in the Ronald Reagan administration redoubled efforts to find ways to reach out to Tehran. Rafsanjani in particular was all too eager for the same thing to happen. Washington decided to overlook his earlier mischiefs, and Rafsanjani's hesitant, venturesome but determined campaign to build bridges with the United States was hence born. Nevertheless, the narrative that Rafsanjani somehow was the sole engine behind an outreach to Washington is a present-day fabrication. It is concocted by the remaining hard-liners in Tehran that are loath to admit to their own role in the process in the 1980s.

§

On November 3, 1986, the Lebanese magazine *Ash-Shiraa* published an article about secret American dealings with Tehran. The *New York Times* picked the story up the following day and the "Iran–Contra" scandal was born. As part of the Reagan administration's effort aimed at a "strategic opening to Iran," the US government had throughout 1985 kept in contact with the Iranians. It was a disorderly affair, involving shadowy Iranian expats that acted as go-between in meetings held in various locations in Europe where officials from the CIA and the Reagan National Security Council joined the talks. To further complicate an already rough operation, the Israeli intelligence services had managed to make themselves into an intermediary albeit under purported disguise. Many in Washington had doubts about the Israeli role while the Iranians have always maintained they knew nothing about it.

It amounted to an unlikely amalgamation of interests that, once it was found out, put Rafsanjani's political life at risk of destruction. He was the leading Iranian figure in the affair and Rafsanjani quickly found out that both foreign and domestic partners turned into rivals wanted him banished or at least thwarted in his agenda in improving the future of US–Iran relations. His profound prudence that followed was therefore justified. He wanted both tight oversight of the process and also deniability in gauging his American options. American considerations, and the subsequent fallout when the covert talks were uncovered, are greatly easier to trace.

President Reagan Sends His Envoy to Tehran

In December 1985, president Reagan's National Security Advisor Robert McFarlane passed a message via Israel's Iranian contact to Tehran that Washington wanted a new start in relations. This was not a fluke. When Reagan was elected in 1980, he had sent a message to Rafsanjani that his administration would be willing to help Tehran with military hardware and specially Phoenix missiles for Iran's F-14 fleet. During his first term in office, Reagan had sent three separate letters to the skeptical Iranians, urging them to improve relations with the United States. He had received no response but he did not give up.[11] Khomeinists were unsavory but Iran falling into Soviet hands was a nightmare scenario for Washington.

As part of this secret channel, the four points that McFarlane emphasized to Tehran were about finding ways to end the Iran–Iraq war on "honorable terms"; convince Iran to end its support for groups the United States had classified as terrorist; foster Iranian–American cooperation against Soviet activities in the Middle East; and for Tehran to exercise its influence over militant groups in Lebanon to free American hostages in captivity in that country. In January 1986, Reagan approved a covert action to accomplish this new set of goals in regard to Iran. On May 15, 1986, Reagan authorized a secret mission by McFarlane. He had on December 4, 1985, resigned as National Security Advisor but was still chosen to lead the secret flight to Tehran.[12]

McFarlane, together with Teicher and other CIA and NSC staff and Israeli and Iranian interlocutors arrived in Tehran on May 25 from Israel to maintain operational secrecy. With them they brought another pallet of spare military parts and huge hopes. This was in contravention of *Operation Staunch*, a worldwide campaign that the United States had launched in 1983 to stop the flow of arms to Iran. Leading up to the mission, the United States had via Israel delivered tons of military hardware as requested by the Iranians such as TOW missiles that could take out the dreaded Iraqi T-72 Soviet tanks.[13]

The Americans had high hopes that providing Iran with much-need US weaponry and parts, and some intelligence about Iraqi military formations, could set the ball rolling toward a new diplomatic chapter. It was not to be. It was all predicated on the premise of United States and Iran hitting the reset button in their troubled relations. But Rafsanjani balked and never agreed to meet the visiting American mission while they waited patiently in a Tehran hotel for four days. Instead, he dispatched three individuals, including his deputy, a 36-year-old Hassan Rouhani, to meet the Americans.[14] Rouhani had taken off his clerical garb to avoid being recognized.[15]

When McFarlane asked Rouhani to meet Rafsanjani, prime minister Mousavi, or president Khamenei, he was told it was "far too soon for that." The Rafsanjani faction was deeply afraid of the reaction of more anti-American elements in the regime if the presence of the US mission in Tehran was somehow revealed. Howard Teicher, the NSC staffer who wrote the American account of the meeting, later recalled that even Rouhani used a pseudonym to protect himself. While nonetheless hopeful that a breakthrough might be in the offing, McFarlane noted that the principal factions in the Islamic Republic "still cannot overcome their more immediate problem of how to talk to the [United States]."[16]

It is safe to say that McFarlane and others in the Reagan administration that had labored for this face-to-face moment with the Iranians were left disenchanted. The men who wielded power in Tehran did not have the fortitude and the foresight to seize the moment. Rafsanjani later on, and very lamely, boasted that "we kept them [the US mission] hostage for four days and let them go." It was a disingenuous account and only aimed to protect him in the cutthroat labyrinth politics of the Islamic Republic. Years later he admitted so much and stated the real reason why the Iranians never sent any senior leaders to meet McFarlane's mission. The Americans, Rafsanjani admitted, had come to engineer a fundamental policy shift in Tehran on the question of the United States. The US mission had hoped for immediate access to the top echelons of power in Iran. But the relatively senior caliber they had sent to Tehran, where there was no prior knowledge of the American group's makeup, had rattled the Iranians.[17] Tehran had not been prepared for such a grand gesture from Washington. The Americans were equally baffled by this lack of preparation and were unwilling just to sit endlessly around in a hotel room while their Iranian interlocutors inched toward a decision.

In the years since, the circle around Supreme Leader Khamenei sought to portray the secret American mission to Tehran as Rafsanjani's brainchild: that he had gone rogue and behind everyone's back in the regime and that his ultimate goal was to secure American support for himself as the best possible heir to Khomeini. In 2014, the older brother of Khamenei, Mohammad Khamenei, hinted that arms-for-hostages in the mid-1980s was an excuse and Rafsanjani had for long wanted to cut a bigger deal with the Americans.[18] This argument amounts to historic forgery. This is at least what Mohsen Kangarloo has to say about it. He was the security affairs advisor to prime minister Mousavi and a key player in the secret talks with the Americans.

Kangarloo, who for the first time broke his silence in 2014, is adamant that all senior leaders at the time, including the then president Khamenei, were aware of the secret channel to Washington. No one figure in Tehran had done this single-handedly. According to Kangarloo, if only McFarlane's delegation had not been so quick to leave Tehran then there could have been a genuine chance for a breakthrough. The Iranian side, he claims, were just too rushed to organize an appropriate response to the Americans who had arrived in Tehran with a key-shaped cake to symbolize the anticipated opening to Iran.[19]

President Reagan had earlier even inscribed a Bible that was given to an Iranian official. Reagan sought to present himself as a man of God to the clerics in Tehran. Reagan wrote in the Bible: "And the Scripture, foreseeing that God would justify the Gentiles by faith, preached the Gospel beforehand to Abraham, saying, 'All the nations shall be blessed in you.'"[20] Rafsanjani's later claimed that Reagan's White House never had a hope in hell in turning him around. What Rafsanjani never admitted was that his American efforts continued even as the McFarlane-led mission left Tehran empty-handed on May 29, 1986. His own nephew, Ali Bahramani, would meet American interlocutors in Belgium and later in Washington, DC.[21] Still, in the next few months, the question of a "strategic opening" was put on the backburner. Instead, US–Iranian engagement was reduced to the American side providing more arms to Iran in the anticipation that Tehran would squeeze pro-Iran Lebanese militants, principally Hezbollah, to release American hostages seized in Beirut. As the American military historian David Crist put it, the entire secret exercise had by now "degenerated into purely an arms-for-hostages agreement."[22]

In June 1986, the US Congress had approved a request from the Reagan administration to fund the Contras in Nicaragua. This diminished the need for arms sales to Iran as a source of funding. The United States still wanted Tehran's help in releasing American hostages in Lebanon. Seven US nationals had been abducted between March 1984 and June 1985. In mid-July 1986, the Reagan administration let the Iranians know through various sources that Washington will not make further moves unless more hostages were released. Iran agreed to do so but it was a step that further fueled rivalries inside the Iranian system.

§

Despite the serious setbacks, proengagement voices both in Tehran and in Washington stayed on course in looking for a broader covenant. A so-called "second channel," where the role of the Israelis as middlemen was eliminated, was born. This channel amounted to Rafsanjani's young nephew—Ali Bahramani—and even two members of the Revolutionary Guards secretly visiting the White House with a message of cooperation.[23] The messengers from Tehran spoke of grand joint US–Iranian efforts against both the Soviets and Saddam's Iraq.[24] But Bahramani's uncle, Rafsanjani, was still overpromising the same way the Reagan administration had found out the hard way in May 1986.

The "strategic opening to Iran" never happened. Unlike McFarlane or Oliver North, who soon became household names in the United States, most of the Iranians involved in the negotiations still maintain uncommonly low profiles. Take Ali Bahramani, Rafsanjani's nephew. There has never been much mention of him in Iran despite him being to this day still one of the handful of individuals affiliated with the Islamic Republic that was able to wander the hallways of the White House. Nor was there much scrutiny from the Western press that either found the secret talks impenetrable or were fed bits and pieces of half-truths or disinformation by the different players. The *Observer*, a London paper, while mistaking Rafsanjani's nephew for his 17-year-old son, reported that president Khamenei had launched an investigation into the secret arms purchases from the United States. Little did the *Observer* know that Khamenei had himself for months been an active participant in the process.

For the Reagan administration, the eighteen months of secret talks in 1985–6 amounted to a sincere effort to overturn the status quo with Iran. While the strategic calculus was sound, Washington's pursuit of this policy objective was at best jumbled nor did it have its ducks in row. The monies the Iranians were paying to the United States for the military hardware was funneled by the Reagan White House to the Contra anticommunist guerillas in Nicaragua. This amounted to breaking American law and hence the Iran–Contra scandal was born in the United States. The performance of the Iranians involved in the affair was mostly a case of the absence of a well-defined national security vision. The amateurish incompetence is also glaring. One notable memory by Kangarloo is that he had overslept the morning he was supposed to meet the American group, a lapse that nearly resulted in McFarlane and his team heading for the airport.[25] Ultimately, though, it was not the poor welcome of the hosts in Tehran that surprised the Americans. It was the depth of their haphazard policy-making process.

At the time, Iran did not have an equivalent to an American National Security Council. A handful of individuals, such as Rafsanjani and Khamenei, with access to and sway over Khomeini exercised the greatest policy influence. These men were also hostages to their past politics where denouncing the United States as Iran's immortal enemy had been sold to the Iranian public as the final truth and destiny of Iran. A quick climbdown on the matter was simply impossible for the Khomeinists. To Reagan, who complained bitterly, the "rug merchants"[26] he had strived to cut a deal with could not see the forest for the trees.

There is also another basic truth. American accounts about what took place with the McFarlane mission in Tehran give an image of feuding Iranian factions hiding the visitors in a hotel in downtown Tehran for four days. The fact is that the mission's presence in Tehran was widely known as soon as the US delegation arrived. No doubt, some inside the regime in Tehran were dead set against revival of diplomatic ties with Washington and yet the public unmasking of the affair still took a few months. The dots can only be connected if one looks for a missing link outside of Iran's borders.

Ash-Shiraa, the Lebanese magazine behind the belated exposé, was at the time close to the Syrian regime of Hafez Al Assad, the source behind the leak.[27] Damascus was ostensibly one of Tehran's very few Arab allies but Assad had his reasons why he did not want to see Rafsanjani succeed in his efforts toward Washington.[28] One CIA assessment later concluded that Assad had a two-pronged objective by exposing the dealings of his ally in Tehran with Washington and Tel Aviv. First, to end the nascent Iranian de-escalation process vis-à-vis the United States and Israel early on. The United States and Israel were, after all, Syria's principal adversaries. Second, the Syrians themselves were at this particular moment in the hot seat with charges of sponsoring terrorism, leading to the UK breaking diplomatic relations with Damascus on October 24, 1986. Assad, who had known about the secret US–Iran dealings for weeks, leaked the information only after he felt more Western countries were about to ditch him.

The Iran–Contra scandal, which Assad divulged in the first week of November, quickly put Syria's role in terrorism on the backburner and focused the attention on Iran and now with its covert negotiations with Washington. The Rafsanjani camp is to this day also certain the Soviets had a role to play. Assad, a Soviet client, no doubt had been encouraged by the Soviets to throw a wrench into the budding US–Iran détente before it took off. The last thing Moscow wanted to see was the return of the American embassy in downtown Tehran.

§

The precise account about who in Iran revealed the secret US–Iran channel to Assad is not yet a fully settled matter in Tehran. During this time, not everyone in Tehran was yet ready to see the direct link between hostage-taking by pro-Iran groups in Lebanon and Iran's costly ostracization from the West. The strongest suspicion has always been on the network of Ayatollah Montazeri, the deputy supreme leader. Montazeri's eldest son, Mohammad, had in the 1970s escaped the Shah's Iran and soon linked up with

Arab militants in Lebanon and Syria. Mohammad, known also as "Ayatollah Ringo" for his militancy and short fuse, was killed in the 1981 bombing of the Islamic Republican Party, but the Montazeri family had other members that followed in his footsteps.

The most infamous figure was Mehdi Hashemi, a brother to Montazeri's son-in-law. Hashemi had been an early member of the Revolutionary Guards but was a man known best for his disdain for all decorum. He had been in prison under the Shah for organizing vigilante killings, including a cleric who had opposed Khomeini's revolutionary agenda. After 1979, Mehdi Hashemi and the Montazeri network remained deeply involved in Iranian efforts in Lebanon by supporting handpicked Lebanese Shia collaborators. This group in Lebanon, meanwhile, very likely came to see Rafsanjani's secret talks with the Americans to release US hostages as a direct threat to their interests.

In Lebanon, the question of what to do with Western hostages, and which faction in Tehran to side with, had resulted in a schism of its own. The relative moderates inside Hezbollah were aligned with Rafsanjani while the more hard-line figures were closer to the Montazeri network.[29] But Rafsanjani was hardly the only powerful figure in Tehran who was tapping into hostages in Lebanon as a way of advancing certain goals. Mohsen Rezai, the head of the Revolutionary Guards at the time and a man today known for his hard-line positions, sent his own special envoy to Beirut to request that Hezbollah release some of the hostages so the United States could resume arms sales to Iran. Not everyone in Hezbollah was happy to see Rezai's envoy. His guesthouse was hit by rocket fire as a way of chasing him out of Beirut.[30] It was Rafsanjani, though, who found himself in the spotlight. There was motion in the Majles to find out what his precise role had been in maintaining the secret channel with the Americans and organizing the McFarlane group's visit to Tehran in May 1986. Rafsanjani had seen this coming. The day after *Ash-Shiraa* had ran its exposé, on November 4, 1986, Rafsanjani sought to stay ahead of the fallout by admitting that an American delegation had been to Tehran but left frustrated and empty-handed.

Khomeini had no prior knowledge about the secret US mission in Tehran. He found out once McFarlane and the US team was already in Tehran. He came to Rafsanjani's aid. Instead of reprimanding Rafsanjani, Khomeini ordered the minister of intelligence, Mohammad Reyshahri, to arrest Mehdi Hashemi and about fifty key members of Montazeri's network. They were charged with sedition within the regime. On November 20, Khomeini publicly reaffirmed his support for Rafsanjani.

There was an interesting and largely forgotten twist in this rancorous episode. In a letter to Montazeri, Mehdi Hashemi claimed that all he wanted was to end the secret channel with the Americans but that the Iran–Contra affair had now become an excuse for Khomeini's son, Ahmad, and Rafsanjani to finish off Montazeri and remove him as deputy supreme leader.[31] The same two men who had put him in the role about a year earlier had by now had a change of heart. Montazeri might have been malleable but key members in his inner circle were set in their uncompromising militancy and on a collision course with the future vision of Iran that Rafsanjani and Ahmad Khomeini were now quietly contemplating. What is beyond question is that Reyshahri, the intelligence minister given the task by Khomeini to get to the bottom of Hashemi's activities, was not impartial. He was the son-in-law of Ayatollah Ali Meshkini, the influential head of the Assembly of Experts, and a man who eyed the deputy supreme leadership for himself only to see Montazeri secure that appointment. Reyshahri therefore had good reasons to try and turn the case of Mehdi Hashemi into a mortal blow for Montazeri.

Washington's Concerns about Rafsanjani's Fate

The McFarlane affair, as it is known in Iran, has always underscored the deep rivalries running behind the veneer of brotherly clerical rule. It continues to fuel wild rumors. One American study, for example, viewed Meshkini as a natural ally of the then president Khamenei since they shared ethnic Azerbaijani background. The CIA at this time was convinced of the existence of a pro-Soviet "Azerbaijani faction" inside the regime led by Khamenei. Profound ethnic or local political interest groups did not, and still does not, exist in the Islamic Republic, and Washington was on this occasion overstating events in Tehran. In the end, the Montazeri faction's campaign had failed to dethrone the triumvirate of Rafsanjani, Ahmad Khomeini, and Ali Khamenei. There is no irrefutable evidence that Montazeri had had a direct role in Mehdi Hashemi's vendetta against the trio but as the patriarch of his network he was always going to be held responsible. That Montazeri would go on to defend Mehdi Hashemi until the day the latter was hanged in September 1987 did not help his position within the system. After the debacle of the Iran–Contra affair, Montazeri's position was on a downward spiral.

Rafsanjani boasted that the antiair missiles that Tehran received from the United States had shot down some fifty Iraqi aircraft. This was not a red herring as such but it was only partially what had motivated Rafsanjani. He never admitted that in 1986 Khomeini's health had taken another turn for the worse and that settling for peace with Saddam was infinitely simpler while he was still alive. Trading with the United States in arms and hostages had a two-pronged purpose: to expedite the ending of the Iran–Iraq war and help pave the way for the post-Khomeini era while providing an opportunity to hit the reset button on the question of relations with the United States.

In Washington, it was Rafsanjani's fate that was monitored with the greatest interest. "Rafsanjani's political survival would not guarantee that Iran will someday turn toward moderation but his demise would be a severe setback for such prospects," the Americans assessed at the time.[32] By now he was still the principal figure in the "pragmatic" faction. This put him in the middle of the "radicals" to the left and the "conservatives" to the right.[33] What Rafsanjani also had, which in essence made him become the "pragmatic," was his access to both the "radical" and the "conservative" factions. But it was an intricate tangle for outsiders to figure out. In November 1986, months after Rafsanjani had begun to turn his back on Montazeri, and orchestrated for Mehdi Hashemi's arrest for revealing the secret talks with the Reagan administration, the American intelligence community was still assessing that Rafsanjani sought to make Montazeri the successor to Khomeini. Unbeknownst to Washington, such valuations were behind the curve. The same CIA assessment, however, got it right when it called Khamenei the "chief rival" to Rafsanjani inside the regime. Few others would have guessed that at the time.

§

The Iran–Contra affair had weakened Rafsanjani's hand. In turn, president Khamenei was in a better position than ever before. He had actively sought to strengthen the Office of the President, and it was starting to work. Khamenei did not have to look far to see it was a realizable ambition. Raw power in the Islamic Republic flows within a few narrow corridors, but the point was and is that it flows. Rafsanjani had demonstrated this by the way he had transformed the position of Speaker of the Majles into a central point. Based on the constitution, the Speakership was hardly the zenith of power but Rafsanjani had turned his position into the de facto No. 2 powerhouse in Iran.

Khamenei was no doubt one of the best public speakers among the senior members of the regime. He was said to consistently attract bigger crowds for his Friday Prayer sermons. But his ambitions were vastly greater than merely acting as one of the regime's engaging mouthpieces. By now Khamenei was still also head of the Islamic Republican Party—the nominal political abode of all the Khomeinists—and used the party's newspaper to attack his rivals. As president of the country, he still had the power to veto parliamentary bills and oversee the performance of the prime minister even though Khomeini, as the supreme leader, could always override him and openly did when he felt necessary. Khamenei charged the parliament to be too slow and too shambolic in producing policy legislation, and he repeatedly clashed with his prime minister, Mir Hossein Mousavi.

Rafsanjani was someone else who viewed the avid president as increasingly too restless to expand his influence. When Rafsanjani and Khamenei publicly clashed, Khomeini was forced to intervene to contain the spat. Khomeini kept a balance between the two men while he lived; collateral damage was unavoidable. On June 1, 1987, Rafsanjani wrote a letter to Khomeini and asked that the Islamic Republican Party be dissolved. Political infighting between various factions within the IRP was threatening regime stability. The IRP had been born in 1979 to generate unity among Khomeinists, Rafsanjani wrote, but it had become a cesspool for plots where different factions among Khomeinists had their knives drawn. Rafsanjani said the IRP was no longer "useful" and Khomeini responded in agreement but told his disciples: "You are all favorites of mine" but remember that "creating divisions at this time would be considered a great sin."[34] Despite the tensions, both Rafsanjani and Khamenei also knew that unless there was an orderly succession the entire clerical regime was at risk. As with the 1979–81 period, the fear of civil war and utter chaos was keeping minds focused.

§

Rafsanjani and Khamenei still agreed on many policy objectives. Above all, they were both against the radical collectivists within the regime that were holding onto semi-Marxist economic ideals. The views of these two men also strongly shaped Iran's policy toward the Iraq war, succession to Khomeini, and policy toward the United States. There were those who felt excluded and openly expressed their anger. Prime minister Mousavi issued a public resignation in September 1988. He was livid about how he had been kept in the dark on key policy issues. He wrote his resignation addressed to

Khamenei, the president, and his nominal boss who had gone from reluctantly accepting Mousavi as his prime minister to actively marginalizing him. "There are five channels of communication with the US—and I, as the head of the Cabinet of Ministers, have no idea of these channels," Mousavi fumed. "Today, the affairs of Afghanistan, Iraq and Lebanon are in the hands of your Excellency [Khamenei]. Letters are written to various countries without the government knowing anything about them," Mousavi rued.

Mousavi was no less critical of Rafsanjani. "The Prime Minister of Japan writes a letter to the honorable Speaker of the *Majles* [Parliament] and the honorable Speaker writes to the Prime Minister of Japan, and I learn about this exchange and the content of the letter in a public ceremony [by accident]." Mousavi left his sharpest attack for the end. "Extra-territorial operations [support for militant groups] take place without the knowledge and orders of the government. You [Khamenei] know better than anyone what great disasters and unfavorable results these have caused for the country up to now." It was a call by a desperate prime minister for an end to the culture of freewheeling and some resemblance of accountability in the policy-making process. The pursuit of narrow factional goals was wrecking Iranian national interests and the prime minister had a front-seat view.

Khomeini interjected and Khamenei never had a chance to seriously contemplate accepting the resignation of the prime minister. Nothing good came from Mousavi's call for streamlining policy making. Take the impact of the Iran–Contra affair in Iran. Unlike in the United States, the Iranians never held public hearings about what had transpired. In the United States, about a dozen men, including a former and the serving national security advisors to the president and top figures from the Pentagon, the CIA, and the State Department, were indicted. Such names as Robert McFarlane, Oliver North, John Poindexter, Elliot Abrams, and Casper Weinberger became synonymous with the Iran–Contra affair. To this day, there is no such an equivalent list of men in Tehran that have admitted or been indicted for participating in the secret talks with the Reagan administration.[35]

In a memorable line in defense of the Reagan administration's project to reach out to Tehran, Oliver North said he had no regrets about exploring ways to "achieve an opening to the strategically vital Iran."[36] He also chastised the members of US Congress for undermining American national security interest by overstepping their mandate in the realm of foreign policy. Ironically, North's Iranian counterparts in the Iran–Contra affair had very solid reason to argue for the need of a strategic opening to the United States, but instead everyone dodged any obligation to speak the truth.

The End of the Iran–Iraq War

In the last year before Khomeini's death, Tehran was under massive domestic and foreign pressure to end the war with Iraq. The immensely costly war campaign had for too long been put on autopilot. Khomeini was ailing and out of day-to-day decision-making. Instead, a nominal five-man team was officially running the country.[37] Of the five, only three men, Ahmad Khomeini, Rafsanjani, and Khamenei, wielded real power. But the war had metamorphosed into a holy crusade and not even the three men could muster the courage to speak the truth about a military victory being beyond reach. By the spring of 1988 the Iranian military had lost some 60 percent of its hardware. The flow of volunteers for the war was way down. The Khomeinists had no option but to accept UN resolution 598, a motion that had been passed unanimously at the UN in July 1987. In Tehran, the top political and military leadership needed an exit ramp but could not say so publicly. The head of the Revolutionary Guards, Mohsen Rezaei, sent a letter to Khomeini with a long list of demands for military parts, including increasing the size of Iran's armed forces seven times. Rezaei, a man with no formal military education, had assessed that for the war to continue for another five years, Iran also needed 2,500 tanks, 3,000 artillery, 300 fighter aircraft, and a capacity to produce laser and atomic weapons. He was asking for the impossible and did so very much deliberately.[38]

There were rumors that the bedridden Khomeini wanted to have some of the IRGC commanders hanged for their incompetence. The origins behind such rumors are still unclear. Rafsanjani, the de facto commander of the armed forces, would recall a tearful Rezaei visiting him in his office and wanting to resign. He was urged to go on television and reject the rumors that he had been arrested and to stay in his job.[39] The Revolutionary Guards' bosses could keep their jobs but Rafsanjani was at this point forcefully spurring them to prepare for an end to the war.[40]

Rafsanjani, and his close associates such as Hassan Rouhani, long after maintained that the top Revolutionary Guards' brass were at a minimum guilty of being blindsided during the latter stages of the war. In one infamous example in April 1988, just a few months before the end of the war, the leaders of the Revolutionary Guards were far away from the military frontlines as they held a workshop on how fielding candidates for Majles elections could give them more political sway in Tehran. As that workshop was held, the Iraqis conducted a blitzkrieg on Iranian forces in Iraq's Faw Peninsula, which Iran had spectacularly captured only two years earlier. Faw's fall to Iran in April 1986 had thrown the Arab Gulf States into a state of panic. Fearing an Iranian onslaught across the region, the Saudis, Kuwaitis, the Qataris, and others had doubled down in financing Saddam's military to the tune of many billions of dollars. They were not alone. After its unsuccessful overtures toward Tehran that blew up in president Reagan's face in the shape of the Iran–Contra scandal, Washington opted instead to cut Iran's wings. The Iraqi recapture of Faw happened the same day as the US military routed the Iranian navy in *Operation Praying Mantis*, the largest naval battle the United States had engaged in since the Second World War. By the end of that day, April 18, 1988, the United States had sunk half of Iran's operational navy.

Then, on July 3, the USS *Vincennes*, an American missile cruiser deployed to the Persian Gulf, shot down Iran Air flight 655 with 290 passengers onboard, including 66 children. The Iranians were incensed. The United States maintains to this day that USS *Vincennes* had mistaken the Airbus A300 for an Iranian F-14 Tomcat. Tehran has never accepted that explanation even though the shooting did happen at a time of open US–Iranian clashes in the Gulf. A year earlier, the United States had begun to escort Kuwaiti oil tankers in response to Iranian attacks. Tehran not only considered the Gulf States such as Kuwait as openly bankrolling Saddam but now judged Washington's interventions as tantamount to explicitly coming to Baghdad's rescue as well.

The last straw, and the factor that many Iranian officials to this day cite as the reason why Iran finally sued for peace, was the international community's obliviousness to Iraq's increasing use of banned chemical weapons in the war.[41] The Iranians were unaware but at this point, the United States was also providing the Iraqis with satellite imagery of Iranian positions to be attacked. Tehran was seriously alarmed by the prospect of Iraqi chemical attacks on big Iranian cities. When US vice president George H. Bush, the leading presidential candidate in 1988's election campaign, said in regard to Iran Air flight 655 that he would "never apologize for the United States of America" and that he did not "care what the facts are," the reading in Tehran was that the United States was taking the gloves off.[42]

§

The leadership in Tehran had for months sought a face-saving way to end the war. The incident with flight 655 had forced the issue. Khomeini's diplomatic off-ramp was via the United Nations. UN resolution 598 could hence avoid giving the impression that Tehran was succumbing to Iraqi and American pressures. But that was exactly what had happened. Tehran sketched its acceptance of the ceasefire as a victory but few bought it. Saddam Hussein had after all asked for a ceasefire since 1982. Khomeini was not ready until the very last minute. "We have told the people we will fight this war even if it lasts 20 years. We don't want to lose the confidence of the people." Rafsanjani claims he was then and there ready to be the fall guy. "If this is the issue, then let me accept [resolution 598]. You can then have me trialed and hanged. But let me take responsibility [for Iran accepting the ceasefire]."[43] Khomeini finally gave in. On July 20, 1988, about three weeks after the shooting down of Iran Air 655, Khomeini finally announced that he would agree to end the war. "I drink this chalice of poison." According to his son, Ahmad, after accepting the ceasefire Khomeini could no longer walk unaided and never again spoke in public. Khomeini's own description, of drinking the cup of poison, was hardly a declaration of victory. Iran avoided a possible military defeat at the hands of Saddam Hussein but the project to export Khomeinism to the rest of the Middle East had come to an acrimonious finale. By one estimate, the eight-year war cost Iran $645 billion.[44]

How Iran came to accept UN resolution 598 is still very much a political football in Tehran. Rafsanjani has ever since been in the middle of this quarrel. At the time of the end of the conflict in 1988, no faction really objected to ending the enervating war. Very few equated accepting Resolution 598 with giving up on exporting the Khomeinist worldwide revolution that was supposed to snatch up Baghdad on its way to spread the revolution to every corner in the Islamic World. Nor did anyone in Tehran really squabble with the fact the United States was a certain enduring power in the Middle East. If anything, the end of the war produced a collective sigh of relief in Tehran. The regime was after all still in power in Tehran, and that was good enough.

From Tehran's vantage point, the sudden external pressures were part of an orchestrated effort to press Iran to agree to a ceasefire. The Reagan administration had been explicit in publicly demanding an end to the war. In his speech at the UN on September 21, 1987, Reagan "welcomed Iraq's acceptance" of the UN resolution to end the war while he said Washington was "disappointed at Iran's unwillingness to accept it." On this occasion, it was Khamenei that represented the Iranian regime at the UN. "I know that the President of Iran will be addressing you tomorrow," Reagan told the UN assembly. "I take this opportunity to call upon [Khamenei] clearly and unequivocally to state whether Iran accepts [UN resolution] 598 or not. If the answer is positive, it would be a welcome step and major breakthrough. If it is negative, the Council has no choice but rapidly to adopt enforcement measures."[45] As the Iranians already know, the Americans were already acting alone and needed not to wait for some kind of endorsement of action from the United Nations. At the UN, Reagan hammered his key point: The United States does "not seek confrontation with Iran" but "finding a means to end the [Iran-Iraq] war with no victor and no vanquished." Unpredictably, Reagan admitted the US desire to see the war end was rooted in its fears that the Soviets were hard at work to turn the Iran–Iraq war into an event that if it continued would go to undermine the US presence in the Persian Gulf.

The day after, Khamenei's much-anticipated debut at the UN morphed into an angry tirade. It was a speech full of indignation, where the Islamic Republic was the sinless party and in which Khamenei sought to rewrite the history of US–Iran relations. He also felt the Americans had willfully deprived him from his moment in the limelight in New York. The day before, hours after Reagan spoke from the UN podium, US forces in the Persian Gulf had seized an Iranian vessel (*Iran Ajr*), which was said to be laying mines. Khamenei called the timing incredible and the charges nothing but American lies and a setup to frame Iran as the bad actor in the region. "I explicitly announce that America will receive a response to this hideous action." He was convinced the Americans were playing a dirty game of pretending to be neutral but aiding Saddam at each pivotal turn in his war against Iran. Khamenei, a man who in the early years of the revolution had reasoned Ayatollah Khomeini should also rule over the Iraqi people, had evidently forgotten why Saddam invaded Iran in the first place.

Harking back to the events of 1979, Khamenei charged that it was the United States that had been the source of the enmity between the Khomeinists and Washington. The United States had incited the Shah to suppress the protesters back in late 1978 and that American hostility toward the Islamic Republic rested on the fact that Tehran had challenged US domination of the world order.[46] The meandering lecture was aimed at a desperate plea for justice for Iran. He hinted that the post-Second World War Nuremburg trials were not only a good precedent to penalize Saddam for his invasion but also to go after the superpowers that had supported Saddam's military in its war with Iran. "The Nuremberg Trials have succeeded in assuring peace and security for turbulent Europe for over forty years. Why not learn from that experience?" The reference to Nuremberg was surreal. One wondered who had advised him, although it is known that a young Javad Zarif was among the Iranian officials based in New York at the time who hosted Khamenei.

Khamenei's UN speech was a missed opportunity for Iran to make its case against Iraq. His starry-eyed call for the world to mobilize against the United States, which Khamenei called an "imminent danger to the entire world," stood in contrast to Reagan's far more narrow mission at the UN to bring about the end of the Iran–Iraq war. As he left New York, American press reported that Khamenei was bitter and believed the United States had fabricated the *Iran Ajr* incident and to have "ruined" his debut at the UN. Khamenei took it personally and it did not help that anonymous US officials went out of their way to kick him while he was down. The *Iran Ajr* incident "undermined his mission [at the UN] and him as a person," said one US official. "He looked very foolish lying in public."[47] That same UN speech by Khamenei is today immortalized by the hard-line camp in Tehran. It is portrayed as the roar of an anti-imperialist lion in the defense of all oppressed people. Khamenei calls himself the only leader at the UN who did not fear the Americans.[48]

§

The Khomeinists, despite the immense isolation and damage that had brought on the country through their insurgent approach to international relations, continued to dig themselves into a deeper hole. Most notably, on the regional level, Tehran's rigid antipathy toward the House of Saud was seemingly impossible to control. The Mecca incident of July 1987 was a prime and lasting example of fragmented policy making in Tehran harming the national interest. Some 400 people had died in Mecca when Iranian protesters who had arrived as pilgrims clashed with Saudi security forces. Khomeini's aversion toward the puritanical Sunni religious establishment of the Arabian Peninsula predated his dislike of the United States and Israel by decades. As early as 1943, Khomeini published his first political polemic, "The Unveiling of Secrets," in which he attacked Iranian Shia reformers by comparing them to "the savages of Najd [central region of Saudi Arabia] and the camel herders of Riyadh." Khomeini's last will and testament referred to the Saudis as "illegitimate" and "puppets" of the United States.[49] He called them the practitioners of the "anti-Quranic religion that is this totally baseless and superstitious religion of Wahhabism." The person who read out the will to the Assembly of Experts was none other than Ali Khamenei who would go on to retain his mentor's anti-Saudi phobias. Khomeini's description of the Saudis as "ungodly" and "daggers that have always pierced the hearts of Muslims from the back" would inexorably become a stubborn mantra for the hard-liners in the Islamic Republic.

The Khomeinists were equally contemptuous of the Soviet bloc and the Europeans. Only a few months before he died, in January 1989, Khomeini wrote his only letter to a foreign leader. The Iranian delegation that brought the letter to Moscow feared they would be arrested as soon as the content was read by the Soviets.[50] In the letter to Mikhail Gorbachev, Khomeini not only forecast the fall of the Soviet Union but urged this most senior of communist leaders to turn to Islam as an alternative.[51] "It is clear to everybody that from now on communism will only have to be found in the museums of world political history, for Marxism cannot meet any of the real needs of mankind," Khomeini wrote.

The long letter could perhaps be admired for its audacity but it was mostly a clue to the still prevalent naiveté found in the Islamic Republic almost ten years after the Khomeinists had come to power. And most likely, the fast ailing Khomeini did not have the mental acumen to write such a letter. The likes of his son, Ahmad, Rafsanjani, Khamenei, and perhaps a handful of other people would have had a hand in its production. To the Islamic Republic's growing base of critics, what topped its ignorance was its cruelty. On Valentine's Day February 14, 1989, Radio Tehran announced that

Khomeini had sentenced Indian-born British author Salman Rushdie to death for allegedly insulting Prophet Mohammad in his novel, *Satanic Verses*.

§

It was after Rafsanjani turned into the nemesis of the hard-line camp, clustered around Khamenei, that he became synonymous with the head of the quitters who had urged Khomeini to agree to a ceasefire with Iraq. He was a befitting prey. Until ten days before the end of the war, Khomeini had publicly called the idea of a ceasefire as betraying Prophet Mohammad himself. It was an empty slogan and meant only to keep the spirit of the armed forces up. Khomeini was sacrosanct, leaving Rafsanjani to be the fall guy.

Rafsanjani had as the de facto day-to-day coordinator of the war effort rebuffed the calls of the Revolutionary Guards to put more of the country blood and treasure in the war effort. He called the young generals in the Guards naive. "The world powers are never going just to let Iran take over Iraq," he told them. And the full national mobilization the Guards had asked for in a letter Mohsen Rezai sent to Khomeini was a pipe dream. By the end of the war, Iran was earning about $6 billion a year from oil sales. Half of the money was to meet basic needs and services of the country and the other half allocated toward the war. Iran's GDP per capita had fallen from some $7,000 in 1979 to hit a low of $3,640 in 1988.[52] There was not much latitude left for more warring. Tagging Rafsanjani as a quitter still stirs hot debates inside the regime. His enemies paint him as the unprincipled operator who betrayed the father of the revolution by shoving the ceasefire down Khomeini's throat. Some of Khomeini's office staff claim that he never again had a smile on his face.[53] His supporters, however, maintain that Rafsanjani had saved Iran from a certain inevitable military defeat and national humiliation.[54]

What is not in question is that back in 1988, Rafsanjani had no intention to marginalize the Guards. All he wanted was to redefine the Revolutionary Guards' mandate with the war over. Hence, when Mohsen Rezai, the Guards' boss, put forward an idea for his men to engage in postwar economic projects, Rafsanjani was supportive. This is how Khatam ol-Anbia (Seal of the Prophets), the massive present-day conglomerate under the control of the Guards with its vast diverse economic interests, was born. Rafsanjani was after all the man who had back in early 1979 endorsed the original charter that lay the foundation for the Revolutionary Guards.[55] They were to be the Praetorian guards of the clerics, a function they had dutifully carried out in the 1980s. All Rafsanjani was doing now was to give the Guards a new direction while all along considering them still as part and parcel of the regime. In time, he would be far less about this viewpoint.

President Khamenei, the future supreme leader, was never put to task for his role in events leading to the end of the war. The fact that he would soon after the war become the highest authority in the land meant that his role in how the Iran–Iraq war ended has never to be scrutinized let alone questioned. This is what is known, however. Khamenei never spoke in defense of Rafsanjani in later years when his old friend was lampooned as the man who had thrown the towel in too early in the war against Saddam. As with the Iran–Contra affair, Khamenei was involved in Tehran's acceptance of UN resolution 598 but he distanced himself. Shirking responsibility and publicly keeping his distance from the West would become Khamenei's flair for operation. In that sense, Rafsanjani was more likely to be true to his word. At least on the question about relations with the West, he insisted it was inevitable that Iran one way or another had to find a way to compromise.

6

(1989–93)—Khamenei: The Second Supreme Leader

I asked the Imam [Khomeini] to resolve the issue of relations with the United States during his lifetime. I told Imam that without him guiding us forward, resolving the issue with the United States will be difficult.

(A. H. Rafsanjani)[1]

If it was up to Rafsanjani, he would have restored relations with America.
(Sadeq Ziba Kalam, prominent Iranian commentator)[2]

The war against Iraq ended in 1988 and the Islamic Republic was still standing. Khomeini had only a handful of months to live and Ronald Reagan was preparing to leave the White House. On the home front, the Khomeinists had routed all opposition: from secular nationalists to a mixed bag of leftists to ethnic separatists such as the Kurds. The disbanding of the IRP in 1987 had not ended squabbling among Khomeinists, and ideological and policy differences were more blurred.

Infighting was driven by shifting personal allegiances among top Khomeinists. The power struggle was compounded by the fact that many of the top figures were related by blood or marriages. Tracing loyalties was no easy feat. Even within the Revolutionary Guards, individual commanders tended to be more loyal to top local clerics than to the central command of the corp. The deputy supreme leader, Ayatollah Montazeri, was so worried about his safety that he replaced a team of Revolutionary Guards protecting him with armed local men he knew well from his hometown. He was far from paranoid.

The Conspiracy behind Khamenei's Rise

Montazeri had every right to be anxious. His camp had exposed the behind-the-scene efforts toward the United States. The same forces—Ahmad Khomeini, Rafsanjani—that had sought to pave the way for Montazeri to become deputy supreme leader now set out to dethrone him. A protracted public relations campaign was launched to tarnish the public image of Montazeri. This would go on long after he died in December 2009.

From late 1986 until the death of Khomeini in the summer of 1989, Montazeri's status inside the regime continued to sink. He was now frustrating Khomeini by questioning not only his political calculations but also the purity of his religious beliefs. It is at this point that Montazeri began his journey to go from deputy supreme leader to become one of the regime's staunchest critics. His calls to limit the powers of the Revolutionary Guards and speaking in defense of political prisoners made him the darling of those inside the regime who were thoroughly despairing by the evolution of the system into a repressive militant Islamist authoritarian model.

As the United States judged that there was "no recent evidence of [Montazeri's] involvement in the use of violence or terrorism to export the revolution," his domestic detractors were peeved by his political transformation. Montazeri's outspoken criticism of Khomeini's approval of the mass hanging of political prisoners in 1988 only distanced the supreme leader further from his deputy. Montazeri wrote to Khomeini: "Do you know that the crimes happening in the name of Islam today in Iran's prison far surpasses anything seen during the days of the Shah?" Somehow the BBC got a copy of the letter and the public humiliation that followed for Khomeini was too much. In a letter, he dismissed Montazeri as his deputy. Montazeri suspected it was Ahmad Khomeini that had done it.[3] He said the crisp handwriting in the letter that finally removed him as deputy supreme leader was likely that of Ahmad Khomeini and not that of the octogenarian elder Khomeini.[4]

The Montazeri family has since maintained that Ahmad Khomeini, Rafsanjani, and others, such as Intelligence Minister Reyshahri, concocted a plan to remove Montazeri. Signaling to the United States was part of this effort. They sought to show the embattled deputy leader to be still a militant radical in order to please the Americans who had long demanded Iranian action against terrorism.[5] This account is the view of the Montazari camp. The duet of Ahmad Khomeini and Rafsanjani had to go back to the drawing board to prepare the ground to take the mantle of leadership after Khomeini. What was possibly concocted by the men remains one of the biggest enigmas of the history of the Islamic Republic. To this day, it is an unfinished chapter.

§

Rafsanjani says he pleaded with Khomeini. "We have to do something. We have this problem." What is known only deepens suspicions about foul play in the months leading to the death of Khomeini. On March 26, 1989, Khomeini responded to Montazeri's concerns in a letter whose authenticity is still in dispute.[6] In that letter, Khomeini calls his deputy a naïve simpleton. "As Allah is my witness, I was from the beginning against your selection [as deputy leader]." "You are easily impressed: stay away from politics and hope God will forgive you."[7] In the letter, Khomeini also accepts Montazeri's offer to resign. This quick turn of events amounted to either convenient after-the-fact wisdom or a genuine admission of sorts by Khomeini that Montazeri had been forced on him.

In any event, in both scenarios Ahmad Khomeini and Rafsanjani would have had to be among those who had whispered loudest in Khomeini's ears. That would be true in Montazeri's selection as deputy leader in 1985 and also his subsequent removal from that post. Khomeini never spoke publicly about Montazeri's sacking. There is only the contested letter that Khomeini is said to have written to Montazeri. In his memoirs, Rafsanjani, somewhat questionably, claims that he and Ali Khamenei had tried to stop Montazeri's fall from grace but that it was too late and the damage too great. Montazeri's removal was not official until June 3, 1989, the day Khomeini died. On that same day, the Assembly of Experts, Iran's equivalent to the Vatican's College of Cardinals, had to make a decision on his fate since this body had the sole power to pass judgment on matters pertaining to the supreme leadership. Rafsanjani, the de facto chair[8] of the body, did not allow for a debate on Montazeri's fate. The bad blood between the Rafsanjani and Montazeri families has continued ever since.

Rafsanjani's speech to the Assembly of Experts was no doubt the most pivotal moment in Khamenei's political life. Rafsanjani told the astounded gathering of senior clerics that immediately before his death, Khomeini had granted an audience to Rafsanjani, Khamenei, prime minister Mousavi, and his son, Ahmad Khomeini. On hearing about a major predicament in the succession process since there were no other grand ayatollahs available or willing to take his place, Khomeini is said to have uttered: "Do not worry. You have a good replacement. "Here, [this] Mr. Khamenei."

Rafsanjani wanted to hammer this point and recalled another anecdote. "When Mr. Khamenei [as president] was [shown on television] visiting North Korea and elegantly stood next to Kim Il-Sung, Imam [Khomeini] said that he truly is worthy of supreme leadership." Khamenei had only days before made a ten-day trip to China and North Korea. It was an awkward performance by Rafsanjani. Even Khamenei appeared unconvinced by Rafsanjani's efforts to make the case that Khomeini had chosen his successor before he died. Looking uncomfortable and rubbing his eyes, Khamenei was just a few steps away from the podium. But he was, of course, on the ruse and played along the scripted act.[9]

Khamenei stood up, walked to the podium, and purported to want to dissuade his fellow clerics from voting for him. "First of all, we should shed tears of blood wailing for the Islamic society that has been forced to even propose me" to serve as a caretaker of the country's leadership.[10] He reminded everyone that he was constitutionally unfit for the job since he was not even an "ayatollah" (the second highest rank in Shia Islam one below grand ayatollah). Worse still, "many of you [senior clergy and members of the Assembly of Experts] will not accept my words as those of a leader. What sort of leadership will this be?" As he put it, his leadership will be "only on paper and not a real one." The charade went on as Rafsanjani dismissed all of Khamenei's worries. He urged those members who back Khamenei to stand up. Rafsanjani then quickly became the first man to stand up.

Video footage from that meeting shows the faces of the members of the eighty-eight-seat Assembly of Experts to express more trepidation than surprise. In those days, the Assembly of Experts still had some independence. Many of its members frowned upon both Rafsanjani and Khamenei. But they feared political chaos and were open to cajoling. That was Rafsanjani's intention in that infamous speech. He more than anyone made the case for Khamenei to be Khomeini's successor. The purported event has been a matter of contention since. Khomeini had explicitly said before his death that nothing, except what was written in his will, should be attributed to him. Nonetheless, on June 3, 1989, a majority in the Assembly of Experts voted—with sixty in favor of the seventy-four members present—for Khamenei as the new supreme leader.[11] Overnight he was hailed by the state-run media as an "ayatollah," a senior rank that everyone knew he had not theologically achieved but the title was given to him as part of his political rise. Many of the bona fide ayatollahs, such as Montazeri, who noted Khamenei's new role, refused to refer to him as an equal. Others who voted for Khamenei to be supreme leader, such as Ayatollah Ahmad Azari Qomi, in time came to denounce him as an illegitimate leader.[12]

Two points are clear. First, the idea of a "council of leaders" was unattractive to most members of the Assembly of Experts. Given nasty factional disputes inside the regime, the outcome of collective leadership would be a certain logjam at the top. Singular supreme leadership could be stabilizing. Khamenei had a few attributes that helped his prospects. He was a senior member of the system, a good speaker, and long in the public limelight. While he lacked Khomeini's religious credentials and personal charisma, Khamenei's claim to be a descendant of the Prophet Mohammad (a *sayyed*) was likely a factor in the degree of support he secured. The irony is that Khamenei was also at the time viewed as a youthful 49-year-old and a moderate figure compared to some of the old dinosaurs who were feared might drag Iran into even more reactionary times. What is almost always forgotten is that Khamenei was appointed only as a caretaker supreme leader. He was to be in that position for one year until a referendum could be organized about the country's political future.

In the Islamic Republic of the present day there are those who say Khamenei's picking up the baton from Khomeini was heavenly preordained. The theatrics of Rafsanjani and Khamenei on that momentous day shows another reality: that elders of the regime chose to put their collective survival above all else and found in Khamenei a candidate the majority could back as a stopgap transitional leader. Nor was this turn of events that eye-popping for outsiders. As early as 1983, an assessment by the CIA concluded that "Rafsanjani and Khamenei will work out a mutually acceptable division of power after Khomeini's death."[13] The CIA's assessment was bang on but more by chance than insight. Not even the Khomeinists had a good sense of how the power transition would pan out. Shia Islam has a history of violent clashes among rival clerical groups in times of transition. The one certainty was that after Khomeini's death the whole regime could collapse unless there was a smooth transition based on a power-sharing agreement.

At the time, the CIA assessed him thus: "Khamenei is more austere and scholarly. He enjoys a significantly better reputation than Rafsanjani with Iran's religious leaders in Qom." Rafsanjani himself did not think he could aim for the top job himself. His reputation as a political hustler only inflated during the 1980s. Many inside the regime disliked him for his increasingly open promarket economic ideas, growing fixation with compromising with the West, and leading the secret talks with the United States that resulted in the Iran–Contra scandal. In comparison, Khamenei was relatively untainted if not innocuous. Little did they know and events to come soon proved them wrong. Many years later, in 2013, Khomeini's daughter, Zahra Mostafavi, claimed that her father had mentioned that Rafsanjani was also a suitable successor.[14] After his death, Rafsanjani's younger brother, Mohammad, claimed that Khomeini had in fact offered the deputy supreme leadership to him but Rafsanjani had no desire to replace Montazeri, his old mentor.[15] There is no corroborative evidence behind such claims. While Rafsanjani's devotees espouse them, the Khamenei camp decry them as a product of retrospective bitterness.

Khamenei's Supreme Leadership

After Rafsanjani had done his part behind closed doors of the Assembly of Experts, the other main architect behind this collusion had to rally public support for the new leader. The function to be played by the family of the late Khomeini was paramount. Hence Ahmad Khomeini quickly released a video of himself declaring his loyalty to Khamenei. He went to see Khamenei the day after he had become supreme leader. "We will not stop ever serving you and may God be with you." Ahmad's act of personal submission was feudal and unpersuasive as the same time.

With both men sitting on ornate Persian rugs, Ahmad's glare avoided Khamenei as he declared: "I am your simple servant, and your wishes are my command."[16] In days and weeks to come, he held more sermons and released more videos urging regime supporters to rally around Khamenei. Over the years serving as the main gatekeeper to his frail father, Ahmad had grown confident in his role if not cocky.[17] That was all buried away as Ahmad made Khamenei's case. He even ignored his father's basic request that he, his son, read out his will when the old man died. Instead, it was Khamenei that read out Khomeini's last will before the Assembly of Experts.[18] It took Khamenei two and a half hours to read Khomeini's full political testament, which he had originally written in 1982 but revised in 1987.

To violate his father's demand in such a conspicuous fashion goes to show how badly Rafsanjani and Ahmad Khomeini wanted to close the deal for Khamenei. An alternative reading of events is that the only real mastermind was Rafsanjani and Ahmad was only an unwitting accomplice. He convinced Ahmad to back Khamenei as a temporary leader but with the promise that the job will be his in due time. After all, he was of Khomeini's flesh, and anyone could see Khamenei was entirely lacking in status to seize the top role for good. Ahmad's personality gives much credence to such a narrative. He was hardly known as a grand political strategist. A jovial man with his deepest passion in life reserved for sports and possessing only a few of the uppity mannerism that the clergy in Iran are known for, Ahmad might very well have been duped. What is certain is that he soon turned on both Rafsanjani and Khamenei.

From 1989 until his suspicious death at the age of 49 in 1995, Ahmad Khomeini turned into an outspoken critic of the regime. Khamenei appointed him to a minor political role but his main function inside the regime was to look after the legacy of his deceased father. The gatekeeper to his father had become the keeper of his father's mausoleum. In the few years left of his life he aged visibly and the bitterness was hardly concealed. The same Ahmad who in 1989 called on Khamenei to keep his father's legacy alive by staying the course of anti-Americanism deplored how the regime made America the scapegoat for anything that was going wrong for Iran. "Is stealing from the people also America's doing?" he deplored.[19] His scathing attacks, openly calling the regime a police state, soon become intolerable. A year before his death, he was put under surveillance, and he died four days after he made his most blunt attack against Khamenei and Rafsanjani.[20] The official account is that Ahmad died of a heart attack. What really happened to Ahmad Khomeini is as of today still an unresolved mystery.

§

The Rafsanjani and Khamenei bargain of 1989 rested on a simple case of a win-win division of power. Khamenei became supreme leader, the top religious guide. That was at least Rafsanjani's purported plan who himself would become the head of the government in the Office of the Presidency. Two issues had had to be resolved first. Khamenei did not have the religious credentials to become supreme leader. For the plan to also work, and for Rafsanjani's appetite for power to be satisfied, the requirement to be a "grand ayatollah" to become supreme leader had to be dropped and the powers of the presidency had to be expanded. Both these objectives could be obtained via a constitutional amendment. This had been craftily arranged in April 1989, while Khomeini was still alive. The amendment was adopted following a referendum on July 28, three weeks after Khomeini's death. An impossible 97.6 percent of the voters had backed the initiative. A presidential election was held on the same day. Rafsanjani was said to have secured an equally impossible 96.1 percent of the vote.

The Rafsanjani–Khamenei sketch also included eliminating the Office of the Prime Minister. Both men saw it as the third but rebel leg of the system put together in 1979. As the new occupant of the empowered presidency, Rafsanjani wanted to rid himself of a rival powerbroker. Khamenei played along and did so happily. As president from 1981 to 1989, he was constantly in conflict with his prime minister, Mir-Hossein Mousavi. In 1985, Khomeini had to personally intervene to force the then president Khamenei to renominate Mousavi as his prime minister for a second term even as the two men could not stand each other. It had not been just a struggle for institutional dominance. Khamenei was a "rightist," someone who defended market economics, and not among the regime's firebrands on questions pertaining to foreign policy. In contrast, Mousavi was a "leftist" inside the system, a proponent of central planned economy, and impulsively an anti-Western radical. Rafsanjani, who had over the years morphed into a free marketeer, tilted the balance and Mousavi was out. As president, he refused even to offer Mousavi or the other so-called radical leftists a cabinet position. Mousavi would spend the next twenty years out of politics.

The ever-callous Khamenei also removed another prominent Khomeini-appointed figure, Ayatollah Abdul-Karim Ardebili, the head of the powerful judicial branch. Ardebili, who himself was a top candidate to succeed Khomeini, was after all senior to Khamenei in all senses of the word. Marginalizing him quickly made abundant sense from Khamenei's insidious vantage point. Both Khamenei and Rafsanjani also initially agreed that the Revolutionary Guards had to underwrite this new chapter in the Islamic Republic. Khamenei's first public appearance was in a gathering of Revolutionary Guards' officers. In the midst of the mostly young men eager to hear what the future would hold for them, Khamenei did not sense the same misgivings as he had done only a few days earlier at the Assembly of Experts.

The Guards were suspicious of Khamenei but he was already breaking tradition to win them over. Khomeini had in his testament implored the Revolutionary Guards not to favor one faction against another. In his first speech to the Revolutionary Guards' commanders, Khamenei told them the opposite. "Without the Revolutionary Guards, the revolution cannot be defended."[21] It was a plea for a pact. The new and still shaky leader was keen to persuade the Guards that they could be good for each other going forward. Khamenei rightly sensed his powerbase inside the system and in society was weak. He needed an anchor. His record with the Guards' commanders had not always been cordial. At one point during the war with Iraq, the Revolutionary Guards forbid him from visiting the frontline. When Mojtaba Khamenei, his second born and an 18-year-old conscripted son, arrived at his regiment the amount of abuse he heard about his father left him with no choice but to ask for a transfer.[22] But the end of the war had also deprived the Guards of a purpose of life. They had joined the revolution exactly a decade earlier and in their own minds sacrificed greatly in the war against Saddam. After the war and Khomeini's death, the Guards wanted to remain relevant and Khamenei's predicament and offer of a mutually advantageous arrangement based on coexistence was seemingly impossible to reject. Khamenei wanted the Guards help him reinforce the shaky scaffolding of institutions built up around the person of Khomeini. To him, there was no other alternative, but he feared the military men nonetheless. Planning against any possible future political challenge from military corners, Supreme Leader Khamenei quickly capped the tenure of senior officers to no more than ten years. No one other than himself should be able to cultivate a cult of personality.

Unlike Khomeini, who could with one speech turn the political tide around, Khamenei needed the power of institutions to carry out his orders. During his ten-year supreme leadership, the number of staff around Khomeini's office hovered around fifty individuals. His son, Ahmad, was his principal interlocutor to the rest of the players in the state. Under his watch, Khamenei was to begin a process of institutionalization with his person at the center. Thousands, mostly hailing from the ranks of the various intelligence services, began to enter service under his personal tutelage. Since the assassination attempt on his life in 1981, Khamenei's appetite for intelligence work had become inexhaustible. Many of his closest advisors and allies from his eight years as president also joined him at the Office of the Supreme Leader.

§

Khamenei, a man of intense personal routine, set out to make his mark. One of his first acts set the stage for the nature of his supreme leadership. He refused to move into *Jamaran*, Khomeini's residence in the last seven years of his life and which he almost never came out of. Khamenei claimed that it was out of respect for Khomeini and his family that he did not chose Jamaran.[23] Cynics pointed out that Khamenei had ordered land and buildings next to the presidential palace to be purchased so he could locate himself next to Rafsanjani. Based on some accounts, he planned a year in advance as far as his political goals were concerned. He was unapologetic about it. "I have read the constitution carefully. I will not give up on an inch of my duties," he would tell his followers. Those alarmed early on interpreted it as him telling the Iranian people that he would rule the way he wanted. His minimum demand was obvious: he expected the same veneration shown politically to Khomeini even as he knew he could not ever fill his predecessor's shoes on matters pertaining to religious authority. Khamenei certainly did not want to be just the top symbolic figurehead as Rafsanjani had likely believed when he engineered Khamenei's rise.

Rafsanjani had been so eager to move into the presidential palace that he committed a number of grave errors that would pursue him for the rest of his life. In the July 1989 presidential elections, he had secured a highly dubious 96.1 percent of the vote. However, only one other candidate had been allowed to run. All other seventy-nine aspirant candidates were disqualified to run by the regime's vetting organ, the Guardian Council, an organ of twelve men whom Khamenei, as supreme leader, controlled through appointment.

Afterward as president, Rafsanjani agreed that the Ministries of Information, Interior, Foreign Affairs, Defense, Higher Education, and Culture and Islamic Guidance should be selected with the supreme leader's approval. Rafsanjani had given Khamenei a veto over all the powerful ministries and paved the way for him to gain what he wanted: more power. In Rafsanjani's mind, what mattered politically was the state of the economy. This was a portfolio he did not give Khamenei a veto power on. But Rafsanjani did not have to wait long to see Khamenei's voracious consolidation moves in play.

Rafsanjani's younger brother, Mohammad, was at the time the head of the country's national radio and television (*Seda va Sima*). He sensed that Khamenei was undercutting him by interfering in daily operations. He saw the writing on the wall and chose to confront Khamenei. When asked if he wanted him to step down, Khamenei turns to Mohammad and says "Your brother brought me into politics; into the Revolution Council and made me the [supreme] leader."[24] He was told he was safe but Mohammad was not convinced and he was right. He was replaced the following year. Khamenei gave the job to a young acolyte by the name of Ali Larijani and made sure he understood that it was he and not Rafsanjani as president that he was answerable to. Khamenei has ever since insisted on appointing the head of the national radio and television. Khamenei's meticulous reshuffling of regime members had just begun.

Khamenei told Rafsanjani, who had been the de facto commander-in-chief during the lifetime of Khomeini, that he was no longer needed in that role. Khamenei became the head of not only the regular military and the Revolutionary Guards but all armed and security forces. In time, anyone from among the first generation of revolutionaries with slightest ability to stand up to him was removed. He proceeded mindfully but by 1994 Khamenei had orchestrated the biggest purge of the history of the Revolutionary Guards when he sent some 4,000 first-generation officers into retirement.[25] When sufficiently confident, he removed the long-time commander of the Guards, Mohsen Rezai, but not until 1997.

After the armed forces Khamenei brought the wealthy *bonyads* under his direct control. These were foundations born from confiscated property from individuals linked to the regime of the Shah. The various bonyads combined controlled billions of dollars in property, investment, and other economic assets and now answered to Khamenei directly. They were so large that they constituted an economy within the national economy. Not only Khamenei's appetite for power grab but also his tendency to micro-manage those that reported directly to him was soon common knowledge.

In one case, Khamenei's office summoned Kamal Kharrazi, Iran's ambassador to the UN in New York, with the aim to offer him the Ministry of Culture, a politically sensitive portfolio given the Islamic Republic's commitment to reengineer the social conventions of Iranian society. Rafsanjani, as president and head of the cabinet, had initially asked Kharrazi but he opted to stay in New York once he realized the extent of the appetite Khamenei had for involving himself in administrative detail. If Khomeini only required the gist of a policy, Khamenei wanted to see the full blueprint before he decided his course of action.

Rafsanjani's Presidency

Rafsanjani, in his elation that he had engineered for a smooth transition of power after Khomeini's death, took his eyes off the ball. He forgot the basic rule of the source of power in the Islamic Republic: control of the armed forces, the intelligence services, and the judiciary. Instead, Rafsanjani set out to build up popular legitimacy for his presidency. The economy was to be his sustenance, his source of popular legitimacy. He, backed by Khamenei to begin with, and amateurishly naïve when it came to grasping the relationship between a country's foreign policy and its standing in international markets, began the post-Iraq economic reconstruction era with one but critical agreement: the old radical and antimarket left of the 1980s had to be destroyed.

As president, Rafsanjani wanted to clear the house. "Some in the system thought the slogan of 'No to the West and no to the East' meant we should not cooperate with anyone. This was wrong. The slogan only meant we should be free from domination by either the West and the East. The [Iran-Iraq] war proved to anyone involved that you don't achieve anything with slogans alone," he would say to the by now ever thinning crowds that attended the Friday Prayers.[26] On the question of the United States, Rafsanjani wanted to undo the bad blood but foresaw an uphill battle. He claimed to have planned this with deep care and consideration.

> I wrote a hand written letter. I did not type it up as I did not want anyone to see it, and gave the letter to Imam [Khomeini]. I mentioned seven points that needed to be resolved while he was still alive. One of them was relations with the United States. Our present policies toward the Americans is unsustainable. They are a world power. Why are they different from China, Russia or the Europeans that we deal with? Let's negotiate, which is not the same as capitulation. If you don't hold our hand on this it will be tough to go around this issue after you are gone.[27]

He was right.

The old radical left, with its trademark phobia for the United States and capitalism, was still very much present and more so in the Majles, the Iranian parliament. With Khamenei's direct intervention, who was himself at loggerheads with the radical left, the two spearheaded an uncanny scheme. The Guardian Council, which had up to this point only dealt with disputes after elections were held, was suddenly in June 1991 given the power to approve anyone running for elected office. This was arguably the moment when the Islamic Republic became an unrepentant theocracy. It was the nail in the coffin of the "Republican" part of the system. The Guardian Council's twelve members, appointed by Khamenei, hence emerged as the regime's topmost filter to keep undesirables out of the already heavily restricted electoral process. In the first parliamentary elections after Khomeini's death, which was held in April 1992, the Guardian Council extensively vetted and disqualified one-third of the 3,150 registered to run, including thirty-nine incumbent members of the Majles. The left of the 1980s was under attack like never before since 1979, and Rafsanjani and Khamenei were the joint and undisputed driving force.

Of the two men, Rafsanjani no doubt felt more comfortable in his position at this particular moment in time. The cleansing of the Majles of the radical left was a big step toward Rafsanjani's mission to herald a new era. His stated goal was to create a new basis of legitimacy for the regime centered on creating a new middle class. This promised new middle class, which the old left always warned against as recreating the old "bourgeoisie" of the Shah era, was to hinge on the expansion of genuine professional expertise within the Iranian society. The number of universities and enrollment shot up and sporting unruly beards alone was no longer a ticket to a job within the state. The new buzz words were economic growth, privatization, linking up to the international economy, and attracting foreign investment. In his memoirs, writing in bullet point format, Rafsanjani takes pride in how a stream of people, from former, present, or aspiring officials, would come to his office in the hope he could change their personal fortunes or those of their constituents.[28] Khamenei claimed that he would pray for Rafsanjani "by name and at least once every day and sometimes more."

§

After Khomeini's death, Rafsanjani and Khamenei were also largely in agreement behind the need to rejuvenate Iranian foreign policy. This was despite the fact that over the 1980s each had shown foreign proclivities that were not always on the same page. Khamenei had in September 1984 become the first president from the Islamic Republic to make a foreign trip. He chose Damascus, and the Soviet-backed Baathist regime of Hafez Al Assad, as his first stop. He then visited Libya and Algeria. He declared his regional trip "very successful." If it meant an ability to procure Soviet-origin missiles—which he did in Syria and Libya—then it was a success. It was also a success in that Khamenei was poking into an open wound of the Arab World. The fact that two Arab states sided with non-Arab Iran was both a blow to Saddam Hussein's pan-Arab image. But it was also a token win for the Islamic Republic that desperately wanted to appeal to the Arab masses around the Middle East and North Africa.

Khamenei claims that Khomeini, when still alive, had told him "Whenever you go abroad, I am nervous. Don't travel so much."[29] There is, of course, only Khamenei's claim that Khomeini ever said such a thing. Then again, Khamenei was hardly the only one rewriting or tinkering with history and he had good reasons: for years he had to justify his accession to the supreme leadership. Khamenei's other foreign trips in the 1980s, as he has never left Iran since 1989, all pointedly avoided the West. In all, he visited fourteen states as president. They included India, Pakistan, Romania, Yugoslavia, North Korea, China, Angola, Mozambique.[30] Most of the states he visited shared his anti-Americanism.³¹ It might have been a case that only these countries were willing to engage with Tehran but that had not stopped Rafsanjani. In 1985, a year after Khamenei went to Syria, Libya, and Algeria, Rafsanjani made his first big debut on the international stage. He chose Japan as his first stop and could not stop raving about the postwar economic miracle that the Japanese had overseen.

Khamenei's proclivities toward the non-Western world only deepened after he became supreme leader. Nonetheless, even as he was far less enthusiastic than Rafsanjani about economic objectives as the pillar of the post-Iraq war foreign policy agenda, Khamenei still stood up to the foolhardiest members of the regime. He had spoken up even when Khomeini was still alive. Days after Khomeini issued a religious death sentence, or a fatwa, against the British author Salman Rushdie in February 1989, for allegedly insulting Prophet Mohammad, Khamenei downplayed the fatwa. He initially also distanced himself from a semi-state foundation that had put a bounty on Rushdie's head.³² At that moment in time, he was yet to become the uber hard-liner that he later became. The biggest foreign policy choice, however, was about how Iran should position itself vis-à-vis the two superpowers, the Soviets and the Americans. Tehran's meandering steps to turn a new page on the issue of the United States was essentially stalled. But occupying a spot in the gray zone in the Cold War setting had already proven to be a bad proposition for Tehran. Hence, less than three weeks after Khomeini's death, and before he was officially president of the Islamic Republic, Rafsanjani became the first Iranian leader to visit Moscow.³³

The trip was not a case of hurried foreign policy. Rafsanjani had as early as 1987 spoken about negotiations with the Soviets about a "defense pact." His trip had been planned for months and followed the historic visit of the Soviet foreign minister, Eduard Shevardnadze, to Tehran four months earlier. Khomeini's death was not allowed to stop what Soviet boss Mikhail Gorbachev called a "landmark event." As Gorbachev put it, Rafsanjani's arrival in Moscow showed the entire world that "Iran and the Soviet Union are two big neighboring states with serious and far-reaching goals."³⁴ The visit was a culmination of months of effort, and it represented a turning point. Washington refused to see it as such. "Rafsanjani's emphasis on national interests has not been demonstrated in a single dramatic change in foreign policy but in a series of incremental shifts," the CIA assessed. The agency instead wanted to believe that Rafsanjani had set in motion a series of efforts to reduce tensions with neighbors and foes far away alike.³⁵ The Soviet component of this broader Iranian de-escalation should not be overemphasized, the CIA reported.

Perhaps the Iran analysts at Langley did not want to alarm the new US president, George H. W. Bush who had just come to office in January 1989. But as soon as Khomeini had himself personally received Shevardnadze at his residence the alarm bells should have gone off at the White House. Khomeini, after all, gave very few audiences to foreign dignitaries. Not only did he urge Moscow to join forces with Iran against the "trouble-making West" but Shevardnadze too criticized the US military presence in the Persian Gulf at the same time.³⁶ A Moscow–Tehran understanding appeared to be under way. Despite the fact that Khomeini had himself blessed this new approach to Moscow, Rafsanjani was still condemned for his overtures to the Soviet. The puritans inside the regime—that were as anti-Soviet as they were anti-Western—rebuked him for his alleged silence against Moscow's repression of Soviet Muslims. As was by now customary, those opposed took action independent of the state. In this instance, an aggrieved faction in Tehran took it on itself to print the Koran in the various languages of the Soviet Muslims and smuggle it into the Soviet Union to incite the Muslims there. This angered Moscow but neither they nor Rafsanjani allowed it to derail the burgeoning ties.

Rafsanjani wanted to undo the American intention to isolate Tehran and the Soviets were offering him a way out. In his June 1989 trip to Moscow, Rafsanjani secured deals to buy arms; to sell natural gas to the Soviets that had been suspended since 1979; and Moscow's approval for Tehran to play the role of a mediator in Afghanistan, which the Soviet military had withdrawn from in February 1989. Iranian accounts of what happened in Moscow during that trip suggest the Soviets saw Rafsanjani as Iran's next strongman even as it had been announced by now that it was Khamenei who had officially become the new supreme leader.

Gorbachev's desire to pocket Rafsanjani's commitment was so intense he practically offered him a blank check on the question of what sorts of arms the Soviets were willing to sell Iran. In Moscow, he showed Rafsanjani a blank piece of paper. "I have the signatures of all the thirteen members of the Politburo on this paper. Just write on the top on the paper what military equipment you want."[37] The unexpecting Iranians were forced to hurriedly improvise but with the help from the Soviets. A $10 billion arms sale, the biggest since the 1979 revolution, was signed. At the main dinner reception in Moscow, Rafsanjani stood up to read out his prepared remarks. When he looked down, he saw the speech was in Russian. No one could find the original version of the speech in Persian, and Rafsanjani had to wing it. He returned to Tehran believing that with Soviet patronage the Islamic Republic could quash American efforts to isolate the regime.

Rafsanjani and Khamenei, the United States and the Radicals in Tehran

George H. Bush in the White House in January 1989 offered a new opportunity for Tehran to reset its policy toward the United States. A Republican, traditionally the American political party perceived in Tehran as the less meddlesome in the internal affairs of other countries, Bush began his presidency with an olive branch. In his inaugural address, Bush vowed "goodwill begets goodwill" as he asked the Iranians to help with the releasing of American hostages in Lebanon by pro-Iran militants. Iran was not only exploring faint hopes for renewed relations. It had the far more specific goal of having billions of dollars of frozen Iranian assets in the United States released. This time, instead of "arms-for-hostages," Tehran wanted "frozen assets-for-hostages." There were also a number of Iranians Tehran believed were held in Lebanon by militant Phalangists, which Rafsanjani wanted freed as part of a deal.

It looked very much like a quid pro quo although the Bush administration—with the memories of the Iran–Contra affair still very much fresh in minds—strongly discouraged that notion. As one Bush official put it, "once the hostages were released, [Iran's assets] could be returned but only after a discrete interval that would preclude the moves being linked as a deal."³⁸ The United States was then open to trade, commerce, and even giving loans to the Iranians since Washington still believed there were "benefits associated with Iran reintegrating itself into the community of nations." Even a tragic natural disaster opened up possibilities. In June 1990, a deadly earthquake that killed some forty thousand hit Iran's Caspian coast. As president, Rafsanjani not only allowed and defended aid and Western teams joining the rescue operation but accepted an American offer of help as well. For the first time since 1979, Tehran was officially open to American assistance.

The symbolism was far more profound than the $300,000 Washington delivered. Excited European diplomats in Tehran believed this might be the moment the dam of mistrust between Iran and the United States is finally broken. "It appears that the Great Satan no more" was how one European diplomat described this sudden Iranian attitude toward the United States.³⁹ "Disaster Diplomacy" was in motion but the road ahead for Iranian–American rapprochement still fickle and tortuous. Tehran also began to quietly experiment with greater enticement for US businesses as a way to garner political goodwill in Washington. On paper, it was a good bet. During Republican presidencies from 1980 to 1992, US merchandise exports to Iran would grow from $140 million to $822 million. The sums were tiny—as compared to the nearly $7 billion in US–Iran trade in Shah's last year in power in 1978—but it was a start.⁴⁰ Rafsanjani's inner circle only reinforced his gut feeling that incentivizing US businesses was an apt way to generate goodwill in Washington and sustain the logic of détente toward Tehran. Among them was Iran's future president, Hassan Rouhani, who was then the head of the Supreme National Security Council (SNSC), the country's key interagency body that oversees strategic policies.

It was never going to be straightforward. Between 1982 and 1992, some one hundred American and other Western nationals had been taken hostage in Lebanon. Not every hostage-taker group was linked to Iran but from 1989 until the last American hostage—Terry Anderson—was released in December 1991 the phenomena of kidnapping foreigners came to an end as did the Lebanese civil war, which officially ended in October 1991. From Tehran's vantage point, however, the United States refused to fulfill its end of the unspoken bargain. At home, the most reactionary forces in the regime called out Rafsanjani's supposed gullibility. He was publicly unrepentant. Only days after Terry Anderson was released, Rafsanjani defended the new course:

> The Islamic Republic now needs a prudent policy, more than it needs anything else … we need a prudent policy, both inside the country in order to strengthen our base, and for our foreign policy, so that we can have a presence and help people without being accused of engaging in terrorism, without anyone being able to call us fanatics. We have no need to speak frantically. We have no need to chant impractical slogans. We do not need to say things which are not acted upon, needlessly frightening people and blocking our own path.⁴¹

Nor was Rafsanjani immunized against the effects of regional events. In May 1989, in a speech aimed to acclaim Tehran's support for the Palestinian struggle against Israel, Rafsanjani said that "if five Americans or Britons or Frenchmen are killed for every Palestinian" then perhaps the West would reconsider its support for the State of Israel.⁴² It was classical Rafsanjani the politician. He was motivated far more by not losing his revolutionary street credibility than demonstrating statecraft for a new era that was just around the corner. The Palestinians knew the harsh messages was largely about the cutthroat politics of Tehran and the pressure Rafsanjani was under from more hard-line elements in the Islamic Republic. The head of PLO, Yasser Arafat, who was blasted by the Iranians to be a sellout for holding peace talks with the Israelis, came out three days later and was explicit in denouncing Rafsanjani: "I reject this call in its totality."⁴³ Arafat could rightly see the Iranian regime had turned Palestine into a political football as part of the race to shape post-Khomeini Iran. Fast forward only a few months until the passing of Khomeini and Rafsanjani was not only calling for a return to normalcy in Iranian foreign policy but exchanging senseless xenophobia about the outside world for the pursuit of practical diplomatic and economic national interests.

Iran and Iraq's Invasion of Kuwait in 1990

Rafsanjani and Khamenei stood shoulder to shoulder against radical elements inside the system that urged Tehran to side with Saddam Hussein against the United States when Baghdad put itself on a collision course with Washington after its August 1990 invasion of Kuwait. To this group, the bigger evil was the United States. Kuwait was anyways viewed as a Western lackey deliberately keeping oil prices down for the benefit of Western consumer states. That Saddam was preparing to attack Israel was the icing on the cake. How Tehran should position itself on the question of the imminent American military attack on Iraq morphed into the first big test for the post-Khomeini partnership of Khamenei and Rafsanjani.

Khamenei and Rafsanjani held a meeting at the Supreme National Security Council and declared Iran to be neutral in the US–Iraq conflict although Iraq was urged to withdraw from Kuwaiti territory.⁴⁴ The day after, radical members of the Iranian parliament, including Khamenei's younger brother Hadi, rejected Tehran's official position as a betrayal of Islam. To them, this was not about defending Saddam but keeping American boots from landing on Muslim lands. They did not have the numbers, however. Rafsanjani's right-hand man Hassan Rouhani, who was then also a member of the parliament, attacked his colleagues. "There are buses outside [the parliament]. Anyone who wants to go to Baghdad is welcome to go." Rouhani was arguing for Tehran's cold and calculated position. "Standing up to the US [in Iraq] is to pick up a war with a 30-nation coalition. And why is it in Iran's interest to see Saddam control Kuwait?" Khamenei said the same although with caveats to defend his credentials as a Muslim leader. On the one hand he criticized what he described as merciless US bombardment of Iraq. But argued this was not a war between Islam and Christian crusaders and Tehran's neutrality was about defending the national interest of Iran.

Those who saw Tehran's handling of the first Persian Gulf War of 1991 to imply a turn toward foreign policy moderation were soon disappointed. An effort to neutralize the exiled Iranian political opposition and events in the world led to a number of very disturbing decisions in Tehran. Among them was the August 1991 assassination in Paris of the Shah's last prime minister, Shapour Bakhtiar. One of the individuals later convicted for the killing was none other than a great nephew of Rafsanjani.[45] Rafsanjani's proclivity to use violence to achieve political goals had hounded him from early on in his career. When he masqueraded as a peacenik, his hard-line opponents would rehash old accounts about how Rafsanjani had been the one to provide a Beretta gun to the Islamist assassin of prime minister Hassan Ali Mansour in 1965.[46] The argument was he was above all an opportunist, shifting lane depending on circumstances. In October 1991, president Bush asked in a press conference, "Does anybody think today, is there anybody out here that would say that this regime under Mr. Rafsanjani is less moderate than Khomeini? Absolutely not." Bush made the point that he wished the "moderates" in Iran all the best, because "I want better relations with Iran."[47]

Throughout the 1980s and the first half of the 1990s, the Islamic Republic carried out dozens of mafia-style assassinations of political opponents, from Europe to the Philippines. In most cases, Tehran relied on deniability to dismiss the charges against it. It was not always possible to do so. The September 1992 killing of four Iranian Kurdish political activists at the Mykonos restaurant in Berlin ended up hanging over Iran's head for years. After a four-year trial, a German court found that leaders in Tehran, including Rafsanjani and Khamenei, had sanctioned the killings.[48]

There were a few other events from the early 1990s that were worrying and clear signposts of the trajectory of the post-Khomeini era. In 1992, for example, Khamenei with Rafsanjani's support approved of an Iranian intervention to support the Muslims of Bosnia in the war against the Serbs. He sent his special envoy, Ayatollah Ahmad Jannati, and a pack of Revolutionary Guards to arm the Bosniaks backed by Iranian funds.[49] The Bosnian war of 1992–5 was a magnet for various foreign players motivated by ethnic and religious reasons, but Iran was hardly alone among governments to intervene. Still, such an intervention in the Balkans so early after the end of the Iran–Iraq war, when Tehran was precisely struggling to find the means to sustain its own postwar reconstruction, demonstrated the still prevalent zeal Tehran had for the Islamic Republic to be among the bigwigs at least on matters relating to the Islamic World. There was otherwise no tangible Iranian national interest at stake in the Balkans in the 1990s or before or since. There were other controversial foreign policy decisions made in this period that would have far more lasting implications than Iran's intervention in the Bosnian civil war. In July 1994, the Jewish Community Center building in the commercial area of Buenos Aires was bombed and eighty-five people were killed. The bombing happened just over two years since the Israeli embassy was attacked in March 1992 that led to twenty-nine deaths. The Israelis each time quickly blamed Tehran. It was judged to be part of Iran's revenge against Israel's assassination of the head of Lebanon's Hezbollah movement, Abbas Moussawi, in February 1992.

§

By the end of his first term as president in 1993, Rafsanjani's reputation abroad as a pragmatic figure was in serious doubt. On his watch, the Islamic Republic was speaking about reform, change, and moderation but its foreign policy actions remained controversial at best. Rafsanjani's pledge of change was faring no better at home. Not only was there no more political freedom than when Khomeini had been alive, and more suppression of opponents was still to come, but his promises of economic development had flopped. In his bid for reelection in June 1993, his percentage of vote went down from the reported 96.1 percent, which was claimed he had secured in 1989, to 64 percent. He was increasingly unpersuasive. His public statements against the West, and the United States in particular, while constantly sending out feelers to Western capitals about an imminent Iranian reorientation, was a case of split personality. No one doubted that Rafsanjani genuinely wanted to kick-start the Iranian economy, to make it the new Japan of the new Middle East. The trouble was he never understood that the kind of economic takeoff that he eyed required fundamental political reform to streamline the policy-making process.

Instead of boldly standing up to those who opposed his agenda, he caved to them. He dreaded giving his opponents a pretext to call him a sellout. The scars left on him from the Iran–Contra affair were still very much fresh. In his mind, the secret talks with the Americans in Khomeini's twilight years might have cost him the supreme leadership. As president, he was not in a mood to go bold in the defense of his agenda of reform. After all, Khomeini was no longer alive to protect him and Rafsanjani had to fend for himself. On the issue of what to do with United States, the Khomeinists had put themselves in an ideological straitjacket. The obsession with Washington had originally been manufactured and then sustained since 1979 by the Khomeinists. After ten years of mobilizing their mass base behind anti-American slogans, it was extremely difficult, if not impossible, for leaders of the Islamic Republic to change their rhetoric. For Rafsanjani, this was particularly so as the domestic political obstacles he faced were still enormous.

§

By the end of Rafsanjani's first term in office as president in 1993, Ali Khamenei was already revealing a political swagger not seen in his early tottering days as supreme leader. Unbeknownst to the Iranian public, it was Khamenei that trekked to the office of the president for their weekly meetings. In his official liaison with Rafsanjani, however, Khamenei needed to impose his authority. Letters to the president amounted to far more than gentle spiritual council. Khamenei's appetite to steer the regime forward touched on anything from the need to limit privatization to encouraging the non-oil-based economy in the country to adhering to the revolutionary principles that had in the 1980s driven Iran's foreign policy.[50] Khamenei was by this point already anxious about Iran's encirclement by the United States. The end of the Soviet Union and the bipolar global order was an open question as far as the future was concerned. The Soviet republics that had comprised Iran's northern flank—Armenia, Azerbaijan, Turkmenistan, and the other new states of the Caucasus and Central Asia—were not only suddenly independent states but with a craving to move closer to the United States. This posed a real dilemma for those in Tehran that regarded further American encroachment into Iran's backyard as an existential threat. For Khamenei and those from his ilk, it was the fear of American "soft power" or "cultural invasion," as Khamenei calls it, that represented the gravest of threats.[51]

In Khamenei's words, the arrival of the United States in Central Asia, and the deployment of US forces in the Persian Gulf states after Iraq was kicked out of Kuwait, combined with the emergence of the anti-Shia and anti-Iran Taliban in Afghanistan, was tantamount to a giant American plot to defang the Islamic Republic. It is unlikely that he himself actually believed in this purported American master plan. In his own publicly expressed statements, he admitted that US policies were less about "regime change" in Tehran than it was about pressing the Islamic Republic to reconsider its foreign policy behavior.

For example, Khamenei bitterly complained that Washington had set out to curb Iran's effort to integrate economically with the rest of its immediate neighborhood. That was certainly the case. American policy toward the Caspian basin in the early 1990s was to prevent new oil pipelines from the region to traverse through Iranian territory to world markets. This was hardly aimed at regime change in Tehran. It was as if Khamenei was deliberately playing ignorant. He wanted the Islamic Republic to remain a "revolutionary" state, to confront US interests across the region while acting surprised when Washington retaliated. Even on matters pertaining to the domestic political situation, including the assassinations of opponents by Iran's own security services, Khamenei would readily blame the *doshman* (the enemy) furthering American and "Zionist" interests. He cast it as an existential struggle. "We say to the US: You have no damn business interfering in the domestic affairs of other countries. Who do you think you are? Go solve your own problems."[52]

By the end of Rafsanjani's first term, Khamenei began to reveal his misgivings about some of the government's policies. In his March 1993 Persian New Year address, he took a shot at the president. "Anywhere we have failed has been because we have more or less deviated from the divine, Islamic, and revolutionary principles. Our external enemies and their agents inside the country try to convince us of just the opposite. Those are lies. What creates problems is deviation from Islamic and revolutionary principles, whether in action or in our thinking."[53] And the United States was again at the heart of Khamenei's case for Iran's problems whether at home or abroad.

> Fifteen years ago the Imam said "America cannot do a damn thing." Some disagreed and feared America. But if we look at where we are today, we see that indeed America could not do a damn thing! Fifteen years later, we have proof. What have they been able to do? So far they were unable to do a damn thing![54]

7

(1993–7)—Dithering in Tehran as the Cold War Ends

What the U.S. wants is to deprive us of our credibility. It wants us to give up. The hostages in Lebanon. We received many messages from the U.S. to use our influence to get them released, and many [American] promises were given. The pressure we exerted did get the hostages freed—and because of that many of our friends are not happy with us. But as soon as the matter was settled, we discovered that the way the U.S. was addressing us had changed [and] became tougher. We [had been] told that the U.S. would release our frozen [financial] assets [which it did not].

(Rafsanjani, May 1993)[1]

Rafsanjani related that Khamenei's selection as the new leader had been welcomed by the West. A day after Khamenei took charge as the supreme leader, on June 5, 1989, Rafsanjani memoirs record him to say that "the Westerners are happy with Ayatollah Khamenei's appointment, which they hope could lead to the rule of moderation and the isolation of the radicals [in Tehran]." The "radicals" did not just pose a threat to American hopes for improved relations with Iran; they were in the way of the joint Rafsanjani–Khamenei plan for economic reconstruction and political consolidation at home and the desire to show a less menacing face to the outside world. The Rafsanjani-led, and UN-mediated, US–Iran negotiations about the future of Western hostages in Lebanon had all been done with the approval of Khamenei. He was also at the time keen to test the idea of a more pragmatic, if not moderate, foreign policy. While Khamenei had in Rafsanjani's first term (1989–93) mostly supported the domestic political policies of the government, the two men began to drift further apart in the president's second term (1993–7). On the question of foreign policy, Rafsanjani soon proved to be more determined to find a breakthrough with the West. Khamenei, disappointed in what he deemed to be American duplicity, very soon would move in a different direction.

This was to be a widening split. It was made more pronounced with Khamenei's insatiable longing for more power. It put the two men on a collision course and removed any doubts Rafsanjani might still have about Khamenei's pliability. As Khamenei felt more comfortable in his role as supreme leader, he began to see his old friend's presidential term as a passing event. He set his eyes on the kind of absolute supreme leadership he believed he was entitled to. For Rafsanjani, Khomeini had been his beloved master and also political cover and enabler. Khamenei could never be another Khomeini to Rafsanjani. If Khomeini was jealous of rivals, Khamenei was doubly so. By the end of Rafsanjani's second presidential term in 1997, Khamenei had robbed him and future Iranian presidents from control over key policy organs.

Rafsanjani's Unlikely "China Model"

Rafsanjani still believed the system needed an iron fist to control the restless population, but this could hardly be the only element to a covenant between the rulers and the masses. As an admirer of the East Asian economies that had by then already entered a cycle of robust growth, Rafsanjani began to see the Chinese model of rapid economic growth and ironclad political control as worthy of emulating. It would be a thinking that was naïve on different levels. As so many of his advisors and backstage supporters told him, economic growth without some form of loosening of the political grip might be possible. The Chinese were, after all, pulling it off. But the Islamic Republic's real challenge lay in the realm of its rebellious foreign policy. To become an integral part of the global economy, as the Chinese had set out to do, Tehran had to reconcile with key international actors and most importantly the United States. This in turn required political vision and courage in the same spirit as Deng Xiaoping had confronted reactionaries in the Chinese communist party before he set out to modernize the Chinese economy.

Rafsanjani had a chance to be Iran's Deng Xiaoping in the early 1990s but missed the mark rather spectacularly. Instead of launching an economic modernization era, rooted in domestic economic reform and a rehabilitated foreign policy, Rafsanjani spent his second term in office buying time. No new major policy steps were taken except controversial privatization measures that only blemished Rafsanjani's image even further as a man who empowered the few already rich at the expense of the working men and women. Khamenei did nothing to help. Khamenei seemed rather to enjoy the heat on Rafsanjani. While the supreme leader could not be publicly criticized, satirical magazines like the mockingly named *Gol Agha* (*Mr. Handsome*) made a living from attacking the Rafsanjani government as a bunch of bloodsucking profiteers.

§

Shortly before Rafsanjani's reelection in 1993, angry protests erupted in a number of towns. From the poor neighborhoods of Tehran's southern suburbs to Khamenei's home town of Mashhad, widespread antiregime demonstrations took the authorities by surprise. The elite Revolutionary Guards, who until only a few years earlier had been mostly deployed in the war against Saddam's Iraq, were mobilized to reimpose order at home. Suddenly the Guards found themselves confronting their kin in towns and neighborhoods they themselves had come from. The situation was tense and smallest sparks could result in mass protest. In one case, a 30 percent increase in the price of bus fares for workers commuting from the suburbs to central Tehran led to outbreak of violent demonstrations.

Rafsanjani was astounded. His team, including his Intelligence Minister Ali Fallahian, who had been preoccupied to hunt down the regime's opponents living in the Diaspora, had failed to detect lurking public rage just under the surface. The people who had come out to protest were not the middle or intellectual classes that the regime could readily dismiss as pampered bourgeoisie. The protesters were from the poorer socioeconomic class, the exact group Khomeini had in 1979 pledged to empower. But Rafsanjani was not about to cave under pressure. He turned to higher powers to assert his legitimacy. "Those who are against Hashemi [Rafsanjani] are against God," the Rafsanjani public relations campaign broadcast to the nation. In time, many of the same plainclothes security forces Rafsanjani sent out to hunt down his opponents would by the late 1990s turn on him.

Rafsanjani's willingness to compromise was no greater when challenged by intellectuals writing in what was left of a functioning press. In one notable case, in early 1990, ninety intellectuals, including many former regime supporters, penned a damning public letter to Rafsanjani. Among the signatories was Mehdi Bazargan, the man Khomeini appointed as his first prime minister in 1979, and Ezzatollah Sahabi, a man who had served alongside Rafsanjani as a member of the Revolutionary Council. It was an incriminating document on so many levels.

"It is not secret that our country is at a deadlock. Our economy is facing unprecedented crisis. The poor are poorer and their numbers are growing."[2] The rule of law is long gone, the letter read, and with every passing day, the people of Iran have fewer and fewer rights to demand political and economic justice. The letter was equally critical on matters of foreign policy. "The once proud nation of Iran is today internationally discredited and isolated and unable to benefit from the international system." Many of the signatories, who had foreseen a harsh response, were soon after coerced to remove their names from the document that became famous as "The 90 Signatories." Rafsanjani without doubt absorbed most of the blame since he was at this point viewed as the man who held most of the power in his hands. But Supreme Leader Khamenei was not sparred, particularly as he began to appropriate more power for his office. His response to criticism was similarly uncompromising. In one case, in October 1993, Khamenei had twenty-two retired army and navy officers arrested for signing an open letter to him that was critical of the regime.

Rafsanjani dismissed the criticism but he knew that intimidation alone would buy him so much time. At the swearing in for this second term, he promised "social justice." "It is not right for a revolution to rob the people of their rights," he conceded. But the people were increasingly restless. Another assassination attempt on Rafsanjani's life in 1994, while he was giving a speech, was a sign of trouble ahead although some accounts put it down as a staged incident.[3] The regime, after all, could best defend itself in circumstances when it could paint a picture of anarchy looming around the corner. The often unnamed *doshman* (enemy) was ever-present and constantly plotting to harm the Islamic Republic, at least that was the joint message of Rafsanjani and Khamenei.

In such a security-centric environment, Rafsanjani's magic bullet—foreign investment—to enhance the regime's legitimacy and his own standing was firing blank. He wanted foreign investment and yet had or wanted to keep the meddlesome world out. Before there was even an opportunity to attract large foreign corporations, there were accounts of personal packages that were coming into Iran that would be opened by customs and anything deemed un-Islamic or antiregime would be stamped with "Islam Is Victorious" and a photo of Khomeini included before shipping it onward.[4] Tehran clearly still had to make up its mind: to remain a revolutionary cause or to free itself from the shackles of militant Islamism and shoot to improve the earthly lot of its people. Rafsanjani also had to wrestle with resistance to his plans from the remaining "radicals" from the 1980s that still roamed inside the ranks of the regime. This camp, nativist in its DNA and still hanging onto notions of an Iran delinked from the West, pushed back and derided Rafsanjani's agenda to attract foreign investment as a sellout. In parliament, the likes of Sadeq Khalkhali—known as the "hanging judge" for his role in the summary execution of Shah-era officials—spoke about resisting the creeping conspiracy that seeks to undermine the Imam's (Khomeini's) line by seeking rapprochement with the West through diplomacy. Rafsanjani had Khalkhali hauled up-front of the Supreme National Security Council (SNSC), and later the flagitious Revolutionary Court, to answer for himself. The radicals, the persecutors of yesterday, found themselves in the firing line of Rafsanjani. If co-option did not work, Rafsanjani's instinct was to turn to suppressing dissent through intimidation, imprisonment, or worse.

When the same radicals, and mostly unreasonably, asked why questioning the course of the country's foreign policy warranted admonishment, the response was either further rebuke or silence. It was in fact quite astonishing that Rafsanjani never took it on himself, not even at the height of his power in the early 1990s, to directly speak to the people and his critics. After all, while arguably inapt about how to execute his vision, his case for a foreign policy rebirth had plenty of merit. Nowhere was this omission more evident than on the question of the United States.

§

After Khomeini's death, the SNSC had become the regime's key policy-making forum. It was made up by about two dozen members, mostly cabinet ministers and top military officials, and headed by the president, Rafsanjani. As supreme leader, Khamenei was represented in the council through his two handpicked representatives, one of whom was Hassan Rouhani. Rouhani had spent most of the 1980s as Rafsanjani's right-hand man. In 1989, Rafsanjani offered Rouhani to be his intelligence minister but he turned it down, preferring the role of the secretary general at the SNSC.[5] It was an understandable decision since it was arguably more of a powerful hybrid role, straddling authority across the regime spectrum. That Khamenei chose Rouhani to be one of his sets of eyes and ears in the council shows two things: that he not only enjoyed a close relationship with Rouhani but that Rafsanjani and Khamenei were at this point still in agreement on broader policy matters. On the question of the United States, the attitude was a case of wanting it both ways.

Anti-Americanism, as a pillar of the Islamic Republic, was not challenged head-on. Rafsanjani would often raise the issue of Tehran wanting to improve relations while Khamenei's bread and butter rested on continuing dedication to the revolutionary creed, including the bombastic line on the issue of the United States he had inherited from his predecessor, Khomeini. It has never been clear if this double-message from Tehran was part of an elaborate effort by Rafsanjani and Khamenei to gently break the taboo of talking to the United States without losing their revolutionary credentials among the shrinking base that still believed in the Islamic Republic. Meanwhile, the views of the Iranian leadership were clearly also shaped by the policies of Washington. Regrettably for Rafsanjani, a good part of his time as president overlapped with the presidency of Bill Clinton (1992–2000). His administration began by adopting the harshest stance on Iran than any of its predecessors. On January 31, 1993, the day he announced his intention to seek a reelection a mere six months later, Rafsanjani felt he was acting boldly when he said improving US–Iran relations was possible but that the ball was in Washington's court. The response could not have been less encouraging. Just about a month later, in early March, the US State Department issued a statement labeling Iran the world's "most dangerous state sponsor of terrorism." Officialdom in Tehran was flustered. The Speaker of the Iranian parliament, the influential Ali Akbar Nateq-Nouri, charged the United States was engaged in a psychological war against his country.

Washington was not about to budge. On March 30, US secretary of state Warren Christopher dubbed the Iranian state an "international outlaw" for its alleged support of international violence and nuclear weapons development.[6] Whether in coordination with Rafsanjani, or perhaps because he saw overtures toward Washington were going nowhere, Khamenei's murmurs suddenly became louder. That same year, on the occasion of the seizing of the US embassy on November 4, Khamenei reiterated the impossibility of resuming relations with the United States.

The Struggle for Foreign Policy

Both Rafsanjani and Khamenei supported the foreign minister, Ali Akbar Velayati. He was a pediatric doctor educated at Johns Hopkins University in the United States, and a dour regime technocrat to his core. He had been foreign minister since December 1981, a feat he achieved due to two abilities. First, he had managed to stay close to Khomeini when he was alive. Second, Velayati throughout his tenure from 1981 until 1997 kept himself close to both Rafsanjani and Khamenei. Nor was Velayati a hustler for power and hence essentially viewed as a harmless messenger to the outside world. And yet, foreign policy was hardly protected from the brewing Rafsanjani–Khamenei struggle. In February 1994, Rafsanjani installed his younger brother as the senior deputy foreign minister. The appointment was announced a day after Khamenei had removed the brother from his job as head of Iran's national radio and television. The firing and quick reappointment were not random acts. It was a prelude to more to come as elbows were sharpened.

Rafsanjani often hinted that his role model and peer was Amir Kabir, a mid-nineteenth-century Persian prime minister who wrestled to keep British and Russian encroachment in Iran limited. In his day, Amir Kabir had looked on foreign meddling as Iran's biggest vulnerability and hindrance to national revival. Amir Kabir, however, was no xenophobe when it came to the outside world. In 1851, he founded Iran's first modern university that in time became the University of Tehran and had no hesitation to tap into European expertise. Rafsanjani shared this trait with his hero. He held no deep-seated phobias against the West. He had visited Europe and the United States before the revolution and was at heart a capitalist, a system he knew was intrinsically a Western concept. But Rafsanjani wanted economic liberalization, foreign investment while at the same time competing with Khamenei for the title of the Islamist militant revolutionary leader.

This paradox was in full swing when it came to Rafsanjani's posturing on policy relating to the Islamic World. Until he died, Rafsanjani reminded anyone who cared to know that he had once in prison written a prelim for a book on the fate of the Palestinian people. He claimed the Shah's regime, which wanted to maintain cordial ties with Israel, had beaten him up for it in prison. "Now you dare write prelims," he had been tongue-lashed. Despite such claims, Rafsanjani was regarded both at home and abroad to be far flexible in his ways than Khamenei. Rafsanjani, the "middle-of-the-road-extremist" as some American observers at the time began to call him, had to be careful not to give cause to have himself labeled Iran's Gorbachev, as someone who inadvertently would end the regime by believing change was inevitable.

This meant, mostly out of necessity than choice, that he took stances that paid homage to the revolutionary ideals of the Islamic Republic but did very little to advance the Iranian national interest. Next door in Afghanistan, in early 1994 and at a time when the blatantly anti-Iran and anti-Shia Taliban movement was on the rise, Rafsanjani called for all Afghan factions to "rally around Islam." His gullible idea that "Islam" is the solution was less a reflection of Tehran's insights into Afghan affairs—the Iranians knew full well that the Taliban was bad news—and more of an affirmation of Rafsanjani's need to keep paying lip-service to "Islam" as the master solution to all things under the sun.

It was also in January 1994 that Rafsanjani showed up in Baku, the capital of the newly independent Azerbaijan, and complained about small numbers of faithful he had seen in the capital's largest mosque.[7] The Azerbaijanis, who had just freed themselves from Soviet shackles, feared that Rafsanjani was hinting that Iran wanted to export its Islamist model to this northern neighbor and only one out of four Shia-majority countries in the world. Rafsanjani had managed to scare Baku, and ironically at the same time his real deeper desire was to see the Azerbaijanis and Iran work more closely on the economic front. Baku soon after agreed to build a pipeline to take its Caspian oil through Turkey to world markets and avoid Iranian territory and hence integration and transit fees for Iran. Rafsanjani later put this loss down to US pressure on Baku to avoid Iran. He never for a second admitted that having unnerved the Azerbaijanis might have played a role in Baku's calculations.

The same reflexive attitude dominated Tehran's position toward the Arab–Israeli conflict and Iran's support for the Palestinians. In February 1994, a few hours after news reached Iran that dozens of Palestinians had been killed at the hands of Baruch Goldstein, a Jewish extremist settler in Hebron, Tehran executed Feyzollah Mekhubad. He was a Jewish Iranian man who had been arrested in 1992 on charges of spying for Israel.[8] To play to the anti-Israel sentiment was still the Islamic Republic's hope to be catapulted to the top leadership role in the Islamic World even as the Palestinians themselves were in the midst of negotiations with the Israelis. A few months later in 1994, Rafsanjani refused to attend the summit of the Organization of the Islamic Conference in Casablanca in protest against the Moroccan government's links with Israel.

Khamenei and Allies Zoom In on Rafsanjani

During Rafsanjani's second term in office, Khamenei began to flex his muscle. He was all in favor of Rafsanjani's crackdown against domestic opponents but began to express dismay at some of the Rafsanjani government's social and cultural policies. It was a case of deliberate disassociation. By now, Khamenei had decided his political domain inside the regime had to be to the right of Rafsanjani. The president was soon compelled to replace a number of his government ministers. Tasting blood, some of Khamenei's closest associates honed in on Rafsanjani as the patriarch of a network that was in essence the biggest rival of the supreme leader. This new, and at first subtle, campaign to undermine Rafsanjani quickly took on a personal nature.

At times, the attacks came from the same government Rafsanjani purportedly spearheaded. In one case, a deputy intelligence minister was caught reportedly fabricating evidence against one of Rafsanjani's sons to implicate him in corruption. The deputy, a man in his mid-20s, was Hossein Taeb. Ostensibly a cleric, he was in reality an intelligence operative and an active member of the Revolutionary Guards, which Khamenei oversaw as the commander-in-chief. Taeb was later transferred to the Ministry of Intelligence, which is accountable to the president. It was here that Taeb as a deputy minister for counterintelligence began to target the president's family.[9]

When president Rafsanjani found out, he asked the Intelligence Minister Ali Fallahian to fire Taeb, which he did. Taeb was quickly soon after appointed as a staff member in the Office of the Supreme Leader, raising all sorts of speculation to this day about what role Khamenei had played in Taeb's anti-Rafsanjani scheme. While Taeb's quest to find incriminating evidence against the Rafsanjanis was politically motivated, the family had already built up a reputation deserving of oligarchs. It would emerge later that Rafsanjani's younger son, Mehdi, had played the role of a behind-the-scene broker for foreign energy giants such as France's Total and Norway's Statoil. Mehdi provided access to his father's government for cash. It was a labyrinth affair that subsequently led to joint US–French investigations and trials, fines, and even the still unresolved disappearance in Dubai of a key Iranian participant in the affair.[10]

The merits of the charges aside, the young Taeb would not have picked up a fight with Rafsanjani without feeling that his back was covered by Khamenei. Khamenei later made Taeb the head of the intelligence branch of the Revolutionary Guards, a rival to the Ministry of Intelligence, which is answerable to the president.[11] Besides a peek into the simmering tensions between the Rafsanjani- and Khamenei-led factions, this incident also exposed fears in parts of the regime about the potential impact on future power and wealth distribution in Iran as Rafsanjani continued to court the world.

§

No doubt that the campaign against the Rafsanjani family was partly about the broader struggle about Iran's relations with the outside world. Rafsanjani had made improving the economy his top priority. This included loosening up state control over the economy and borrowing money from the outside to finance the reconstruction era. During his two terms as president, foreign imports ballooned while exports increased far less. Meanwhile, foreign debt piled up, reaching a record of almost $25 billion by 1993 although it dropped after that.[12] Inflation was up, many state subsidies were eliminated, and the gap between the poor and the rich widened. Western governments hoped Rafsanjani's policy of détente in foreign affairs and economic restoration would succeed but had deep doubts. "Rafsanjani could be killed at any time, which is in the tradition of Iranian politics, and then what?" said an exaggerating Western ambassador in Tehran as early as 1991. Even the most optimists expected that rolling back the policies of the dark 1980s would take many years.[13]

Khamenei had initially been onboard but in time he came to see economic integration to the outside world as slippery ground. To him, economic liberalization meant forfeiting political control, and no counterargument, such as the example from China on freeing the economy while maintaining tight political control, could convince him otherwise. From the perspective of Khamenei, change was an invitation to strip himself of influence. Pro-Khamenei figures began to attack Rafsanjani's economic plans as destructive. They claimed borrowing money from the outside world made Iran into a dependent entity and beholden to the diktat of Western-led institutions such as the International Monetary Fund and the World Bank. On top of that, Rafsanjani's economic reform agenda was painted as a golden opportunity for the wealthy class to become wealthier. Khamenei pitched himself as the guardian of the poor and the champion of social justice. The promise of social justice has always had mass appeal in Iran, but Khamenei was not interested in the political capital such posturing created for him in society.

He had more pressing concerns: to shield the economic enterprises that he controlled from Rafsanjani's unpredictable reform plans. Khamenei controlled a countless number of large economic enterprises—from thousands of properties confiscated from those linked to the previous regime of the Shah to religious foundations that brought in billions of dollars each year. He wanted to keep his sources of economic power out of the Rafsanjani government's purview. In other words, Khamenei was not about to let Rafsanjani's flunkies with their modernization ideas to eat into what some viewed as his "juggernaut with real estate, corporate stocks, and other assets."[14]

That Khamenei's allies, and principal protectors, in the Revolutionary Guards had amassed an economic empire of their own, and jealously protected it, meant that Rafsanjani had to face off a formidable hurdle. This should not have surprised Rafsanjani. He was after all the patriarch of a distinct powerful clique himself. This group's political, economic, and foreign interests often did not converge with those interests coalescing around Khamenei. The Rafsanjani network was an amalgamation of old acquaintances from the Bazaar going back to before the revolution. At the time, Rafsanjani's observable supporters were mostly found in the Motalefeh, an anti-Shah, Islamist but pro-market political grouping established in 1963 that represented the interests of the old Bazaar. Motalefeh had backed the revolution against the Shah and was handsomely rewarded for it afterward. By the mid-1990s, Motalefeh and other supporters of Rafsanjani believed economic integration with the outside world was on balance to the benefit of them and the Islamic Republic. To propagate this message, a large number of media outlets supportive of Rafsanjani began to market the pro-reform economic agenda of his government.

Rafsanjani was not oblivious to the fears of Khamenei or the Revolutionary Guards but prioritized the latter. He had in his first term agreed with Khamenei to create a new conglomerate to oversee the various economic interests of the Guards. Known as the "Khatam-ol Anbia" (Seal of the Prophets), Rafsanjani had hoped this new entity would divert the attention of the Guards away from politics. The conglomerate, with its considerable technical capacity—such as building roads, dams, and other construction projects—was meant to become a money-making enterprise and keep the Guards busy and placated. It was a compromise. Rafsanjani had in the final year of this Speakership of the parliament sought to merge the Guards into the regular armed forces, the Artesh. After Khomeini's death, however, the pushback from the senior bosses at the Revolutionary Guards was accentuated when Khamenei also opposed the de facto disbandment of the Guards. Hence the marriage of convenience between Khamenei and the Guards was born. The year was 1989.

One could even say the Guards were now in debt to Khamenei and judged the Rafsanjani circle of the so-called liberals (also known as the "technocrats") as the common rival for power. The contrasts were great in more ways than one. In particular, from the perspective of social class, the differences between the two camps were quite deep. The leadership of the Revolutionary Guards was made up almost exclusively by men who were in their late teens or early 20s when they in 1979 joined Khomeini's movement for an Islamist utopia. They hailed predominantly from poor urban or rural backgrounds and had ripened during the Iran–Iraq war.

The technocrats were also once young Islamist revolutionaries, but instead of donning the uniform of the Revolutionary Guards, they had manned the civilian ministries in the 1980s. Rather than rising out of poverty, they mostly came from middle-class homes. Many had lived and been educated in the West before the Shah's fall. For example, the long-time head of the Guards was Mohsen Rezai, a shepherd from a poor provincial family who barely had any formal schooling.[15] Another top commander was Qassem Soleimani, a man who years later would go on to haunt the Americans in places like Iraq and Syria. His family was so poor he had had to drop out of school and work on construction sites. In contrast, Rafsanjani's cabinet was packed with ministers who had at one point or another studied abroad and attended institutions such as the Massachusetts Institute of Technology, University of California, Iowa University, and so on. Rafsanjani's younger brother, Mohammad, had studied at the University of California in Berkeley.

Both groups were forged in the chaos that immediately followed the 1979 revolution, but each took a different lesson from that period. At the ministries in Tehran, the technocrats learned firsthand how revolutionary fanaticism—cutting off trade with the outside world, for example—could lead to international isolation, harm the economy, and create poverty. The Guards, meanwhile, found that same fanaticism indispensable for mobilizing a small yet determined base to advance its interests, first on the battlefield against Iraq's Saddam Hussein and later against opponents on the home front. Unsurprisingly, the technocrats and the generals of the Guards held very different views on the merits of political and economic reform. The former, clustered around Rafsanjani, wanted to bring Iran into the global economy. The latter, by this point increasingly clustered around Khamenei, feared that the arrival of Western capital and technologies would endanger their interests and possession of power in the Islamic Republic.

Tehran Fails to Grasp the Consequences of the End of the Cold War

Aside from bickering about how to handle the economy, there was the question of American opposition to Tehran's efforts to become a "normal" economy. President George H. Bush had vowed to restore ties with Tehran if there was "goodwill" demonstrated from the other side. Rafsanjani looked for ways to demonstrate this required goodwill, including facilitating the release of Western hostages. But then Bush lost in his reelection bid in 1992 to Bill Clinton. He launched the so-called Dual Containment policy in May 1993—aimed to contain both Iran and Iraq—and it culminated in the 1996 Iran Sanctions Act (ISA). The latter barred US and foreign investments of more than $40 million in the development of Iran's energy sector. As early as May 1993, Clinton's special assistant for the Middle East, Martin Indyk, called Iran a "bad investment in both commercial and strategic terms." Rafsanjani was undeterred, believing that adding more incentives would overturn such American calculations.

The Rafsanjani government's tantalizing offers to US energy firms to return to Iran was to transform Washington's attitude but it failed. On March 15, 1995, president Clinton issued an executive order formally blocking a $1 billion contract between Conoco and Iran to develop a huge offshore oil tract in the Persian Gulf. A deflated Iran instead awarded the oil contract to the French firm Total. The Clinton White House insisted on punishing Iran for its sponsorship of militant groups such as Lebanon's Hezbollah or the Islamic Jihad and Hamas of the Palestinians and Tehran's opposition to the US-brokered Arab–Israeli peace talks. There was also a growing American concern during Rafsanjani's presidency about Tehran's push to develop an indigenous nuclear industry.

From Iran's perspective, in the post-Cold War era, the Clinton White House had opted to make the Islamic Republic its whipping boy, at least while America was still engaged in formulating a new global grand strategy. While some US business interest groups—such as USA*Engage—pushed for an American rethink of Washington's Iran policy, the moderates in Tehran, who believed in the profound utility of restoring diplomatic ties with the United States, faced the daunting reality of having very few possible collaborators in Washington. If the Reagan and Bush Republican administrations kept the door open for possible talks, the Democratic Clinton team went out of its way to keep the Iranians at arm's length. In one famous episode in the spring of 1995, Washington and Delhi butted diplomatic heads after the Indians failed to give the United States early warning that president Rafsanjani was in the Indian capital at the same time as the US Secretary of Treasury Robert Rubin who said he would have postponed his trip if he had known.[16] The acrimony was bare for anyone to see.

Tehran was not at all ready to address these American concerns. The sense here was that the Democrats wanted simply to punish the ayatollahs in Tehran since the seizing of the US diplomats in 1979 had given the Republicans control of the White House for twelve straight years. From Tehran's point of view, Iran was seemingly at the center of the universe. The fact the Cold War had ended in 1991 and reordered US policy priorities in the Middle East was somehow not comprehended in Tehran the way it should have been. In retrospect, the Bush presidency of 1989–93 was yet another big missed opportunity. As with Reagan's bid to end the stalemate with Tehran in the mid-1980s, domestic politics was not only paralyzing Tehran but baffling to the Americans. To focus minds in Tehran, Washington chose to go for the jugular. From 1994 onward, Washington made it harder for Iran to borrow money from the outside. Rafsanjani's reconstruction plans were at risk but he put on a brave face. "The state of our economy is such that American sanctions will have no impact." Rafsanjani said the Clinton administration was scoring an own goal. "It is an embarrassment as no other country except Israel and no non-American companies are taking part [in the boycott of Iran]." He told German and Russian press that it was the United States and its companies that are the biggest losers from sanctions on Iran. But he knew all along the sanctions were disastrous to his plans. Years later and long after he left the presidential palace, Rafsanjani called the sanctions his cabinet faced as unbearable.

Another admission by Rafsanjani was that he had as president wanted to meet the Americans half way and bring an end to the hostilities. He claimed Khamenei would not hear of it.[17] What is still not known is how far the pro-Khamenei faction—the "deep state" inside the regime—might have gone to scuttle any effort to normalize ties with Washington. Rafsanjani claimed that he had wanted Khomeini to work out a solution when he was still alive. That never happened but Rafsanjani likely supposed the resolution of the American conundrum to be a big legacy to leave behind as his second presidential term was coming to its end. He might have even viewed such a development as prolonging his political shelf-life. He was already contemplating ways he could stay on even though the Iranian presidency is capped at two four-year terms only.

In the midst of Rafsanjani's machinations, one single event stopped him in his tracks. On June 25, 1996, a truck bomb exploded outside the Khobar Towers, a housing complex in eastern Saudi Arabia where some 2,500 US military personnel were stationed. One Saudi and nineteen Americans were killed. The finger was quickly pointed at a hitherto group called the "Saudi Hezbollah," an entity with alleged ties to Tehran and Hezbollah in Lebanon. This one incident was like a hand grenade thrown at Rafsanjani's efforts to reduce tensions with Riyadh and Washington. In June 2001, a federal grand jury indicted thirteen Saudis and a Lebanese for the bombing, stating they were given support by Iran. In 2006 and 2018, US judges ordered Iran to pay millions of dollars in compensation to the victims and their families.[18]

Iran's precise role in the bombing has never been conclusively proven. What is known is that the purported bomber, the Saudi national Ahmed Al-Mughassil, had fled to Iran where he subsequently was able to live for many years.[19] Rafsanjani claimed that he heard about possible Iranian involvement in the Khobar Tower bombing from the Iranian ambassador to Riyadh. Prince Nayyef, the powerful Saudi minister of interior, had let it be known that the Syrians had told the Saudis that Mughassil and three other Saudi suspects were in hiding in Iran. "They [Riyadh] wanted direct negotiations with Tehran," Rafsanjani wrote in his memoirs, and "want to forget the past and turn a page in relations." The Saudis were telling Rafsanjani that they were keeping the Americans out of the loop but that Iran had to cooperate or the Americans might find out sooner or later. If so, Prince Nayyef warned Rafsanjani, "bad things" can happen at the hands of the Americans.[20]

Nayyef had no idea if Rafsanjani's rivals in Tehran had facilitated the bombing to undermine Rafsanjani.[21] Nor did Rafsanjani insinuate that this might have been a rogue Iranian action by elements that wanted to undercut him at every turn. He had squarely blamed "fanatics" to have been behind gunrunning into Saudi Arabia in 1986.[22] A decade later, Rafsanjani stayed silent about who, if any, in Iran might have had a role in the Khobar Tower bombing that was about to unravel his agenda vis-à-vis the Saudis and the Americans.

§

That Rafsanjani had to watch his back when it came to his dealings with the West still does not excuse his unimaginativeness. He criticized past mistakes but only halfheartedly. He would instead look for excuses. During his April 1995 trip to India, when asked about whether Tehran intended to carry out the death sentence of Khomeini against Indian-born Salman Rushdie, he called the entire affaire a storm in a tea cup. He said Iran had no intention to send out death squads to kill Rushdie and described the fatwa against the author of *The Satanic Verses* as an issue of "Islamic jurisprudence." It was the West, he said, that was endangering Rushdie's life by "turning the death edict into a political issue."[23] He sidestepped the need by the West to see measurable action to corroborate shift in Tehran's attitude. Khamenei maintained that the death sentence was "irreversible" and to this day insists that the verdict is based on divine verses and, just like divine verses, it is "solid and irrevocable."[24] Shortly after he returned from Delhi, in June 1995, France sentenced six Iranian agents to life imprisonment for the 1991 assassination in Paris of former Iranian prime minister, Shapour Bakhtiar.

Unable or unwilling to free himself from the excesses of the regime, Rafsanjani again turned to what he knew best and always, and mistakenly, believed would yield result: cutting transactional deals. In January 1997, in one of his last shots at a foreign policy success, Rafsanjani ordered his oil minister, Gholam Reza Aghazadeh, to incentivize British and French companies by putting on the table the development of some of Iran's largest hydrocarbon deposits such as the South Pars natural gas field, the world's largest. "Reaching a deal with them [two veto-wielding members of the UN Security Council) will prevent the UN to impose sanctions on Iran," Aghazadeh told him. Rafsanjani, constantly on the lookout for a shortcut, ordered a meeting to be held.[25] It would turn out to be another mirage.

§

Demoralized by his inability to break the stalemate with the West, Rafsanjani doubled down on reinforcing existing ties with two principal non-Western states: Russia and China. Unlike his efforts aimed at the West, his domestic rivals in the pro-Khamenei camp in Tehran demonstrated no objections. The spring of 1997, a handful of months before Rafsanjani ended his final presidential term, witnessed a flurry of activity. Purchases and agreements, involving products ranging from Russian aircraft engines to Chinese locomotives and from Russian ballistic missile system to Chinese anti-air defense systems, symbolized an Iranian foreign policy shift that has to this day not been reversed. Within a handful of years, China would overtake Germany as Iran's biggest trading partner.

On paper Moscow accepted US sanctions on Iran but proceeded to sell Iran sensitive equipment, and over US objections, when the financial revenue was hard to pass over. A year earlier, Moscow had agreed to help Iran build ballistic missiles in violation of a 1994 US–Russian accord. In 1995, Moscow sold to Tehran nuclear reactors that Washington claimed would speed Iran's acquisition of nuclear weapons. President Boris Yeltsin, a man the Iranians had at first disparaged as an American asset, refused to back down in the face of US pressure. By 1996, American media were reporting that Iran was buying around $500 million a year in military equipment from Moscow, which accounted to about 85 percent of all of Iran's imports from Russia.[26]

The West, and particularly the United States, watched as Chinese anti-ship missiles and Russian-made submarines delivered to the Iranians began to look like a military buildup in the Persian Gulf. It was tantamount to a strategic shift by Iran toward Russia and China, but Washington chose to downplay it. When the United States in May 1997 named five Chinese individuals for "knowingly and materially" contributing to Iran's chemical weapons program, as Secretary of State Madeline Albright put it, the Americans made sure to separate the sanctioned individuals from the Chinese government. "The sanctions are against these individuals and entities, and not against the governments of China," State Department spokesman Nicholas Burns said in the statement.

There was nothing inevitable about this strategic shift toward Russia and China, and certainly not a key goal of Rafsanjani when he had first entered the presidential palace back in 1989. Tehran and Moscow at times came close to blows even as the notion of strategic relationship was pursued. In January 1995, for example, the same month as Russia agreed to build a number of nuclear reactors in Iran, Rafsanjani was forced to publicly scold Moscow for its military operation in the Muslim-majority republic of Chechnya in Russia's Northern Caucasus.

Moscow hit back at Tehran and told it to stay out of the Chechen war and prevent Islamist mercenaries to use Iran as transit.[27] By all accounts, the Iranians quickly acquiesced, knowing that infuriating Russia would only deepen Tehran's international isolation. It was a sanctimonious moment for the Islamic Republic. On the one hand, Tehran had let a fictional book by one author, Salman Rushdie, cause a major crisis with the entire membership of the European Union. But when Russia launched a bloody military invasion of Chechnya, Tehran chose to look the other way and promptly accepted Moscow's ultimatums.

Rafsanjani Shoots to Preserve Post-Presidency Relevance

Sometime during his second term, feeling he had not achieved his goals and his legacy in danger, Rafsanjani took a quiet chance to stay for a third term as president. People close to him, such as his vice president Ataollah Mohajerani, who a few years later had to flee the country, and his protégé Hassan Rouhani, began in media interviews to hint at amending the constitution to remove the clause on two-term presidential limit.[28] It was met with negative reaction. Newspaper editorials called it an attempt at "permanent sovereignty," a step that would lay the foundation for authoritarianism; and qualms were raised that Iran was no "North Korea, Syria or Libya to have a lifetime president."[29] In the Islamic Republic, where there has never been much of press freedom, it was not hard to trace much of this pushback to have originated in the Office of the Supreme Leader.

Khamenei, in public entirely ignoring the chatter about a possible extension of Rafsanjani's presidency, immediately began to signal that he already knew who he preferred as the next president. That man was Ali-Akbar Nateq-Nouri who was at the time the Speaker of the parliament. Nateq-Nouri had been an ally of Rafsanjani but the latter's appetite to stay on as president had created bad blood. And Nateq-Nouri was not the only one that felt Rafsanjani's vision of the future had little room for many from among the old guard. In tandem with his elusive style to suss out a way to stay on as president, Rafsanjani set out to prolong his legacy by sponsoring the birth of a new political party. In 1996, sixteen members of his cabinet formed a new party called *Kargozaran-e Sazandegi* (the Executives of the Construction). This was the first time since the dissolution of the Islamic Republican Party in 1987 that an organized party platform had been born. It promoted itself as the "modern political right." This was a deliberate punch at Khamenei. Rafsanjani's "neoliberal" or "technocrat" government hired younger and hipper consultants to differentiate themselves from the "traditional right," which grouped around the supreme leader.

It was marked in a roundabout way but the party's creation represented the most profound split between Rafsanjani and Khamenei to date. In that year's parliamentary elections, the new party came second to pro-Khamenei candidates as Rafsanjani's supporters charged that voter fraud had taken place in the provinces. The accusing finger was pointed at the Revolutionary Guards, the organization that had once been suspicious of Khamenei but now saw him as the preferred patron over Rafsanjani. Even before accusations of fraud were raised, the Khamenei-controlled Guardian Council (GC), the regime's vetting agency, had disqualified some half of all candidates for ostensibly not being committed to the "Islamic Republic."[30] After the death of Khomeini, GC had become nearly indiscriminate in disqualifying anyone remotely suspected to want to pursue significant political change in Iran. The question of fraud was not allowed to lead to intraregime bloodletting, but it was evident that Rafsanjani and Khamenei were about to sharply veer away from each other.

Rafsanjani could take solace from the fact that his brainchild was now the second largest faction in the parliament. But Iran has never had much of a culture of political parties. Power is drawn not from parties but from informal and fluid networks clustered around prominent political heavyweights. No one knew this basic rule better than Rafsanjani. He knew increasingly also that he was fallible. During the previous parliamentary elections (1992), many had campaigned as pro-Rafsanjani candidates only to declare loyalty to Khamenei once elected. There was a rising inevitability about his lapse as the kingmaker and Rafsanjani was incapable to turn the tide around. That is precisely why he set out to reinvent himself to maintain political relevance.

§

The purpose of Rafsanjani underwriting the birth of Executives of Construction party was to fend off Khamenei's seize of more power at every opportune moment. With a supportive faction in the parliament, Rafsanjani had hoped to pave the way for a better flowing policy-making process. At the very least, Rafsanjani wanted to negate the possibility of public embarrassment at the hands of parliament members. Early on in his second term parliamentarians had started an impeachment process against two of his cabinet ministers, an event that Rafsanjani found deeply degrading.

Khamenei could see the writing on the wall and doubled down on his own coalition building. On top of the partnership he had initiated with the Revolutionary Guards when he took over as supreme leader in 1989, Khamenei began to chisel away at Rafsanjani's political base of support. Khamenei, the man who throughout the 1980s stood side by side with Rafsanjani in defending market economics against the collectivists among the Khomeinists, now spoke about the dangers of the president's economic liberalization ideas for the poor. In the background, Khamenei championed the presidential bid of Nateq-Nouri who was a member of the Motalefeh, the pro-market group with which Rafsanjani had had a sporadic courtship. Khamenei's calculations rested on a simple goal: a Nateq-Nouri presidency, believed to be deferential to Khamenei, would elevate the overall power of the Office of the Supreme Leader. Rafsanjani's supporters could see he was heading for the cliff. Some urged him to speak directly to the public. His younger brother, Mohammad Hashemi, urged his brother to go on and give a sermon at the Tehran Friday Prayer and turn the tables on Khamenei. Rafsanjani hesitated. He expressed deep misgivings and warned that an open schism with Khamenei could turn Iran "into another Afghanistan," in reference to the ravaging civil war going on in Iran's next-door eastern neighbor. To invoke the idea of a civil war was a surprisingly glum and clearest sign that the Khamenei–Rafsanjani partnership was heading for the cliffs.

The self-evident reality was that most observers or the public at the time did not believe Rafsanjani to be the moderate he claimed to be.[31] He was after power and was being outplayed by Khamenei. It was that simple. His second-best option was to make a temporary tactical retreat and buy time. In the meantime, he could cultivate his image as a genuine economic modernizer if not a political "reformer." The quest for reinvention had been amply evident when Rafsanjani's youngest daughter, Faezeh, ran for a seat in the parliament in 1996 and came second in Tehran.[32] Her candidacy and agenda were no doubt meant to help her father's effort to remake himself. The country was despairing for taboo-breakers and Faezeh's rebelliousness—which in this context could be as little as wearing jeans in public—was widely welcomed in society.

Later on, she spooked the Khamenei circle when in 1998, and while still serving as a member of the parliament, she launched a women's magazine, *Zan (Women)*.[33]

The magazine not only openly challenged key regime dogma—such as the need for compulsory veil in society when the majority in public were clearly against it—but the outlet had the support of Rafsanjani.[34] Unlike Khamenei, whose wife and two daughters have rarely ever been seen in public or heard, Rafsanjani accepted, if not encouraged, his wife and particularly his two daughters to represent the family in public.

With his shifty plans to change the constitution so he could stay on as president going nowhere, Rafsanjani had to make up his mind about his post-presidential future. By now, and against the advice of some of his closest confidants, Rafsanjani elected to steer clear of an open conflict with Khamenei. The question was whether to accept Khamenei as his overlord and for Rafsanjani to end his drive to reengineer the Islamic Republic and hope for the supreme leader's benevolence. Rafsanjani opted for a third option. He and his supporters chose to take a stance against Khamenei but only vicariously. The context was to be the 1997 presidential elections. They threw their weight behind the opponent of the Khamenei-backed Nateq-Nouri. That man was a former detractor of Rafsanjani. His name was Mohammad Khatami.

By the 1997 presidential elections, which was soon recognized as an epic turning point, the political "right" of the 1980s, which Rafsanjani and Khamenei had both once belonged to, had all but disappeared. Rafsanjani and his supporters moved to back Khatami. He was a midranking cleric and a member of the old "radical" (left) faction when Khomeini had been alive. They had throughout the 1980s opposed market economic reform and remained avid defenders of revolutionary foreign policy. Both Khatami and the old left in the Islamic Republic were shedding their old clothes, and it was at this juncture that Rafsanjani first viewed them as opportune companions on the political journey ahead.

Rafsanjani's backing for Mohammad Khatami in the 1997 elections might have been in a roundabout way but it was unmistakable. First, he dissuaded other potential candidates from among his supporters to run for president in order to prevent splitting the anti-Nateq-Nouri vote.[35] He then put his formidable network behind Khatami. While preferring to keep his options open and keep a distance from Khatami's campaign in the public, Rafsanjani's disciples in various roles in the official bureaucracy pushed for a Khatami win. A huge endorsement came from none other than the City Council of Tehran. The mayor, a major Rafsanjani ally by the name of Gholam-hossein Karbaschi, came out in support for Khatami. Tehran's publicly funded *Hamshahri* daily newspaper was instrumental in introducing the otherwise relatively unknown Khatami to the nearly 8 million citizens of Tehran. In Iranian politics, the mood in Tehran both shapes and is a harbinger to what the rest of the country ends up preferring.

Rafsanjani was, in his own words, closer to Khatami in preferring a dialogue with the rest of the world and allowing for more social and cultural freedoms for ordinary Iranians. This was not surprising. Khatami had been Rafsanjani's advisor on cultural affairs for a number of years in the early 1990s. Rafsanjani was, however, still unsure about Khatami's economic or foreign policy plans. The aspiring president had in the 1980s been an ideological ally of prime minister Mir Hossein Mousavi who had stood in the way of any economic liberalization initiatives that Rafsanjani pursued at the time as the Speaker of the Majles. Rafsanjani soon overcame his reservations. While he still withheld an explicit endorsement, he did something more consequential. One week before the election day on May 23, 1997, Rafsanjani spoke about the dangers of fraud in the election. "There is no bigger sin than to steal the votes of the people."[36] It is impossible to know the significance of this intervention but what is known is that large-scale fraud had been feared by the Khatami campaign. The fact that the election was held in a relatively orderly manner on the day meant that Rafsanjani's sounding off alarm against fraud never got much attention at the time.

§

Khatami won against Nateq-Nouri in a landslide with just under 70 percent of the votes. In the 1997 vote, only 4 men were allowed to run while 234 candidates were disqualified as "unsuitable." While elections in Iran are highly regulated, the 1997 vote was notable for the genuinely high voter enthusiasm. About 80 percent of those eligible to vote did so. That was a reflection of the entrenching popular anger at the system in its entirety. The faint hope of his supporters was that Khatami could genuinely unclench the fists of the Islamist regime, which he himself had paradoxically belonged to since its birth in 1979. To the ordinary voter, unaware of the tug of war behind the scenes, Khamenei and Rafsanjani both epitomized the "regime" or as is referred to in Persian, *hakemiyat* ("the ruling class").

With his 20-million-strong voter support base, Khatami became the father of the newborn bloc called "reformists." He adopted a whole new vernacular about political change at home and in Tehran's dealings with the outside world. He spoke of empowering the people. He was cheered when he spoke about confronting "dictatorship." It was interpreted by the restless public not only as an attack on Khamenei but also as an attack on Rafsanjani. Few had any idea at the time that without Rafsanjani's tacit support a Khatami presidency might have never happened in the first place.

Khamenei had foreseen this turn of events but had ultimately been unable to prevent the rise of the "reformists." The voter enthusiasm for Khatami had deeply surprised Khamenei. His dilemma was hugely shaped by the fact that Khatami and his cohorts were hardly fringe elements that could be dismissed as counterrevolutionaries. Khatami and the other top figures in this new reformist movement had been the core of the so-called radicals in the 1980s. Not only had they been part of the Islamic Republic from the inception of the regime but they had a prior track record as the most devoted among Khomeini's supporters. Instead of crushing the leaders of the new reform movement, Khamenei could only belittle their agenda and fight it tooth and nail.

On foreign policy, he called them naïve if not clueless. "I wonder if the young people [who voted overwhelmingly for Khatami] have studied the last 150–200 years of Iranian history? To see what the West did to Iran?"[37] He felt this naïveté and Khatami's call for "dialogue among civilizations" was providing the Western adversaries of Tehran a backdoor option to return to Iran. Khamenei prepared agencies and resources under his control—from pro-Khamenei media to the Revolutionary Guards—to mobilize against the incoming Khatami government and its promise of transformational change.

As Khamenei was calibrating his approach to this new and popular reformist president, he might have found himself regretting not enabling Rafsanjani to amend the constitution in order to stay on as president. Khamenei and Rafsanjani had

had a litigious partnership-rivalry dating back to 1979 but it had been a contained competition and mostly took place behind the scenes. Khatami's challenge was different. His jabs at the shortcomings of the Islamic Republic were interpreted by Khamenei as targeting him personally in full public view. Khomeini was never publicly chided by regime figures insubordinate to him in the power pyramid. Khamenei was not about to accept anything less. In his mind, Rafsanjani was not as hard-pressed with the coming of his successor, president Khatami. On the contrary, Rafsanjani had plenty to be happy about. His gamble to help have Khatami elected soon paid off. Many of Rafsanjani's inner circle ended up in the new Khatami government, including taking over the cash cow, that is, the oil ministry. Not only had Rafsanjani helped bring about this new era of reformism but he began to also disassociate himself from Khamenei and the record of the Islamic Republic. He was in effect running away from his own record as he hoped the public's memory would be short.

Rafsanjani succeeded in seeing his acolytes secure majority of the cabinet seats in the Khatami government. The Iranian public's memory, however, proved to be long as far as his personal file and persona were concerned. During the entire two terms and eight years of the Khatami presidency, public opinion regarded Rafsanjani not as the man who yearned to be the antithesis to Khamenei. Instead, he was still the encapsulation of the Islamic Republic's worst sins. He was unconvincing as a reformer, and his reputation was blighted further when his associates, including family members, were periodically entangled in corruption scandals.[38]

For the grassroots reformist movement, both Khamenei and Rafsanjani deserved to be set aside for Iran to be able to move forward. Khamenei was in the crosshairs. He readied his supporters for a clash inside government institutions and in the streets. Rafsanjani, transfixed by the outpouring of popular support Khatami's reformist campaign had unleashed, looked for redemption. To his deep disappointment, the reform movement looked at Rafsanjani as the easier object for criticism. Being a regime elder was in itself no immunity and he had little capacity to strike back. It was a godsend of sorts for Khamenei as Rafsanjani took the bulk of the blows handed out by the reformist class. Khamenei was by now also excited he no longer needed to share the prime stage. In 1994, Ahmad Khomeini had died. And now Rafsanjani had vacated the presidency. Khatami could after all never be his equal in both political stature and biography. Khamenei admitted so much on national television on the day Khatami had been elected. "It makes no difference to me who is elected president. But, of course, no one [president] will ever be the same for me as Hashemi [Rafsanjani]. I hope the next president will be for the people what Rafsanjani was for me."[39] For now, both Khamenei and Rafsanjani pretended still to be inseparable despite evidence to the contrary.

§

In the realm of foreign policy, Rafsanjani departed the presidential palace after eight years with his ambitions largely unfulfilled. Despite the initial promise of softening the image of the Islamic Republic, and in fact making some headway early on, Tehran was still barely anymore respected on the international stage as when he had begun as president back in 1989. Some of the fault lay not with him but with the vindictive elements outside of his control in the regime that remained unapologetic for their diehard and pernicious beliefs. Just a few months before the end of Rafsanjani's presidency, an organization under Khamenei's control, the "15th Khordad Foundation," raised the bounty for the death of the British writer Salman Rushdie from $2 million to $2.5 million. Either Khamenei had little control as supreme leader over the vast political empire he had manufactured Or, alternatively, he was purposely sabotaging the president's agenda.

In 1989, both Khamenei and Rafsanjani had dithered when Khomeini issued his death sentence (in a religious decree or a *fatwa*) against Rushdie. A stonewalling Rafsanjani declared that if anyone killed Rushdie then "it should not be linked to the Islamic Republic of Iran" while Khamenei said at the time that it was possible for Rushdie to apologize and "people will pardon him."[40] And yet, in 1992, as supreme leader, Khamenei went on to reaffirm the same fatwa. He was by this stage busy consolidating his position and figured throwing some red meat at the most zealous supporters of the regime would do him good. Khamenei, knowingly or unwittingly, was insensitive to its impact on Tehran's international image. After the increase in the bounty in early 1997, a disenchanted Rafsanjani again indicated the 15th Khordad Foundation as a "non-governmental foundation" and said it was operating independently.[41] The statement was a shot at keeping up an appearance. Rafsanjani realized very well that without Khamenei's implied endorsement the foundation never had the gall to increase the bounty.

If Khamenei did so to undermine Rafsanjani's foreign policy legacy then he succeeded. But he dragged himself further down as well in the process. The Rushdie saga was only one element in an otherwise plummeting relations with Europe, which at the time comprised Tehran's primary trading partners and hopes for diplomatic rehabilitation. Shortly after, on April 10, 1997, a German court found four men guilty in the 1992 slaying of four Iranian, ethnic Kurdish, opposition members at the Mykonos restaurant in Berlin. The German judges had determined the assassinations had been ordered by a "Committee for Special Operations." Members of this committee were said to be Khamenei, Rafsanjani, Iran's foreign minister, Ali Akbar Velayati, and a handful of other senior Iranian officials.

A diplomatic crisis was inevitable. Berlin and Tehran expelled a number of each other's diplomats while the European Union suspended its "critical dialogue" with Iran.[42] This had been an initiative launched in 1991 to keep communications open in the hope of influencing Iran's policies. Of the fifteen EU states, only the ambassador of Greece stayed in Tehran. As the president of the Islamic Republic, Rafsanjani was embarrassed and undermined. Throughout the first half of the 1990s, Germany had not only emerged as a key European champion of dialogue with Tehran but German Chancellor Helmut Kohl had offered to mediate between Iran and the Americans. All that was now down the drain. But Rafsanjani was hardly blameless. Thirteen months earlier, Germany had issued an arrest warrant for Rafsanjani's intelligence minister, Ali Fallahian, for his role in the Mykonos killings.[43]

Rafsanjani did nothing but to stand by his controversial minister. He did not even attempt to give up Fallahian as the sacrificial lamb in order to mitigate against the highly costly diplomatic fallout. Rafsanjani put the regime's cohesion and continuity over looking at it as a chance to purge the Islamic Republic of its worst excesses. As with his performance during the US embassy hostage crisis in 1979, or his role in the Iran–Contra Affair in the mid-1980s, Rafsanjani did not speak up when it mattered the most. Then again, how could he? The opaqueness of policy making in Tehran; the propensity to put short-term narrow political goals over the long-term national interest; and dodging responsibility were as much the making of Rafsanjani's conduct as they were Khamenei's doing.

§

From the moment he left the presidency in 1997, Rafsanjani basically spent the next twenty years until his death in 2017 witnessing his political clout diminish and his record constantly coming under fire. He remained, though, very much eminent if not still celebrated by many of the regime's elite. For Khamenei, going forward, Rafsanjani had to therefore be handled with care. He was not just a book of knowledge about the inner workings of the regime, much of it still very inconvenient to Khamenei if it came out, but Rafsanjani's tentacles spread across every level of the political and bureaucratic setup. To prevent Rafsanjani from becoming a spoiler, Khamenei had no choice but to keep him close by. He kept him as the head of the Expediency Council, a body set up in 1988, to advice the supreme leader when there is disagreement and policy paralysis among the regime's institutions. Rafsanjani's image with the public ebbed and flowed, all depending on how he placed himself against the covetous, and increasingly unpopular, supreme leader, Khamenei.

Rafsanjani liked to tell Iranian media that Khamenei had once said he preferred to die if the choice was between himself and Rafsanjani. He claimed that he held the same stance vis-à-vis the supreme leader and that he would give his life for him. Such dramatics were impossible to believe and very few did. It became even harder to believe this tale of the inseparable union of the two men when Khamenei, despite his occasional public tribute to Rafsanjani, did nothing but only to stifle his old friend from ever again being able to return to the political center stage as someone equal to the supreme leader.

Figure 1 The Shah of Iran and Henry Kissinger. Photo by Keystone Pictures via Alamy.

The Shah of Iran and US Secretary of State Henry Kissinger in 1975. From 1941 to his downfall in 1979, the Shah was a close ally of the United States, a relationship he believed served Iran's national interests.

Figure 2 Ayatollah Khomeini in exile in Paris in 1978. Photo by GAROFALO Jack via Getty Images.

To the majority of those who supported Khomeini's anti-Shah movement, he was a man of God with little interest in politics. It was a colossal misreading of Khomeini's intentions.

Figure 3 Iranian women as militant Islamism's first victims. Photo by Bettmann via Getty Images.

Khomeinists quickly managed to mobilize much of the Iranian population against themselves. A policy of forced veil in public resulted in the first big protest movement against Khomeini. Militant Islamist intransigence was soon to transform Iran's relations with the world as well.

Figure 4 Israel, the first foreign target of Khomeinists. Photo by Kaveh Kazemi via Getty Images.

The Shah and Israel maintained cordial relations from 1948 to 1979. Iran's leftists and Islamists had many ideological differences but shared animosity toward Israel. El Al's offices in Tehran under attack in November 1978.

Figure 5 Rafsanjani, the Speaker of Majles (parliament), President Khamenei, and Prime Minister Mir Hossein Mousavi (standing next to Khamenei). Photo by Kaveh Kazemi via Getty Images.

Despite the public commitment to a militant foreign policy, by mid-1980s, Rafsanjani and Khamenei were behind-the-scene looking for ways to break Tehran's international isolation, including overtures to Washington.

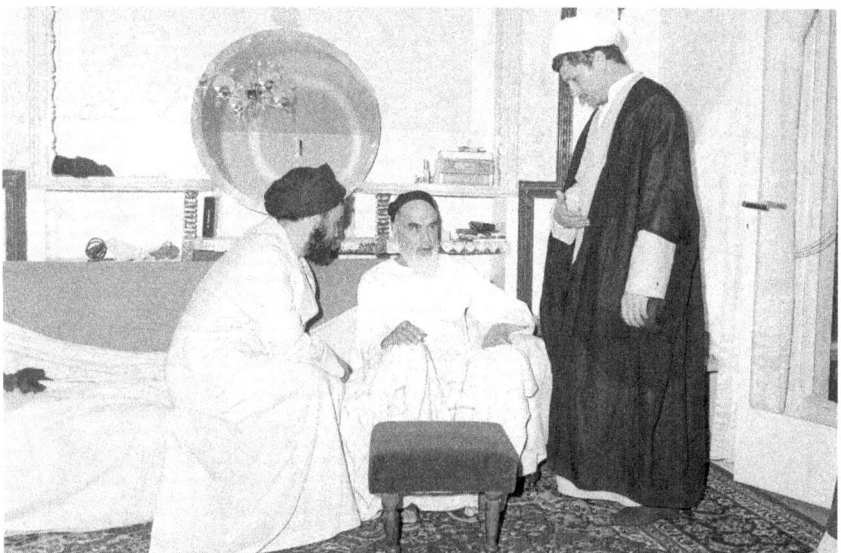

Figure 6 Rafsanjani and Ahmad Khomeini as gatekeepers to the old ayatollah. *Source*: Wikimedia Commons.

By 1986, Ayatollah Khomeini's closest advisors were his son, Ahmad, and Rafsanjani. They would go on to shape the succession process more than anyone else.

Figure 7 Rafsanjani and Khamenei. Photo by Kaveh Kazemi via Getty Images.

While as president (1989–97) Rafsanjani was mostly busy with an economic reconstruction agenda, Khamenei consolidated his control over military, security and intelligence agencies. Rafsanjani's shadow was on Khamenei as long as he lived but he was ultimately outplayed.

Figure 8 Mohammad Khatami. Photo by Bloomberg via Getty Images.

President Khatami secured two landslides election victories in 1997 and 2001. He never stood up to Khamenei. He was the greatest of disappointments to the reform movement. Seen here in 2007 with US Senator John Kerry at Davos.

Figure 9 Mahmoud Ahmadinejad. Photo by ATTA KENARE via Getty Images.

Mahmoud Ahmadinejad played the role of the obedient servant to Khamenei but had ulterior plans. A political opportunist, he stood up to Khamenei in ways no one had done.

Dithering in Tehran as the Cold War Ends 125

Figure 10 US Secretary of State John Kerry meets with Iranian Foreign Minister Javad Zarif in Vienna. Photo by KEVIN LAMARQUE via Getty images.

US Secretary of State John Kerry and Iran's Foreign Minister Javad Zarif in Vienna in January 2016. From 2013 until President Donald Trump withdrew from the 2015 Iran nuclear deal in May 2018, American and Iranian diplomats held rounds of face-to-face meetings. Such encounters had been very rare since 1979 but still failed to shift the trajectory of US-Iran relations.

Figure 11 Rouhani, Putin, and Xi. Photo by VYACHESLAV OSELEDKO via Getty Images.

Rouhani had wanted to move Iran closer to the West after the 2015 nuclear deal. But President Trump's "maximum pressure" campaign against Iran forced Tehran to instead deepen its relations with China and Russia. Khamenei was fully supportive since he never trusted the Western states.

Figure 12 Khamenei and the Revolutionary Guards. Photo by Anadolu Agency via Getty Images.

Immediately after the American assassination of General Qassem Soleimani in January 2020, Khamenei reiterated that Tehran would continue its regional agenda despite US warnings. The Khamenei-Revolutionary Guards alliance continues to be the cornerstone of hardline power in Tehran.

Map 1 Iran. *Source*: Alamy ID: H46D18.

Map 2 Iran and its neighbors. *Source*: Alamy ID: P6AYFT.

8

(1997–2005)—The Era of Reformist Hope: Rafsanjani under Fire; Khamenei Hits Back

> *I will treat whoever emerges as the winner from this ballot box the same way as I treated Hashemi Rafsanjani the last eight years [as president]. But for me personally, no one can be another Hashemi [Rafsanjani].*
>
> (Khamenei, May 1997)[1]

Mohammad Khatami had not anticipated to win the presidency on May 23, 1997. He had been reluctant to run, expecting Khamenei to do all he could to deprive him from a win at the ballot box. By some accounts, even Khatami's supporters told him he would not win. They told him that he could secure a few millions of votes and the election was sustenance for the cause of reform. The movement could then gradually strengthen and push back against Khamenei's devouring style of rule.[2] It only later emerged that Rafsanjani had done his bit for this nascent battle for reform. The night before Khamenei's weekly sermon, just two days before the elections, Rafsanjani paid Khamenei a visit. He told him that any expression of support for Nateq-Nouri would be seen by the pro-Khamenei circles—such as the Revolutionary Guards—as greenlighting election fraud against Khatami. Khamenei reluctantly accepted this reasoning, and in his sermon the following day he did not mention Nateq-Nouri by name. His anger was discerning. When Khatami's supporters branded Nateq-Nouri as an Iranian version of the Afghan Taliban, Khamenei interpreted it as an arrowhead aimed at him personally.

§

Khamenei viewed Khatami and the reform movement as an obstacle to his ultimate ambitions. Swords were drawn and in the next eight years and two-term Khatami presidencies, Iran witnessed a new battle for the soul of the regime. Khamenei and his supporters were pitted against a mixture of political forces pulled from various corners. Much of the energy came from disillusioned members of the system that believed only a major settling up with the past might save the Islamic Republic's future. The appeal of nonviolent gradual reform even attracted supporters who long ago had given up on the regime being remediable. Hence, the one thing that kept this reform movement together was a vague notion of the birth of Islamic Republic 2.0.

A startled Khamenei had to edge closer to his armed protectors in the Revolutionary Guards. This meant further distancing himself from his contemporaries among the politicized clergy, like Rafsanjani, who in greater numbers found the call of reform not only a public demand but prudent politics to survive. Khamenei could have jumped on this bandwagon but this was against his instincts not to mention his obstinate character that rarely changes course and holds a grudge. After all, the leading personalities of the reform movement—such as Khatami—had been a longtime critic of his. Ironically, during the 1980s it was Khatami and his close associates that had been starry-eyed about the ingredients needed to keep a political system sustainable. They had been the unabashed ideological puritans. Life, and a spirited Iranian civil society, eventually caught up with them and they mellowed. Khatami's personal transformation was the most shining example. As culture minister from 1982 to 1992, he evolved, ending up so tolerant toward licensing books, newspapers, and movie productions that he was ultimately forced to resign under pressure from the reactionaries.

He had, however, been less transformed over the years when it came to foreign policy. An avid reader of Western philosophy, as president he took great pains to distinguish between Western politics, which he invariably cast as imperialistic and overbearing, and Western civilization that he believed contained much good. He had briefly lived in West Germany in the late 1970s, as head of the Islamic Center in Hamburg, and enough for him to stop seeing the West as a forbidden fruit. As he put it, Western ideals of liberty and freedom are "the most cherished values for humanity in all ages" and in the West he saw societies that had "freed humans from the shackles of many oppressive traditions."[3] His predecessor, Rafsanjani, had never spoken in such elegant terms.

For Rafsanjani, the Islamic Republic's history had been greatly shaped by backroom deals. Invoking Western philosophy or alluring the civil society as a vehicle to power, in Rafsanjani's mind, was rather redundant and not serious endeavors. He failed to grasp that hard political power can emerge from appealing to basic aspirations and ideals of a population. He saw the slogans of reform as a means to him to pressure Khamenei to make concessions and share power. But reformism was not an end in itself, at least not to Rafsanjani. Despite the fact that he had been instrumental in enabling Khatami's election win, Rafsanjani chose to occupy the middle ground in the clash between Khamenei and the reform movement.

To Khamenei's supporters, Khatami was a revisionist. He took this insult as a badge of honor. To defend himself, he cited no other than Khomeini who once said "In Islamic government there should always be room for revision."[4] An anxious Khamenei, uncertain how to confront this election sensation, was determined to see Khatami not as an end to his ambitions but as a temporary hurdle. Khatami could, and did, slow Khamenei's plans but never had the slightest chance to stop him entirely. The institutional distribution of power in the Islamic Republic, which favors the unelected supreme leader over the elected president, was still left intact despite Khatami's epic election win in 1997. Khamenei used his control over the judicial and security forces to curb Khatami at every turn through arrest, harassment, and imprisonment.

§

Khatami and the reform movement were fully conscious of the troubles that lay ahead. Still, the earliest days of the Khatami presidency were the most sanguine and audacious. Support came not only from the streets but also from deep within the clerical corners upset about Khamenei's rule. Ayatollah Montazeri, who had been unceremoniously removed as deputy leader in 1989, for the first time publicly questioned the religious qualifications and hence legitimacy of Khamenei's ascent to the supreme leadership. Rafsanjani, true to form, stayed on the sidelines in what can only be described as another ignominious display of political survival instinct.

An indignant Khamenei arranged for Montazeri's offices to be stormed as he warned he would not put up with anyone questioning his reign. He called for charges of treason against Montazeri and put his old mentor under house arrest for the next five years. There were other examples of heavy-handed responses. Tehran's mayor, Karbaschi, was suddenly arrested and faced corruption charges by the Khamenei-controlled judiciary. His real ostensible transgression was his support for Khatami. Rafsanjani wrote an open letter expressing regret over Karbaschi's arrest but was unable, probably more like unwilling, to stick his neck out much more. Khamenei in turn said he was not willing to issue a pardon. He did, but seven months later. This was his way to let everyone know who is the boss.

On a formal level, a solution to this political impasse was to push for a quick amendment to the constitution to redistribute power in the system. President Khatami did in fact create a five-man committee to ensure implementation of Iran's constitution, which was a fainthearted move to squeeze Khamenei. But proper constitutional change was a far-fetched ambition that was occasionally aired but rarely pursued by the reformist leaders. Like Rafsanjani before him, Khatami opted not to grab the bull by the horns. When he did, it was lackluster performance. He pushed unsuccessfully to reduce the powers of the Guardian Council, the Khamenei-controlled body that has to approve all candidates and legislation. Behind the mask of the Guardian Council, Khamenei would go on to wield immense ability to micro-manage any state affair that he lay his eyes on. Khatami's supporters were disappointed but recognized that the popular president had no institutions with hard power—such as the military and security forces—at his disposal and hence no way to flex muscle.

But what was often omitted in analyzing Khatami's timidity was not political persuasions but personal constraints imposed on him due to his family's ties. The Khatami and Khamenei households are related through marriage.[5] This reality no doubt lowered Khatami's gusto for an all-out showdown with Khamenei. Instead, Khatami and his supporters turned to the public to generate more legitimacy as ammunition to push for change. In the midst of this campaign to win the hearts and minds of the people lay the battle for a freer press.[6] Pro-Khamenei and state-funded newspapers such as regime mouthpiece *Kayhan* were left in the dust as the reform movement launched dozens of papers with such names as "Participation" (*Mosharekat*), "New Dawn" (*Sobeh Emrooz*), and "Message of Freedom" (*Payam-e Azadi*).

Khatami knew the public was desperate for oxygen in the country's political discourse. He also knew that this project of increased freedom for the press was on borrowed time until the moment Khamenei felt uneasy about its direction. In due time, Khamenei did come out against the idea of a more lively and inquisitive press, which he called "press charlatanism."[7] By April 1999, Khamenei ordered the head of the judiciary, who he has the power to appoint, to close down about a dozen of reformist newspapers. The era of prying press fast closed, but Khamenei's onslaught against the reformist movement did not end there. The core of Khamenei's criticism was that the new and more inquisitive press that had been born with the coming of the Khatami presidency was giving rise to disillusionment. "Some of the press [in Iran] are platforms for the enemy," he said. "They are doing the work of the BBC, the Americans or the Zionists." By this he meant that the Iranian press had started to ask tough questions about the state of affairs in the country. He claimed a conspiracy, backed by foreign powers, was afoot.

Concepts such as press freedom, constitutionalism, and people power meant only one thing to Khamenei: him being stripped of the authority he had so dutifully amassed since 1989 as supreme leader. He was right. When the public was giving any leeway, it had chosen the most anti-Khamenei alternatives available to them. That was true for the presidency of Khatami as it was for the two parliamentary elections of 1996 and 2000. To stop this reformist front rising from the streets, Khamenei had to turn to hard power.

Khamenei, through his legion of appointees, charged the Khatami government with agitation and the abandonment of the principles of the 1979 revolution. Khatami's effort to derive legitimacy from the people was eventually bound to create a duality of power—the supreme leader and the president. Khamenei, though, had no intentions to share the center stage. In his worst nightmare, the reform movement was part of a vast Western scheme. He was said to keep a "Yeltsin list," reflecting his belief that the downfall of the Soviet Union had been achieved through American infiltration of the Soviet system. Those on the "Yeltsin list" were individuals within Iran's political system that had the potential, and maybe motive, to subvert the political order from within.[8]

It shaped his actions. In one example, unsure about the loyalty of the Ministry of Intelligence, Khamenei ordered the creation of a new organ, an intelligence organization under the control of the Revolutionary Guards. With this single step, Khamenei compounded the dilemma of rivalry among agencies under the auspices of the elected government pitted against those only answerable to the Office of the Supreme Leader. He appointed a junior cleric by the name of Hossein Taeb, in his early 30s at the time of his appointment, to lead the new force. Taeb was a confidant of Khamenei's second son, Mojtaba. He was the same man who a few years earlier had been tasked by the Office of the Supreme Leader to gather incriminating information about the Rafsanjani family. The return of Taeb, a ruffian who has since been sanctioned by the United States and the EU for human rights violations, was a prime example of how Khamenei believed he could see off the challenge of the reform movement by setting up new counterinstitutions managed by handpicked loyalists.

The generals at the Revolutionary Guards needed very little persuasion from Khamenei to go on the attack. The then head of the Guards, Yahya Safavi, called the reform movement a Trojan horse bent on diluting the militant Islamist revolutionary agenda to appease the West. "Can we withstand American threats and [America's] domineering attitude with a policy of détente? Can we foil dangers coming from America through dialogue between civilizations?"[9] In adopting the exact same catchwords uttered in the early 1980s when Khomeinists demolished any opposition, leaders of the Revolutionary Guards warned about the "liberals" (reform movement) and how the youth of Iran was at risk of indoctrination by Khatami's reform and West-obsessed government. This was more than a war of words. In a throwback to the anarchic early post-revolution days, political violence returned to the streets of Tehran. Pro-Khatami members of the parliament were heckled at the podium when defending the government. Two of Khatami's cabinet ministers were beaten up in the street by thugs linked to the Khamenei camp.

When Khamenei let his proxies loose against the president, Rafsanjani stayed more or less mute. As a regime elder, and still head of the Expediency Council, he had options to come to Khatami's aid but did not. Perhaps it was his revenge for pro-Khatami media rightly blaming him for cronyism. In any event, the time was yet not ripe for a partnership between Rafsanjani and the Khatami camp. The reformist camp, believing the ammunition they needed was the mandate from the people, made a blunder in not seeing Rafsanjani as a bulwark against Khamenei. They would come to regret it. Reformist attacks only tarnished Rafsanjani's image further. His inability to hit back was perceived as his declining sway. Khamenei was the real winner. In truth, though, Rafsanjani's regal style made it arduous to incorporate him in the reform movement's message of change. He did not fathom the optics of this new age. After his presidency, he moved into the Marble Palace, a confiscated Shah-era building that dripped in lavishness.[10] The overseer of the building was a foundation under Khamenei's control. But Khamenei had more sense than to turn down a request by a man who not only had assured him the supreme leadership but still could hurt him. Unlike the leaders of the reform movement, Khamenei kept Rafsanjani close at hand, if not appeased, for now.

Khatami Hoping for Better Fortunes Abroad

President Khatami faced similar impediments put in his path when it came to reorienting Iran's foreign policy. His hope was to build on Rafsanjani's limited foreign policy success from 1989 to 1997.[11] On the one hand, it took a lot of soul-searching within his camp since many of its most prominent figures had previously been deeply suspicious of the West under the omnibus flag of combating Western imperialism. Meanwhile, for Khamenei, the struggle to shape Iran's foreign policy was merely an extension of the ongoing struggle over the identity of the Islamic Republic, which at this point had been in power for some thirty years. At the very beginning of his presidency, Khatami had some leeway but it turned out to be short-lived.

§

On August 4, 1997, the day after he officially took over as president, Khatami reappointed Hassan Habibi as his first vice president. The position was mostly symbolic but the fact was Habibi had been Rafsanjani's vice president too and his reappointment signaled continuity of sorts. While Khatami removed Ali Akbar Velayati as foreign minister—a role he had held since 1981—he appointed Kamal Kharrazi as his foreign minister. Kharrazi was hardly a groundbreaking choice. He had lived in the United

States and was partly educated in Texas but he was also the son of an ayatollah. He had been Iran's top envoy at the UN during the Rafsanjani presidency from 1989 to 1997. On top of all of that, Kharrazi, as with Khatami, was also related to Khamenei through marriage.[12] With such political pedigree, and family ties, it is in hindsight perplexing that so much hope existed at the time about the Khatami government reversing course in foreign policy.

For the reform movement's grassroots, it was a disappointment. His supporters wanted big and bold measures as when he had refused in the campaign to express support for the death sentence against Salman Rushdie, and instead urged for détente with the United States.[13] Uncertain about Khatami, the Clinton administration was not yet ready to tango. As if to test Khatami's resolve, Washington on August 7 announced that it would penalize companies that spent $20 million or more a year in developing Iran's oil and gas fields instead of the $40 million originally stipulated in the Iran–Libya Sanctions Act that had been passed the previous year.

The case with Europe showed more promise. One month after the Americans tightened the sanctions regime against Iran, Kharrazi announced that EU ambassadors could return to Tehran "any time at their pleasure." They returned by November after a ten-month hiatus. Few days later, Khatami said during his first press conference that he hoped to establish a dialogue with the American people. It was a remarkable admission given the hostile history of Iran and the United States since 1979, but it was also a clumsy overture to officials in Washington.

Khamenei took no chances. Within a few weeks of the arrival of the new reformist government, he appointed the outgoing foreign minister, Ali Akbar Velayati, as his special advisor on foreign affairs. The message to Khatami was clear. The supreme leader, creating yet another office to curb the latitude of the government, was letting it be known that Velayati was his backchannel to foreign leaders. Velayati's frequent calls to Moscow, Beijing, or Damascus tallied well with Khamenei's dream of a world in which the West was less influential and Iran could tie its destiny to non-Western powers. As the highest elected official, Khatami had to do better than pursue illusions of a non-Western bailout for Tehran. All these years later, the elephant in the room was still the question of what to do with the United States.

Washington Sees an Iranian Cleric It Can Work With

The straitjacket that Iran's American policy was in was all too evident a few weeks later when Khatami gave his famous interview to CNN's Christiane Amanpour. He praised American history and culture, and came closest by any Iranian official to admitting regret over the seizing of the American embassy in 1979. "I do know that the feelings of the great American people have been hurt, and of course I regret it," he said in reference to the momentous event.[14] That interview also showed him not to be that apart from Khamenei in seeing the US government as inherently sinister and a source of instability around the world. He also conjured the idea of American impotence about Iran. "Certain foreign policy decisions of the US are made in Tel Aviv and not in Washington," he said without blinking. An editorial by the *New York Times* the following day called Khatami's criticism of US government policy to be "crude and rigidly ideological" and a missed opportunity for genuine dialogue.[15] This much was clear as Khatami squarely rejected direct talks with Washington, and all he could do was to propose cultural and educational exchanges.

Khatami's performance, ruling out talks with Washington but welcoming dialogue with the American people, was exactly the kind of wariness Supreme Leader Khamenei wanted to see as the regime in Tehran as a whole moved forward on this most sensitive of foreign policy files. It was a performance that made sense in keeping the Iranian regime boat steady; it made far less sense as a solid gesture to the Americans.

§

From the Clinton administration's perspective, embroiled as it was in the Monica Lewinsky crisis, it could have done without Tehran's hard-to-get performance. It was difficult to judge whether Khatami was a real force able to deliver change. He had the popular mandate, but Washington was aware that the president was not the ultimate voice in Tehran. Clinton responded in kind. In a message to the Muslim World broadcast by the Voice of America, he called for more cultural exchanges between Iran and the United States and that such exchanges would lead to better relations with Iran. The first-term Clinton presidency had begun with a barrage of sanctions against Tehran, unprecedented in scale up until that point. Clinton's second term (1996–2000), coinciding with Khatami coming to power, was more of a mixture but included plenty of people-to-people diplomacy. When an American wrestling team arrived in Tehran in February 1998 for an international wrestling competition, the US flag was displayed for the first time since 1979. Shortly after, Washington announced that it would ease the visa process for Iranians.

Washington also issued waivers to a number of international companies—such as France's Total, Russia's Gazprom, and Malaysia's Petronas—to carry out commercial energy projects in Iran. US Secretary of State Madeline Albright called on Iran to join the United States in drawing up a "road map" to normalize relations between the two countries. Echoing Robert McFarlane's frustrations, when he met with his unprepared Iranian interlocutors back in 1986, Washington wanted to forge ahead but Khatami had to pace himself. All Tehran would agree to were baby steps.

By the end of December 1997, Iranian and American officials sat together at a UN working group in New York on the future of Afghanistan under Taliban rule. And yet, as a regime, the Islamic Republic kept harking back to its radical roots. That same month, Tehran hosted the Organization for Islamic Conference (OIC).[16] As an expression of rejection of Iran's militant position on the Arab–Israeli conflict, most heads of states from Arab countries such as Egypt, Morocco, and Algeria did not attend the conference. But the presence of delegations from fifty-five Muslim-majority countries evidently made Khamenei feel leadership of the Islamic World was within his grasp. It merely required doses of anti-Americanism and strong denunciations of Israel.

A few weeks after the conference, Khamenei again ruled out any dialogue with Washington. Instead of staying silent, Khatami mimicked him in saying Iran would never again be "enslaved" by the United States. It was fast becoming apparent that Khatami, despite his big talk of "dialogue among civilizations," was far less daring than his predecessor, Rafsanjani, to put foreign policy dogma of the Islamic Republic to test. Khamenei set the tone, and the lower ranks dared not question his wisdom. In September 1998, Iran's Kamal Kharrazi even famously ducked out in the last minute at a UN meeting where the Americans had expected the first face-to-face meeting between him and Madeline Albright. And yet, the baby steps continued. Khatami welcomed the "change in tone" from Washington but said Tehran was waiting "for a change in [American] action." In the meantime, the fate of Khatami's economic plans—including securing foreign investment—very much depended on the outcome of this US–Iran dance.

The global investor community wanted to rush into the large and mostly untapped market but waited for the prompt from Washington. When the American and Iranian football teams met in France for the 1998 World Cup, sports diplomacy was at its peak. Iran won by 2-1 and Khamenei could not resist the temptation to revel. "I did not want to stay up and watch the game. It was late at night and time for me to go to sleep, but when I saw the opening minutes of the game [when Iran scored the first goal], I decided to watch it until the end." Later he kissed the forehead of the Iranian player who had headed his team to victory.[17] The episode was indicative about the deep grudge Khamenei still held against the United States. It was called the most political match in the history of the World Cup.[18]

Khatami, meanwhile, was still mostly talk and very little action. He asked for change in American actions but did not, or could not, do anything when a bus full of US businessmen came under attack by stones on an official visit to Tehran. They had been invited by his own government. The culprits, members of a small radical group called *Fedayeen Eslam*, were Khamenei loyalists. But they were never chastised by the supreme leader even as such actions clearly undermined Khatami's modest foreign policy pursuits.[19] Khatami could have come clean and admitted that the incident was rooted in the dichotomy that is the Islamic Republic.

Even Khamenei's own younger brother, Hadi, a reformist, was attacked at a mosque in Qom. There was more. Political violence, including assassinations of prominent critics of the regime, was again on the rise. A few weeks before the bus carrying American businessmen had been pelted with stones, prominent political dissident Dariush Forouhar was killed in his home along with his wife. Forouhar's offense, who had been a nationalist anti-Shah activist who once served in the interim government alongside Ali Khamenei, was to speak against the concept of a "Supreme Leader." In the weeks that followed Forouhar's killing, the bodies of more dissident writers and journalists were found. What would become known as the Chain Murders, some eighty individuals—from singers to political activists, from journalists to poets—were killed at the hands of the Ministry of Intelligence and other intelligence services. Some were killed in Iran, and some abroad. The common sin they shared was to question the political order. The paper trail was strong but the whole truth has never been allowed to come out. A key intelligence official involved, Saeed Emami, was scapegoated and said to have committed suicide in prison. The most senior figure to fall was Khatami's minister of intelligence. He merely lost his job but faced no charges. The political trajectory was crystal clear to anyone who cared to pay attention and Khatami pretty much acquiesced.

§

When Khatami was elected in 1997, the *Economist* magazine had a cover of him beaming with a smile. The headline read: "Iran's new face." The truth was the world desperately wanted the Islamic Republic to change but Khatami turned out to be a ruse. Khatami once told Mohsen Makhbalbaf, a famed film director, that "every ideological entity will come to an end and so will the Islamic Republic; I will no longer fight but will go back to my library to read." A baffled Makhbalbaf hit back: "But you read books to arm yourself against tyranny!"

In Iran's context, fighting tyranny meant only one thing above all else: standing up to Khamenei. This Khatami never really did. Instead, he traveled far and wide to market the illusion of an Islamic Republic under transformation. In the first trip by an Iranian leader to Europe since 1979, Khatami, the purported reformer from the East, told his Italian hosts in March 1999 that Iran is "choosing a new way." At the Vatican, the issue of Christian–Muslim relations and human rights in Iran were raised with Pope John Paul II. Khatami spoke in grand, promising terms, but detecting the long shadow of Khamenei over his every step was easy. Khatami dropped plans to visit Paris because his French hosts insisted on having wine, which is religiously forbidden in Islam, present during a state banquet at the Elysee Palace.

Khatami was not going to give his enemies in Tehran a free pass and dropped the banquet part of his state visit. The episode spoke volumes about his place in the pecking order in Tehran. The credibility of his "dialogue among civilizations" was badly bruised. Wine, merely present at the table in wine-mad France, was frowned upon at the same time as foreign female visitors to Tehran were required to veil up in respect of Islamic customs. The sanctimony aside, there were many other such cases of Khatami second-guessing, and humiliating, himself in this fashion at home and abroad only in the hope to prevent the wrath of Khamenei.

The ideological straitjacket was also a factor in Tehran's approach to the Arab World. As with his European trip, Khatami made history in May 1999 by being the first Iranian president to visit Saudi Arabia since 1979. A year earlier, Rafsanjani had led a major delegation to Riyadh to pave the way for the trip. The Saudis deemed Rafsanjani as a man they could work with.[20] There was euphoria. Crown Prince Abdullah even defended Iran's right to increase its military power. "All the countries of the world follow the same path," he told the London-based Saudi-owned newspaper *Asharq Al-Awsat*. "Why should a question be raised over Iran?" The olive branch was as unmistakable as it was generous but not everyone in Tehran heard, or wanted to hear, the message from Riyadh. That very same month, Tehran municipality, under the control of reformists, renamed a street that had been named after the 1981 assassin of Egypt's president Anwar Sadat. Cairo had made this renaming a precondition for any normalization in relations. Even then, pro-Khamenei activists blasted the reformists for betrayal. Such kneejerk objections were typical of those opposed to Khatami's presidency even as they themselves had little new to offer in terms of ideas to overturn the staleness of the regime.

For the Arab states, and particularly the oil-rich Persian Gulf states that looked to Washington for protection, it was the course of US–Iran relations that gave hint of Tehran's international rehabilitation. The state of affairs on this front remained decidedly uncertain. In May 1999, the Clinton administration dropped the designation of Iran as the leading state sponsor of terrorism. This was a few months after Tehran had once again renounced the death threat against Salman Rushdie, the British author. London had quickly restored full diplomatic ties with Tehran. Washington eagerly awaited Tehran's response. Iran's next move was, to put it mildly, discouraging.

Just a few short weeks later, intelligence services in the Iranian city of Shiraz arrested thirteen local Jews on charges of spying for Israel's Mossad and the Americans. The ancient Jewish community of Iran was in a daze when Khamenei supporters, such as the head of the judiciary, Ayatollah Mohammad Yazdi, called for their execution before a trial had even been held.[21] Khatami's response was scarcely reassuring. "Some people are using almost any method to ruin the plans of the government," he said. But he did not dare mention anyone by name. Those who had voted for him were again left disappointed.

The most common reading in Tehran was that the arrest of the local Jews was meant as a signal by Khamenei to Washington and others that he controls Iran, and Khatami's enthralling speeches should not be mistaken for ability to dictate policy. Once Khamenei had made his point, and after much international pressure, the thirteen Jews were gradually released and flown to Israel, the last ones leaving Iran in February 2003.[22] One of the key intermediaries, UN diplomat Giandomenico Picco, recalls how he over meetings kept pressing on Khatami about the damage to Iran's international image.

He found that "Khatami balanced protecting relations with the West with the limiting domestic political atmosphere." Such an observation suggested Khatami was under pressure but still the one calling the shots. There is, however, no palpable proof that Khatami had a hand in the manufactured crisis or its conclusion. But his subordination to Khamenei was never in question. Even then, when he was abroad and spoke about "dialogue among civilizations"—as he did in September 2000 with US Secretary of State Albright in the audience at the UN in New York—Khatami still mustered big crowds that admired his message of coexistence. For the Iranian public, it was his impotence that was impossible to miss.

Iran's "Deep State" Strikes Again

Khatami's reform agenda never really took off, and its certain death knell was unmistakable. On July 9, 1999, pro-reform students clashed with Ansar-e Hezbollah, another small group of pro-Khamenei thugs armed with clubs and knives. The students barricaded themselves in the dormitories and pleaded with Khatami to help. No help came, the dormitories were raided, and the student protest spread from Tehran to other cities. A week of unrest followed with a handful of deaths and hundreds arrested.

Khatami called the student protesters, who had essentially risked their lives for the sake of his reform agenda, a "threat to national security." The sense of betrayal was manifest yet another time. The images of young students from Tehran University, who had had to jump through many hoops to be admitted to this elite institution, being hit, kicked, and slashed were to date the most graphic illustration of who held power in the Islamic Republic. Khatami was wrong in thinking he had covered himself politically by not standing on the side of the students. Once the dust settled, Khamenei still chose to disarm Khatami even more.

§

The July 1999 protests only reaffirmed that Khatami's election in 1997 had not overturned the fundamental dynamics that guide the system. None of the personalities the students had hoped for a helping hand came to their rescue. Khatami bailed on them. Rafsanjani, the regime elder who could have intervened and was begged by the students, remained hush. A certain Hassan Rouhani, who was then still the head of the Supreme National Security Council (SNSC), even threatened to crush the students "mercilessly and monumentally" if they "dare to show their faces."[23] In the moment of truth, the regime as a whole had closed ranks.

The protests happened exactly ten years after Khamenei had become supreme leader. It was a wake-up call for him as much as anyone else. When the angry protesting students burned his pictures, he must have relived the scenes of 1979. Only this time it was Khamenei's, and not the Shah's, pictures that were burnt in the streets. There was no sign of remorse on his part, however. "If they tear up my pictures, do not do anything," said a crying Khamenei at a Friday sermon. "I have a crippled and feeble body but am ready to sacrifice it for the sake of the revolution," he wept.[24] This political theater was to reassure his minions that he was still in the game, and for the long haul. In the days and weeks that followed, the arrested protesters suffered some of the worst beatings, and more, handed out to political protesters since the early 1980s.

It was also in July 1999 that Khamenei's armed protectors from the Revolutionary Guards arrived on the political scene in an inconspicuous way and on equivocally the side of Khamenei. During the protests, rattled as they were, twenty-four top commanders from the Guards wrote a letter to Khatami and gave him an ultimatum. He should end the protests fast, or the Guards would take matters in their own hands. The letter was to put Khatami on notice and humiliate him in the process. After all, the Guards did not need Khatami's blessing to crack down in the streets, which they had done from the very beginning of the protest.

This was the moment for the Guards to flex their political muscle. This they did in matters pertaining to not only domestic but also foreign and economic policy. Soon after, when Khatami introduced his first five-year economic plan, which called for a "total restructuring" of the economy, the Guards grumbled. Thanks to their political clout, they had already become the country's largest conglomerate with various ownerships of economic enterprises in such fields as construction, telecommunication, and energy. When president Rafsanjani had a decade earlier opened the door to the Guards entering the economic realm, his hope had been it would be a distraction from politics. He had never in his wildest dreams foreseen the Guards' appetite. That was a colossal underestimation. The Guards were even emerging as Tehran's principal decision-makers in regard to regional affairs. In volatile places like Afghanistan or Iraq, it was the Guards and its arm on foreign operations—the Quds Force headed by General Qassem Soleimani—that called the shots. The Khatami-controlled Foreign

Ministry was already frequently on the backburner. Opportunities for the Guards to expand their regional operations only grew in the coming years with the US invasions of Afghanistan and Iraq in 2001 and 2003, respectively.

§

In one of the last parting shots at diplomacy by the Clinton administration, US Secretary of State Madeline Albright told an audience at the Asia Society in Washington, DC, in May 2000 that the United States was ready for normalization of relations. Iran, she said, is "what much of the world reasonably considers to be the center of the world." It might have worked if she had targeted her adulation at Khamenei. She did the opposite. "Respected clerics speak increasingly about the compatibility of reverence and freedom, modernity and Islam. An increasingly competent press is emerging despite attempts to muzzle it," she said. The collective reaction in Tehran to the speech was one of surprise. The thinking among Iranian officials was if this was a trick and what the Americans were up to.[25]

Albright's Jewish background made the Iranians even more skeptical of her intentions. As Albright later wrote in her memoirs, the Iranians "thought the influence of American Jews was too strong [in Washington] to permit real flexibility in the U.S. position" on Iran, in other words, that the road to US–Iran reconciliation travels through Tel Aviv, and the Iranians were not ready to embark on that journey. Obsession with the role and power of American Jewry aside, which was always a subject of interest to the leaders of the Islamic Republic, Khamenei had more personal grounds to be worried.

From Albright's remarks, it was not hard to guess who was doing the muzzling in Tehran. "As in any diverse society, there are many currents swirling about in Iran. Some are driving the country forward; others are holding it back. Despite the trend towards democracy, control over the military, judiciary, courts and police remains in unelected hands, and the elements of its foreign policy, about which we are most concerned, have not improved." But, she added, "the momentum in the direction of internal reform, freedom and openness is growing stronger." Albright had probably no idea but she had just sharply undermined the cause of reform in Iran, or what was left of it. She had in essence divided the ruling clerics in Tehran into "good" and "bad" ones.

Khatami and his reform movement were the good guys. Khamenei and his Revolutionary Guards constituted the bad guys.[26] That speech sent shivers down the spine of Khamenei. He hinted that the United States, which in his view had engineered the rise of Mikhail Gorbachev and his programs of Glasnost and Perestroika only to bring about the collapse of the Soviet Union, might want to pull off the same trick in Iran. He had his reasons to believe such a scenario. Back in 1996, a year before Khatami's election, Thomas Friedman of the *New York Times* had rhetorically asked in his column "What produces a Mikhail Gorbachev?" In the case of Iran, Friedman claimed, change in Iran "was not going to come by the Shah's son riding back on a white horse to oust Iran's Islamic leadership." He continued: "No, if Iran is to become the more pragmatic, fully law-abiding member of the world community that the West seeks, it will only be because an Iranian Gorbachev emerges from the Muslim leadership that now thoroughly dominates this nation and is able to forge a more moderate, but still Islamic, course from within."[27]

Khamenei knew, of course, that Friedman's column had been a product of a visit he had just earlier made to Tehran. He wondered who this prominent, and Jewish, American columnist had met on his trip. To Khamenei, Khatami, whether he knew it or not, was the Islamic Republic's "Ayatollah Gorbachev," as Friedman had forecast Iran would one day see. In a speech two months after Albright's gesture of peace in May 2000, Khamenei basically claimed that Khatami was credulous if he believed he can control the momentum of the reform movement.[28] In Khamenei's mind, if Khatami was Gorbachev, the Americans were determined to introduce a figure like Boris Yeltsin into the political stage in Tehran to finish off the Islamic Republic once and for all.

As expected, Khamenei threw a wrench into the yet-to-deliver US–Iran détente that had slugged forward since 1997. He berated those pushing for resuming diplomatic ties with Washington as either "simpletons or traitors." Albright had only reinforced Khamenei's belief that the Islamic Republic he wished to govern required anti-Americanism as a pillar of its dogma. At the UN General Assembly in New York in 2000, president Clinton stayed after his speech and listened to Khatami's speech. The American president had hoped for an impromptu exchange of words with Khatami, but the latter chose to hide in a bathroom in the UN building to avoid a handshake that could haunt him back home.[29] Even simple steps, as when the United States asked for permission to engage in consular cooperation, were rejected by Tehran in the months that followed before the election victory of George W. Bush in November 2000.

The shamefaced Iranian president told a group of students that he lacked the power to implement his vision of a "democratic Islamic system." "Every nine days a new crisis is manufactured for my cabinet!" In any other political model that was even remotely representative of the popular will, this confession should have been followed by a resignation as an expression of ultimate despair. Khatami had secured 70 percent of the popular vote in 1997 but his reform train had still not left the station. The Iranian voters still remained desperately hopeful that gradual reform is possible within the parameters of the Islamic revolution. In the February 2000 Majles elections, reformist candidates managed another grand slam: of 290 seats, 222 were picked up by Khatami's reformist allies. In his reelection bid in 2001, Khatami himself secured even more popular support, almost 77 percent of the vote. Reform, however, was not to be. Khamenei stuck to his game plan of obstructing anything substantive that the reform movement sought to implement. That was true for domestic as it was for foreign policy.

§

During Khatami's years of playing cat and mouse with Khamenei, Rafsanjani mostly waited around but he was still very much a voice to be reckoned with. The bifurcation of power in the Islamic Republic, and frequent policy paralysis, did not eliminate entirely the requirement for the occasional collective regime judgment. When the anti-Iran Taliban killed a number of Iranian diplomats and Revolutionary Guards' officers in the Afghan city of Mazari Sharif in 1998, there were those in Tehran that suggested an invasion of Afghanistan to punish the Taliban. In this case, Rafsanjani came out to warn the Revolutionary Guards about the consequences of a new war. He knew all too well from his Iran–Iraq war experience that military conflicts are like quicksand. At a public level, as the head of the Expediency Council, Rafsanjani pledged "revenge." Behind the scenes he pushed for restraint. The collective verdict from the Supreme National Security Council was to stay out of Afghanistan. It was said to be easy to go into that country but impossible to know how to come out again.

Still, Rafsanjani was not content with merely playing the role of the behind-the-scene elder statesman. He had plenty of political appetite left in him and wanted to move back to the center stage. Rounds of humiliation awaited him. The first one came in February 2000. He ran as a parliamentary candidate, hoping he could return to his old job as the Speaker of the parliament. In the event, this once most powerful of men in the Islamic Republic received the fewest votes in his district in Tehran. Humiliated, he gave up on the seat when rumors swirled around even the authenticity of the number of votes he claimed he had secured.

Khamenei was not bothered. He did nothing to help Rafsanjani in his bid for a mere seat in the parliament. They might have both been in the firing line of the reform movement but that did not mean Khamenei wanted to see the return of Rafsanjani as he had after all a claim to be his coequal regardless of the office he held. In the previous year, in 1999, Khamenei had published a volume of his memoirs. It was hardly warm toward Rafsanjani. Here, while Khamenei very generously refers to himself as a "grand ayatollah," he could not bear calling his once-promoter an "ayatollah," a junior title. Khamenei had no more religious qualifications but that was not the point. Khamenei by now had amassed the greatest power inside the regime. He had no intention to allow Rafsanjani to return.

As far as the outside world was concerned, given his fears, if not paranoia, Khamenei continued to prioritize the non-Western world. He thought he would be a fool if he did not look at the fate of the Soviet Union to make sure the same did not befall the Islamic Republic. "Through an intelligent 3–4 year plot, spending some funds, buying off some people, and using propaganda, the Americans could destroy the Soviet Union over last 6–7 months [of its existence]," Khamenei claimed. This was said in a speech he gave shortly after Vladimir Putin had been elected president in May 2000.[30] Putin would become a frequent visitor to Khamenei in the years to come. In time, Khamenei would even ban criticism of Russia in Iranian school books.

Another frequent visitor to Tehran was Syria's Bashar Al Assad who took over from his late father in July 2000. The Iranian–Syrian relationship dated back to 1979 but it was always a marriage of convenience. During a visit to Syria in 1999, Khatami had asked his Syrian hosts to repay Tehran for years of financial assistance. The Syrians stalled and only agreed to return Iran's money in the form of Syrian pounds and only if it was to be invested in Syria or used to purchase Syrian goods. The Syrians knew they could be scornful toward Khatami because Khamenei needed Damascus' cooperation to keep a lifeline open to Hezbollah in Lebanon, which was by now one of Khamenei's most prized foreign policy projects. It boiled down to opposing the United States and Israel, and Khamenei's drive to establish partnership with similarly anti-American entities in distant lands.

With Khamenei's blessing, the likes of Hugo Chavez of Venezuela, Daniel Ortega of Nicaragua, or Evo Morales of Bolivia would be as welcome foreign dignitaries in

Tehran in the 2000s as Yasser Arafat of Palestinian Liberation Organization (PLO), Muammar Qaddafi of Libya, or Cuba's Fidel Castro had been welcomed in the 1980s and 1990s. To Khamenei, participating in any international anti-American parade was never really about foreign policy as an instrument to advance the national interests of Iran. It was about him, and protecting the Islamic Republic, as he wanted it to be, from a certain downfall if the United States were given a free hand to do as it liked. In his mind, all American overtures to Tehran were smokescreen for that ultimate objective.

The 9/11 Attacks and Iran Included in the "Axis of Evil"

Mohammad Khatami's second term, which began in August 2001, coincided with the Al Qaeda terrorist attacks on the United States in September 2001. The Iranian public sentiment was undoubtedly on the side of the grieving Americans, with spontaneous mass vigils held in Tehran. The tragic events were also an opportunity for the United States and Iran to hit the reset button. The George W. Bush government soon after launched the "War on Terror," a mighty endeavor with no expiration date or limited to any geographic boundaries. Unsurprisingly, the US interventions in Afghanistan in late 2001 and in Iraq in March 2003 generated much anxiety in Tehran about whether Iran was on the list to be the next American target.

In both the US interventions in Afghanistan and in Iraq, Tehran played a cautious double game. It has never been clear, though, if this was by design or merely a result of the policy rift among factions in Tehran. On the one hand, Tehran condemned the United States for its use of military force in the Muslims countries. "Islam condemns the massacre of defenseless people, whether Muslim or Christian or others, anywhere and by any means," Khamenei said in his first public reaction to the 9/11 attacks. "Based on the same principle, Iran condemns a possible attack on Afghanistan which could lead to another human catastrophe."[31]

Behind the scenes, Iranian intelligence services handed all the intelligence they saw fit to the Americans with the aim of bringing about the destruction of the Taliban. Ambassador James Dobbins was the Bush administration's point man to bring about the new post-Taliban order in Afghanistan. At the meetings that culminated in the 2001 Bonn Declaration, the Iranians reached out to him directly, which did not surprise Dobbins.[32] Tehran was ecstatic about a new beginning in Afghanistan. His Iranian counterpart, a younger diplomat by the name of Javad Zarif, was part of the Khatami government. The real tangible benefit the United States secured from Iran was intelligence on the Taliban, including the location of its bases, which the US air force proceeded to raze to the ground once identified. That intelligence-sharing was overseen by Qassem Soleimani who was head of the Quds Force, the branch of the Revolutionary Guards that operate outside of Iran's borders. Such tactical information-sharing turned out to be easy. This moment, however, was not to become a bigger political opening. Neither Washington nor Tehran was ready. Zarif's description to Dobbins about the possibility of broadening the dialogue was precisely accurate. "After all, Jim, we are both way out ahead of our instructions on this issue, aren't we?" the Iranian diplomat said.

US secretary of state Colin Powell sent Ryan Crocker to meet with the Iranians in Geneva. According to David Crist, "as a cover, the Italians and Germany were included to avoid the appearance of direct talks."[33] In Tehran, this subtle collaboration, with exchanges of information in hotels in Europeans capitals in late 2001, was believed to buy Iran time if not lead to easing of tensions between Tehran and Washington. But the Iranians pushed back when the Bush administration publicly scolded Iran. For the revolutionary Islamic Republic, it was about balancing against any rash US action versus keeping up an appearance. When president George W. Bush on January 10, 2002, warned Tehran to "contribute in the war against terror" and support the post-Taliban Afghan government of Hamid Karzai or else, even Rafsanjani had to respond. He called Bush's warnings "rude and impudent" and said such tough talk was "counterproductive."

Bush had also asked Tehran to hand over the Al Qaeda members it had captured fleeing Afghanistan after the US invasion. But those Al Qaeda members were not in the custody of the Khatami government but in the hands of the Revolutionary Guards. The captured Al Qaeda members were chips the Guards wanted to hang onto and cash them only at a future opportune moment. Given the depth of mistrust in US–Iran relations, it made more than good sense as any foreign policy realist will concur. The anti-US voices in Tehran soon felt vindicated. A few weeks of US–Iranian tactical cooperation over Afghanistan was not about to wash away the bad blood. On January 29, 2002, in his first State of the Union speech since the 9/11 attacks, George W. Bush labeled Iran as part of an Axis of Evil. The other two states were Saddam's Iraq and North Korea.

Khatami had not seen it coming. He called Bush's speech "bellicose and insulting" and him a "warmonger." On a political level, Bush's "Axis of Evil" speech no doubt enhanced Khamenei's position. Khatami again reiterated that he had no intention to negotiate with the Americans over Khamenei's head. He asked the supporters of the reform movement to abide by Khamenei's guidance and policy preferences. But Tehran was rattled by Washington's "War on Terror" and what it possibly meant for Iran. Tehran quickly vowed it would never seek nuclear weapons for any reason. Defense Minister Ali Shamkhani said a nuclear arms race in the Middle East was hardly in Iran's interest. On the question of Afghanistan, the Iranians soon after closed down the operations of an anti-US Afghan faction leader, Gulbuddin Hekmatyar. The Hezb i-Islami leader, who had lived in Iran for several years, had denounced the interim post-Taliban government in Kabul as illegitimate and he was expelled from Iran about a month after Bush's speech.

How Iran ended up in George W. Bush's Axis of Evil is still a bit of a mystery. The American scholar Kenneth Pollack has argued that Iran might have just been "road kill" in this instance. "Iran was just a prop needed to make a point—the [Bush] speech writers had come up with a great line and they needed a third country to make up the Axis."[34] That might have well been the case but a number of conspicuous events did lead up to Tehran's designation by Bush. Just a few weeks earlier, on January 3, the Israelis stopped an Iranian vessel in the Red Sea by the name of "Karin A." Inside the vessel, weapons were found and the Israelis claimed it was bound for militant Palestinians in Gaza. Within a span of a handful of months after the 9/11 attacks, US–Iran relations went from clandestine intelligence cooperation against the Taliban to the Bush White House asking American nuclear war planners to include Iran as part of a potential target for the Strategic Command's mission.[35] The reversal of fortunes was as swift as it was serious.

§

For Khamenei, the lesson was clear: the United States is not to be trusted. The Khatami government was far more unsettled on what to do with the United States. It continued to prod and jab away at the American question. Taboo topics were not beyond reproach, including the issue of Israel. Khatami's vice president, a cleric by the name of Abdollah Nouri, spoke for the Iranian people when he boldly asked, "Who are we [Iran] to be in the way if Israelis and Arabs want to have peace?" "When the world pushes for diplomacy and we argue for militant resistance, no wonder the world labels us a terrorist regime." This was a plea for the Islamic Republic to quit its quest to be the self-appointed guardian of the Palestinians. Nouri was throwing a wrench in the regime's ideological machinery, but Khatami's role was unclear. He himself certainly never uttered such fearless sentiments even if he deemed Nouri to have a point. In due time, Nouri was sentenced by a Special Clerical Court, under the control of Khamenei, to prison for his taboo-breaking viewpoints.

Tehran continued to hold secret talks with the Americans but it followed the same clandestine approach each time this had been tried before since 1979. Hence, the Khatami government denied holding talks that was evident to everyone. To feign ignorance, Khatami would order his intelligence minister to investigate whether Iranian and US officials had held any secret talks. On the public level, in an effort to protect its image and its final say over policy decisions, the Khamenei camp manufactured its own pantomime. The Khamenei-controlled judiciary banned the media from reporting any possible talks between the United States and Iran. The edict was about preserving the pecking order in Tehran. It emphasized that all key foreign policy decisions are directed by Supreme Leader Ayatollah Ali Khamenei.

The Bush administration was far less inclined to go along with this charade put up by Tehran than had been the case with the Clinton administration. In July 2002, the White House announced that it had decided to halt overtures to Khatami. Bush's advisors told him Washington was better off appealing directly to the Iranian opposition and raise the specter of possible American support for regime change in Tehran. Khatami's second term (2001–5) foreign policy agenda was to be hugely undermined by pressure from Washington. The unfolding Iran nuclear crisis was soon to be a major aspect of the escalation in tensions. In January 2000, the CIA, in a "sharp departure from its previous assessment of Iran's nuclear capacity," had informed the Clinton White House that Iran might be able to make a nuclear weapon. In Washington, the new evaluation touched off a debate about Tehran's nuclear capacity and the CIA's ability to monitor it.[36]

It was after Bush came to office, and after his inclusion of Iran in the "Axis of Evil," that the Americans decided to openly squeeze Tehran in regard to her nuclear ambition. In August 2002, the anti-Khomeinist MEK opposition group held a press conference in Washington, DC, and revealed that Iran had secretly been working on two nuclear-related sites in Natanz and Arak.³⁷ The information had very likely not been collected by the MEK. They were only tapped by the CIA and Israel's Mossad to deliver the news to the world.³⁸ In late February 2003, just a few weeks before the United States invaded Saddam's Iraq on March 20, 2003, a group of UN inspectors visited Natanz, a nuclear enrichment center. American officials were quoted in the press to claim the UN findings about Iran's nuclear advances to be "startling" and "eye-opening."³⁹ Tehran had not been legally obliged to inform the UN about the Natanz plant until it was operational, which it was not at the time, but the international impression was that it had been caught red-handed.

The Iranians were far less concerned about their international image than avoiding giving ammunition to a combative Bush White House that Tehran deemed to be looking for a pretext to go after Iran once its invasion of Iraq was complete. What followed was an offer of peace from Tehran, which had support from president Khatami and some of Supreme Leader Khamenei's closest confidants if not himself. Dubbed a "grand bargain," Tehran sent a two-page fax to the US Department of State through the Swiss government, the country that has represented US interests in Tehran since official diplomatic rupture between the two countries in May 1980. It was an offer of broader dialogue between Iran and the United States on a long list of issues. "In essence, the proposal was a peace treaty to end hostilities between the two states," Iran's former ambassador to Germany, Hossein Mousavian, observed.⁴⁰ Tehran was offering to address US concerns ranging from Iran's nuclear intentions to its support for terrorism, including revisiting its military support for Hezbollah, and a pledge to stop acting as a spoiler in the Arab–Israeli peace process.

When news leaked about the infamous fax, both the American and the Iranian sides were reluctant to admit to it. As so many times before in this tormented relationship, each side feared damage being done to their image if an impression of weakness was given. There is to this day a disagreement about whether Khamenei himself knew the details of the fax as was claimed by the American press.⁴¹ In Tehran, there are still those who claim that Khamenei had not seen the offer before it was given to Washington. This is unlikely for two main reasons. Khamenei is a micro-manager and no other issue has mattered to him as much as relations with the United States. Moreover, the fax that arrived in Washington on May 4 was only the last version of three drafts that the Americans and the Iranians had been exchanging in the weeks before. The key individuals who oversaw the operation on the Iranian side were Foreign Minister Kamal Kharrazi; his nephew, Sadeq Kharrazi, who was Iran's ambassador to Paris; and Javad Zarif, who was at the time Tehran's ambassador at the UN in New York. All three men are so close to Khamenei that the suggestion that they had exchanged three drafts of a "grand bargain" with the Americans without keeping Khamenei in the loop is unimaginable.⁴²

The Americans never officially responded. There was apparently doubt about how sincere Iran was or how far it was willing to go in its concessions. National Security Advisor Condoleezza Rice had not been sure. "We had people who said, 'The Iranians want to talk to you,' lots of people who said, 'The Iranians want to talk to you,'" she later testified. "But I think I would have noticed if the Iranians had said, 'We're ready to recognize Israel.' … I just don't remember ever seeing any such thing."⁴³ In any event, it was another missed opportunity. Next it was Tehran's turn to doubt the intentions of the Americans. In early January 2004, following a deadly earthquake in the ancient town of Bam, the United States offered to send a delegation to Iran as part of a relief operation. It was to be led by US Senator Elizabeth Dole. Her seniority was probably what gave the Iranians cold feet. The fact was that on December 30 two US C-130 military aircraft, with some two hundred personnel and 150,000 pounds of medical supplies, had landed in Iran.[44] Refusing Senator Dole's request should not have been a surprise to anyone who had spent tracking the number of times Tehran was second-guessing itself about what the Americans were really up to. Then again, the Iranians very likely felt they had good reasons to question the dispatch of an American senator to Iran only a few months after Washington had snubbed Tehran's offer of a "grand bargain."

Khamenei never publicly hinted of his approval for any change in direction vis-à-vis the United States. The manager of a government-affiliated think tank was jailed on charges of spreading lies after his agency published an opinion poll showing broad public support for a dialogue with the United States.[45] All such die-hard steps fitted nicely when considering Khamenei's aversion to the United States had only risen over the years. If change was to come on the question of what to do with the Americans, it would not be the sentiment in society that led the way. That would, after all, set a dangerous precedent. Only Khamenei could change course if conditions ever allowed for it. The future of US–Iran relations was seen by him and his supporters in the hard-line camp to be intimately tied to the future of the Islamic Republic itself. When this basic reality was disputed, a steady burst of charges was hurled at the Khatami government: they were said to be looking at building ties with the United States as part of the ultimate mission of turning Iran into a secular state.[46]

The Rise of Iran's Militant Proxy Model in the Middle East after 2003

As the Bush administration's War on Terror in the Middle East took root across a number of theaters, the Khatami government and the Khamenei–Guards partnership went in different directions. It was as much destined due to the institutional division of labor in the system as it was a reflection of the different priorities of dominant factions in Tehran. Khatami and his foreign ministry had to crack on with tackling the consequences of international trepidation about Iran's nuclear program. That was a protective, or preventative, exertion. Tehran desperately wanted to avoid its nuclear file ending up at the UN Security Council for arbitration.

The Guards, on the other hand, had a different focus. They assessed the power vacuums that had resulted from the US military interventions in the Middle East, specifically in Iraq, as a once-in-a-lifetime opportunity to reinvigorate the Shia Islamist revolutionary spirit. Besides, by helping to bog down the Americans in Iraq Tehran could tie America's hands if it ever chose to go after Iran. The Guards, and Khamenei who wholeheartedly backed his project, deemed this course of action as imposed on them by the Americans. After the United States invaded Afghanistan in 2001, the collective mood in Tehran was to give cooperation with Washington a chance. It was also very much self-serving. President Bush's January 2002 "Axis of Evil" speech did not change this basic reality: if the Americans were about to remove any of the regional foes of Iran, why stand in their way? In the same way Tehran helped in thrashing the Taliban, it organized for pro-Iran Iraqi Shia political–militant groups, such as the Badr Corp, to play their part in the US-led mission to remove Saddam from power. Once that mission was complete, with Saddam's capture in December 2003, the Revolutionary Guards shifted gear and set out to create a quagmire situation for the US military in that country. Washington's long-term goal to establish a pro-American rule, perhaps even a democratic one, in Iraq could only represent a dangerous counter-model to the Islamic Republic.

The Guards were adamant that Shia-majority Iraq, where Tehran's historic and political ties run deep, was Iran's backyard and not to be made into a research lab for the Bush administration's doctrine of spreading democracy around the Middle East. While Khamenei let the Guards loose in Iraq to bog the Americans down, and create post-Saddam's Iraq in the mirror image of the Islamic Republic, Khatami's ailing effort at democracy in Tehran was all but crumbling.

§

The eight-year-long presidency of Mohammad Khatami was the beginning, and the end, of political reform in the Islamic Republic. Khatami did not become Iran's Gorbachev. He secured more popular votes than anyone before or after him. Still, he tiptoed around standing up to Khamenei and never really did so in any fundamental way. His heart was not in it. He repeatedly declared himself not only loyal to the Islamic Republic but Khamenei as the ultimate source of power. It was a colossal letdown for anyone who had vested any hope in him. The reform movement had had big ideas: to weaken Khamenei's powers or those of the Guardian Council; to neutralize the Revolutionary Guards as a political predator by merging it with the regular armed forces; to enable for a freer press; and to show a new face to the world beyond. None of these measures succeeded as they were never truly pursued.

On the other side, Khatami's big election wins in 1997 and 2001, and the landslide win by reformist parliamentary candidates in 2000, convinced Khamenei that he needed to invest more in the parallel structures of power to render reformist politicians effectively powerless. In that, Khamenei was very successful, so much so that the public by and large lost any hopes in gradual nonviolent reform. But despite the deep public anger, Iran was not yet in a prerevolutionary phase. This generation of Iranians was far more prone to apply for a visa to a Western country and abandon the homeland than to risk their lives by speaking truth to power. The unflagging Khamenei set his eyes on the post-Khatami era with all his guns blazing. If the reform movement's power came through the ballot box, Khamenei was determined to choke it then and there. He ordered the Guardian Council, his filter and firewall to screen out candidates and policies he did not approve, to show no mercy. In the 2003 and 2004 elections for city councils and the national parliament, reformist candidates were overwhelmingly barred from running, paving the way for pro-Khamenei figures.

One relatively unknown populist personality, who at first proclaimed his out-and-out loyalty to Khamenei, was a diminutive man by the name of Mahmoud Ahmadinejad.

He became the mayor of Tehran in 2003, his trebuchet to the presidency in 2005. The Khatami government was suspicious of him and had sought to prevent his mayorship on grounds that he was a questionable character. But Khamenei's entourage in the Office of the Supreme Leader intervened and Ahmadinejad was appointed mayor by Tehran City Council.[47] Khamenei's support for Ahmadinejad was unmistakable and his reasons would soon become clear. In the 2005 presidential elections, Khamenei and the Revolutionary Guards came all out in his support. For presidential candidate Ahmadinejad, the big obstacle to climb over was Rafsanjani. The former kingmaker and two-term president believed the time was ripe for his return as he declared his intention to once again return to the presidential palace. The outcome was surely certain. Ahmadinejad had never been a top-tier figure in the Islamic Republic while Rafsanjani had always been a cornerstone in it. The trouble was Khamenei had explicitly told Rafsanjani not to seek the presidency again.[48]

9

(2005–13)—The Election of Mahmoud Ahmadinejad

Let them pass as many sanction resolutions against Iran until they run out of resolutions.[1]

(Ahmadinejad, November 2008)

They [Western governments] have succeeded in decreasing our oil revenues (In October 2012, Ahmadinejad admitted for the first time that sanctions were badly hurting the Iranian economy).[2]

Rafsanjani acted as if his decision to run for the presidency again in 2005 had been reached in close consultation with Supreme Leader Khamenei. "I have no intention of being elected president again as there is no shortage of qualified individuals in Iran." He omitted that he had sought to extend his presidency back in 1997 but met with stiff resistance from Khamenei. Fast forward to the 2005 elections, and Rafsanjani's account was that he and Khamenei had at first tried to agree on a single candidate to support but that this had not been possible. When he realized Ahmadinejad would run, Rafsanjani throw his hat in. He never said this was in contravention to Khamenei's wishes, which was the case. All Rafsanjani would admit to was that "Naturally, [he] thought that we could not put the country in the hands of someone like that [Ahmadinejad]."

Rafsanjani said many groups, such as senior clergy in Qom and Najaf (Iraq), were urging him to stand and to "perform his duty." He claimed that among those who had urged him to run was the wife of the late Khomeini.

> "In whose hands do you wish to entrust the country? The Imam put it in the hands of people like you, now to whom do you want to pass it on?" Rafsanjani claimed to have been shaken and turned to the Koran. I took an augury [one opens the Koran reads the first lines to see whether they are positive or negative] after the evening prayer and I decided to come forward. The following day was the last day for the registration [of the candidates].

§

Rafsanjani's message in the 2005 elections proved to be unconvincing to the voting public. As a candidate, he placed himself between the dreamers from the reformist camp who had a record of failing to deliver on their lofty promises of political change and an unknown entity by the name of Mahmoud Ahmadinejad. The latter's message was simple: the government had no business telling Iranians how to live their lives in the private space. Equally important, he vowed that every Iranian family would come to see a share of the country's oil wealth.[3] Rafsanjani had no option but to speak in the same vein of wanting to do more for wealth distribution but by the 2005 elections he simply had much political baggage that was unhelpful to him at best in his bid.

The reformists continued to knock him as an out-of-date and out-of-touch cleric who had no vision for transformational change and who engaged in gimmicks when he offered himself as the passageway to a fresh future. Some of Rafsanjani's supporters expressed concern. They told him he would do well in the first round among a polarity of candidates but that his share would be less than 50 percent of the vote. In that case, in the two-man race in the second round, he would lose to Ahmadinejad.[4] That is exactly what happened. Ahmadinejad's 62 percent against Rafsanjani's 36 percent would be the former president's last run for office. Rafsanjani said the election had been engineered in a way to assure his defeat but his gripes went nowhere.[5]

§

No one doubted that Khamenei wanted to see an Ahmadinejad victory in 2005. In fact, his son Mojtaba worked tirelessly behind the scenes to make sure his father's old friend did not return to the presidential palace.[6] Another partaker in the scheme to land Ahmadinejad in the presidential palace was the Revolutionary Guards. In his brief stint as mayor of Tehran, Ahmadinejad had redirected many contracts to businesses linked to the Guards. The generals saw in Ahmadinejad someone servile that would not be in the way of their political and economic ambitions. One of Ahmadinejad's closest associates, a millionaire by the name of Sadeq Mahsouli, had begun his career in the ranks of the Revolutionary Guards. Figures like Mahsouli, intersecting the two worlds, acted as intermediaries. In the 2005 presidential campaign, this Ahmadinejad–Revolutionary Guards alliance denounced Rafsanjani as the proponent of so-called American Islam. Ahmadinejad was himself more unequivocal. At his nicest, he said Rafsanjani was too old and had to step aside. At his most spiteful, he said Rafsanjani and his entourage represented ground zero of the ravaging problem of corruption in Iran.

The extent of the fraud and overt support by pro-Khamenei supporters for Ahmadinejad has never been made clear. The main reformist candidate, Mehdi Karroubi, wrote an open letter at the time and blamed Khamenei's son for rigging the election results. Like Khatami, Karroubi had been a stalwart regime member right from 1979, and one of Khomeini's earliest most senior appointments. None of that mattered as he was now in the way of Khamenei's grand vision. Karroubi famously said that he had following the election "slept for two hours and woke up to find out I had lost in the [first round of the] elections." When his pleas were ignored by Khamenei, Karroubi resigned from all his posts in the state, including as an advisor to Khamenei. It was rather bold.

Rafsanjani was characteristically far less audacious, missing another opportunity to confront Khamenei. In public, all Rafsanjani threatened to do was to take his complaints to God. He threatened in a letter that "there were matters [he] could but would not say." In private, he went to Khamenei and confronted him. "What are you thinking? How can Ahmadinejad win [the presidency?]." It was too late. To this day, the Rafsanjani camp maintains they had been perfectly tricked. According to this line of argument, Khamenei's strategy had all along been to engineer the elimination of the main reformist candidate—Karroubi—in the first round. Rafsanjani would be routed in the second two-man race, which is what happened. Khamenei had managed to keep the reformist and Rafsanjani camps apart while paving the way for the emergence of his intended pawn, Ahmadinejad.

Election engineering and outright fraud aside, there was nonetheless no doubt that by this time the reform movement had lost its allure. In contrast, Ahmadinejad ran on an anti-corruption platform—taking mostly aim at Rafsanjani—while promising wealth distribution exactly the same way Khomeini had promised income from oil exports to be handed to every single Iranian family. Ahmadinejad's flagrant populism and all its promises could not stand scrutiny and yet enough desperate Iranian voters believed he might just be able to change the status quo.

Ahmadinejad's Rowdy Domestic Agenda

It is commonplace to read from Western observers that the 2005 election win of Ahmadinejad was as a result of the American rejection of Tehran's "grand bargain" and George Bush's inclusion of Iran in the "Axis of Evil." In this logic, Khamenei was tired of looking for a breakthrough with the West. If Khatami's "dialogue of civilization," the tepid venture that it was, was not enough for the West it was perhaps time to show them some teeth in the form of the unrestrained Mahmoud Ahmadinejad. That was likely a factor that helped pave the way, but Ahmadinejad's election had a more profound driver behind it—the desire by Khamenei and the Revolutionary Guards to further consolidate power at the expense of the reform movement and the Rafsanjani network. Ahmadinejad, the lightweight meant to be deferential to Khamenei, was elevated for this reason only. It made perfect sense as Khamenei had strived since he became supreme leader in 1989 to weaken the role of elected officials and institutions. Khamenei wanted no more Rafsanjani or Khatami or anyone else with a slightest independent streak to have to grapple with.

§

At first, Ahmadinejad very much played along. At his swearing-in ceremony, Ahmadinejad kissed Khamenei's hand, the way courtiers of the late Shah had a habit of doing. Rafsanjani and Khatami would never dream of doing such a thing. Khamenei's elated expression conveyed his delight of having this 48-year-old son of a poor blacksmith be his submissive president. Ahmadinejad was the first non-cleric to become president since Bani Sadr fled Tehran for Paris in 1981. Up until he had become mayor of Tehran, Ahmadinejad's national profile was nearly zero. But he had been an Islamist student activist since before the 1979 revolution. There were rumors that he had been one of the hostage-takers at the siege of the US embassy. This led to a wild goose chase in Washington. It turned out Ahmadinejad had advocated for seizing the Soviet embassy at the time. "The biggest problem in this country is atheism and that's why we should go after the Soviet embassy," he had urged his fellow student revolutionaries.

Despite his early start in Islamist politics, his only other role was that of a governor of a minor province in the northwest of Iran for a handful of years during Rafsanjani's presidency. Rafsanjani recalled that there were no problems between the two men. Their status was incomparable. One was the president; the other appointed to be a governor of a small province by Rafsanjani's interior minister. While the earliest interactions between Rafsanjani and Ahmadinejad remain an enigma, Rafsanjani claimed that all was good until the moment Ahmadinejad decided to run for the presidency in 2005.[7]

Ahmadinejad had been replaced as governor after Khatami became president but Ahmadinejad had stayed close to Rafsanjani. In 2000, Ahmadinejad was a district campaign manager in Rafsanjani's election campaign when he humiliated himself running for a Majles seat. Rafsanjani's unpopularity, when he came last in Tehran, had rattled Ahmadinejad. It was as if he had banked on the former president to be his flight of stairs to political power only to see his would-be-benefactor fall flat on his face. This account paints Ahmadinejad as driven purely by a quest for power. Personal allegiance or a fixed ideology was not the driver behind his rise.

What is certain is that Ahmadinejad made a U-turn at this point and marketed himself as the antithesis to Rafsanjani. With that he set out in the 2005 elections as the only candidate to fix his message as the anti-Rafsanjani platform. It is at this point that the Khamenei *bayt* (household) moves distinctly closer to Ahmadinejad. And what is also known is that once in the presidential palace, he let loose against Rafsanjani, his legacy, and anyone associated with him. The venom and the explicitness of his charges were remarkable by the standards of the Islamic Republic where behind-the-scene backstabbing had been far more ordinary. In his first term, Ahmadinejad and the new political camp that he put together took a hammer to the Rafsanjani network. Anyone seen to be part of the Rafsanjani clique was replaced or pushed out. Not even Rafsanjani's family was immune. Charges of corruption against the family and personal attacks by pro-Ahmadinejad media not only became the new norm but the average member of public should have been forgiven if believing that a quiet revolution was underway.[8]

But Rafsanjani was most bitter over the fact that Khamenei was not only quiet but in fact giving Ahmadinejad a free pass. The national television, which Khamenei controls, became a reservoir for anti-Rafsanjani chronicles. Figures close to Khamenei, from clerics to senior media commentators, spoke about those against Ahmadinejad as being against God's wishes. Ahmadinejad was impervious. He had packed his cabinet with people that hailed from the ranks of the Revolutionary Guards. To some, Ahmadinejad was moving Iran from a theocracy toward a military dictatorship. All Rafsanjani could do at this point was to give speeches to friendly audiences and warn against a Revolutionary Guards takeover of the system. He warned Khamenei that he was in the process to open up a can of worms. He would point to Egypt. In that country, the military's control of the political realm is so strong, he would say, that people do not see a point in voting. "I believe that a political system without people's participation will not last," he liked to say. When Rafsanjani said "bullies are always armed," the bosses in the Revolutionary Guards perceived it as a direct assault.

Ahmadinejad barred foreign visitors, who sought to abide by diplomatic protocol, from seeing Rafsanjani. The same was true for top provincial officials, many of whom had come up through the ranks during Rafsanjani's heyday in the 1980s and 1990s.[9] The new president had a core of close confidants but his populist politics was inherently erratic at home and abroad. He broke the record in the number of cabinet members he fired from his government.[10] Unlike Rafsanjani, who protected his political surrogates, Ahmadinejad did not flinch in creating enemies for himself by sacrificing allies in order to promote an image of no-nonsense administrator. This was a habit that he would eventually come to pay a dear price for.

But at the beginning, his scorched-earth approach delighted both Khamenei and the Revolutionary Guards. Khamenei famously called Ahmadinejad's first-term government the best since the Constitutional Revolution of 1906. For now, Ahmadinejad stayed off their backs, but that would change. On the other hand, Rafsanjani's supporters increasingly insinuated that Ahmadinejad was a Western Trojan horse on a mission to destroy the Islamic Republic from within.[11] All sorts of outlandish gossip about him came out, including the charge that his family had Jewish roots, as a prominent Rafsanjani ally by the name of Mehdi Khazali claimed.[12] There were other suggestions that he was propagating the anti-clerical doctrine of the Bahai, a persecuted religious minority. An undeterred Ahmadinejad remarked that "we have to climb up the clerical ladder and destroy it once on the top."[13]

Ahmadinejad's Foreign Policy Chaos

The anticipation from the outset was that Ahmadinejad's ability to shape Tehran's foreign policy would be hugely limited given Khamenei's proven track record in micro-managing all sensitive domestic and foreign files. In fact, Khamenei tightened the noose even more. In the first year of the new president's term, Khamenei created the five-member Strategic Council on Foreign Relations (SCFR) to "engage experts, devise foreign policy approaches, and facilitate decision-making."[14] The former foreign minister under Khatami, Kamal Kharrazi, who is related to Khamenei, was given the job to oversee SCFR. Ahmadinejad had no time for meddling coming from this Khamenei-appointed council and ignored it.[15] He refused to meet its members or listen to the council's recommendations.[16] Ahmadinejad was firm in protecting his turf and managed to make his mark but only as long as he stayed close to Khamenei's worldview.

The closest Ahmadinejad the candidate had come to brandishing a foreign policy doctrine was when he declared that his government would foremost occupy itself with Iran's immediate neighbors. Prior to his election, Ahmadinejad hardly discussed relations with the United States or his intentions regarding Iran's nuclear program. After taking office, his time was to be dominated by these very two issues. The unsuspecting

Iranian voters who had seen in him not a foreign policy ideologue but a Robin Hood of sorts to go after cronyism, corruption, and nation-building at home were in for a rude awakening.

Seemingly clueless about international power structure and dynamics, Ahmadinejad used his first visit to the UN General Assembly in September 2005 to urge for a restructuring of the UN Security Council. There are more than fifty Islamic countries in the world and they are not represented at the UNSC, he complained. "Nor does the continent of Africa have a voice in the UNSC and all of Asia has only one voice at the SNSC [China]."[17] This concept of upending global power distribution would become one of his signature international rallying calls. The American UN delegation had decided to skip the speech and were not in the hall to hear Ahmadinejad's list of grievances. And while the new Iranian president's call for reordering global order was aimed at more than just the United States, he was explicit in asking the UN not to bend to Washington's pressure over Iran's nuclear program. Thanks to Russia and China, the United States could not move the UN against Tehran but the story was different at the headquarters of the IAEA in Vienna. A momentum was gathering here to vote on a resolution that Tehran was in noncompliance. Ahmadinejad soon after coming to power had abandoned all the nuclear restrictions the Khatami government had agreed with international powers.

There was a third topic that the world would come to associate with Ahmadinejad more than anything else: his avid skepticism concerning the historic veracity of the Holocaust. A few weeks after his visit to the UN in New York, he called for Israel to be "wiped off history pages." While the Islamic Republic had always been hostile to Israel, Ahmadinejad soon took off in policy directions that were bizarre and with little apparent strategic value for Iranian national interest. The timing and only possible logic suggested Ahmadinejad wanted to quickly land himself on the map of international politics as the new fearless figure, a global Islamist warrior. No doubt he had audiences in the Islamic and developing worlds in mind, exactly the same way Khomeini had them in mind when he declared his infamous fatwa against Salman Rushdie in 1989.

Ahmadinejad would go on to attend the UN General Assembly each year, reflecting his exaggerated sense of himself. In contrast, in his eight years in office president Rafsanjani never attended the UN annual gathering. Rafsanjani had not wanted to tap into international bodies as megaphones to transmit grandiose messages. His vainglory was confined to him fabricating an account of his presence at the UN but retold only in his memoirs. "When my speech [at the UN] ended, the applause [by international dignitaries] began and it was hard to see how it would come to an end," he wrote about a trip to New York in December 1991. There is, however, no evidence that Rafsanjani had visited the United States again after 1979.[18] Still, no one can accuse Rafsanjani to have intentionally desired to be a renegade on the global stage. His aspirations for Iranian foreign policy had been far more conventional by the standards of the Islamic Republic.

As with the Rushdie affair, Ahmadinejad's Holocaust denials would also come at a great cost to the Iranian nation. It not only resulted in American and European condemnation, but even the Russians protested. Israel's Defense Minister Shaul Mofaz, who hailed from an Iranian Jewish family in Tehran, warned that Israel would consider "all options" to prevent Iran from becoming a nuclear armed state. Even the Foreign Ministry in Tehran was taken aback and quickly released a statement pledging that Tehran had no intention to violate the UN charter by using force against another UN member. This just irked Ahmadinejad who removed some forty senior diplomats and ambassadors that he denigrated as remnants from the Khatami administration. He doubled down and his government organized a conference in Tehran to question the historical veracity of the Holocaust. Ahmadinejad again called it a "myth" as the likes of David Duke, the former American Ku Klux Klan leader, and other international Holocaust-denying A-list figures were invited to Tehran.[19] Khamenei stayed silent, signaling his endorsement.

The random zigzagging was bewildering. Ahmadinejad wrote an eighteen-page letter to US president George W. Bush by arguing that his foreign policy was surely in contrast to his Christian faith. Bush called the letter "interesting" but that it had not addressed the issue of Iran's nuclear ambition. "That is the issue at hand," Bush said, and that the United States had "no beef with the Iranian people."[20] It is hard to believe but this one letter, and the rather apathetic response by Bush, was the first official direct communication between an Iranian and an American president since 1980. In that sense, Ahmadinejad was an insurgent. Iranian officials from 1979 onward had a miserable record in cultivating any personal ties or even appealing directly to American leaders. Iran's Islamist rulers tended to speak in a sanctimonious style, which the Americans had always quickly dismissed as aimless ostentation. The American side was often not much better in its response. Bush's comment that Ahmadinejad's letter was "interesting" suggested the Americans had no idea how to respond to this oddball Iranian president. He was of a different breed.

When the president of Columbia University, Lee Bollinger, controversially invited Ahmadinejad to give a lecture he proceeded to introduce him as a man who "exhibit all the signs of a petty and cruel dictator."[21] Ahmadinejad took the unexpected body blow rather well and went on to attack American policies. "If you have created fifth generation of atomic bombs and are testing them already, who are you to question other people [Iran] who just want nuclear power?" Based on the boisterous outcry, the *New York Times* guesstimated the student body was 70 percent against and 30 percent for Ahmadinejad. Two topics enraged this American audience more than anything else: his condemnation of Israel as a colonial power, and an absurd comment he made that was quickly taken as a suggestion that homosexuality does not exist in Iran. No one in his entourage of seventy-eight people had evidently any serious understanding about American society or basic political instincts about issues to steer away from while on US soil.[22] Neither issue was of national security interest to Tehran and should have never been allowed to eclipse this momentous opportunity to speak directly to the American people. Instead of specialists in American culture and politics, Ahmadinejad's large entourage to New York would each year be made up mostly of family members of his closest advisors whose shopping habits often overshadowed any policy proposals the Iranian president might have had to offer. Ahmadinejad had hired many relatives and former colleagues from his days as a university professor with the aim of forming his own enduring political network.

Ahmadinejad's bombastic style had the tacit support of one man, Khamenei, whose 1987 indignant speech at the UN might just as well have been the model on which Ahmadinejad based his style on. As he grew in confidence, in 2007 Ahmadinejad fired Iran's UN ambassador, Javad Zarif, who called it "the biggest favor in history" that anyone had done for him.[23] Khamenei did not intervene despite the fact that he had a personal relationship with Zarif that is both long and believed to be deep. Khamenei was not just enabling Ahmadinejad's costly foreign policy positions but he seemed to have genuinely become an admirer.[24] For both men, assailing the American opponent outweighed much else even as Washington was mobilizing international backing to launch a series of sanctions against Tehran that the world had rarely seen.

Nonetheless, back in Iran, Ahmadinejad's idiosyncrasies, naiveté, and exaggerations were openly mocked. Once on returning from New York, Ahmadinejad told a group of clerics that when he delivered his speech from the UN podium, a light from above surrendered him.[25] He said the "the world is rapidly becoming Ahmadinejad-ized."[26] Rafsanjani sneered at him, hinting that Ahmadinejad viewed himself as the earthly representative of the Hidden Imam (the Islamic messiah). If so, this was surely heresy even in the otherwise rule-bending theocracy that is the Islamic Republic. But Rafsanjani's blow was intended for Khamenei, without whom Ahmadinejad would have never been given the opportunity to speak as the Iranian president at the UN. Look what you have done, appeared to be Rafsanjani's criticism of Khamenei's judgment. Khamenei took Rafsanjani's jabs on the chin but he himself knew Ahmadinejad needed to be kept on a short leash. Despite kissing his hand and other routine flattery, the president had fast shown himself to be fickle to even Khamenei. In regard to Iran's nuclear dossier, Ahmadinejad's reversal of course might have been quietly blessed by Khamenei, but the perception of the public was that he was challenging the supreme leader's past judgment. Within a few days of taking over, he had removed Hassan Rouhani as Iran's top nuclear negotiator. Ahmadinejad called Rouhani "submissive" in dealing with the Europeans during rounds of nuclear negotiations from 2003 to 2005. Everyone seem to forget that Rouhani had negotiated with Khamenei's backing and as the head of Iran's Supreme National Security Council (SNSC), a role he was appointed to way back in 1989 by Khamenei.[27]

But Khamenei had not come to Rouhani's defense. Rouhani's successor as the head of the SNSC, Ali Larijani, did not last much longer either. Larijani, who had also been a contender in the 2005 presidential elections, resigned after less than two acrimonious years in the job. His disagreements with Ahmadinejad, who disparaged the influential Larijani family at any opportunity, were not only personal but also a broader epiphany. The attacks on the Larijanis and Rouhani was also an attack on Khamenei. Strategic foreign policy matters are above all the prerogative of the supreme leader and an expression of the collective opinion of the SNSC. And who did Khamenei have as his two personal emissaries in the SNSC during the Ahmadinejad presidency? It was Rouhani and Larijani, two men Ahmadinejad had repeatedly vilified in public. This clear effort by Khamenei to keep Ahmadinejad under control only made sense from the vantage point of domestic power play in Tehran. Given the immense costs of sanctions on Iran, to have a disjointed and prolonged nuclear crisis otherwise made no sense.

§

Ahmadinejad's antics on the world stage quickly wore off. Even those who had voted for him believed Ahmadinejad's routine of demagoguery and in-your-face belligerence toward the West was erasing sympathy from the developing states and sped up a sequence of events where the possible outcome was to be further economic isolation. Although a good part of the public at this point backed the idea of a civil nuclear program, they were exasperated by Ahmadinejad's handling of the nuclear crisis and Tehran's priorities. The Robin Hood in Ahmadinejad never came out either. The elite that Ahmadinejad had promised to confront remained largely untouched, although the Rafsanjani network stayed in the firing line. Instead, the Iranian public got to taste Ahmadinejad's megalomania. "Over one hundred international leaders have in conversations with me requested that Iran play the role of the global administrator," he once boasted.[28] As Khatami's former deputy foreign minister, Mohammad Sadr, observed, Ahmadinejad suffered from a combination of amateurish incompetence, delusion, and "profound ignorance." As Sadr put it, "He doesn't know that he doesn't know, so he doesn't ask anyone."[29] Within a year of coming to power, Ahmadinejad had managed to unite the UN Security Council, which imposed sanction on Iran in July 2006.

In all, during Ahmadinejad's presidency from 2005 to 2013, the UNSC voted to sanction Iran on eight separate occasions. Trade with the outside world was hampered; Iranian banks faced restrictions; the country's shipping and airline industries were put under strict monitoring, while a long list of materials was banned to be exported to Iran in fear of aiding the country's nuclear and ballistic missile programs. These were the measurable costs associated with noncompliance with the UNSC. It was impossible to know the true figure but international investors, in fear of breaching the sanctions regime and incurring penalties, also stayed out of the Iranian market.

It was also during the Ahmadinejad presidency that capital flight reached new records. Between 2006 and 2016, some $135 billion was moved out of the country by nervous Iranians.[30] Ahmadinejad downplayed the sanction resolutions as scrap paper by "pathetic" world powers fearing "Iran's hidden human power."[31] Iran's human capital, however, was not as much hidden as it was anxious. Iranians were leaving the country in droves. One estimate put the annual cost of the brain drain at $150 billion.[32] As one example, about 90 percent of Iranian doctoral students who studied in the United States preferred not to return to Iran. Meanwhile, lines for visas outside foreign embassies in Tehran grew longer and longer. Tens of thousands of Iranians were permanently leaving the country every year.

Life under Ahmadinejad was particularly bleak for Iranians with hopes for less intrusion in their daily lives. Campaign promises of increasing social freedoms never became policy. Instead, he sought "a purge of the liberal and secular" influences in society. This was not that Ahmadinejad cared much either way, but he had to do Khamenei's bidding to buy time and until he was strong enough to break free from the supreme leader. Khamenei, after all, had in mind the making of an Islamic Civilization on his watch. The rate of confiscation of satellite dishes went up to keep the dreaded Western influence out; Western music was banned from state-run television and radio and soon the religious police increased its patrols to crack down on failing to comply with mandatory veil for women. Ahmadinejad even reversed an earlier decision to allow women into sports stadiums after Khamenei expressed his disapproval. The man who had as candidate asked "Is the style of haircuts of the youth really the business of the state?" backpedaled and felt he had no choice. It was a catch-22: by now Ahmadinejad's biggest enabler was the Revolutionary Guards. The generals, meanwhile, had no intention to loosen the pact with Khamenei for the sake of Ahmadinejad's phantasm of a "new beginning," a hodgepodge of ideas that left most baffled.

§

Despite his public submission to Khamenei's plans for domestic policy, Ahmadinejad was still so apt at creating global unease that Khamenei had to restrain him. Rafsanjani had lost in the election in 2005 but as head of the Expediency Council he was tasked by Khamenei to play a bigger role in supervising the Ahmadinejad government's performance. Khamenei might have come to reconsider the size and speed of change that had arrived with Ahmadinejad. He yearned for some past nostalgia. In the December 2006 elections for the Assembly of Experts, Khamenei accepted a win by the pro-Rafsanjani faction that opposed Ahmadinejad on all levels. For a brief while, it seemed that the Rafsanjani camp was back. Rafsanjani claims that Khamenei had pleaded for him to run as the most important job of the Assembly of Experts is to choose the supreme leader. "What will happen if I die and you are not in the Assembly of Experts?"[33]

Khamenei's doubts about Ahmadinejad opened the door to large-scale attacks on his government. In a rare move, 150 members of the parliament signed a letter blaming him for high unemployment, rampant inflation, failure to deliver a budget on time, and economic mismanagement. Governors complained that on his visits to provinces Ahmadinejad made outlandish pledges of new economic projects that he or the state had no ability to deliver. Ahmadinejad was also blamed for worsening relations with the UN Security Council. His nuclear strategy was scorned as nothing but a platform for him to engage in grandstanding on the international stage. And yet, the fact that Ahmadinejad could engage in nuclear grandstanding on his own demonstrated one or two realities: that Khamenei was supportive of at least some of his views or that the collective policy-making process was broken.[34] Both points were to a large extent true, and Khamenei was hardly blameless.

In March 2007, shortly after a new round of UN sanctions on Iran, the Revolutionary Guards arrested fifteen British sailors for allegedly straying into Iranian waters from their base in Iraq. The British were held for some two weeks before Ahmadinejad gave them new suits and sent them home but not before he had them paraded in front of media cameras. He said the return was a gift on the occasion of Christian Easter. The entire episode—from the seizing of the British (who may or may not have entered Iran's territorial waters) to the television confession interviews of the sailors to parading them before their release—smelled of 1979. It was as if all the lessons of the takeover of the US embassy in 1979 had been forgotten.

The rank and file at the Foreign Ministry were alarmed but had no say in the matter. The Revolutionary Guards had taken the action. Ahmadinejad was happy to jump on the bandwagon for the sake of the limelight that it gave him. He even claimed the British prime minister Tony Blair had written to him personally and "apologized" and promised a change in British policy toward Iran.[35] London said no such letter was ever sent to Ahmadinejad. Khamenei, meanwhile, had just witnessed another example of Ahmadinejad's ego but again did not intervene. There were other examples of the dysfunctional and increasingly faction-ridden policy-making process. Shortly after the British sailors were released, a key associate of Rafsanjani, Hossein Mousavian, was arrested for spying for Western powers. He had been a top member of Iran's nuclear negotiating team during the Khatami presidency. Mousavian, a former ambassador to Berlin, was later charged and briefly detained before he moved to the United States in 2009.

Mousavian, and his then boss Rouhani, viewed Ahmadinejad as a simpleton. In August 2005, when Rouhani told Ahmadinejad that Tehran needs to be careful in how he treats the IAEA, because most of its budget comes from Western states, the president had a solution at his fingertips. "Call El-Baradei [the Egyptian head of the IAEA] right now and tell him Iran will pay the IAEA's full budget!" Rouhani was evidently stunned about how little the president knew about how international organizations operate.[36] A reluctant Rouhani was even more stunned about Ahmadinejad's belief that he was the pinnacle of policy wisdom in Tehran. "I am instructing you and you should obey." Rouhani resigned and Khamenei said nothing in his defense.

At the same time as Mousavian was arrested, Haleh Esfandiari, an Iranian-American academic, was also arrested. Charges of spying were also leveled against Esfandiari. These arrests were not coincidental. The intra-regime fight was once again mounting. Ahmadinejad warned the "people who have access to money and power" in Iran's political system to cease their activities and support Iran's nuclear stance. This was in no doubt targeted at officials such as Rafsanjani, but Khamenei was not immune. The president was basically saying only his elected government has the right to formulate foreign policy. As with the hostage crisis of 1979 or the squabble in Tehran around the Reagan administration's secret missions in 1986, this latest fight was again erupting around domestic power politics. And invariably, the fight was sucking foreign actors into the eye of the storm.[37]

After he was released, Mousavian visited his mentor Rafsanjani. "He told me that some reliable sources had informed him that a series of arrests targeting the moderate and reformist camps had been planned after my arrest." Mousavian's arrest was supposed to be a prelude to a major campaign to "destroy Rafsanjani, Khatami, and Hassan Rouhani." The intention was also to show Western states how little power Rafsanjani and his network had left in Iran. In his book, Mousavian has a first-hand anecdote from Rafsanjani: "I am convinced their main target is the Supreme Leader [Khamenei] but they need to eliminate me [Rafsanjani] first." But Ahmadinejad had no hard power to carry out a purge along these lines as Rafsanjani claimed to have foreseen. If that was true, then the Revolutionary Guards must have been on the plan. In the months to come, this presumption was put under intense trial.

§

In the midst of this fight in Tehran, the Bush administration released its 2007 National Intelligence Estimate. It found that Iran had halted its nuclear weapons program in

2003 when Khatami was president. But was that a source of comfort or anguish? Khatami had, after all, at least sought to deescalate tensions with the West. As one academic in Tehran put it, "during Khatami's presidency, Iranian national identity was distinguished by the heavy weight of republicanism; national interests were pursued according to defensive and economic interests and the framework of the world order." Ahmadinejad, meanwhile, wanted to take a sledgehammer to the world order.

Khatami had wanted to confront the realities of life with the tools he had in his toolbox. Ahmadinejad wanted to create alternative realities but came short. Take his government's pursuit of new alliances in Africa and in Latin America. In the case of the latter, the glue that held it together was a common dislike of the United States that Ahmadinejad shared with the likes of Hugo Chavez of Venezuela or Evo Morales of Bolivia. That was the start and end of the strategic partnership. The best that came out of such attempts in far-flung lands was the so-called nuclear compromise deal of 2010 that was brokered by Brazil and Turkey. And the Obama administration's rejection of this proposal again underscored the inevitable front-seat role that the United States wanted to preserve for itself in any resolution of the Iranian nuclear deal.

Undeterred, the adamant Ahmadinejad doubled down on his "East and South" (meaning East Asian states and those from Africa and Latin America) foreign policy agenda. But Ahmadinejad's big bet on Africa had even less good news for Tehran.[38] His government began to increasingly import goods from African states on a spectacular scale. In 2008, imports from Africa rose by 101 percent. But African imports from Iran stayed the same as before. It was all symbolic and with little tangible return. In 2006, Ahmadinejad famously attended the African Union summit in Gambia as a guest of honor. But in November 2010, Gambia broke diplomatic relations with Tehran and expelled all its diplomats. The official reason for the fallout was Iran's shipment of arms to Gambia, which Nigeria had uncovered a month earlier when it intercepted an Iranian ship.

The Iranians maintain that the real reason was American pressure on Gambia to cut Ahmadinejad loose. Regardless of the true reason for the diplomatic rupture, it was very clear that making diplomatic inroads into the African continent was much harder than Ahmadinejad's beaming photo opportunities with various African leaders suggested.[39] Nor did he even manage to secure African support at the UN. In 2010, African UN Security Council members Gabon, Nigeria, and Uganda voted in favor of sanctions against Iran for its nuclear program. The vote, which resulted in UN Resolution 1929, came a few months after Ahmadinejad's lobbying tour of Africa.

One undeniably potent factor that did help the otherwise bungling Ahmadinejad government was record crude oil price. His eight-year government received "some $700—compared to $440 billion received by all previous administrations since the revolution, and five times the receipts between the discovery of oil in 1908 and the end of the [Shah] regime in 1979."[40] Thanks to this oil income, Iran's imports grew at a fast pace. It made it possible for Tehran to perform a strategic foreign policy shift. Trade between Iran and China increased from US$4 billion in 2003 to $36 billion in 2013, making China Tehran's biggest trading partner by far.[41]

Europe's position as a top trading partner of Iran was sliding. Much of China's imports were Iranian oil. The unexpected oil-income windfall also allowed

Ahmadinejad to embark on the most comprehensive structural economic reform since 1979. The populist, whose mass injection of imports had sharply increased inflation while crippling the local manufacturing sector, experimented with removing basic subsidies for everyday goods. Instead, families would receive monthly cash subsidies. It was the kind of reform the IMF had urged Tehran to introduce for years.[42] That Ahmadinejad, the self-declared foe of global financial order, should be the person to launch such an initiative just made his resume even more confounding.

§

Ahmadinejad's overtures to China, or other non-Western powers, faced no objections from Khamenei. In fact, he was largely supportive. China, in his mind, never posed a threat to his supremacy in Tehran. China is, after all, also an authoritarian state that had been amply content to work with the Islamist ruling elite. However, like his two predecessors, shifting policy toward the United States was not to be Ahmadinejad's call. As Sadeq Kharrazi, the former Iranian ambassador to France whose uncle was former foreign minister Kamal Kharrazi, put it: "The government of Iran executes foreign policy decisions made by Iran's Supreme Leader." Ahmadinejad, who unlike the Kharrazis or the Khatamis had no family ties to Khamenei and was far more brazen, wanted to be different, but his options beyond sloganeering on strategic policy questions were hugely limited.

To Ahmadinejad's outrage, Khamenei's trusted personal advisors such as Ali Larijani and Ali Akbar Velayati continued to negotiate with foreign governments at the leader's personal discretion. The effects of this kind of obscure shuttle-diplomacy as sanctioned by Khamenei were bewildering to the outside world. In one example, in 2009, Ali Larijani traveled to Cairo with the aim of normalizing relations. The Ahmadinejad government rejected it as a "private visit." Larijani told journalists that just because the trip had been "unofficial" it "did not mean that it had no political content." As so many times before, such ongoing conflicts in Tehran confused foreigners on how to approach Tehran. To ask who really runs the show in Tehran was a legitimate question when Ahmadinejad publicly charged his domestic political rivals—be it Khamenei, the reformists, or the Rafsanjani clique—sabotaged his government. As with presidents before and after him, he deplored his lack of power. In a shot aimed at Khamenei, he declared that "no one is above the president." In a dig at the Rafsanjani network, he claimed certain individuals from inside Iran had "decided to sit down with the enemies of the country" and had given "Iran's enemies information about the situation inside the country." He resented the fact that he, as president, was just playing a supporting role in the making of Iranian foreign policy. All he could do was to display fits of anger as when he fired his foreign minister, Manouchehr Mottaki, while the latter was on a visit to Senegal and found out about his sacking by his hosts. Ahmadinejad later explained that Mottaki had never been his choice as minister but did not risk saying so when he was still in the presidential palace.[43]

§

On January 3, 2008, Khamenei once again sought to remind domestic and foreign audiences about his stature in Tehran. Stating that "cutting off relations with the US" was one of the "principal policies" of the Iranian regime, but that he would be the "first person to endorse these relations" if it benefited the Iranian people, Khamenei secured news headlines. The statement was less about shifting sands in US–Iran relations. It was to remind Ahmadinejad not to let the title of president to go to his head. Khamenei meant he was ready to turn a page in the American file if and when it served his interests. As time would show, benefiting the Iranian national interest was a secondary concern.

By late 2008, as one commentator in Tehran saw it, Ahmadinejad's golden era was over and his honeymoon with the supreme leader had finished. "He has problems even meeting the supreme leader." "The countdown to his dismissal has already begun."[44] That turned out to be a spectacular misreading of Khamenei's initial reasons to support Ahmadinejad or his future plans for the pestering president. For sure, Khamenei had begun to doubt Ahmadinejad's loyalty but there was still no good alternative available. The reformists or the Rafsanjani camp posed problems of their own to Khamenei. Some sources claim that a year before his first term had ended, Khamenei had told Ahmadinejad to prepare himself for a second term. Perhaps the conflicting signals were all part of a master play by Khamenei.

Meanwhile, Khamenei and Rafsanjani continued having their weekly meetings.[45] Rafsanjani had in July 2007, following the death of long-time chairman Ayatollah Ali Meshkini, become the chairman of the Assembly of Experts. This was on top of his chairmanship of the Expediency Council. The latter had a membership of regime elders who would step in and mediate when there was gridlock in the policy-making process involving the Majles, the presidency, and the Guardian Council, which clinches Khamenei's power. Through his control of the Guardian Council, Khamenei decides who can run for elected office and what sorts of legislation can be passed at any level in the Islamic Republic. It was his ultimate filter.

While Rafsanjani had failed in his bid for elected office in 2000 and 2005, for the parliament and presidency, respectively, his continued presence in key regime agencies spoke volumes about his remaining clout. It also spoke about Khamenei invariably choosing to continue to accommodate, and limit Rafsanjani when needed, instead of seeking to entirely neutralize him. In the 2005 presidential elections, Rafsanjani had not expected the opposition he faced from Khamenei and the hard-line camp. But at the time of the 2009 presidential elections, Rafsanjani knew that Ahmadinejad's unbridled populism and idiosyncrasies had begun to seriously worry Khamenei. Above all, Ahmadinejad's absurdities were undermining the religious foundations of the Islamic Republic.

He once famously said the Americans had invaded Iraq in 2003 to prevent the coming of the Islamic messiah, the Hidden Imam.[46] The proposition that the American government can anticipate and prevent the coming of the messiah was not only an assault on the sanctities of Islam. His promotion of what many viewed as naked religious superstitions was not just awkward for the clerics; Ahmadinejad was already beginning to sound like an agitator who urged Iranians to have a direct relationship to God and skip the orthodox structured religious path to Allah. When he said he wanted to hasten to emergence of the messiah, the clerics told him to watch where he was stepping.[47] He was shaking the pillars of the organized theocracy established in 1979.

For the chief cleric, Khamenei, this was a menacing new test, but circumstances meant he still had to live with Ahmadinejad's behavior. The opposite was true for Rafsanjani. He was as determined as ever to see the back of Ahmadinejad who had humiliated him in public as no one else. Rafsanjani recognized he was still unpopular with the public. And he was loath to repeat the experience of the 2005 presidential elections. Instead of running himself, he chose to play the role of the chief organizer to unseat Ahmadinejad. In 1997, he had been the savior for Mohammad Khatami's candidacy when he intervened and made sure Khatami would not be robbed by Khamenei. In 2009, Khatami was urged to run again but declined. Rafsanjani and Khatami chose to back the former prime minister from the 1980s, Mir Hossein Mousavi. At this juncture, anyone opposed to Ahmadinejad backed Mousavi. Despite his growing misgivings about the incumbent president, Khamenei doubled down in supporting Ahmadinejad's reelection.

The 2009 Green Movement and Khamenei's Falling Out with Ahmadinejad

As Iran prepared for the June 12, 2009, presidential elections, a new American president arrived in the White House. Barack Obama had been elected on a platform of reaching out to all the foes of the United States without precondition. That included Iran. In March of that year, Obama taped a video statement aimed at the Iranian public where he spoke about his desire to see normalization of relations between the two nations. For Khamenei, he offered something specific: an "engagement that is honest and grounded in mutual respect."[48] The Iranian state press later called it a first since 1979. It was, however, a sentiment that US presidents had conveyed to Tehran since the days of Jimmy Carter. The difference was that Obama was explicit about which Iranian leader's perceptions he wanted to shape.

In the weeks and months to come, the Obama team honed on Khamenei and Ahmadinejad was entirely ignored. From mid-2009 to October 2014, Obama wrote four letters to Khamenei. The Iranian leader responded to each outreach publicly or privately.[49] Khamenei was at best lukewarm but did not shut the door to dialogue. "This new U.S. president had nice words. He has given us messages repeatedly—spoken and written [messages]—saying: 'Let's turn the page, let's create a new situation, let's work with each other to solve the world's problems,'" he said. "If you change, we will change too," was the best Khamenei could offer Obama. In between, Khamenei managed to maintain the burst of public denunciations of alleged past American sins against Iran. Unbeknownst to Ahmadinejad, he also approved for a secret line of negotiations to be established with the Americans. The country of Oman had offered its services as a mediator and would soon host rounds of meetings between Iranian and American officials.[50]

§

The two main challengers to Ahmadinejad in the 2009 presidential elections were both long-time regime insiders. The more prominent one was former prime minister Mir

Hossein Mousavi. The other was former Speaker of the parliament, Mehdi Karroubi. Unlike the clerics he had spent so much of his life with—and who spend much time in seminaries refining the art of oratory—Mousavi was a flat speaker when he was prime minister some thirty years earlier. Karroubi, on the other hand, was a straight shooter and the occasional hothead. Not wanting to fall short of what the United States offers its electorate during elections, authorities in Tehran organized a number of debates. It would be the most explosive political television ever aired in Iran. Mousavi put Khamenei on the spot when he said: "I sensed danger and that is why I am running for president."[51] Ahmadinejad called Mousavi and Karroubi marionettes played by Rafsanjani and accused him of bankrolling his challengers. "People need to know I am not standing against another candidate [Mousavi]; I am standing against an organization backed by Rafsanjani and Khatami."

Around midnight on election day on June 12, 2009, Mousavi declared himself the winner. It was not to be. The following afternoon, the Ministry of Interior declared Ahmadinejad as the official winner with almost 25 million votes. The minister of interior was none other than the former Revolutionary Guards commander-turned-Ahmadinejad ally, Sadeq Mahsouli. This purported figure meant that Ahmadinejad had secured eight million more votes than in 2005. It was beyond incredulous.

An angry, and restless, public looked to vent its anger at this patent case of election fraud. In this instance, not only Rafsanjani but his entire family played a leading role in mobilizing the people. Unlike the invisible female members of Khamenei's family, women in the Rafsanjani household took up a front seat. Effat Marashi, Rafsanjani's wife, asked Iranians to come out to the streets to protest.[52] Rafsanjani's younger daughter was so forceful in her rejection of the election result that she was twice arrested in the mayhem that followed. Senior members of Rafsanjani's network were also arrested.[53] The stage was set for the most epic schism inside the Islamic Republic since 1979. It was at this point, the summer of 2009, the Green opposition movement was born.

§

Unlike 1989, when Mousavi had quietly allowed himself to be pushed off the political stage after the office of the prime minister was abolished in the constitutional reform, he decided to hold his ground. He rejected Khamenei's repeated calls for him to accept the election outcome. In 1989, both Rafsanjani and Khamenei had basically come together to push Mousavi to the side so they could share power. Now, an aggrieved Rafsanjani sided with Mousavi and the Green opposition movement. That explained the existing immense hope that on this occasion the opposition was not limited to street protesters. A big limb of the regime was falling off.

In the weeks that followed, street protests proliferated from Tehran to the rest of the country. For the first time since the student protests of 1999, Khamenei was gripped by fear. On the first Friday Prayer after the June 12 elections, he literally gave the protesters an ultimatum: go home or else.[54] "I ask everyone to stop this. This approach is wrong. If they don't stop this [protesting], then they will bear the responsibility and the consequences of this chaos," he said in what was clearly aimed not only at the street level but also at Mousavi and Rafsanjani.[55] This was not just a green light for a brutal crackdown that followed. Khamenei, for the first time, openly denounced

Rafsanjani and his support for the Green opposition movement. In claiming that his views on politics, economics, and social issues were much closer to Ahmadinejad than Rafsanjani, Khamenei had just turned a new page in his relations with his old friend.

In the public perception, Rafsanjani was still the éminence grise. Surely, he would hit back, but how? Rafsanjani was the master of the behind-the-scene deal-making but Khamenei had just invited him to a public duel. It was unchartered territory. His once frequent weekly meetings with Khamenei were a thing of the past. He had no choice but to accept Khamenei's dare as the two men set out to mobilize support both in the ranks of the regime and within the public. A few weeks later, as the street protests refused to die down, Rafsanjani took to the same podium as the Friday Prayer leader at Tehran University—the same place that had made both him and Khamenei into big political players in 1979. It would become his most iconic speech, and the last time he was ever again given the lectern at Tehran University.

Rafsanjani, while still characteristically soft in tone, pummeled Khamenei. He criticized not only the handling of the election but called on the Khamenei-controlled police and security forces to end the use of violence against protesters. He demanded that those arrested be freed. He was booed by the Khamenei supporters in the crowd and his speech repeatedly interrupted. Khamenei was livid but Rafsanjani's admonishment continued. In a letter that was widely distributed, he further lectured the supreme leader. The concept of an "Islamic Republic," he wrote, is not just a ceremonial word. It is both a "republic" and "Islamic." If either is damaged then that is the end of the Islamic Republic.[56]

In that infamous letter, in which he does not greet his old friend with the customary "Salam Alaikum" (which translates as "Peace Upon You" or simply the customary "hello"), Rafsanjani let Khamenei have it. "Those arrested in the protests have to be released. Let them go back to their families." That part was to enhance his appeal to the public. There was a more intricate point to his speech in which he basically pleaded with Khamenei for a return to earlier political coexistence that had shaped their relations for so long. In Rafsanjani's implicit words, the responsible person for the political turmoil in Iran was Khamenei. But he could salvage the situation by walking away from Ahmadinejad. For a discreet man, Rafsanjani was speaking unusually boldly.

Rafsanjani had no option but to up the ante. He had during the elections complained about Ahmadinejad's attacks on his family and called it an orchestrated campaign that was not limited to the incumbent president but had the explicit support of the "deep state." Khamenei, the closest thing to a taskmaster of the "deep state," had not lifted a finger for him. Rafsanjani's pitch was that Khamenei too was under attack. He had after all been alongside Rafsanjani and part of the same Khomeinist system since 1979.[57] The letter was a desperate plea by Rafsanjani for Khamenei to change course and quit seeing Ahmadinejad as a useful sycophant. "I am not asking you to remove [Ahmadinejad] or wish to see him have same fate as [President] Bani Sadr [who had to flee to France after Khomeini denounced him] but to act to prevent things to move in that direction." It was a warning to Khamenei that more such letters will be written unless Khamenei put the brakes on the attacks on the Rafsanjani family. "In due time, I will let the people know what has happened." Reminding Khamenei about their years of friendship and collaboration, Rafsanjani asks Khamenei to "put this fire out," in reference to Ahmadinejad. It was signed: "Your friend, companion, brother-in-arms, yesterday, today and tomorrow." At least in public, Khamenei never replied, despite the fact that Rafsanjani was clearly looking to cut a deal with him and not eclipse his supreme leadership.

Rafsanjani and his clique had not been behind the Green movement. The movement's key strength was organic and linked to the popular anger that poured into the streets. But Rafsanjani and Mousavi were happy to ride this wave. There was anti-Khamenei momentum elsewhere. A number of Iranian diplomats in Europe defected as hundreds of figures close to Rafsanjani, Mousavi, and the reformist camp were rounded up and put through televised mass trials before imprisonment. Khamenei genuinely seemed to believe Rafsanjani was spearheading a "color revolution" against him. When Rafsanjani told the Revolutionary Guards to stay out of the election debacle, Khamenei read that as an attempt to disarm the supreme leader who by now depended on the guns of the Guards unlike any time before. Khamenei's anxieties rose even more when Rafsanjani appealed to the better senses of the Revolutionary Guards to be neutral in the fight. Rafsanjani still had some sympathizers in the ranks of the Guards. He warned Khamenei about the militarization of the political system the way of Egypt or Pakistan. "Bullies are always armed," he insisted. Others were far less hopeful. Mousavi, in particular, was glum. "I don't think power will any longer peacefully change hands" in Iran, he said.

By December 2010, when the anti-regime protests were still very much alive in Iran, a young Tunisian fruit vendor by the name of Mohamed Bouazizi set himself on fire in the town of Ben Arous on the Mediterranean. This was the spark that led to popular uprising across North Africa and Middle East to be known collectively as the "Arab Spring." Khamenei had good reasons to fear the turmoil in the Arab lands. It could be a reinvigorating factor for the faltering Green movement in Iran. Thinking time was not on his side, he set out to strangle the opposition movement before it was too late.

§

Rafsanjani's gamble did not pay off. In the end, the Revolutionary Guards, the intelligence and security services stuck to Khamenei. In the process, some one hundred protesters were killed in the crackdown. The Islamic Republic had experienced a monumental schism but the defied supreme leader had managed to keep the regime together. Now, it was payback time. Mousavi and Karroubi, the two presidential candidates that had refused to accept the official election result, were by February 2011 put under house arrest where they remain to this day.

Rafsanjani avoided that fate but slogans of "death to Rafsanjani" were now aired on national television. His daughter, Faezeh, was assaulted in the street and taunted as a "whore" by pro-Khamenei thugs.[58] It was captured on film and was incredibly personal, but Rafsanjani seemed helpless. A number of his close associates, including his relative and former chief of staff, Hossein Marashi, were swiftly imprisoned. By the late spring of 2011, the Green movement was off the streets, as its leaders had fled the country, were in prison, or were under house arrest. Leaked videos from a conference attended by the leadership of the Revolutionary Guards, including its top boss General Mohammad Ali Jafari, show them admitting that the organization had indeed intervened to make sure Ahmadinejad won in the first round.[59]

The cantankerous Ahmadinejad had had his way.[60] Khamenei and the Revolutionary Guards had for now rendered Rafsanjani harmless. He soon decided to give up his position as chairman of the Assembly of Expert after Khamenei pressured each of the eighty-eight members of the body to shun Rafsanjani and not vote for him. Rafsanjani had not looked this impotent since the fall of the Shah in 1979. But the same man who had been the catalyst for his fall, Ahmadinejad, also threw him a lifeline by acting evermore brazenly against Khamenei.

By the late spring of 2011, as the Arab Spring uprisings raged across the region, Ahmadinejad quickly ignored who had kept him in the presidential palace. It seemed he believed he had to be ahead of the popular curve that surely in Iran too would travel in the same direction as in the Arab countries: a demand for fundamental change of the political order. Ahmadinejad began to defy Khamenei in any way he could. Khamenei kept him increasingly on a short leash particularly on foreign policy. At the UN General Assembly in 2011 in New York, Ahmadinejad wanted to have two Americans detained in Iran released. Khamenei made sure it did not happen.[61]

Unlike when Khatami came to power in 1997, who staffed his team with many figures from the previous Rafsanjani government, Ahmadinejad had his own core group of loyalists when he began his presidency in 2005. In his second term, his team became even more distinct and with weaker links to Khamenei. Ahmadinejad had in his first term often spoken about how he received his "orders" from the "Hidden Imam," the Islamic messiah. In essence, this notion that he had a line open to Allah made the Islamic Republic, and its clerical ruling class, redundant. Ahmadinejad was promising the advent of a post-clerical world.

Ahmadinejad's Messianism Morphs into Anti-Clerical Nationalism

Khamenei was late in seeing this challenge coming from Ahmadinejad, but he did organize for Ahmadinejad's unorthodox "messianic" messages to be confronted. In his second term, Ahmadinejad challenged Khamenei from a whole and unexpected new angle: he began to play the Iranian nationalist card. He dabbled in glorifying Iran's rich pre-Islamic past. On the occasion of the Persian new year, the Norouz, which Khomeini had derided as a "pagan" event, Ahmadinejad invited twenty heads of state to Persepolis, the ancient capital of the Persian Empire.[62] Perhaps Ahmadinejad did not see it that way but the similarities to the Shah's veneration of Iran's pre-Islamic history were unmistakable. There was only difference. The Shah was sincerely in awe of the history of Iran before the Arab armies brought Islam to Persia in AD 651. For Ahmadinejad, the carpetbagger that he was, it was just good politics since the Iranian public was sick to death of Islamism and nostalgic for a past long gone.

Worried about Ahmadinejad's nationalist messaging, Khamenei had to find new ways to elevate his prestige. Sometimes his efforts were bizarre. In one incident, one of Khamenei's clerical subordinates claimed that the supreme leader had shouted "Ya Ali" as soon as he was delivered from his mother's womb. Ali is the name of the first Imam in Twelver Shia Islam. In other words, Khamenei's birth had been a miracle. That this absurd claim should first surface at a time when Tehran was abuzz about the potential impact of the Arab Spring on Iran and Ahmadinejad's sudden newfound nationalism was hardly by chance. Khamenei was desperate for legitimacy, and unlike Ahmadinejad his options to maneuver were limited.[63] Khamenei decided to double down to market himself as heavenly chosen. Friends and rivals alike warned him but were also surprised by the turn of events. Nateq-Nouri, the failed 2005 presidential candidate who was by now a top advisor to Khamenei, said about the claim: "This sort of nonsense is an insult to the Supreme Leader," although he said it without admitting Khamenei must have approved of this gimmick to idolize him. Rafsanjani was candid. "What are these rumors they are spreading about you? Why don't you unequivocally reject this sort of absurdity so even the simple pious people don't lose faith?" Khamenei reassured Rafsanjani the story was true. "I summoned my sister and she confirmed this is what happened when I was born. It is the truth."

Once such stunts boomeranged on Khamenei, he opted to deal with Ahmadinejad's insubordination through another tried-and-tested approach: intimidation and suppression. Many of the same people who used to say anyone who opposes Ahmadinejad is opposed to God now said the ungrateful president was under the spell of a deviant faction of infiltrators. The chief infiltrator was Ahmadinejad's right-hand man, Esfandiar Rahim Mashaei, said to be a modern-day Iranian Rasputin. The strong bond between two men, who were related through the marriage of their children, was one Khamenei chose to break as a way of capsizing the Ahmadinejad presidency and his plan to have Mashaei succeed him in the 2013 presidential elections. Mashaei had anti-clerical bona fide. He had as early as 2004 declared "Islamism to have run its course." He called into question the state's enforcement of strict interpretations of Islamic customs, such as forcing the mandatory veiling for women in public.

In the foreign policy domain, Mashaei's most stinging remark was when he in 2008 said, "Iran today is friends with the people of America and Israel." By saying that, he took a shot at the heart of Khamenei's worldview. Khamenei called Mashaei's statement "illogical" and he was from then a marked man.[64] When, after the 2009 elections, Ahmadinejad appointed Mashaei as his vice president, Khamenei vetoed the decision. All the backstage lobbying on Ahmadinejad was clearly not working. The supreme leader chose to humiliate him publicly to teach the unthankful president a lesson and put him in his place. It was not, however, a path without risks for Khamenei. Ahmadinejad was a very different man than either Rafsanjani or Khatami who preferred to either submit or cut deals with him. Ahmadinejad had no intention to go away quietly. He gave Mashaei another senior role and kept him close at hand. Next, Ahmadinejad's decision to fire his own minister of intelligence, Gholam-Hossein Ejei, who he, and rightly, accused to be an operative for Khamenei, almost brought the government down.

Khamenei then took another unusual step and appointed Ejei's successor, even though this was over the president's head.[65] Humiliated, a sulking Ahmadinejad disappeared for eleven days and refused to go to work. It was a prolonged political paralysis unlike anything modern-day Iran had witnessed. It was a test of nerves between a rabble-rouser president and a supreme leader who on paper saw himself as God's representative on earth. He would not succumb to a mere mortal. In the two years remaining in his presidency, Ahmadinejad was gradually sidelined almost to irrelevance but had to still be handled with care.

As his own defense minister, Hossein Dehghan, later remarked, Ahmadinejad "was like a fireball in your hand. You could toss it from hand to hand, but you could not let it fall down."[66] The populist president quickly found out the real source to his power was not the support of the people but Khamenei's backing. Without that backing Ahmadinejad turned out to be rather helpless even though he had stood up to Khamenei unlike his two predecessors. Khamenei was so frustrated with Ahmadinejad that he implied on more than one occasion that the office of the presidency might be abolished altogether. Rafsanjani called that a bad idea.[67] In the meantime, the same Revolutionary Guards that had been instrumental in bringing Ahmadinejad to power were by now on an all-out assault on Ahmadinejad's political network.[68] In due course, a number of his closest allies, including Mashaei, were thrown in prison.

10

(2013–Present)—The Coming of President Hassan Rouhani

There will be no war. And we will not negotiate [with America].
(Khamenei, May 2019)

Ahmadinejad's betrayal and the devastating international sanctions imposed on Iran over her nuclear program left Khamenei with no option but to look for a shake-up of the domestic political situation and an end to the turmoil in Iran's foreign policy. The 2013 presidential elections presented an opportunity to shift gear. But when Rafsanjani hinted he might be still up for another stab at the presidency, Khamenei's rejection of such an idea was not only unambiguous but eerily cruel. Through an interview Khamenei's older brother, Mohammad, gave to a newspaper, Rafsanjani was not only warned to drop the idea to run again but also branded an "American asset."[1]

Khamenei and his supporters would attach the label of "American Islam" to anyone who opposed them. It was meant as the ultimate insult and disqualifier. Khatami, Mousavi, Ahmadinejad, and many others in the regime had been labeled this way when they stood in Khamenei's way. But it was a first for Rafsanjani. To Khamenei, Rafsanjani's support for the Green opposition had revealed his true colors as someone willing to throw the supreme leader under the bus if an opportunity presented itself. He was closely watching him. Rafsanjani's family lawyer claimed the Ministry of Intelligence, under Khamenei's control, repeatedly asked him to record his conversations with Rafsanjani.[2]

Khamenei's hard-line supporters in Qom even sought to disrobe Rafsanjani of his religious credentials. Rafsanjani had no choice but to strike back. "In [the 1,400 years] history of Shia Islam, there is not even one reference to demotion of the status of a cleric by another group of clerics. The Shiite scholars receive their status from the people."[3] Rafsanjani knew Khamenei was behind it all and said he "smelt conspiracy." In truth, however, very few among his fellow clerics spoke up for Rafsanjani. Over preceding years, Khamenei had diverted huge sums of funds from state coffers in Tehran to seminaries around the country that traditionally had been sponsored through private charitable donations. With Khamenei's control over the purse strings, majority of the clerics selected to stay out of his latest brawl with Rafsanjani.

Instead of stripping Rafsanjani of his official privileges as a regime elder, Khamenei used formal levers at his disposal to prevent him. A few weeks before the elections, the Guardian Council declared Rafsanjani too old to run for the presidency.[4] This was a pretext as he was hardly the oldest among the top regime figures. But the decision smacked of desperation by Khamenei. Rafsanjani, the man who was the most senior living founding father of the Islamic Republic, was stifled as an individual but his political squad was too big to simply disappear. By most accounts Rafsanjani's rather quick acceptance of his disqualification to run rested on the fact that a close ally of his had been approved to run. That was Hassan Rouhani.

A case can be made that Rouhani was in effect Rafsanjani's most successful disciple. But Rouhani also shared very close ties to Khamenei. In that sense, Rouhani stood out among the eight candidates that were given the green light to run in the 2013 presidential elections. No other candidate had this same level of closeness to both Rafsanjani and Khamenei. Rafsanjani, the leaders of the reform movement, and much of the regime supported Rouhani's candidacy. For Khamenei, a Rouhani presidency was more than just an opportunity to keep Rafsanjani out. It was an end to the increasingly wayward populist politics of the Ahmadinejad era.

§

In the weeks leading up to the 2013 presidential elections, the Iranian electorate was positively not impressed. Among the eight presidential hopefuls, none had a trademark political platform to sell. The common slogans were hardly ingenious: each candidate vowed to fight mounting inflation and to bring (what's left of) the oil money to peoples' tables; promised to end the ever-evasive corruption; made fuzzy pledges to fix the economy; and vowed to overcome the huge economic difficulties resulting from international sanctions.

The declared candidates had one more thing in common: none of them dared to question the so-called red lines of the Supreme Leader Khamenei. The foremost "redline" was that no one—including any elected president—should suppose they can go around the leader to shape Tehran's relations with the United States. Khamenei made sure this message came out loud and clear. Just a few days before election day, a top figure close to Khamenei, Ayatollah Emami Kashani, warned that presidential candidates should "not interfere in the fundamental policies of the Islamic Republic" and for example "make statements about [Iran's] policies toward America." If anyone was left in any doubt, Kashani made sure to clarify: "Such policy decisions are neither within the responsibility or capacity of [any] president." In other words, only the supreme leader can guide the course toward Washington.

Whoever could challenge this lopsided bottom line in Tehran was almost guaranteed to capture the attention of the Iranian voter. And no candidate came closer to questioning Khamenei's sacred red lines than Rouhani. But he did so mostly through Rafsanjani who began to throw grenades at Khamenei's rock-hard ideological dogma. In terms of foreign policy, Rafsanjani effectively impugned Tehran's stance on Israel. He offered that Iran should not be in the business of confronting Israel. "If the Arabs end up in a war with Israel, Iran can provide material support to the Arabs," but that is it and no more. Rafsanjani was raising the ante and even challenging the regime's long-held immovable enmity toward the Jewish Israel. The insults hurled at him when he said that were not only what Rafsanjani had anticipated but also what he craved. It helped him cultivate the image that he so desperately desired: a man who admitted ideological zealotry that he had once helped establish as the norm in the Islamic Republic was choking the country. It was another effort at distancing himself from Khamenei, at least in the eyes of the public.

On June 14, 2013, Rouhani won with more than 18 million votes or 50.7 percent of the share in the first round. It was the smallest margin of victory as compared to the ten previous presidential elections since 1979. Rouhani's win was enough to avoid a second round but hardly a landslide. The cynics thought this was Khamenei's way to signal his qualified acceptance of Rouhani as the new president. Rafsanjani was still over the moon and called the election the most "democratic in the world." That was hardly true. What was true was the sense of vindication that was evident in Rafsanjani's demeanor. Not only did Rafsanjani reiterate that Khamenei's backing of Ahmadinejad had brought the Islamic Republic to its knees but that Khamenei should not be in the way of the newly elected president to pursue profound policy reorientation.

There can be no doubt that the 2013 presidential election result was a personal triumph for Rafsanjani. Rouhani, who initially only had 8 percent of the support of the voters, was the beneficiary of Rafsanjani's network endorsing his candidacy. Many of Rafsanjani's closest allies quickly found their way into the Rouhani government. The country had by now been under severe US-led sanctions for three years and bleeding badly. If there was a swift fix, it was to have the sanctions lifted the soonest possible. However, while Rouhani was arguably one of the regime's most seasoned hands when it came to international diplomacy, the open question was whether he would be a transactional president, as had been the case with Rafsanjani, or a truly transformative one.

§

After he helped him win the presidency, Rafsanjani was speaking the language of the necessity of transformation at home and abroad. Just as Rouhani won the presidency in the summer of 2013, Rafsanjani began to question Tehran's rising military support for Bashar Al Assad's war against the Syrian opposition. "The Syrian prisons are so full they have to round people up in stadiums while the [Syrian] government drops chemical bombs on its own people."[5] He said this as the Khamenei-backed Revolutionary Guards were deploying more and more so-called volunteers to Syria to keep Assad in power in Damascus. Rouhani was far more preoccupied with the American question, and he wrongly believed he could compartmentalize Tehran's foreign policy files. It would turn out to be a grave error.

Before he was inaugurated, Rouhani told Iraq's prime minister Nouri Al Maliki to pass on a message to Washington: Iran wants direct talks with Washington. This seasoned politician still thought he could have it both ways. It took him only a few days to create a furor in the West after he arrived in the presidential palace when he told state television that Israel is a "sore that has been sitting on the body of the Islamic world for many years." It was a flashback to the kind of reckless comments Ahmadinejad had become famous. But Rouhani had not spoken off the cuff. His jab at Israel was his ill-judged attempt to keep the ideological zealots in Tehran pleased. It was an early indicator that Rouhani too was an unlikely candidate to become a transformative president. It was certainly very unlike what Rafsanjani had said about Israel just a few months earlier.

After the predictable backlash, and as a way of making amends, Rouhani sent his younger brother to Tehran's only Jewish hospital, the Dr. Sapir Hospital, with a $400,000 financial donation. There were other clumsy steps early on that revealed this new Rouhani government was hardly a panacea in waiting. He even nominated one of the hostage-takers from the US embassy incident from 1979 to the role of Iran's UN ambassador in New York. He only withdrew Hamid Aboutalebi when the Obama administration made it clear the nominee would never be granted an American visa.[6] Rouhani and his team, the best and professional foreign policy cadre that the Islamic Republic could muster, were ham-fisted.

None of this, however, was to prevent Iran and the United States to sign a nuclear deal. A provisional agreement was first signed in late November 2013. It was between Iran and the P5+1 (the United States, the UK, France, Russia, China, and Germany). A saga that had begun in 2002, when Iran's secret nuclear program was exposed by the CIA and the Mossad, appeared to be finally over. In the weeks that followed, Khamenei feared Rouhani might start to see the agreement as a first step in a major recalibration of Iran's approach to the world. He did not have to say it but it was clear he would oppose such a direction, and yet he had to give Rouhani some space while waiting for the benefits of the nuclear deal to kick in. Khamenei kept Rouhani on a short leash. When Rouhani had a fifteen-minute phone conversation with president Obama on September 27, 2013, while in New York to attend the UN, he was accused of disloyalty to Khamenei. A Khamenei mouthpiece, the *Kayhan* newspaper, led the charge. Rouhani had to apologetically assure that without the phone conversation the nuclear deal would not have been possible.

For the twenty-one months between the provisional and the final agreement in July 2105, the Revolutionary Guards watched the nuclear negotiations nervously but kept quiet. They were never particularly worried that Iran would lose its nuclear program; rather, the senior Guards' commanders feared the domestic political clout Rouhani would reap from the resulting international deal. As long as the Guards were not cut out from foreign policy decision-making entirely, they seemed prepared to go along. Khamenei delivered on that. He made sure it was crystal-clear to everyone that while Rouhani-controlled Foreign Ministry would be in charge of the nuclear negotiations, the Guards would continue to hold onto files related to militarized conflicts, principally those in Iraq and in Syria. Rouhani's foreign minister, Javad Zarif, openly admitted that, even as the Foreign Ministry handled nuclear negotiations, Iran's Syria policy was "not in the hands of the Foreign Ministry in Tehran."[7] From Khamenei's perspective, this division of labor worked out: Iran's diplomats possessed the credentials and ethos that resonated with the West. They stood in stark contrast to former president Ahmadinejad's provincialism and learn-on-the-job routine.

This act of balancing factions inside the regime was not a new management style for Khamenei. In September 2013, shortly after he became president, Rouhani gave the Revolutionary Guards an ultimatum of sorts: Revolutionary Guards should be open to compromises both at home and abroad on issues ranging from not playing an excessive role in Iran's economy to acquiescing to more regional cooperation and de-escalation of tensions with Iran's rivals. The day after, Khamenei echoed the president's words in front of those same generals. Khamenei had no choice. In 2013, Iran was faced with historic painful sanctions that few nations had ever had to endure.

Sanctions were not to be lifted before early 2016 and after Iran had done its part to curtail back its nuclear program. The race was on to maximize the number of Western stakeholders in the Iranian nuclear deal's fate. Many of the top Rouhani advisors had been involved in incentivizing American businesses—such as the 1995 deal with oil giant Conoco—in the first half of the 1990s. With the same logic, they once again pushed for big deals with major Western firms to build on the nuclear deal. Hundreds of Western businesspeople arrived in Tehran, and hundreds of commercial Memorandums of Understanding (MoUs) were signed. In the case of cooperation with American firms, past obstacles persisted. A case with a deal with Boeing was illustrative. In 2016 and 2017, Tehran and the American aerospace giant Boeing announced $20 billion in deals for 110 aircraft. The mammoth deal soon came under congressional attack in Washington with credible threats by both Democratic and Republican lawmakers to stop it. The Iranians had still made no friends in Washington. Rouhani had seen it all before in the early 1990s when commercial outreach to US firms had failed to overturn the deep-seated opposition to the Islamic Republic in parts of the American government.

In 1992, Rouhani had turned down to become Rafsanjani's minister of intelligence. He chose to become the head of the Center for Strategic Research (CSR), a think tank established to give direction to Tehran's various strategic interests. As Kayhan Barzegar, a former CSR staffer and prominent foreign policy voice in Tehran put it, Rouhani wanted to "cultivate some of the country's brightest moderate minds" in order to push for a more pragmatic approach to domestic, cultural, and foreign policy. Rafsanjani had established the think tank in 1989 in one of the first major acts of his presidency. CRS was to push for Iran "playing a constructive role" in world affairs and to reintegrate into the world economy. As Barzegar described it, however, while Iran's system "grants some independence to the president, particularly in domestic affairs, his ability in directing political change or making changes in the security policy of foreign affairs in contrast to the leader's [Khamenei] preference is, at most, trivial."[8]

Indeed, the dichotomy of the Iranian system was still in the way. After the 2015 nuclear deal, the generals in the Guards were still acting with near impunity in the region's conflict zones. Despite the Foreign Ministry's reservations about the Guards' strategies and goals in Syria and Iraq, the Rouhani government kept quiet and opted to choose its battles carefully. Rouhani would in his 2017 reelection campaign break new ground when he claimed he sought reelection "for the sake of Iran and [then] Islam."[9] He was nibbling at the idea of being the "nationalist" president, meaning putting Iranian national interests first. But Khamenei and the Guards stayed loyal to the idea of transnational Islamism, and all the havoc that came with it, and were in no mood for Rouhani to even tone down their agenda. It was not hard to see who had the upper hand. On January 2, 2016, just as international sanctions were to be rolled back on Iran, a pro-Khamenei mob attacked the Saudi embassy in Tehran in retaliation for

Riyadh's execution of a Shia dissident cleric by the name of Ayatollah Nimr Al Nimr. Riyadh promptly cut diplomatic ties with Tehran, and a number of other Arab states recalled their ambassadors from Iran. With one act, the pro-Khamenei street mob, organized by higher-ups among the hard-liners, had quashed Rouhani's game plan of marching toward foreign policy rehabilitation.

§

From Khamenei's perspective, the 2015 nuclear agreement achieved his goal of lifting international sanctions against Iran. Once that goal was achieved, he opted to put the brakes on the rest of Rouhani's agenda. The ayatollah made it very clear that the warming of US–Iranian relations that came as a result of Rouhani's bargaining proved irksome. In a letter to Rouhani that expressed support for the nuclear deal, Khamenei closed his message with a curious but explicit demand: "Importing any consumer materials from the United States must be seriously avoided." Khamenei's point was not about US consumer goods, which are readily available in Iran, but to firmly nudge Rouhani away from broadening the diplomatic dialogue with Washington, which he suspected was the moderate president's ultimate policy objective.

Khamenei's displeasure toward potential rapprochement with the United States again revealed his own insecurity. He still viewed Washington as both intending to and capable of bringing down the Islamic Republic, with nuclear negotiations serving as a trap. In this conception of US grand strategy, Rouhani was at best cast as a naive enabler and, at worst, a willing agent of Washington, as some of Rouhani's most hardened critics, such as Guards' boss General Mohammad Ali Jafari, openly suggested at times. Nor was this, of course, the first time Khamenei has reined in an Iranian president. It was all too reminiscent of what Khamenei did to Khatami when he had become too ambitious in his plans for political change (including overtures toward Washington that went over Khamenei's head) and was censured. The same was true when Ahmadinejad acted as a loose cannon in the last two years of his presidency (2011–13).

But in clamping down on Rouhani, Khamenei had jumped the gun. If anything, he may have forced the president's hand. The half sentence admonishing US–Iranian trade in Khamenei's letter to Rouhani took on a life of its own; after its publication, the Revolutionary Guards and their resources—media outlets, their minions in the Iranian parliament, and other lackeys in the state machinery—all ripped into Rouhani's government. Everything it stood for was now a fair target. Khamenei had provided the Guards with a blank check to "identify threats to the political order" and address them as they saw fit. This measure was bound to receive pushback from Rouhani's faction.

Obama's Outreach to Khamenei and the 2015 Nuclear Deal

By publicly mandating unelected Revolutionary Guards' generals to act as a check on a popularly elected president, Khamenei crudely pitted two centers of Iranian power against one another. But in doing so, Khamenei merely raised the stakes in an intra-regime power struggle. One, however, might have caused the supreme leader to lose control within Tehran's political decision-making process. Khamenei, the master ideologue, had concluded that Ahmadinejad-era intransigence in foreign policy, which he had himself encouraged, could not continue.[10] With Rouhani's election, Khamenei set out to reverse course. As soon as the nuclear deal was signed, though, Khamenei had to make sure no one misunderstood this to be the all-clear for normal relations. The "arrogant" United States could not prevent Tehran from supporting its allies in the region, a reference to Iran's support for the Assad regime, the Lebanese Hezbollah, the Palestinian Hamas, and other militant Islamists. "Even after this deal, our policy toward the arrogant U.S. will not change. We don't have any negotiations or deal with the U.S. on different issues in the world or [in] the region."

History will probably conclude that president Obama took a gamble on the Islamic Republic and fell short of his expectations. "Yes, we can" was Obama's powerful antidote to all sorts of obstinate policy challenges. In the realm of foreign policy, the cold war between the United States and the Islamist ruling class in Tehran had perilously lingered since 1979. In the interim, the 2002 discovery of Tehran's nuclear ambitions had elevated the Iranian question as a US national security priority. Obama's pitch was simple: engaging with Tehran was the only way forward. And yet, in all of his laudable efforts, Obama failed to foresee another equally simple proposition: that the tip of power in Tehran had little desire to sincerely engage with Washington. Anti-Americanism was a pillar of the Islamic Republic's ideology. Khamenei wanted to keep it that way. Obama had set out to pursue "tough, direct presidential diplomacy with Iran without preconditions." He was clear-eyed about the division of power in Tehran and about who ultimately had the clout to deliver results on the Iranian side. He had ignored Ahmadinejad and aimed directly at Khamenei. As Obama's team got Iran's power pyramid right, they woefully misread Khamenei.

It was clear early on in the Obama presidency that Khamenei was at best good for narrow tactical concessions if circumstances called for them. He never had any intention of swinging the strategic pendulum away from anti-Americanism. It was only after the Obama administration successfully built an international coalition to confront Iran's nuclear ambition that Khamenei succumbed to the pressure. Knowing full well that in the long run Iran's economy could not withstand international sanctions, he had permitted secret talks to be held with the Americans. Tellingly, the end goal in his mind was a narrow policy objective: to find a way to end the nuclear saga and have the sanctions lifted. Khamenei spoke of respect begetting respect, but his ideological rhetoric kept the United States in place as Iran's impeccable foe.

Some of the posturing was no doubt about saving face. Khamenei is stewarding a system that has for nearly four decades devotedly nourished a worldview in which the United States is the angel of darkness and a superpower that has to be confronted at every turn. For the purportedly foolproof Khamenei a climbdown on the American question would be tantamount to fallibility. In his March 2012 Persian New Year message, almost two years after he had approved secret talks with the Americans but just as international economic sanctions were starting to seriously bite, Khamenei went on the offensive. He spoke about "economic self-sufficiency," saying that the United States and other Western nations were in no position to act against Iran militarily. But this was pure brinkmanship. Khamenei knew that Iran is no North Korea, which can cut itself off from the rest of the world.

Worsening economic conditions had a direct impact on the extent of popular mobilization against the regime. Khamenei was cornered and close to overseeing the implosion of the economy. His call for "self-sufficiency" had over the course of months been superseded by his call for "heroic flexibility," a code for making any concessions necessary to safeguard the future of the Islamic Republic. It was a perfect moment for the Obama White House to drag Khamenei out of his comfort zone and aim to broaden the basis of the talks between the United States and Iran. As it turned out, the July 2015 nuclear accord ended up being solely focused on the number of centrifuges Iran could spin and other nuclear-specific limitations imposed on the country for a specific time period.

The litany of other concerns about Tehran's behavior—from its suppression of its own people to its expansionist agenda in the post–Arab Spring Middle East—were left basically unaddressed by the agreement that the world powers reached with Tehran. In its defense, the Obama administration maintained that a comprehensive bargain that might have tackled all of the concerns of the United States and its allies, such as Israel and the Gulf Arab states, was never a realistic goal. Still, this presupposition downplays how fearful Khamenei was in the lead-up to the 2015 nuclear deal about his grip on an increasingly anxious Iranian population. The skeptics in Washington and among the Iranian opposition felt Obama could have forced Khamenei to concede more on nuclear-related matters but that he was too engrossed with the idea of cutting any deal with Tehran and that he was after a signature foreign policy achievement rather than extracting the maximum possible concessions from Khamenei at a time when Obama clearly had the upper hand and much international support to bank on.

While that assessment might be uncharitable, there is no doubt that Obama wanted to be the anti-Bush. He wanted to be the US president who learned the lessons of the disastrous US military invasion of Iraq in 2003 and sought to defuse challenges emanating from the Middle East through the art of diplomacy. In his furthermost expectations, Obama had believed a nuclear deal with Iran would pave the way for normalizing relations between Washington and Tehran. And while on Obama's watch the United States and Iran came the closest to having functioning diplomatic ties since the 1979 Iranian revolution, resumption of ties with Washington was never seriously on the cards for Khamenei.

§

Rafsanjani defended the 2015 nuclear agreement until the day he died. "The Americans wanted to have Iran settle for an oil-for-food scheme [a reference to sanctions on Iraq during the 1990s]." In his view, Rouhani had achieved a far superior deal. "Now I can die [in peace]," Rouhani alleged Rafsanjani had uttered after the deal had been signed.[11] Rafsanjani maintained that he had discussed the need for an end to the nuclear standoff with Khamenei before Rouhani was elected in June 2013. Rouhani and his Foreign Minister Javad Zarif were by some accounts unaware that secret direct talks had been ongoing between Iran and the Americans through Omani mediations from the days when Ahmadinejad still sat in the presidential palace.[12]

That Khamenei would have kept Rafsanjani in the loop in regard to his secret negotiations with the Americans is still a mystery. If there ever was a coordinated Khamenei–Rafsanjani game plan, the objectives were not hard to identify. First, to turn a page after the eight-year Ahmadinejad presidency. For Khamenei, accepting a Rouhani presidency was not only a compromise with Rafsanjani but a way to let the Iranian public let off some steam by pretending that their votes had brought about this turn of page. Rouhani's promise of change soon turned out to be as empty as the pledges Khatami had made when he ran for the presidency in 1997. Still, Rouhani's 2013 election did provide a temporary relief to an Iranian political system that was on the edge. Khamenei, as he did with Rafsanjani, could have blocked a Rouhani candidacy but saw him as a cover to shift policy.

The Khamenei–Rouhani Tango

Rouhani's pitch to the Iranian public was simple: he was to be the economic fixer that would end the devastating sanctions. And to address the problem of Iran's free-falling economy, Tehran had to strive for structural changes on both the home front and its dealings with the world, particularly the West. Rafsanjani and Rouhani sought to convince Khamenei to shift gear and to build on the 2015 nuclear compromise rather than to double down on the standoff against Washington. Aiming for maximum impact, Rafsanjani again chose to argue for course of policy by invoking the long-dead Khomeini.

He mournfully said,

> Ultimately, the policy that we are now adopting, to neither speak with the US nor have relations with it, is unsustainable. The US is the world's superpower. And what difference is there between Europe and the US, China and the US, or Russia and the US? If we can negotiate with them, why can't we negotiate with the US? Negotiating does not mean that we surrender to them. Negotiations means that if they accept our positions or we accept theirs, it's done. I wanted to open negotiations with the Americans based on the conditions that I had set forth, but we were unable to.[13]

The haziness around what Rafsanjani was saying was deliberate. As many times before, he craved space for deniability. He warned against open-ended and costly foreign policy adventurism and specifically questioned the nature of Tehran's support for Lebanon's Hezbollah and the Syrian regime of Bashar Al Assad. He would allude to the importance of nation-building at home but step back when forcefully challenged by Khamenei's hard-line supporters. On one occasion, Rafsanjani had to go as far as to claim that his voice had been faked when a tape recording of one of his speeches, critical of Iran's adventurist regional policy, emerged.[14]

Rouhani, the president, was hardly any more courageous than his arch sponsor. In fact, Rouhani's critique of Iran's foreign policy record was predictably much more guarded, but it was not any less profound if he could institute what he was preaching.

For example, he urged for a rebalancing in how Tehran dealt with the West versus non-Western states such as Russia and China. The latter, members of the Rouhani cabinet sincerely believed, would not alone be able to deliver what Tehran desperately needed: foreign investment, technological know-how, and the offer of new markets for Iran's top exports such oil and natural gas.

In his first speech at the UN in 2013, Rouhani had promised a new era. *"Be relentless in striving for the cause of Good / Bring the spring, you must, / Banish the winter, you should* (emphasis mine).["]15 This beautiful medieval Persian poetry was widely welcomed when he uttered those words. But could Rouhani deliver on his end? He could but only as long as Khamenei let him. That is why Tehran made enough compromises that enabled for the nuclear deal to be signed by 2015. But the nuclear compromise, which Khamenei had himself initiated when he accepted to hold secret talks with Washington, would soon turn out to be a one-off.

§

The American presidential elections of November 2016, and the election of Donald Trump, resulted in a new round of squabbling in Tehran. Trump had vowed to take the United States out of the 2015 nuclear deal and the question was how Tehran should respond. For Khamenei, the nuclear deal was principally about removing international sanctions. He did not care whether the United States imposed unilateral sanctions on Iran or not. Rouhani was not so sure. He sought to make the case that Washington under Trump could still harm Iran badly even if he sought to do it unilaterally and against the objections of international opinion. That is exactly what Trump did.

As a candidate, Trump's statements about US foreign policy and Iran had been a mixed bag. On the one hand, some of his statements suggested a willingness to cut deals with America's adversaries—such as Iran—as long as the benefits cut both ways. It even carried a hint of the type of transactional relations that Iran had sought to cultivate with Republican presidents going back to Reagan and Bush Sr. in the 1980s. In contrast, the Democratic Party and its 2016 presidential candidate, Hillary Clinton, were feared as meddlesome liberal internationalists who would poke their noses in Iran's internal affairs.

In Tehran, Clinton was never really considered as an heir who could build on what Obama had achieved with Iran. Her solid record of support for Israel and president Bill Clinton's record in confronting Iran in the 1990s were definitely a cause of introspection in Tehran. Her closeness to the Arab states of the Persian Gulf, such as Iran's rival Saudi Arabia, was also a cause of interest in Tehran. Reports that the Clinton Foundation had received funding from the Arab Gulf States, including $25 million from the Saudis, certainly generated plenty of coverage in Iranian state-run media. Trump, to the delight of many in Tehran, had on the other hand been critical of the Saudis, calling them "freeloaders" who would not last as a country without US protection.

Tehran also initially welcomed Trump's views on the situation in Syria: like Tehran and Moscow, Trump lumped the multifarious Syrian opposition together with the Islamic State (ISIS). In that equation, he judged Assad as the lesser evil. This was music to the ears of Khamenei. Iran's generals took their cue from statements by Russia's influential ambassador in Tehran, Levan Dzhagaryan, who called Trump's comments on Syria a few days after the 2016 US election "hopeful." Dzhagaryan's words echoed his optimism that Trump could undo what they saw as the Obama administration's mistakes in the Middle East. Yahya Safavi, a top military adviser to Khamenei, even expressed his anticipation that Trump might rethink the United States' posture toward Iran. Safavi, who was from 1997 to 2007 the head of the Revolutionary Guards, pointed to Syria and Iraq as the two crucial arenas in which the United States might move closer to the Iranian and Russian positions. And he at least urged other Iranian officials to avoid prematurely judging the American president-elect. His remarks were, in many ways, unprecedented. Revolutionary Guards' generals had long relied on unconditional anti-Americanism. It was safe, however, to assume that Safavi was speaking in close coordination with Khamenei's office.

Hard-liners in Tehran clustered around Khamenei also saw another immediate benefit to a Trump presidency. He was found to be a figure bound to galvanize European and international public opinion against the United States. In doing so, Trump would make the reimposition of any new set of international sanctions on Iran much harder. In other words, a Trump presidency was a win-win for Khamenei. Due to the 2015 nuclear deal, he would see the burden of international sanctions on Iran continue to be removed without having to endure the treacherous dialogue with Washington. Rouhani was unconvinced. He said that such a scenario was too good to be true. He would turn to be far more accurate in his expectations from a Trump presidency.

Almost four decades after Ayatollah Khomeini capitalized on it as a way to mobilize his core supporters, the American question was still a pawn in an intra-regime fight. Rouhani's so-called moderate camp, as Rafsanjani had begun to articulate from the late 1980s, believed détente with the United States was a source of domestic and international empowerment. The hard-line camp still viewed it as a direct challenge to their narrow domestic and foreign interests. Trump's victory soon turned out to be far worse for Tehran than even the worst scenarios imagined by Rouhani. It was about this time that Rafsanjani's attacks against Khamenei and his supporters again became explicit. It was even more damning than his condemnation of Khamenei's handling of the 2009 presidential election debacle.

"Who gave you the right to have arms, the broadcasting [media] or choosing Friday prayers," he said in a dig at Khamenei.[16] Whispers in Iran grew louder that Khamenei was turning the Islamic Republic into a Taliban-like nightmare, with himself as the sole judge, jury, and executioner. Rafsanjani, one of the last remaining founding fathers of the Islamic Republic, felt the need to declare remorse. "Constitutions change everywhere [around the world] and we have to work on it too," he implicitly said about Khamenei's endless appetite for power and micro-management.[17] Rafsanjani's assault was so severe that it raised serious questions about whether he could avoid imprisonment or house arrest.

The Impact of the Death of Rafsanjani in 2017

On March 10, 2016, Khamenei met with a group of elderly clerics from the Assembly of Experts—Iran's equivalent to the Vatican's College of Cardinals. That morning, sitting in a small hall with whitewashed walls, an animated Khamenei had something particular in mind: he wanted to speak about his successor. The assembly, made up of eighty-eight senior Shia Muslim clerics, was created with two key functions in mind: to oversee the leader's performance and to choose his successor. That morning, they were convened to discuss the latter. The 77-year-old Khamenei turned to his audience and made his basic, but powerful pitch to the clerics, including those recently reelected for another eight-year term. I will not be around forever, he said, but "a supreme leader has to be a revolutionary." "Don't," Khamenei implored, "be bashful" when it comes to choosing the next man.

The loaded remark, and the insinuation that some of the gathered figures lack a revolutionary zest, was a shot at the man sitting next to Khamenei, Rafsanjani. Khamenei and Rafsanjani, symbolizing the status quo versus the promise of reform, each saw the succession process as both a pivotal juncture for Iran and their individual legacies. The regime had only gone through a succession process once before, in 1989, when Khamenei became supreme leader. That last succession process turned out to be a protracted affair, spanning at least five years and involving plenty of intrigue and turns and twists. This latest succession process was likely to be even more beleaguered by intra-regime personal and factional competition.

Twenty-seven years after Rafsanjani had brokered Khamenei's rise to become supreme leader, it was easy to see that he had outmaneuvered his on-and-off ally and rival. And yet, he was still unable to extinguish Rafsanjani's influence or the many secrets he frequently threatened to reveal. Rafsanjani kept calling himself the principal enabler behind the moderate government of Rouhani, and he frequently hurled himself into fights against the moderate president's hard-line opponents. In these battles, he believed he was winning; Rafsanjani's sense of confidence about the future was on vivid display a few weeks later on the cover of *Shargh*, a top reformist newspaper. It simply ran a headline quote by Rafsanjani, "Now I can die peacefully."

But could he? Khamenei's speech on March 10 and the jab at those lacking revolutionary credentials signaled his fears about Rafsanjani's ability to engineer his succession, the same way Rafsanjani brought Khamenei to power in 1989. Khamenei had fired the first shot. Leading up to the last elections for the Assembly of Experts in February 2016, Rafsanjani had launched a campaign to elevate the candidacy of Hassan Khomeini, a 43-year-old reformist-leaning grandson of Ayatollah Khomeini. The young Khomeini was touted by pro-Rafsanjani circles as ideal to succeed Khamenei as supreme leader. But he was rejected by the Khamenei-controlled Guardian Council, the regime's vetting filter. The reasons given for Hassan Khomeini's rejection were hardly convincing—including his age, even though younger candidates made the selection—but Hassan Khomeini and his allies took it on the chin. The Rafsanjani circle knew better than giving pretexts for all-out assaults on them by Khamenei and his forces and chose to stall for time.

§

On January 8, 2017, the lifeless body of the 82-year-old Rafsanjani was found in a swimming pool in Saad Abad Palace in upscale north Tehran. Few were willing to believe the official explanation that he had had a heart attack and subsequently expired in the water. Unlike Khamenei, who had recently battled prostate ailments, Rafsanjani had been in good health. All sorts of theories were raised. When, a few days later, Tehran's iconic Plasco high-rise building collapsed after it caught fire in a moment captured on live television, rumors swirled around that the catastrophic incident had been manufactured to take attention away from Rafsanjani's suspicious death. Such was the public's distrust and indignation.

The fate of Plasco raised other questions. "Iranian missiles can reach any target in Tel Aviv but the fire trucks of Tehran municipality cannot reach above 10th floors," was a joke that made the rounds. That the building was owned by a multi-billion-dollar organization, the Foundation of the Oppressed and Disabled, under Khamenei's control deepened the public anger. The organization had repeatedly violated building codes but it was untouchable under Khamenei's auspices. The event illustrated the problem of lack of transparency and accountability in the country. Instead of spending on basic services and safeguards on the home front, the Iranian state was busy with military interventions in Iraq, Syria, and elsewhere. The overlap of Rafsanjani's death with the haunting image of the collapse of Plasco happened as Donald Trump entered the White House on January 21, 2017. Trump had promised that he would abandon the 2015 nuclear deal. His national security advisor, Michael Flynn, immediately put Iran "on notice" and Washington issued a sudden ban on all Iranian travelers to the United States. In the weeks following Rafsanjani's death, coinciding with the arrival of Trump, a sense of national alarm gripped Iran.

Meanwhile, the same pro-Khamenei circles that had spent nearly decades attacking him as a seditionist and counterrevolutionary were suddenly out in big numbers praising his record. In their recollections, it was Rafsanjani as the second-in-command to Khomeini in the 1979–89 period that was eulogized. The more recent version of Rafsanjani, the supporter of Khatami's reformist movement or the sponsor of Rouhani's platform of political moderation, was conveniently kept out of the tributes. The praise and the sudden shift in tone were shameless. But Rafsanjani was gone, and the pro-Khamenei camp no longer needed to fear his machinations, and complimenting him now came at no cost.

But statements by his family fueled speculation that Rafsanjani had been murdered. Swimming was routine for him and only a week earlier a doctor had given him a clean bill of health. "Mr. Hashemi [Rafsanjani] has easily another 10–15 years left in him," one of his daughters said a doctor had assessed shortly before his death. The family had demanded an autopsy but this was denied. The Rafsanjani family were soon told to stop speaking to the media about his death.[18] They were informed the matter would be handled by the Supreme National Security Council (SNSC). Its head, Ali Shamkhani, told Rafsanjani's daughters that "radioactive particles had been found" in his urine but then the investigation went cold and nothing more has come from it since. The family also claimed that intelligence agents had immediately taken away all surveillance tapes from the swimming pool hall the very same day Rafsanjani had died. More ominously, Rafsanjani's personal files, including his political will, had been taken away from his office safe immediately after his death.

His eldest daughter, Fatemeh, implicated Khamenei but without naming him. "As soon as my father passed away, they quickly emptied his safe. We very much like to know what happened to his will. They think we have some important information and secrets of the regime."[19] It is still an unresolved riddle. Perhaps the mystery is linked to the fact that Rafsanjani had supposedly written a new will before he died.[20] The remaining Rafsanjani family members seem to deliberately keep the rumor mill alive. "My dad was smarter than leave secret documents behind just like that," said Faezeh, the younger daughter. "If they exist, it should not be hard to publish them."[21] The disappeared political will and files from Rafsanjani's safe might just be insurance against further harassment of the family. In the weeks and months that followed, the anti-Rafsanjani campaign would resurface but his family were more or less left physically untouched but would go on to experience phased-in marginalization.[22]

§

By the end of his life, Rafsanjani strived to be compared to Amir Kabir—the political reformer of the mid-nineteenth-century Persia. In one of his last recorded speeches, he read aloud from a book about how Amir Kabir had dispatched an envoy to Europe (Austria and Prussia) to recruit teachers for a new modern and secular school established in Iran. "I invited them to Persia but I am no longer in power and I fear my successor (as prime minister) will not welcome these Europeans the way I would have," Amir Kabir was quoted by him to have said. Amir Kabir was a modernizer but reactionary forces had him killed. Rafsanjani wanted to be seen in the same modernist light. With tears rolling down his face, the small group of his visitors could be in no doubt that Rafsanjani was not only comparing himself to Amir Kabir but that he so deeply regretted failing short in his own political mission in life.[23] The anti-modernizer in the story he quoted was no doubt Khamenei. Rafsanjani's point was that when he was gone the process to modernize Iran would be halted. He had been the guardian of reform in the Islamic Republic.[24] It was, to be sure, an exaggeration. But Khamenei's monopolization of power was by now so extreme that even his old accomplice wanted to reforge his record. Rafsanjani wanted history to recall him as a reformer and not as Khamenei's once brother-in-arm.

Rafsanjani did not expressly signal who should be his political heir, but Hassan Rouhani was the most natural candidate. The Iranian press at the time mentioned other names, such as Hassan Khomeini, the 44-year-old grandson of Ayatollah Khomeini, and Mohammad Khatami, the former president. None of these men, however, could fill Rafsanjani's big shoes. Rouhani was soon to shift into survival mode as the return of US sanctions on Iran decimated the economy. Hassan Khomeini, despite his reformist leanings, chose to remain neutral to preserve any fighting chance to one day put himself forward as a candidate to replace Khamenei as supreme leader. And Khamenei did not need to nor intended to let Mohammad Khatami replace Rafsanjani as his go-between with political forces outside the hard-line camp. Whoever aspired to seize Rafsanjani's mantle had to be able to be a bridge between the reformists and Khamenei. It turned out that no political figure in the Islamic Republic could do that. Unsurprisingly the so-called reformist and moderate wings of the regime began a steady but pronounced decline after Rafsanjani's death.

Rouhani Faces Trump in the White House

Two weeks after Rafsanjani's death, Donald Trump walked into the White House as Iran entered its own presidential election season. Incumbent president Rouhani, having achieved no notable reform of any kind, had one claim to success and that was the 2015 nuclear deal. That was now hanging by a thread as Trump was preparing to withdraw from it. On top of it all, Rafsanjani, Rouhani's long-time protector against Khamenei, was dead. Rouhani's political fortunes looked distinctly uncertain and it was about to deteriorate. Within 48 hours of the Trump administration banning Iranian travelers to the United States on January 27, 2017, Iran test-fired a ballistic missile in the Persian Gulf as a symbol of resistance. Washington then responded within 48 hours by naming another twenty-five individuals and companies in Iran to the list of sanctioned entities by the United States. However, even as Washington was introducing new sanctions, Rouhani's inner circle maintained that Trump was surely open to cut a deal with Tehran. The usual tired incentives were dangled: Oil Minister Bijan Zangeneh repeated that "US [oil and gas] companies face no ban to enter Iran's oil industry" and should act. Rouhani's Transportation Minister Abbas Akhoundi wondered the Americans surely would not cancel the $20 billion deal for 110 passenger jets, signed with Boeing as recently as in December 2016. In Tehran, the Boeing deal was the one litmus test that was watched carefully. The stunned Iranians soon had to endure seeing Boeing leave Iran under pressure back in Washington.

A new dangerous cycle of quid pro quo was set in motion. Trump's first National Security Advisor Michael Flynn had been the first to put Iran "on notice." Flynn held the job for one week only but the question of pressuring Iran was to become a fixed feature of the Trump administration. Pressure for the sake of it appeared to be the entire strategy. For Khamenei, Trump epitomized the bullying of American power, and he was unequivocal. "Iran will burn the [2015] nuclear agreement if Trump tears it apart," he insisted. Khamenei knew very well what the Trump administration wanted from Iran, even if it was not at first plainly formulated. Washington wanted Iran to roll back its regional agenda and support for movements such as Hezbollah in Lebanon or the Palestinian Hamas and other militant regional groups. Trump was unwittingly asking Khamenei for an ideological makeover, and the Iranian leader was not willing to even ponder it. Not knowing if Trump might next push for a policy of "regime change" in Tehran, Khamenei had even before the reimposition of sanctions had to determine how best to maintain political stability in Tehran as pilling American pressure coincided with Iran's 2017 presidential elections.

§

On April 9, 2017, Ebrahim Raisi, a longtime behind-the-scenes operative of the Islamic Republic closely associated with Khamenei, declared his candidacy in the May 19 presidential elections. He was something of a consensus candidate of the Islamic Republic's array of handful of factions representing hard-line positions. Raisi was neither charismatic nor known by the Iranian public. Unless there was mass vote-rigging, his chances of unseating Rouhani were next to nothing. But Rouhani's camp had reasons to fear that Khamenei's inner circle would resort to just such tactics. For months, Raisi's name had been mentioned as a likely successor to Khamenei who was now in his late 70s.

The 57-year-old Raisi's sudden jump into the presidential fray made most sense as part of a broader campaign by the hard-line anti-Rouhani camp to engineer a Raisi win and place him on the path for supreme leadership when Khamenei had died. In an event that was highly publicized by state media, the top brass of the Revolutionary Guards went to Khamenei's hometown of Mashhad to pay Raisi an official visit. Just a year earlier, in March 2016, Khamenei had appointed him to become the head of the Imam Reza shrine, Iran's largest religious shrine and a multibillion-dollar business enterprise. The Guards are widely believed to be among the principal voices, if not the kingmakers, on the question of choosing the next supreme leader—the image of the top Guards' generals, such as Qassem Soleimani, sitting at Raisi's feet in Mashhad elevated his political profile even further.

Raisi's campaign pledge was to "save the nation." "I deeply believe that the (current) situation can be changed and that bringing back mobility, vitality and (economic) boom [growth] to people's lives is possible with the help of God." Raisi's focus on the economy, unemployment, and combating corruption was certainly not coincidental. It looked like a repeat of the 2005 election was underway with a simple pitch from the hard-line camp: accept the political status quo and be economically rewarded in return. But Raisi was no Ahmadinejad. He was ill-equipped to play the role of the populist or surprise candidate the way Ahmadinejad had done in 2005. If real power in the Islamic Republic runs through the Office of the Supreme Leader, as it does, the notion of Raisi as a candidate of change was nonsensical and roundly dismissed by the public. No doubt that Khamenei preferred Raisi over Rouhani. But he was not about to risk popular backlash as in 2009 and test the public's patience by ramming Raisi through to the presidency.

While Rouhani had hardly made good on every pledge he made when he ran for office in 2013, Iranian voters have a proven track record of opting for the most moderate of candidates available if given an opportunity. Raisi's only sources of hope were his impeccable hard-line credentials and the trust he enjoyed from Khamenei himself. The ground was fertile for an epic fight but Khamenei backed away. There was no sign of any major intervention to strong-arm a Raisi win. Rouhani was reelected with 57 percent of the vote, a bigger margin that he had secured as a presidential candidate in 2013. Afterward, unsure about how to position himself vis-à-vis Khamenei, Rouhani decided to go on the offense but it would not last long. In June 2017, the two men clashed in the nastiest way to date. Rouhani had kept complaining about "forces" that stand in his way to bring about change. Basically, it was a call to action and the need to change and create trust on the other side, the West, so Iran could free itself from self-inflicted global isolation.

Soon after, Khamenei gave a speech where Rouhani was in attendance, and basically said to the president: stop complaining. You are the president, get on with it. Typical for him, Khamenei was not about to accept any blame for Iran's laundry list of socioeconomic problems and deep anger in society about the state of affairs. Instead he hinted again, as he did when Ahmadinejad was in office, that the role of the president could be abolished altogether if Rouhani kept up his defiance. Khamenei was so incensed with Rouhani that he sought to formalize an unspoken rule that has long been practiced under his watch: for his minions, armed or otherwise, to bypass the government and act independently in whatever way they saw fit to preserve the Islamic Republic and with Khamenei as its crux. In the Persian language, his diktat was hair-raising. In English, "Aatash Be Ekhtiar" is best summed up as "fire at will [when you see fit]." He was issuing a license for vigilantism and risking chaos. Even Khamenei's supporters struggled to rationalize the instruction.[25]

The extraordinarily strained regional environment reinforced Khamenei's inkling for policy consolidation in Tehran. On June 7, 2017, the rabidly anti-Iran and anti-Shia Islamic State (ISIS) staged a number of deadly attacks in Tehran, including the Majles building and the mausoleum of Ayatollah Khomeini, killing eighteen people. Tehran retaliated by firing ballistic missiles at ISIS bases at Deir Ezzor in eastern Syria. The ISIS attack was a stark reminder of the dangers of blowback from Iran's multiple interventions in the Arab world. Those in Tehran who questioned Tehran's Arab policy argued that without some kind of introspection, Iran would likely remain in the line of fire of Sunni jihadists for a long time to come. Some of Rouhani's foreign policy counselors, such as Mohammad Sadr, had long argued for a more even-handed approach to the Syrian civil war and more prudent Arab policy.[26] Khamenei and the Revolutionary Guards will have none of it. "We have to fight them in Iraq and Syria so we don't have to fight them at home."

The Guards said the retaliation was a "warning message" to ISIS and "regional and international allies." Khamenei saw fit to use the event to respond to Trump since he had a few weeks earlier on his first foreign visit, which took him to Riyadh, called Iran the godfather of terrorism in the Middle East. "You [the United States] and your agents are the source of instability in the Middle East," the Iranian leader charged. "Who created the Islamic State? America [did]."[27] The contrast with Rouhani was self-evident. The Iranian president did not explicitly blame the United States or Saudi Arabia for the June 2017 ISIS attack in Tehran. But Rouhani's bandwidth to quarrel with Khamenei on Iran's Arab policy was extremely limited.

This round of tug-of-war between Khamenei and Rouhani in the summer of 2017 was followed by truce. It was again Rouhani that caved. On August 3, 2017, at his official inauguration to commence his second term, he had another opportunity to make his mark. It was a moment for him to display his intentions to more aggressively stand up for political change. Instead, Rouhani's speech was cautious and uninspiring. He had nothing to offer in the much-awaited speech that can be construed as a challenge to Khamenei. On foreign policy, Iran's policies in the Arab world were left unquestioned. Rouhani accepted that Khamenei's ideas of a "revolutionary" approach to the world would be the order of business of his second presidential term. For Khamenei, "revolutionary" means giving the generals of the Revolutionary Guards—such as Quds Force chief Qassem Soleimani, who was assassinated by the United States in a drone attack in January 2020—a free hand to determine Iran's approach to the Arab world. The Revolutionary Guards had by now become so brash they did not see a need to pretend Rouhani and Zarif mattered. It came to a boil in late February 2019 when Soleimani brought Syria's President Assad to Tehran to meet Khamenei while keeping Zarif in the dark. The insulted Zarif resigned but was persuaded not to go. You might say it was the clearest example since 1979 of the impotence of the Foreign Ministry in Tehran. When all is said and done, the Foreign Ministry does not call the shots as evident by Zarif's multiple resignation attempts, which were nothing but efforts to generate some leverage for himself against his rivals inside the regime. Despite his often-shameful misrepresentations about the Islamic Republic's record at international forums, the cosmopolitan Zarif could not shake off the doubters in the Revolutionary Guards.

The Guards' experience from involvement in multiple regional wars had taught them that plenty of Arab constituencies are receptive to Tehran's militant Islamist agenda. The trouble for Rouhani was that a militant foreign policy, even if successful in the region, nullified his hopes to make Iran into a "normal" country that the badly needed mainstream international foreign investors might look at with serious eyes. Another challenge for Rouhani is how far Tehran can continue to provide patronage to militant allies in the Arab world and at what cost. If Tehran is as committed to intra-Arab conflicts as Khamenei suggests, it could remain militarily tied up for years to come. To this day, the Iranian state has revealed little information about the financial cost of its operations in Iraq and Syria, with most estimated in the $20–$30 billion range.

Rouhani also again pledged that Tehran was not to abandon the 2015 nuclear deal. It was a signal to the Europeans and part of Rouhani's attempt to isolate Trump. He told the 1,200 local and foreign guests who attended the inauguration that Tehran was not about to succumb to "those who are new to politics," in a dig at the US president. Rouhani ignored the entrenched hostile reality of relations that long predated Trump. No doubt, Trump's arrival had energized the Iranian opposition and Tehran's regional rivals. In one case, a few months after Trump arrived, the Saudis financed the birth of *Iran International*, a first-class television channel with a multi-million-dollar annual budget, headquartered in London and operated by Iranian exiles. Meanwhile, throughout 2017 and 2018 a stream of US politicians, including former New York mayor Rudy Giuliani and Senators John McCain, Roy Blunt, John Cornyn, and Thom Tilis, all visited the MEK leadership based at their displaced persons camp in Albania. McCain told Maryam Rajavi, the MEK leader, that "Someday, Iran will be free. Someday, we will all gather in that square [Shahyaad in Tehran]." Tehran did not respond publicly but could only conclude that a strong current in Washington still aspired to topple the system in Tehran if it could. And it was obviously not limited to Trump and his supporters as plenty of figures from the Democratic Party, and anti-Trump Republicans like McCain, were also backing MEK's agenda.[28] If Rouhani was hoping for an American opening so he could question Khamenei's anti-American mantra, Washington was not giving him much to play with.

Besides his pledge to resist any pressure for Iran to abandon the 2015 nuclear deal, Rouhani focused on Tehran's eagerness to continue to attract foreign investment. He repeated the call that the Islamic Republic is not split into two hostile factions and that foreign investors should feel confident to invest in Iran where investments are "safe," as Rouhani put it. The fact that the head of the Revolutionary Guards, General Mohammad Ali Jafari, did not attend the inauguration was a strong signal that contradicted this message that regime factions were in harmony. The shadow of the Revolutionary Guards continued to put off international investors and this was a real problem for Rouhani. Job creation was to be one of his key priorities in the next four years and Tehran simply did not have enough financial capital on its own to underwrite big job-creating projects.

Rouhani dithered also on how to mobilize the old Rafsanjani network to come to his aid. After his reelection in 2017, Rouhani did not mention Rafsanjani at his inaugural speech. This upset Rafsanjani's family. Some saw it as Rouhani's attempt to be his own man. He did not want to be seen to owe his presidency to Rafsanjani.[29] Yet, the reality was that without Rafsanjani and the support from the reformist movement, Rouhani would have never become president. Others believed he was not engaging in rewriting his political past and debts, but that he was looking to the future. His lame disassociation with Rafsanjani was perhaps a signal to the hard-line camp that he was not a Rafsanjani proxy but a man in his own right with his own agenda. It suggested he wanted a buy-in from the hard-line camp to at least consider him as a possible compromise candidate for the supreme leadership when the day comes. It smacked of opportunism. As Mohammad Khatami and other senior reformists said it, Rouhani had in the 2017 elections bagged the votes of 24 million people desperate for political change but was looking to deliver for the 16 million that had not voted for him.[30]

No one in power in Tehran was willing to see Trump and his "maximum pressure" campaign against Iran as an opportunity to adjust domestic or foreign policy. Instead of exploiting Trump's pressure tactics on Iran to urge Khamenei to agree to change, Rouhani, Khatami, and many others from the moderate camp called for "national unity." It was a missed opportunity that kept Khamenei in the driver's seat. Rouhani refused to accept Trump's request for a meeting in New York when he was attending the UN in September 2017. The failure to meet was partly because Rouhani was a handcuffed president and because Trump was alarmingly unpredictable and unclear what he was after in his Iran policy. Just before he requested a meeting with Rouhani, Trump had called the Islamic Republic a "murderous regime" in a speech to the UN. Words matter, and in this case, it had shut the door to diplomacy. While Rouhani had managed to rationalize his brief phone conversation with Obama in 2013, this time around with Trump the hard-liners in Tehran would have been far less forgiving. They were constantly waiting for Rouhani to blunder, and in particular seek to paint him as weak and unpatriotic.

From Trump arriving at the White House in January 2017 to when the United States officially left the 2015 nuclear deal in May 2018, Tehran and Washington did not really bother to salvage the deal. There was a couple of face-to-face encounters as part of UN-arranged meetings but any Washington–Tehran channels of communication established after the nuclear deal soon ceased to exist altogether. Foreign Minister Javad Zarif was soon banned from US soil to even attend meetings of UN agencies. Proponents of the nuclear deal in the Trump administration, such as Secretary of State Rex Tillerson and H. R. McMaster, were fired in the spring of 2018. They were replaced by Mike Pompeo and John Bolton, respectively, and both well-known for deep loathing of the Islamic Republic. Washington shortly after withdrew from the agreement. Washington issued a twelve-point demand of Tehran that was far more sweeping than the deal from 2015: from insisting Iran give up nuclear enrichment altogether instead of just limiting it for a certain time to halting its ballistic missile program to end what Pompeo called Tehran's threatening behavior toward its regional neighbors such as Israel, Saudi Arabia, and the United Arab Emirates (UAE). The concessions demanded were invariably regarded in Tehran as a call for capitulation. An aghast Rouhani pledged Iran would "win" in this "economic war" by the Americans. In case anyone needed a reminder of the history behind the enmity, Washington chose the date of the return of US-imposed sanctions to be on November 4, 2018, on the anniversary of the seizing of the US embassy in 1979.

Rouhani was livid since the return of sanctions was happening just as foreign investors were returning and Iran was now selling oil at volumes last seen before president Obama had imposed sanctions in July 2012. To put it in perspective, Iran secured roughly $40 billion in Foreign Direct Investment (FDI) in the past twenty years—and of that amount, $8 billion had come after the 2015 nuclear deal. The economy grew at around 7 percent per year in 2016 and 2017. Now a crashing halt was underway. That said, the Iranians also assessed that Trump was not a war president per se. Trump had campaigned to end "the stupid endless Mideast wars" and Tehran believed him. Trump had reportedly told the famously anti-Iran Bolton that he would become his national security advisor only on the condition that he quit pushing for militarily confronting Tehran. With a possible war off the table, the one scenario he could not risk, Khamenei was willing to force the Iranian people endure another round of economic sanctions if that was as far as Trump was willing to go. And yet, there was a third option in between war and sanctions, and that was engineering a "regime change" in Tehran. Trump never convincingly played that card either, and the Iranians judged his hawkish sanctions-centered position on Iran as an end in itself. They saw it as geared toward appeasing anti-Islamic Republic interest groups in the United States such as the American Israel Public Affairs Committee (AIPAC) or lobbies in Washington linked to the oil-rich Arab states of the Persian Gulf. On this point, Javad Zarif kept prodding Trump on Twitter not to let the likes of Pompeo and Bolton to lead him into another war in the Middle East. "@realDonaldTrump is 100% right that the US military has no business in the Persian Gulf. Removal of its forces is fully in line with interests of US and the world. But it's now clear that the #B_Team is not concerned with US interests—they despise diplomacy, and thirst for war." The #B_Team was a reference to Israeli Prime Minister Binyamin Netanyahu, the Saudi Crown Prince Mohammad Bin Salman, and the Crown Prince of the UAE, Mohammad Bin Zayed. Zarif wanted to convince Trump that he was being deceived.

§

In February 2019, the fortieth anniversary of the Islamic Republic, Khamenei issued a lengthy statement to younger Iranians on how to keep the revolution alive. This much-anticipated statement had been promised to be a "strategic" message but there was nothing "strategic" about it. It was the usual sort of statement that Khamenei always gives. In regard to domestic policy and the ideology of the system, there was no sign of admission of guilt by him or that regime needs to change course in any way. The same intransigence was also evident about foreign policy. Khamenei again reiterated that "there is no point in talking to the Americans" as they cannot be trusted. He said Europeans are not much more reliable than the Americans. It was a pretentious speech that did not offer anything new. It was widely condemned by independent commentators as a sign of Khamenei's detachment from present-day Iranian realities.

Anger about political repression and a crumbling economy led to the broadest nationwide protests that was to be termed "Bloody November" in 2019. Dozens of towns erupted. Unlike before, these protests were leaderless and spontaneous and the demands of the protesters were nothing but the removal of the political Islamist order. This new generation of protesters, mostly young and from the smaller towns, was lashing at Khamenei himself. The opposition had not been this radicalized since the early 1980s and the deeply alarmed regime felt only an iron fist could force the protesters to go home. Hundreds were killed but Tehran roundly rejected any investigation into the number of killed.

Nor was Khamenei moved by a chain of events that rocked the country in 2020. The number of sudden "accidents" at various sensitive points in the country certainly suggests a systematic campaign of sabotage was under way. An explosion at the Natanz nuclear enrichment facility in July 2020 was by far the most significant given its strategic value. The finger was pointed at a joint American-Israeli campaign, suggesting that the Trump administration and the Israelis had concluded that Khamenei would not change any of its policies while Trump was in the White House. The central role of Israel was not in doubt. In January 2018, Mossad agents had broken into Iran's secret nuclear archives in a commercial district outside of Tehran and walked away with about 50,000 pages and 163 compact discs worth of intelligence about Iran's nuclear program, which provided fodder for Trump's "maximum pressure" campaign against Tehran.

Many in Tehran speculated that Trump either wanted to roll back Iran's nuclear and missile programs as much as possible before he left office or, alternatively, that it was a trap to force Iran to retaliate and set in motion a broader military confrontation. Tehran, however, basically accepted the losses it incurred and simply continued its nuclear program as before. For Iran, though, one troubling aspect that went beyond the nuclear issue was the perception that the country was awash with CIA and Mossad agents running around carrying out attacks with impunity and undermined the regime. There were signs of panic. A hardline parliamentarian, Javad Karimi Ghodousi, claimed that "50% of the members of the Majles want to topple the regime [Islamic Republic]." Infiltration on such a scale was highly improbable. Instead, such charges spoke far more about the state of paranoia that was increasingly shaping policy in the faction-ridden regime. Minister of Intelligence Mahmoud Alavi went after any official that held dual nationality. It was yet another defeat for Rouhani who had hoped to attract Iranians from the Diaspora for top government jobs in Tehran.

Rouhani still could not make up his mind about whether he wants to be a transformative president or an obedient subordinate to Khamenei. He made headlines in September 2019 by declaring that people should not have expectations from him since he has "no power" as a mere president. In reference to his government's performance, he said: "What do you want from someone that has no power?" Rouhani's comment that "no change in Iran is possible until distribution of power is changed" was not only an attack on Khamenei but again showed that he was wavering. He simultaneously berated the political system—including on occasions pushing for a popular referendum to reassert the limitations of power at the hands of the supreme leader—but always avoided a showdown with Khamenei. In the meantime, US-imposed sanctions were choking the country. The economy would shrink by almost 10 percent in 2019. Trump's repeated calls for talks were rebuffed as the Iranian officialdom collectively judged him as too unreliable to negotiate with. Rouhani took pride in denying Trump. "Since imposing sanctions on us, the Americans have at least asked 23 times to meet me."[31] Trump constantly moving the goalpost compounded Tehran's misgivings. Trump's national security advisor John Bolton summed it up this way: "Trump simultaneously wanted to sound tough on Iran and strike a deal with them. Trump's dilly-dallying about his ultimate Iran objective made Tehran sit on the fence."

The fortieth anniversary of the Islamic Republic coincided with Iran being rocked by the largest and deadliest protests since 1979. Two waves of protests hit the country in late 2018 and again in November 2019. Corruption, mismanagement, and general unaccountability and no light at the end of the tunnel brought out anti-regime protests across some one hundred Iranian cities and towns. But yet, there was still no sign that Khamenei would consider any fundamental policy change. He put the blame at the door of Rouhani for failing to provide for the basic needs of the people. Then he ordered the security forces to launch a merciless crackdown against the street protesters. More people were killed and arrested in seven days in November 2019 than during the 2009 protests that lasted seven months. Use of physical force and imprisonment was also the standard in dealing with the enraged civil society. With the economy in a free fall, the security forces cracked down on any show of civil disobedience: from those playing music or dancing in the streets to women who in public removed the compulsory veil, the response was nearly always more arrests. The fear was that a soft response to calls for more political or sociocultural freedoms would quickly escalate to more demands for change.

Khamenei would brush the protests off as if nothing had happened. He was more concerned about the image of the Islamic Republic. Rouhani was no different. Just few short weeks after hundreds had been killed in anti-regime protests, Khamenei called on Iranians to take part in elections for the parliament to be held on February 21, 2020. Those who went to the polls would "neutralize many of the evil intensions of the Americans and [Israel]," he announced. This was classic Khamenei. Always pointing the finger at the outside world when the massive public apathy is a result of the domestic political situation and the futility of elections in the Islamic Republic. A younger generation of Iranians no longer play along with this charade. As expected, the turnout for the elections was a historic low. Thanks to his control over the 12-man Guardian Council, Khamenei still decides who can run for any office. He can also literally veto anything any elected office puts forth as policy, including those coming from the presidential palace.

For a brief while, starting with Mohammad Khatami's reformist landslide in 1997, there was a glimmer of hope that gradual political reform is possible in Iran. Today, prominent reformist personalities openly accept that they no longer appeal to the general public as they are viewed by the public as either pawns in the hands of Khamenei or incapable to confront him. In particular, the youth have clearly given up on the idea of peaceful gradual reform. They are increasingly turning to political messages that speak of the need to replace the Islamic Republic and that the regime is irreformable. The mood in Tehran is that Khamenei has decided that the Islamic Republic can only survive if the entire regime is in the hands of hard-liners. No alternative voices will be allowed to run or to win. Khamenei's plea for the Iranians to take part in a political theater that only advances his absolute power while massaging his ego is truly a case of disregard of the intelligence of the Iranian public.

Epilogue

Commander-In-Chief [Khamenei], resign, resign.
The Revolutionary Guards are our ISIS.
            (Street chants by Iranian protesters in January 2020)

The death of Ayatollah Akbar Hashemi Rafsanjani on January 8, 2017, marked a major turning point for Iran. For nearly forty years, his undisguised hunger for power combined with his knack for deal making had made him the most proven power broker of the Islamic Republic. In fact, without Rafsanjani, Iran's two most important living political personalities—Supreme Leader Ayatollah Ali Khamenei and president Hassan Rouhani—might never have risen through the ranks. For his part, Rouhani, stayed more or less loyal to Rafsanjani until the very end. Khamenei, however, parted ways with Rafsanjani many years ago, as soon as he succeeded in consolidating his position as supreme leader. The two former friends became the severest of rivals, spearheading different portions of the *nezam* (the political order) in the quest for preeminence. To begin with, theirs was not really an ideological difference, although Rafsanjani masqueraded as the moderate and Khamenei as the die-hard Islamist militant revolutionary. Rather, their dispute was always about power.

With Rafsanjani's death, it was Rouhani who was best suited to fill the role of the elder of the so-called moderate camp. With time, his grit to even want to fill Rafsanjani's big shoes came under serious question. Other candidates for the role, men such as former reformist president Mohammad Khatami, would never be given the political space by Khamenei to attempt such a thing to begin with. Nor did they ever want to risk Khamenei's wrath. Despite Rafsanjani's controversial and mixed political record, he did leave behind a vacuum. For good or bad, he had become the face of hope for moderation and gradual change in the Islamic Republic, and only he had the stature to stand up to Khamenei. His death could, and has, weakened the factional struggle in Tehran.

For generations of Iranians, Rafsanjani's beardless face had come to symbolize factionalism. His nickname, the shark, was also a reflection of his canny ability to stay at the top political level. Politics was in the DNA of this more than anything else. His biggest achievements were as a result of his machinations concocted behind the scenes, but he always craved the public limelight and, with age, popular admiration. His most decisive plot, to elevate Ali Khamenei to the supreme leadership in 1989, was also Rafsanjani's pivotal faux pas. In Rafsanjani's calculations, Khamenei was to be only a symbolic leader without the kinds of political powers that Khomeini had amassed for himself. His underestimation of Khamenei's appetite for more than just symbolic religious leadership proved to be Rafsanjani's most consequential mistake.

At first, the Rafsanjani–Khamenei duet had worked but only because the novice supreme leader had to find his footing. During his two terms as president, which lasted from 1989 to 1997, it was Rafsanjani who was mostly in the headlines. He launched what was to become known as the "reconstruction era," during which time the centralized war economy was to be dismantled. When he opened up Iran's oil and gas sectors for foreign investors in the early 1990s, Rafsanjani deliberately set aside a number of fields to be open only to American firms for bidding. He knew more than anyone else how dearly the Islamic Republic's enmity toward the United States was costing the country in geopolitical and economic terms. And he accepted that the Iranian public desperately wanted to see normalization of diplomatic relations with Washington. This period of economic liberalization, though, was also the first time the Rafsanjani family became associated with corruption, a label the politician was never able to shake off and always limited him.

He was a merchant-turned-politician and one who throughout his career prized expediency over ideology. While he was no admirer of the West as such, in power he quickly accepted the necessities of compromise if Iran wanted to rid itself of its pariah state. That made it easy for his hard-line critics, particularly in the later years, to paint him as an opportunist at best and an agent of foreign powers at worst. All the while, Khamenei was quietly consolidating his power base. Most importantly, he brought all the military, security, and intelligence agencies under his control. By the mid-1990s, Iranian politics had become binary, with Khamenei emerging as the head doyen of the hard-liners while Rafsanjani emerged as the godfather of a rival political network whose many members continue to serve in the highest echelon of power in Iran. Many of those who first served under Rafsanjani remained close to the influential ayatollah. Rafsanjani sought repeatedly to make political comebacks. In 2005, a presidential bid ended in a humiliating defeat at the hands of an unknown figure by the name of Mahmoud Ahmadinejad. The fact that the Office of the Supreme Leader had played an active role in assuring an Ahmadinejad victory made the loss that much more bitter for Rafsanjani.

In 2009, Rafsanjani backed Ahmadinejad's challengers in an election that ended up producing the millions-strong Green opposition movement, which protested mass voter fraud. Rafsanjani's open support for the Green movement turned him into a prime target for the Khamenei camp, which viewed the protests as a threat to Khamenei's tight grip on power. In 2013, the once mighty Rafsanjani was again humiliated when he was told he was too old to run. He accepted the ignominy and began instead to push forward his devotees. He felt vindicated, if not emboldened, when his long-time confidant, Hassan Rouhani, secured the presidency in 2013. It seemed Rafsanjani had put the cause of reform ahead of his ego. Or perhaps he had in reality no other choice.

A prolific writer of memoirs, Rafsanjani was always much preoccupied with how history would remember him. He wanted to shape that narrative to the extent possible. As such, there is no doubt that his published memoirs have been highly selective in the revelations they have offered. And yet, despite his best attempts, he was never able to whitewash his involvement in regard to some of the worst atrocities of the Islamic Republic, including mass execution of political prisoners in 1988 or the chain murders of political dissidents in the 1990s. But what is known beyond doubt is that, in the course of his political career, Rafsanjani morphed from Islamist hard-liner to someone that in the later years was regarded by Iran's youthful reformist masses as a potential savior. If Rafsanjani had been so instrumental in imposing the repressive theocracy on the nation, he surely could do something to help undo it.

That was at least the idea. It never came to pass. Nor can those reformist hopefuls ever know for sure if that was really what Rafsanjani intended to do if he ever got to call the shots again. For now, the big question is whether the broad network that Rafsanjani leaves behind will stay together. His loyalists are found in many of Iran's political institutions, in the economic sector, in a good part of the media, and elsewhere inside the regime. What is also equally important is whether Rouhani will choose to pick up the mantle from his old mentor. In the Islamic Republic, it has always been the role of informal political networks that matter the most in shaping outcomes. The country's official political parties are not much equipped for popular mobilization. For that reason alone, Rouhani's steps were bound to be decisive not only in preserving the Rafsanjani clique as an alternative to the hard-liners but also in steering the trajectory of the Islamic Republic.

In early 2019, on the second anniversary of the death of Rafsanjani, the Rouhani government put up a big show to celebrate the man many today like to portray as a "moderate." Rouhani took the lead and praised him in ways few have praised Rafsanjani in public since his death. Rouhani's comments were directly aimed at Khamenei. He said that Rafsanjani was the reason Khamenei became supreme leader in 1989. He also said that Rafsanjani was the reason why Iran could stand up to Iraq militarily and not be defeated by Saddam. But most importantly, according to Rouhani, Iranians had a revolution in 1979 so "no son will follow his father in power," a jab at Khamenei. He said this as there continues to be speculation in Tehran that Khamenei has plans for his son, Mojtaba, to succeed him.

§

There are those who say Khamenei's picking up the baton in 1989 from Khomeini was heavenly preordained. In reality, the elders of the regime chose to put their collective survival above all else and found in Khamenei, a midranking cleric, a candidate the majority could back as a stopgap transitional leader. The necessary adjustments were quickly put in motion to keep the succession process orderly and quick. A constitutional amendment was swiftly arranged so the leader no longer needed to be a "grand ayatollah," since Khamenei had far subpar religious qualifications. Accepting his limitations as a religious figure, Khamenei turned to the Revolutionary Guards for help. He offered them a deal. They would protect his supreme leadership and he would give them political cover to pursue their interests in any field they wished, which is exactly what they have done on Khamenei's watch.

Khamenei set out to dictate what course the "revolution" would take and the Revolutionary Guards would ensure his orders were implemented, although this has not meant the Guards do not have their own agenda and ability to shape Khamenei's calculations. During Iran's two biggest opposition protests, in the 1999 student uprising against the regime and in 2009 when the opposition Green movement mobilized millions against Khamenei's rule, it was the Revolutionary Guards that saved the day for Khamenei. Furthermore, Khamenei has not been content with just his rule in Iran. He has long set his eyes on the Islamic World and aspired to gain a leadership mantle among the world's nearly 2 billion Muslims. Here, his political-ideological doctrine has had a two-pronged objective.

First, he has argued that the main objective of the 1979 Islamic revolution was to create a new Islamic Society and that there are four major stages to reach this goal. The stages are: "The Islamic Revolution; The Islamic Government; The Islamic Society," and finally "The Islamic Civilization." "We were truly dead; Imam [Khomeini] made us alive. We were lost; he guided us. We were negligent of our grand human and Islamic duties; he woke us and showed us the way."[1] In truth, Khomeini never ever articulated such a vision of internationalizing the revolution of 1979 as Khamenei has proceeded to do since 1989. Khamenei's quest for influence in the Islamic World is supposed to enhance his legitimacy within Iran but the opposite is much closer to reality. The average Iranian finds Khamenei's commitment to exporting the message of the Islamist revolution to places like Lebanon, Syria, and Iraq to be both costly and oftentimes counterproductive. For every Arab Tehran recruits to its militant Islamist cause, many more non-Islamist Arabs are lost.

Second, Khamenei subscribes to the idea of "forward defense" against the United States. Accordingly, to deter Washington from attempting a policy of "regime change" in Tehran, Iran should take the fight to the Americans and their allies in the Middle East and beyond. Khamenei often reminds the Revolutionary Guards and its proxy allies, such as Lebanese Hezbollah, Palestinian Hamas, the Houthis in Yemen, or the pro-Iran Shia Iraqi militias, that they should not limit their operations to specific regional boundaries. This is no doubt a warning aimed at the United States and its regional allies. "Do not build walls around yourself and stay within those walls," he once told the senior commanders of the Revolutionary Guards.[2]

§

All the presidents that have served under the watchful eye of Khamenei—from Rafsanjani, Khatami, Ahmadinejad, to Rouhani—have had to endure a relentless push by the Office of the Supreme Leader to rob them of powers that are according to the constitution vested in the office of the president. Khamenei's ability to veto anything he dislikes that comes from the presidential palace or the Majles has all but voided the "republic" component of the "Islamic Republic." No serious observer would today claim that the source of power in Iran is through the ballot box. Khamenei has a proven thirty-year track record that he wants absolute power; he does not want to share the stage with anyone else and is set in his ideological ways. The presidency, the Majles, or any other elected office is a subterfuge and a convenient scapegoat when Khamenei's stewardship fails as it has repeatedly done since 1989.

When it comes to his succession, he trusts the generals from the Revolutionary Guards more than anyone else, including his fellow clerics. They are well-placed to make sure his legacy lives on after he is gone. That is why Khamenei periodically asks the Revolutionary Guards to think outside of the box and be ready for "big events." But giving carte blanche to the Guards to confront their common enemies is not without risks. The escalating fight between the Rouhani government and the Guards, involving leaks, disinformation, and daily charges that the other is badly undermining cohesion in the regime, suggests this is a competition that could get out of hand. And most importantly, and far more than was the case in 1989, the Guards are today seen as the principal agent of repression in Iran.

The Guards continue to be embroiled in various political and corruption scandals, further focusing public anger on the predatory nature of the organization and its role as the key obstacle to political reform. Instead, Khamenei is callously asking the Revolutionary Guards to go on the offensive at home and abroad. The question for the Guards, and their long-term interests, is whether they should double down against the Rouhani government and the Iranian public or perhaps start thinking of a new formula to maintain their political and economic interests as the Islamic Republic looks beyond the reign of Ali Khamenei. What should not be expected of Khamenei is a volte-face while he lives. He is ready to take all his mistakes with him to the grave and will never apologize for his decisions. This reality is not because of a lack of trying to shift his calculations. Washington has certainly over the years looked at a variety of carrots and sticks approaches but so far to no avail.

No US president probed Khamenei's stamina for a shooting war with the Americans as much as Donald Trump. On January 3, 2020, Trump approved of the assassination of top Revolutionary Guards general Qassem Soleimani outside Baghdad international airport. He was the master architect behind Tehran's "forward defense" strategy of proxy warfare. Soleimani had been instrumental in expanding Tehran's influence in the region. It was Washington's highly controversial and risky way to let Khamenei and the Guards know that the United States was serious about rolling back Iranian advances made across the region. In the days that followed, tensions reached record levels as Tehran fired off a number of ballistic missiles at US forces deployed in Iraq. In this fog of war, the Revolutionary Guards accidently shot down a Ukrainian airliner that was departing Tehran. Some 176 passengers, overwhelmingly Canadians of Iranian origin, were killed. A new, but well-established, cycle was in motion: an act of regime incompetence was followed by popular protests by the Iranian people followed by a harsh crackdown at the hands of the authorities.

About a week later, Khamenei came out to give the Friday sermon at Tehran University, something he had not done for almost a decade. Amazingly, there were those expecting him to apologize for the event, or even offer to resign. It was a case of phenomenal misreading of the man. Khamenei did not offer to resign. He did not really even apologize or accept any responsibility as the commander-in-chief. Instead, he defended the regime to the end and reassured his core supporters that the regime was not collapsing.³ He vowed "severe revenge" from Washington and quickly appointed Soleimani's successor.

The US assassination of Soleimani was so unprecedented that many feared that any move afterward might lead to all-out war between the United States and Iran. After four decades of tense rivalry in the Middle East, the American use of an armed drone to target a military official widely viewed as one of the most powerful man in Iran signaled a precipitous climb up the escalation ladder between Washington and Tehran. Yet, Soleimani's assassination and the increased tensions vis-à-vis the United States and the fluidity of the geopolitics of the Middle East have brought into the open questions in Iran about the long-term costs, benefits, and risks of the state of hostilities between the United States and Iran. As of the time of this writing, Ayatollah Ali Khamenei still believes the path of confronting the United States is the only righteous course, and he shows nothing but apathy toward any contrary view. His message to those who are still holding out for talks with the Americans is loud and clear. As he put it in August 2020, "I have laid out the reasons for not negotiating with the U.S. many times, but some [domestically] either don't understand or pretend to not understand."

In Tehran, the joy in seeing Donald Trump defeated in his reelection bid in November 2020 was crystal clear. What was also clear was that Tehran has yet to come up with a robust strategy to turn Joe Biden's election as the 46th president of the United States into a moment to fundamentally steer US–Iran relations in a different direction. That strategy might quietly be in the making or it might not at all be under consideration. Still, if Tehran is readying itself for a "grand bargain" with Washington under Biden, it was not showing in those early days after the American elections. The initial reaction from the hard-line faction that handles Tehran's key foreign relations, namely Supreme Leader Khamenei and the Revolutionary Guards, has been one of contempt not just for Trump but for the American system of government.

Put simply, the hard-liners' message is that US hostility toward the Islamic Republic is a fixed feature regardless of who is in the White House. The reality is the reverse. It is the hard-line camp in Tehran that would be thunderstruck if it one day had to give up on anti-Americanism as a principal pillar of its worldview. That's why the hard-liners have constantly engaged in erecting barriers to a meaningful dialogue with Washington. Meanwhile, the so-called moderate wing of the regime clustered around President Rouhani could not make a meaningful outreach to President-elect Biden without buy-in from Khamenei and the Revolutionary Guards. But at least the moderate faction goes through the trouble of showing a possible path for negotiations. What Rouhani and his team were asking for was a return by the United States to the 2015 nuclear deal and the removal of sanctions. In turn, Tehran will once again put a cap on its nuclear activities. Rouhani also asked for compensation and an apology from Washington for Trump's "maximum pressure" campaign, but that was just tough public talk to protect himself from his hard-line rivals in Tehran.

By the time of Biden's election win in November 2020, Rouhani had about seven months left in office and his entire political legacy was tied to how much of the 2015 nuclear deal he could salvage between the time Biden arrived at the White House in January and Iran's presidential elections in June 2021. Figures close to Rouhani readily admitted that not only détente with the United States but also rehabilitation of the badly hurting Iranian economy requires Tehran to make major adjustments in the realm of foreign and economic policy (such as ratifying international financial standards) as well as contemplating negotiating with Washington about Iranian policies in the Middle East.

But the general consensus in Tehran was that the prerequisite for US–Iran talks to be broadened to include Iran's regional actions is a successful return by both sides to the 2015 deal. That all said, the sad reality is that the American question is still a political football in Tehran. The hard-line camp, which is far more powerful, still believes anti-Americanism serves its narrow political interests at home and its militant Islamist ambitions in the Middle East. There likely will be some limited new talks between the Biden White House and Tehran, but there is no evidence that Ayatollah Khamenei and the Revolutionary Guards intend to shift course in a major way as far the United States is concerned.

Rafsanjani and other senior members of the Islamic Republic that put Khamenei on the pedestal are almost all dead or marginalized. Within the ranks of the system, there are very few personalities that can push back against Khamenei's political instincts. Pushback against him now only comes from the streets, from an Iranian public that is so deeply dismayed by the realities of domestic and foreign policies of the country.

Notes

Prologue

1. The exact number has never been confirmed.
2. M. A. Tabaar, *Religious Statecraft: The Politics of Religion in Iran* (New York: Columbia University Press, 2018), Chapter 5.
3. *Revolution Anniversary—39 Years of News Control and Censorship in Iran*. Reporters without Borders (February 13, 2008).

1 (1978–9)—Khamenei and Rafsanjani: Waiting for Khomeini to Return from Paris

1. Y. Alpher, *Periphery: Israel's Search for Middle East Allies* (Lanham, MD: Rowman and Littlefield, 2015), p. 22.
2. R. E. Huyser, *Mission to Tehran* (New York: Harper and Row, 1986), pp. 91–101.
3. Interview with Shapour Bakhtiar: Sarzamin Kohan (2016), available at: https://www.youtube.com/watch?v=WL8Fus2sU70 (last accessed May 18, 2020).
4. B. Moin, *Khomeini, Life of the Ayatollah* (London: I.B. Tauris, 1999), pp. 182–98.
5. CIA: National Foreign Assessment Center, "Iran: The Seizure of the Embassy in Retrospect" (November 1, 1981). https://www.cia.gov/library/readingroom/document/cia-rdp06t00412r000200560001-7.
6. CIA: National Foreign Assessment Center, "The Politics of Ayatollah Ruhollah Khomeini" (November 20, 1978). https://www.cia.gov/library/readingroom/docs/CIA-RDP80T00634A000500010002-9.pdf.
7. Others have claimed that the meeting between the two men first happened in Karbala, Iraq, but that it was the sermon of Ayatollah Damad that brought them together as friends. "When Did the Friendship of Ayatollah Khamenei and Ayatollah Rafsanjani Begin?" *Entekhab.ir* (January 22, 2011). https://www.entekhab.ir/fa/news/85/دوستی-آیت-الله-خامنه-ای-و-آیت-الله-هاشمی-از-کجا-آغاز-شد.
8. A. R. Summitt, "For a White Revolution: John F. Kennedy and the Shah of Iran." *Middle East Journal*, 58(4) (2004): 560–75.
9. For a discussion, see S. A. Arjomand, *The Turban for the Crown: The Islamic Revolution in Iran* (Oxford: Oxford University Press, 1989), pp. 80–94.
10. Hashemi Rafsanjani, *Years of Resistance (1934–1979)* (Daftar Nashre Maaref Enqelaab (Office of Education about the Revolution), 1st vol., 2nd ed. (Tehran, 1997), pp. 221–5.
11. H. Asadi, *Letters to My Torturer, نامه هائی به شکنجه گرم* (London: H&S Media, 2013), p. 113.

12 See, for example, A. Khamenei, "Persian Poetry Has Always Been Virtuous (May 30, 2018). Available at: http://english.khamenei.ir/news/5714/Persian-poetry-has-always-been-virtuous.

13 "Khamenei's Night of Poetry," *BBC Persian* (June 2, 2018). https://www.bbc.com/persian/arts-44341690.

14 "The Story of the Shared House of the Khamenei and Rafsanjani Families," *Khabar Online* (March 21, 2017). https://www.khabaronline.ir/news/647962/ماجرای-خانه-مشترک-خانواده-آیت-الله-خامنه-ای-و-هاشمی-رفسنجانی.

15 Y. Unal, "Sayyid Qutb in Iran: Translating the Islamic Ideologue in the Islamic Republic." *Journal of Islamic and Muslim Studies*, 1(2) (November 2016): 35–60.

16 For more background, see J. Calvert, *Sayyid Qutb and the Origins of Radical Islamism* (New York: Columbia University Press, 2010).

17 A. Khamenei, "You Have Spoken against Israel and the Jews," *Khamenei.ir* (February 3, 1998). https://farsi.khamenei.ir/memory-content?id=24647.

18 A. Alfoneh, "Supreme Leader Ali Khamenei: A Secret Russian Life?" American Enterprise Institute (February 23, 2014).

19 A. Fakhravar, *Comrade Ayatollah: Soviet KGB's Role in the Islamic Revolution & the Rise of Ali Khamenei to Power in Iran* (Los Angeles: Ketab, 2016).

20 "A Look at the Life of Ayatollah Khamenei," *Khamenei.ir* (March 21, 2014). https://farsi.khamenei.ir/memory-content?id=26142.

21 It was later claimed that the pilot had been planted on the flight by the French intelligence service.

22 E. Abrahimian, *Khomeinism* (Los Angeles: University of California Press, 1993), pp. 60–70.

23 "Rafsanjani's Interesting Answer about Hejab," Aparat, https://www.aparat.com/v/yclHn/پاسخ_جالب_هاشمی_درباره_حجاب (last accessed June 23, 2020). Until he died, hardliners constantly reminded Rafsanjani that as a younger statesman he had strongly favored compulsory veil for women. See, for example, "Rafsanjani: Badly Veiled Women Are Thieves and Counter-Revolutionary," *Mashregh News* (February 3, 2016). https://www.mashreghnews.ir/news/530844/هاشمی-رفسنجانی-زنان-بدحجاب-دزد-و-ضد-انقلاب-هستند-صوت.

24 "Why Did the Imam Go to Refah School?" *Jam-e Jam* (February 7, 2012). https://jamejamonline.ir/fa/news/455771/چرا-امام-به-مدرسه-رفاه-رفت.

25 "Rafsanjani: Refah School Was the Identity Card of the Islamic Republic," *Mehr News* (February 3, 2007). https://www.mehrnews.com/news/443097/مدرسه-رفاه-شناسنامه-انقلاب-ماست.

26 "A Look at the Life of Ayatollah Khamenei," *Khamenei.ir* (March 21, 2014). https://farsi.khamenei.ir/memory-content?id=26142.

27 "The Council of Islamic Revolution," Political Studies and Research Institute. https://psri.ir/?id=fn50bclv (last accessed June 23, 2020).

28 "Memories of Ayatollah Rafsanjani about the Formation of the Council of the Revolution," Department of the Institute for Compilation and Publication of Imam Khomeini's Works (February 3, 2016). http://www.imam-khomeini.ir/fa/c13_25265/خاطرات/خاطرات_شخصیت_ها/روایت_آیت_الله_هاشمی_رفسنجانی_از_تشکیل_شورای_انقلاب.

29 Navab Safavi was executed for acting against the national security of Iran in January 1956.

30 "The Memory of Ayatollah Khamenei about the Leader of the Fadayan Islam," *Alef* (January 17, 2018). https://www.alef.ir/news/3961027179.html.

2 (1979–80)—Bloodletting between the Reds and Islamists to Seizing the US Embassy

1. Ayatollah R. Khomeini, *Imam's Sahife*, vol. 4 (November 1978): 244.
2. M. Aidani, *Narrative and Violence: Ways of Suffering amongst Iranian Men in Diaspora* (London: Routledge, 2020), p. 34.
3. Interview with Mohsen Sazegara, Alexandria, Virginia, May 24, 2016.
4. Two other men were important Islamist revolutionary figures in Mashhad: Ayatollah Mahmoud Vaez Tabbasi and Abdul Karim Hashemi Nejad.
5. Phone interview with Abol-hassan Bani Sadr (June 4, 2015).
6. A. Gheissari and Vali Nsar, *Democracy in Iran: History and the Quest for Liberty* (Oxford: Oxford University Press, 2009), p. 84.
7. B. Baktiari, *Parliamentary Politics in Revolutionary Iran* (Gainesville: University Press of Florida, 1996), p. 55.
8. A. Alfoneh, *Iran Unveiled: How the Revolutionary Guards Is Turning Theocracy into Military Dictatorship* (Washington, DC: AEI Press, 2013), p. 13.
9. M. Parsa, *States, Ideologies and Social Revolutions* (Cambridge: Cambridge University Press, 2000), pp. 249–51.
10. The job was given to another key Khomeini deputy, Ayatollah Morteza Mottahari.
11. M. Khalaji, "The Iranian Clergy's Silence," *Current Trends in Islamist Ideology*, Hudson Institute (July 12, 2010). https://www.hudson.org/research/9870-the-iranian-clergy-s-silence-.
12. M. Moslem, *Factional Politics in Post-Khomeini Iran* (Syracuse, NY: Syracuse University Press, 2002), pp. 26–31.
13. M. Milani, *The Making of Iran's Islamic Revolution* (New York: Routledge, 2018), pp. 29–31.
14. Baktiari, *Parliamentary Politics in Revolutionary Iran*, p. 62.
15. Central Intelligence Agency, "Iran: Debate on the Draft Constitution" (July 20, 1979). https://www.cia.gov/library/readingroom/document/cia-rdp81b00401r000500100034-1.
16. "Why Was Brzezinski Quietly after Beheshti?" *BBC Persian* (February 4, 2015). https://www.bbc.com/persian/iran/2015/02/150203_u01_beheshti_americans.
17. Arjomand, *The Turban for the Crown*, p. 137.
18. A. Rafsanjani (1997), "Memoirs of Ayatollah Rafsanjani: Years of Resistance," 2nd vol. https://rafsanjani.ir/records/خاطرات-آیت-الله-هاشمی-رفسنجانی-دوران-مبارزه-خاطرات-زندان/آیت-الله-هاشمی-رفسنجانی-رفتار-ساواک-در-زندان/print.
19. Audio of Ayatollah Taleghani's speech. https://www.youtube.com/watch?v=xxqFkcNqoRU (accessed May 18, 2020).
20. "Ayatollah Talaghani's Offspring: My Father's Marginalization Was Orchestrated," VOA last page (2013), https://www.youtube.com/watch?v=jvIFAmllFc0 (accessed May 18, 2020).
21. Extensive interview with Mehdi Taleghani's son, "New Information about Deceased Talaghani and Ayatollah Khamenei," *Tasnim News* (September 11, 2016). https://www.tasnimnews.com/fa/news/1395/06/21/1182265/ناگفته‌هایی-از-ارتباط-مرحوم-طالقانی-با-آیت-الله-خامنه‌ای-ماجرای-اختلاف-افکنی-بهزاد-نبوی-بین-امام-و-آیت-الله-طالقانی-هاشمی-خودمرکزپندار-است.
22. That son was Mehdi Taleghani.

23 "Was the Suspicious Death of Ayatollah Talaghani the Work of the Russians or the British?" *Khabar Online* (September 10, 2017). https://www.khabaronline.ir/news/705764/مرگ-مشکوک-آیت-الله-طالقانی-کار-روس-ها-بود-یا-انگلیس-ها.

24 J. Kifner, "Iranians Take to Streets to Mourn Ayatollah Taleghani, a Key Leader," *New York Times* (September 11, 1979). https://www.nytimes.com/1979/09/11/archives/iranians-take-to-streets-to-mourn-ayatollah-taleghani-a-key-leader.html.

25 "Children of Ayatollah Talaghani: If Our Father Was Alive, a Lot of Events Would Not Have Happened after the Revolution," Zamaneh (September 7, 2016). https://www.radiozamaneh.com/297847.

26 "Talaghani and Montazeri: They Were One," *BBC Persian* (December 21, 2009). https://www.bbc.com/persian/iran/2009/12/091221_na_mb_taleghani_montazeri.

27 "Was It the Tobacco in the Cigarette or the Soviet Ambassador's Ring That Made Ayatollah Talaghani Have a Stroke?" *Jamaran* (September 10, 2017). https://www.jamaran.news/بخش-بازنشر-59/737966-توتون-سیگار-باعث-سکته-آیت-الله-طالقانی-شد-یا-انگشتر-سفیر-شوروی.

28 "Ghotbzadeh: Talaghani Died, We Lost," VOA last page (October 20, 2013). https://www.youtube.com/watch?v=fxM4b3pzXyc.

29 W. Branigin, "Iranian Leftists Battle Way into U.S. Embassy," *Washington Post* (February 15, 1979). https://www.washingtonpost.com/archive/politics/1979/02/15/iranian-leftists-battle-way-into-us-embassy/5d58ffcd-566a-440e-a288-496f12a37643/.

30 Memoirs of Supreme Leader (Moass-e Farhangi Qadr-e Velayat) (Tehran, 1378), p. 104.

31 Central Intelligence Agency, "Iranian Islamic Assembly Debate on Past Relations with the US" (September 19, 1980). https://www.cia.gov/library/readingroom/docs/CIA-RDP85T00287R000102110002-7.pdf.

32 "CIA's Envoy in Tehran: Meeting with Bazargan, Secret Visit to Beheshti?" *BBC Persian* (November 4, 2014). https://www.bbc.com/persian/iran/2014/11/141104_u01-cia-beheshti.

33 W. H. Sullivan, *Mission to Iran* (New York: W. W. Norton, 1981), 200.

34 "The Secret Message of Abolqassem Kashani to Eisenhower," *BBC Persian* (February 14, 2018). https://www.bbc.com/persian/iran-features-43053577.

35 S. Bakhash, *The Reign of the Ayatollahs: Iran and the Islamic Revolution* (New York: Basic Books, 1986), p. 225.

36 Ibid., p. 54.

37 "Imam Khomeini: A Pity to Call America a Lion," *Khabarland* (November 6, 2017). https://khabarland.com/news/772113/حکایت-امام-خمینی-ره-از-تهدیدات-امریکا-حیف-است-به-امریکا-بگوییم-شیر-فیلم.

38 Y. Hovsepian-Bearce, *The Political Ideology of Ayatollah Khamenei* (New York: Routledge, 2015), p. 57.

39 Ibid.

40 "Interrogator of Abbas Entezam: It Was Never Proven He Was a Spy," *BBC Persian* (July 14, 2020). https://www.bbc.com/persian/iran-53404949.

41 "American Officials Speak of Secret Meetings with Beheshti," *BBC Persian* (November 2, 2014). https://www.bbc.com/persian/iran/2014/11/141101_u01-beheshti-main. Also see H. Precht, "The Association for Diplomatic Studies and Training Foreign Affairs Oral History Project: Interview with Henry Precht," The Association for Diplomatic Studies and Training (2001). https://www.adst.org/OH%20TOCs/Precht,%20Henry.toc.pdf.

42 Milani, *The Making of Iran's Islamic Revolution*, p. 126.

43 "What Happened to the Members of the Constitutional Experts?" *BBC Persian* (May 24, 2016). https://www.bbc.com/persian/iran/2016/05/160524_l10_fgh_assembly_of_experts_for_constitution. For background see R. K. Ramazani, "Constitution of the Islamic Republic of Iran." *Middle East Journal*, 34(2) (1980): 181–204. S. Randjbar-Daemi, "Building the Islamic State: The Draft Constitution of 1979 Reconsidered." *Iranian Studies*, 46(4) (2013): 641–63 (661). See also S. K. Farsoun and M. Mashayekhi, *Iran: Political Culture in the Islamic Republic* (London: Routledge, 1992), p. 96.
44 A. Parsons, *The Pride and the Fall* (London: Jonathan Cape, 1984).
45 Foreign and Commonwealth Office. (Diplomatic Documents; 1979–80, Batch 81-5, p. 97. The cable mistakenly refers to him as "Asghar Moinfar."

3 (1980–1)—The Second Purge: Chaos at Home and War Abroad

1 "The Story of Imam Khomeini's Heart Attack," *Tarikh Irani* (June 4, 2014). http://tarikhirani.ir/fa/news/4370/۶۵-سال-در-خمینی-امام-قلبی-ایست-ماجرای.
2 R. Shipp, ed., "Enter, Iran's New Regime; Exit, Revolutionary Council," *Christian Science Monitor* (September 12, 1980).
3 The second round was held in May 1980.
4 The Iranian parliament, the Majles, has 290 seats today.
5 CIA: Director of Central Intelligence, "A Soviet 'Best Case' for Military Intervention in Iran" (February 19, 1980). https://www.cia.gov/library/readingroom/docs/CIA-RDP81B00401R000500130018-7.pdf.
6 Ibid.
7 "Khamenei Visits U.S. Hostages," *Radio Free Europe/Radio Liberty* (November 3, 2009). https://www.rferl.org/a/Khamenei_Visits_US_Hostages/1868607.html
8 J. Cooley, "Aftermath of Rescue Attempts Makes Another Try Tougher," *Christian Science Monitor* (May 12, 1980). https://www.csmonitor.com/1980/0512/051265.html
9 R. Halloran, "Soviet Buildup Near Iran Tested Carter," *New York Times* (August 27, 1986). https://www.nytimes.com/1986/08/27/world/soviet-buildup-near-iran-tested-carter.html
10 CIA: National Foreign Assessment Center, "Iran: The Seizure of the Embassy in Retrospect" (August 12, 1981). https://www.cia.gov/library/readingroom/document/cia-rdp06t00412r000200560001-7.
11 CIA: National Foreign Assessment Center, "Iran: Factional Conflict and Political Instability" (June 27, 1980). https://www.cia.gov/library/readingroom/docs/CIA-RDP81B00401R000500110031-4.pdf.
12 Ibid.
13 "Sahifeh Imam Khomeini," vol. 9 (August 19, 1979), p. 300. https://emam.com/صحیفه-امام-خمینی/#book9.
14 Interview with Behrooz Sarshar, Vienna, Virginia (April 15, 2015).
15 For more details on relations between Arab and Iranian militants prior to 1979, see Chapter 6 in Afshon Ostovar, *The Vanguard of the Imam* (New York: Oxford University Press, 2016).
16 Ali Afshari, "Why Is Khomeini Guilty in the Making of the Iran-Iraq War," Radio Zamaneh (September 26, 2014). https://www.radiozamaneh.com/178187.

17 O. Seliktar and F. Rezaei, *Iran, Revolution, and Proxy Wars* (Germany: Springer International, 2019), pp. 5–10.
18 Ibid.
19 "What Happened on the First Day of the War," *BBC Persian* (September 21, 2015). https://www.bbc.com/persian/iran/2015/09/150921_l10_ma_iran_iraq_war35th_anniversary.
20 "The First Message That Was Broadcast after the Outbreak of War," Islamic Revolution Document Center (October 2, 2019). http://irdc.ir/fa/news/5200/اولین-پیامی-که-بعد-از-حمله-عراق-از-رادیو-تلویزیون-ایران-پخش-شد.
21 "Bani Sadr: Mr Khamenei Was Way Behind the Revolutionary Clerics," *BBC Persian* (September 17, 2011). https://www.bbc.com/persian/iran/2011/09/110916_l13_banisadr_interview_on_khamenei.
22 B. Alikhani, "Popular War Songs and Slogans in the Persian Language during the Iran-Iraq War." *Cambio*, 3(6) (2013): 212.
23 Baktiari, *Parliamentary Politics in Revolutionary Iran*, p. 103.
24 FCO cable from August 13, 1980.
25 "Hassan Karroubi and the Secrets He Did Not Reveal," *Tarikh Irani* (March 13, 2015). http://tarikhirani.ir/fa/news/4981/حسن-کروبی-و-اسراری-که-فاش-نکرد.
26 R. Parry, *Trick or Treason: The October Surprise Mystery* (New York: Sheridan Square Press, 1993), pp. 82–5.
27 Interview with Taghi Karroubi (Son of Mehdi Karroubi) (October 8, 2018).
28 J. Drinkard, "Probe of 1980 GOP Hostage Dealings Reveal Covert CIA Operation," *Associated Press News* (November 24, 1992). https://apnews.com/article/aced9401e8837998832ee4c0643508cf
29 G. Sick, "The Election Story of the Decade," *New York Times* (April 15, 1991). https://www.nytimes.com/1991/04/15/opinion/the-election-story-of-the-decade.html. For a detailed account see Gary Sick's *October Surprise* (London: I.B. Tauris, 1991).
30 A. Bani Sadr, *My Turn to Speak: Iran, the Revolution and the Secret Deals with the U.S.* (Ann Arbor: University of Michigan, 1991).
31 CIA: National Foreign Assessment Center, "Iran: The Seizure of the Embassy in Retrospect" (August 12, 1981). https://www.cia.gov/library/readingroom/document/cia-rdp06t00412r000200560001-7.
32 Bakhash, *The Reign of the Ayatollahs*, p. 140.
33 Speech by Bani Sadr about Religious Tyranny in the Aftermath of the Revolution, YouTube (last accessed June 26, 2020). https://www.youtube.com/watch?v=s1tXl3shRQU.
34 Speech by Khamenei in the Majles, "Ayatollah Khamenei and Bani Sadr's impeachment," YouTube (last accessed June 26, 2020). https://www.youtube.com/watch?v=BQM9NxlROrg.
35 "Union of Rouhani and Bani Sadr at Qods Day of 2017," *BBC Persian* (June 24, 2017). https://www.bbc.com/persian/iran-40393357.
36 "Assassination of Khamenei: 35 Years Later," *BBC* (June 26 *Persian*, 2016). https://www.bbc.com/persian/iran/2016/06/160626_l10_ha_khamenei_assassination_attempt.
37 "Mr. Bani Sadr, Who Had a Hand in the Explosion of the Islamic Republican Party?" YouTube (last accessed June 26, 2020). https://www.youtube.com/watch?v=55KmiocRslo.
38 A. Amanat, *Iran: A Modern History* (New Haven: Yale University Press, 2017), pp. 799–800.

39 "If Rajaei Had Lived He Would Have Stood Up to Khomeini," *BBC Persian* (August 30, 2013). https://www.bbc.com/persian/iran/2013/08/130828_l39_rajaei_jalal-yaghoobi.
40 FCO 81. 4. p. 39.
41 Ibid.
42 R. Eder, "Bani-Sadr Says Killing 5 Key Men Can End Regime," *New York Times* (August 25, 1981). https://www.nytimes.com/1981/08/25/world/bani-sadr-says-killing-5-key-men-can-end-regime.html.
43 "Khamenei: In Newly Revealed Speech Says Most of Those Involved in US Embassy Takeover Have Apologized," Radio Farda (January 26, 2018). https://www.radiofarda.com/a/khamenei-on-us-embassy-hostage-crisis/29000202.html.
44 Rafsanjani explains how Khamenei became supreme leader, BBC Monitoring Middle East, London. BBC Worldwide Limited (March 14, 2015). Translated from article in Iranian reformist newspaper Sharq (March 10, 2015).

4 (1981–5)—Rafsanjani and Khamenei Sharpen Knives for Each Other

1 Sahifeh-e Imam Khomeini, "Documents of Imam Khomeini: "If America and Israel say "La ilaha ill Allah [Allah is Great]," we do not accept it," vol. 15 (2008): 339. http://panahian.ir/post/4002#gsc.tab=0 (accessed November 20, 2020).
2 Khamenei, *Memoirs of Supreme Leader* (Moass-e Farhangi Qadr-e Velayat) (Tehran, 1378), p. 90.
3 A. Ganji, "Rafsanjani and Khamenei: A Brief History," Al Jazeera (September 23, 2013). https://www.aljazeera.com/opinions/2013/9/23/rafsanjani-and-khamenei-a-brief-history/.
4 "The Saga of the 99 Where Khamenei Was the 100th," Radio Farda (October 19, 2010). https://www.radiofarda.com/a/f3_khamenei_history_against_mousavi/2194883.html.
5 "Second Majlis: Unfolding of the Differences between Khamenei and Mousavi," *BBC Persian* (February 26, 2016). https://www.bbc.com/persian/iran/2016/02/160214_ir94_second_majlis.
6 Speech by Prime Minister Mehdi Bazargan, "Bazargab: The Man Who Predicted Today 30 Years ago," Daily Motion (last accessed June 27, 2020). https://www.dailymotion.com/video/x2vb892.
7 "Reviewing the Most Sensationalist Political Fights," *Nameh News* (January 12, 2015). https://bit.ly/3hqN2XT.
8 CIA: Directorate of Intelligence, "Iran's Air Force: Frustrations of a Former Power" (September 1, 1984). https://www.cia.gov/library/readingroom/docs/CIA-RDP85T00314R000300020001-7.pdf.
9 CIA: Director of Central Intelligence, "Implications of Iran's Victory over Iraq" (June 8, 1982). https://www.cia.gov/library/readingroom/docs/CIA-RDP85T00176R001100130001-6.pdf.
10 Bakhash, *The Reign of the Ayatollahs*, p. 234.
11 "Iran's Lost Opportunities in the War," *BBC Persian* (last accessed June 27, 2020). https://www.youtube.com/watch?v=qVL3cr-DKNM&feature=youtu.be&ocid=socialflow_twitter.
12 "Rafsanjani: Imam Khomeini' Willed That I and Khamenei Stand by Each Other," *Asr Iran* (February 9, 2013). https://bit.ly/2ZzdWqn.

13 Bakhash, *The Reign of the Ayatollahs*, p. 44.
14 "Why Did Velayati Become Foreign Minister?" *Bahar News* (June 5, 2018). http://www.baharnews.ir/news/151604/علت-اینکه-ولایتی-وزیر-خارجه-ایران-شده.
15 CIA: Directorate of Intelligence, "Khomeinism: The Impact of Theology on Iranian Politics" (November 1, 1983). https://www.cia.gov/library/readingroom/docs/CIA-RDP84S00927R000100150003-5.pdf.
16 J. Crystal, *Kuwait, the Transformation of an Oil State* (New York: Routledge, 1992), p. 113.
17 I. Rabinovich and S. Haim, *Middle East Contemporary Survey: Volume Ix, 1984–1985* (Boulder: Westview Press, 1987), p. 403.
18 "More on Sa'ud al-Faysal's Meetings," Tehran International Service (May 20, 1985).
19 "Current Directions in Iranian Foreign Policy," Foreign Broadcast Information Service (April 11, 1985).
20 Bakhash, *The Reign of the Ayatollahs*, p. 257.
21 CIA: Director of Central Intelligence, "Iran: Outlook for the Islamic Republic" (May 24, 1983). https://www.cia.gov/library/readingroom/docs/CIA-RDP86T00302R000801310007-5.pdf.

5 (1985–9)—The Beginning of the End of Khomeini

1 G. Fuller, *The Center of the Universe: The Geopolitics of Iran* (Boulder: Westview Press, 1991), p. 255.
2 A. Shahrough, "The Thought and Role of Ayatollah Hossein'ali Montazeri in the Politics of Post-1979 Iran." *Iranian Studies*, 41(5) (2008): 645–66.
3 Baktiari, *Parliamentary Politics in Revolutionary Iran*, p. 95.
4 U. Von Schwerin, *The Dissident Mullah* (London: I.B. Tauris, 2015).
5 Bakhash, *The Reign of the Ayatollahs*, p. 231.
6 Data on all arms sales to Iran from 1980 to 1988 from the Stockholm International Peace Research Institute (SIPRI).
7 J. Wallach, "The Artful Ambassador," *Washington Post* (December 8, 1985). The list of attendees was confirmed to the author by David Ignatius.
8 CIA, "Recent Developments in Iran" (July 19, 1982). https://www.cia.gov/library/readingroom/docs/CIA-RDP84B00049R001603990009-0.pdf.
9 Ibid.
10 According to Shaul Bakhash, no one can find the original source for this quote and the statement itself cannot be found in databases and published collections of Khomeini statements and speeches.
11 D. Crist, *The Twilight War* (London: Penguin Books, 2013), p. 181.
12 The Reagan administration's arms-for-hostages was feared by those opposed to the project (such as Shultz and Weinberger) to undermine the containment of Iran and Operation Staunch.
13 For more details, see *The Tower Commission Report* (New York: Bantam Books, 1987).
14 The other two individuals were Mohammad Ali Hadi and Fereidoon Vardinejad.
15 "If McFarlane Could Have Met Hashemi [Rafsanjani], This Affair Would Have Ended very Differently," *Entekhab* (September 28, 2019). https://bit.ly/33tx5em.
16 S. Harris, "When Rouhani Met Ollie North," *Foreign Policy* (September 26, 2013). https://foreignpolicy.com/2013/09/26/when-rouhani-met-ollie-north/.

17 "McFarlane's Visit Based on an Eye Witness," *Iranian Diplomacy* (May 5, 2014). http://irdiplomacy.ir/fa/news/1932372/سفر-مک-فارلین-به-روایت-شاهد-عینی.
18 "Advisor to Imam [Khomeini]: Mohammad Khamenei and the Israelis Both Lie," Kaleme (January 3, 2015). https://www.kaleme.com/1393/10/13/klm-206480/?theme=fast.
19 "Preliminary Inquiry into the Sale of Arms to Iran and Possible Diversion of Funds to the Nicaraguan Resistance," US Congress, Senate Select Committee on Intelligence (February 1987), p. 26.
20 "White House Verifies Reagan Did Write in Bible Sent to Iran," *Los Angeles Times*, (January 30, 1987). https://www.latimes.com/archives/la-xpm-1987-01-30-mn-1803-story.html.
21 Interview with Ali Hashemi, *Entekhab* (September 28, 2019). https://bit.ly/35xhvkM.
22 Crist, *The Twilight War*, p. 195.
23 "Rafsanjani's Nephew: I Did Not Visit Israel as Part of Negotiations with the Americans," *Khabar Online* (July 13, 2020). https://bit.ly/32qcFnm.
24 M. Byrne, *Iran Contra: Reagan's Scandal and the Unchecked Abuse of Presidential Power* (Lawrence: University Press of Kansas, 2014).
25 "Advisor to Imam [Khomeini]: Mohammad Khamenei and the Israelis Both Lie," Kaleme (January 3, 2015). https://www.kaleme.com/1393/10/13/klm-206480/?theme=fast.
26 "President Reagan's White House Diary Entry: May 28, 1986," Ronald Reagan Presidential Foundation and Institute, Simi Valley, California.
27 Some sources claim that the Soviets gave the information to the Assad regime. S. T. Hunter, "The Real Reason Iran's Hardliners Don't Want to Talk to America," Lobe Log (May 21, 2019). https://lobelog.com/the-real-reason-irans-hardliners-dont-want-to-talk-to-america/.
28 National Security Agency, "How the Iran-Contra Story Leaked" (released July 29, 2014). https://nsarchive.files.wordpress.com/2014/11/1989-00-00-cia-studies-in-intel-syria-leak-to-ash-shiraa-iran-contra.pdf
29 For a good discussion, see M. Ranstorp, *Hizb'Allah in Lebanon: The Politics of the Western Hostage Crisis* (London: Palgrave, 1997).
30 "Reassessing the Secret Ties of the Sepah and America," *BBC Persian* (April 22, 2019). https://www.bbc.com/persian/iran-features-48016253.
31 "The Controversial Haj of 1365 [1987]," Radio Farda (October 12, 2018). https://www.radiofarda.com/a/commentary-on-motazeri-rafsanjani-confrontation/29539895.html.
32 CIA: Directorate of Intelligence, "Iranian Factionalism: Implications for the United States" (November 14, 1986). https://www.cia.gov/library/readingroom/docs/CIA-RDP86T01017R000807980001-8.pdf.
33 CIA memorandum, "Iran Economic Indicators" (November 10, 1986). https://www.cia.gov/library/readingroom/docs/CIA-RDP88G01116R000500450001-7.pdf.
34 "Decree to Disband the Islamic Republican Party," Iran Data Portal (June 1, 1987). https://irandataportal.syr.edu/decree-to-disband-the-islamic-republic-party-june-1-1987.
35 R. Cheit, ed., "Understanding the Iran-Contra Affair: The Hearings, Brown University." https://www.brown.edu/Research/Understanding_the_Iran_Contra_Affair/thehearings.php.
36 AmericanRhetoric.com (2018), "Oliver North—Iran Contra Hearing," YouTube. (accessed May 18, 2020). https://www.youtube.com/watch?v=ct3UxB696D4.

37 As Ayatollah Khomeini's health deteriorated, a five-member council took over the matters of running the country. This council included Mir-hossein Mousavi, prime minister; Mousavi Ardebili, chief justice of the Supreme Court; Khamenei, the president; Ahmad Khomeini, the son of Ayatollah Khomeini and his chief of staff; and Hashemi Rafsanjani.
38 "Why Did Khomeini Want Commanders Responsible in War Defeat Hanged?" *BBC Persian* (September 23, 2014). https://www.bbc.com/persian/iran/2014/09/140923_l39_file_iran_iraq_war.
39 Ibid.
40 "Rafsanjani's Peculiar Comment to Rafiqdoost about Ending the War," *Jahan News* (July 19, 2018). http://www.jahannews.com/news/628024/جمله-عجیب-هاشمی-رفیق-دوست-پایان-جنگ.
41 According to CIA records, Iraq first used chemical gasses against Iran in August 1983. Central Intelligence Agency: Director of Central Intelligence (1988), "Impact and Implications of Chemical Weapons Use in the Iran-Iraq War." Multiple sources report that Iraq used chemical weapons during the al-Faw campaign in April 1988. According to Russel in *Weapons Proliferation and War in the Greater Middle East: Strategic Contest*,

> Iraq began to fully integrate CW into its successful offensives ... Iraq made heavy use of chemical weapons. For example, in the April 1988 battle to recapture the Al Faw Peninsula, we estimate that the Iraqis used well over 100 tons of CW agent. The suddenness and severity of this attack disrupted Iranian command and control, decimated key units, and threw the Iranian defenders into disarray. (44)

Another frequently cited *Foreign Policy* article states that Iraq used mustard and sarin gas in four offenses throughout the spring of 1988. The article also states that the CIA provided Iraq with satellite imagery to conduct the attacks. https://www.cia.gov/library/readingroom/docs/DOC_0001079783.pdf.
42 P. Razoux, *The Iran-Iraq War* (Cambridge, MA: Harvard University Press, 2015), pp. 455–62. In 1996, the United States "recognized the aerial incident of 3 July 1988 as a terrible human tragedy and expressed deep regret over the loss of lives caused by the incident." Washington agreed to pay Iran $131.8 million, including $61.8 million to the family members of the deceased.
43 "I Told the Imam [Khomeini] to Put Us on Trial and Hang Us," *BBC Persian* (January 10, 2017). https://www.bbc.com/persian/iran-38568792.
44 "Iran's Networks of Influence in the Middle East," IISS (November 2019), pp. 11–38. There are no precise figures available about the cost of the war for Iran. One study published by Iran's Khabar Online news site put the direct and indirect losses relating to the war at $437.08 billion. ("How Much Did the 8-Year War Cost?" *Khabar Online* [September 21, 2013].) https://www.khabaronline.ir/news/313910/خسارت-های-جنگ-8-ساله-چندمیلیارد-دلار-بود.
45 R. Reagan, "Address to the 42nd Session of the United Nations General Assembly" (September 21, 1987), United Nations Headquarters, New York.
46 A. Khamenei, "Leader's Speech at UN General Assembly" (September 22, 1987), United Nations Headquarters, New York.
47 D. Ottaway, "Mine-Laying Episode Put Iran's President on Defensive at U.N." *Washington Post* (September 26, 1987). See also S. C. Pelletiere, *The Iran-Iraq War: Chaos in a Vacuum* (New York: Praeger, 1992), pp. 131–2.

48 Memoirs of Supreme Leader Khamenei, p. 199.
49 R. Sleiman-Haidar, "The Iranian Threat: The Saudi Perspective," London School of Economics and Political Science (June 15, 2018). See also Baharaan (2010), "Imam Khomeini's Last Will and Testament—Part 1/11 [English Sub]." https://www.youtube.com/watch?v=RQAFYgemWOc (accessed May 19, 2020).
50 "Publication of Hidden Details of Relations between Tehran and Moscow in Final Days of Soviet Union," *BBC Persian* (December 5, 2012). https://www.bbc.com/persian/iran/2012/12/121205_l23_iran_su_hashemi_rafsanjani_tehran_moscow.
51 "Imam [Khomeini's] Historic Letter to Gorbachev," *Jamaran* (January 1, 2011). https://www.jamaran.news/بخش-سیاست-12/16291-نامه-تاریخی-امام-خمینی-به-گورباچف. In English "Ayatollah Khomeini's Only Written Message to a Foreign Leader," American Herald Tribune (December 31, 2016).
52 "GDP per Capita (Constant 2010 US$)—Iran, Islamic Rep." World Bank national accounts data, and OECD National. https://data.worldbank.org/indicator/NY.GDP.PCAP.KD?end=1989&locations=IR&start=1979.
53 "The Most Bitter Moment for Imam Was Accepting UN Resolution 598," *Dana* (April 13, 2015). https://www.dana.ir/news/282474.html/حاج-احمدآقا-تلخ-ترین-خاطره-عمر-امام-ره-پذیرش-قطعنامه-----بود--توسلی--دیگر-خنده-بر-لبان-امام-ره-ندیدیم.
54 "An Account about Differences between Hashemi [Rafsanjani] and Mohsen Rezai," *Nameh News* (September 23, 2018). https://bit.ly/2Ftncp3.
55 "IRGC: Defender of the Islamic Revolution Sanctioned after Four Decades," Radio Farda (April 8, 2019). https://en.radiofarda.com/a/irgc-defender-of-islamic-revolution-sanctioned-after-four-decades/29868846.html.

6 (1989–93)—Khamenei: The Second Supreme Leader

1 "Rafsanjani: 'I Requested That Imam Resolve the Issue of Relations with the Americans in His Lifetime,'" *BBC Persian* (April 3, 2012). https://www.bbc.com/persian/iran/2012/04/120403_l39_rafsanjani_iran-us_relations.
2 "Ziba Kalam: 'Hashemi Rafsanjani Probably Wrote the Letter to Imam about Relations with America in 1365 [1986],'" *Khabar Online* (April 11, 2012). https://www.khabaronline.ir/news/207483/زیبا-کلام-هاشمی-رفسنجانی-نامه-به-امام-درباره-رابطه-با-امریکا.
3 "Ali Motahari's Skepticism about Montazeri's Dismissal Letter," *BBC Persian* (February 13, 2019). https://www.bbc.com/persian/iran-features-47231687?ocid=socialflow_twitter.
4 Montazeri's son claimed the letter that dismissed his father was not written by Khomeini but by his son Ahmad. See Agaahi, "Montazeri Son Blame Khomeyni Son Ahmad of Forgery" (2010). https://www.youtube.com/watch?v=vyObfbnjtWI (accessed May 19, 2020).
5 "New Information about the Arrest and Execution of Mehdi Hashemi," Radio Farda (May 5, 2019). The saga with Mehdi Hashemi is still unresolved. https://www.radiofarda.com/a/mehdi_hashemi_arrest_execution_hosseinian_account/29921992.html.
6 H. Dilip, *Neighbors, Not Friends: Iraq and Iran after the Gulf Wars* (London: Routledge, 2003), p. 21.

7. "The Office of Ayatollah Khomeini's Legacy Has to Respond to Charges of Corruption against Ayatollah Montazeri," *BBC Persian* (May 6, 2019). https://www.bbc.com/persian/iran-48176717.
8. The nominal chairman of the body was Ali Meshkini but the real power in the Assembly of Experts was Rafsanjani.
9. In his memoirs, Rafsanjani claims that on his deathbed, Khomeini had grabbed his hand and urged him to "hasten the revision of the constitution" so that Khamenei could be qualified to succeed him as supreme leader. "How Did the Last Days of Imam [Khomeini] Go?" *Boyer News* (June 3, 2016). http://boyernews.com/193465/193465/.
10. "Shocking Video Clip from 1989 Shows Khamenei Elected Only for One Year as a Caretaker," Radio Farda (January 9, 2018). https://en.radiofarda.com/a/video-showing-khamenei-election-supreme-leader/28963611.html. See also S. Golkar, "Iran after Khamenei: Prospects for Political Change." *Middle East Policy*, 26(1) (2019): 76.
11. "Why Did Khamenei Become Leader and Hashemi Did Not?" Radio Farda (June 7, 2019). https://www.radiofarda.com/a/Iran-leadership-why-khamenei-and-not-rafsanjani/29986610.html. See also "A Recounting from Imam: You Become leader," *Tarikh Irani* (June 12, 2019). http://tarikhirani.ir/fa/news/6634/نقل-قول-ناگفته-امام-شما-رهبر-بشوید.
12. "Why Was Azeri Qomi Transformed?" Kadivar.com (February 12, 2014). https://kadivar.com/13174/. See also K. Amirpur, "Contemporary Critics of the Velayat-e Faqih," Oasis Center (March 30, 2020). https://www.oasiscenter.eu/en/iran-critics-guardianship-jurisconsult.
13. CIA: Directorate for Intelligence, "Khamenei and Rafsanjani: Rivals for Power in Iran" (December 3, 1983). https://www.cia.gov/library/readingroom/docs/CIA-RDP84S00927R000200110004-7.pdf.
14. "Revelations from Unpublished Video about Election of Khamenei to Supreme Leadership," *BBC Persian* (January 10, 2018). https://www.bbc.com/persian/iran-features-42630586.
15. "New Details about the Offer of Deputy Leadership to Hashemi [Rafsanjani]," *Tabnak* (June 9, 2020). https://bit.ly/3iqEi5e.
16. "Statements of Haj Ahmad Khomeini about Supreme Leadership of Imam Khamenei," Aparat (unknown date). https://www.aparat.com/v/Jv8dz/سخنان_حاج_احمد_آقا_خمینی_در_مورد_رهبری_و_ولایت.
17. "Let Us Get to Know Ahmad Khomeini and His killers," VOA (April 5, 2013). https://www.youtube.com/watch?v=HUONy50RECo.
18. "Imam Khomeini's Last Will and Testament," Al-Islam (February 15, 1983). https://www.al-islam.org/imam-khomeini-s-last-will-and-testament/testament.
19. "20 Years Has Passed since the Suspicious Death: Who Was Ahmad Khomeini?" Radio Farda (March 16, 2016). https://www.radiofarda.com/a/f14_20_years_after_suspicious_death_of_ahmad_khomeini/26902390.html.
20. "Was Ahmad Khomeini Killed by Saeed Emami?" *BBC Persian* (November 24, 2013). https://www.bbc.com/persian/iran/2013/11/131120_l39_analysis_ahmad_khomeini_saeid_emami.
21. "The First Meeting of the Sepah with Khamenei," *Akharin Khabar* (April 10, 2019). http://akharinkhabar.ir/politics/5159011.
22. "The Mojtaba Khamenei Circle," Radio Farda (2019). https://www.radiofarda.com/a/30119166.html.
23. "Why Did 'Agha' [Khamenei] Not Go to Jamaran?" *Quds Online* (June 9, 2016). http://www.qudsonline.ir/news/390517/چرا-آقا-به-جماران-نرفت-بیت-رهبری-چگونه-ساخته-شد.

24 Interview with Mohsen Sazegara.
25 S. Haeri, "Tehran 'Purges 4,000 Guards,'" *The Independent* (July 18, 1994).
26 "Hashemi and His Decisions to Negotiate with the Americans," *Fararu* (April 2, 2012). https://bit.ly/3imJqHD.
27 Ibid.
28 "Memoirs of Ayatollah Hashemi," *Entekhab* (October 13, 2019). https://bit.ly/33sNPmb.
29 Khamenei memoirs, *Memoirs of Supreme Leader* (Moass-e Farhangi Qadr-e Velayat), (Tehran, 1378), p. 201.
30 Ibid., p. 203.
31 Ibid., p. 216.
32 S. Randjbar-Daemi, *The Quest for Authority in Iran: A History of the Presidency from Revolution to Rouhani* (London: I.B. Tauris, 2017).
33 R. Parks, "Iranian Gets Warm Soviet Welcome," *Los Angeles Times* (June 21, 1989). See also S. Shajari, *Chain Reaction and Chaos: Toward Modern Persia* (New York: UPA, 2014), p. 164.
34 E. D. Moore, *Russia-Iran Relations since the End of the Cold War* (London: Taylor & Francis, 2014), pp. 17–19.
35 CIA: Directorate of Intelligence, "Redirecting Iranian Foreign Policy: Rafsanjani's Progress" (June 1, 1990). https://www.cia.gov/library/readingroom/docs/DOC_0000602680.pdf.
36 P. Tyler, "Shevardnadze, Khomeini Meet in Tehran," *Washington Post* (February 27, 1989).
37 "Publication of New Information about Tehran and Moscow Relations in Last Days of the Soviet Union," *BBC Persian* (December 5, 2012). https://www.bbc.com/persian/iran/2012/12/121205_l23_iran_su_hashemi_rafsanjani_tehran_moscow.
38 M. Dowd, "Iran Is Reported Ready for a Deal to Recover Assets," *New York Times* (August 9, 1989).
39 G. Nada, "If Sanctions Are Lifted, Here's What Trade between Iran and the U.S. Could Look Like," Quartz (April 24, 2015). See also I. Kelman, *Disaster Diplomacy: How Disasters Affect Peace and Conflict* (London: Taylor & Francis, 2011), pp. 21–4.
40 Y. Hovsepian-Bearce, *The Political Ideology of Ayatollah Khamenei* (New York: Routledge, 2015), p. 153.
41 Ibid.
42 N. Macfarquhar, "Rafsanjani Calls on Palestinians to Kill Westerners," *Associated Press* (May 5, 1989). See also R. S. Litwak and R. Litwak, *Regime Change: U.S. Strategy through the Prism of 9/11* (USA: Woodrow Wilson Center Press with Johns Hopkins University Press, 2007), p. 204.
43 "Arafat Denounces Iranian's Call For Revenge Killing of Westerners" *New York Times* (May 8, 1989). https://www.nytimes.com/1989/05/08/world/arafat-denounces-iranian-s-call-for-revenge-killing-of-westerners.html.
44 "Khalkhali's Jihad and Rouhani's Prudence in Persian Gulf War," *Tarikh Irani* (August 2, 2014). http://tarikhirani.ir/fa/news/4556/جهاد-خلخالی-و-تدبیر-روحانی-در-جنگ-خلیج-فارس.
45 K. Pollack, *The Persian Puzzle: The Conflict between Iran and America* (New York: Random House, 2005).
46 A. Alfoneh and M. Gerecht, "The Death of Ali Akbar Hashemi-Rafsanjani, a Machiavellian Prince," *Washington Examiner* (January

9, 2017). https://www.washingtonexaminer.com/weekly-standard/the-death-of-ali-akbar-hashemi-rafsanjani-a-machiavellian-prince.
47 Public Papers of the Presidents of the United States: George Bush, 1991 (1992). (United States: Best Books), p. 1, 268.
48 For a detailed account, see R. Hakakian, *Assassins of the Turquoise Palace* (United States: Grove Atlantic, 2011).
49 "Presence in the Bosnian War in the Balkans; the Peak of the Qods Force," *BBC Persian* (June 5, 2019). https://www.bbc.com/persian/iran-48535731.
50 "Fundamental Policies of the Second Development Plan," *Khamenei.ir* (November 9, 1993). https://farsi.khamenei.ir/news-content?id=2692.
51 Khamenei, *Memoirs of Supreme Leader* (Moass-e Farhangi Qadr-e Velayat), (Tehran, 1378), pp. 346–8.
52 Ibid., p. 159.
53 Ibid., p. 160.
54 Ibid., p. 167.

7 (1993–7)—Dithering in Tehran as the Cold War Ends

1 "Rafsanjani's Advice to the 'Great Satan,'" *Time Magazine* (May 31, 1993). http://content.time.com/time/magazine/article/0,9171,978611,00.html.
2 "The Letter of 90 Signatories in 1990," *Ensaf News* (April 11, 2018). http://www.ensafnews.com/108603/متن-نامه-90-امضایی-سال-1369-به-هاشمی/.
3 S. L. Simmons and E. F. Mickolus, *Terrorism, 1992–1995: A Chronology of Events and a Selectively Annotated Bibliography* (United Kingdom: Greenwood Press, 1997), pp. 552–3.
4 "Rafsanjani's Memoirs: Tequila, Yasser and the Camels," Radio Farda (October 26, 2019). https://www.radiofarda.com/a/Jalal-Saeidi-satire-e62/30236323.html.
5 "What Is Happening in Iran's Intelligence Ministry," *BBC Persian* (January 23, 2019). https://www.bbc.com/persian/iran-46906435.
6 "News Summary," *New York Times* (March 31, 1993). https://www.nytimes.com/1993/03/31/nyregion/news-summary-582693.html.
7 A. Yunusov, "Malicious Mapmaking (in the Price of Freedom)." *Bulletin of the Atomic Scientists*, 50(1) (January/February 1994): 19.
8 "One Person's Story: Feyzollah Mekhobad," Abdorahman Boroumand Center. https://www.iranrights.org/memorial/story/-3463/feyzollah-mekhoubad.
9 "All the Files That Hossein Taeb Manufactured," Radio Farda (September 16, 2016). https://www.radiofarda.com/a/hossein_taeb_cases_security_intelligence_service/29492891.html.
10 A. Dehghan and O. Bowcott, "Wife of UK Businessman Who Vanished in Dubai Demands Answers from SFO," *The Guardian* (December 26, 2013).
11 A. Alfoneh, "*The IRGC v Rohani: Spy v Spy*," *Arab Weekly* (June 19, 2015).
12 S. Maloney, *Iran's Political Economy since the Revolution* (Cambridge: Cambridge University Press, 2015), p. 235.
13 P. Tyler, "Hostage Issue: Test for Iran's President," *New York Times* (September 13, 1991).
14 S. Stecklow, B. Dehghanpisheh, and Y. Torbati, "Exclusive: Reuters Investigates Business Empire of Iran's Supreme Leader," *Reuters* (November 11, 2013).

15 E. Mehrabi, "Mohsen Rezaei: Loser of War, Economics, and Politics," *Iran Wire* (April 19, 2019). https://iranwire.com/en/features/5978.
16 "U.S, Iran exchange barbs in India," *UPI* (April 18, 1995). https://www.upi.com/Archives/1995/04/18/US-Iran-exchange-barbs-in-India/8776798177600/.
17 A. Eshraghi and Y. Baji, "Debunking the Rafsanjani Myth," Al Jazeera (February 21, 2012). https://www.aljazeera.com/opinions/2012/2/21/debunking-the-rafsanjani-myth/.
18 J. Stempel, "Iran Ordered to Pay $104.7 Million over 1996 Truck Bomb Attack: U.S. Judge," Reuters (September 10, 2018). https://sports.yahoo.com/iran-ordered-pay-104-7-million-over-1996-201247199.html.
19 D. Kenner, "Saudi Arabia Bans National Geographic Cover Featuring Pope Francis," *Foreign Policy* (September 8, 2015).
20 "Memoir of Ayatollah Hashemi," *Entekhab* (October 13, 2019). https://bit.ly/33tzHJe; "What Was the Secret Message of the Saudi Ruler to Hashemi?" *Nameh News* (February 2, 2019). https://bit.ly/2Fizhh3.
21 There are other theories about the identity of the culprits, including this five-part investigation that claims that it was done by al Qaeda, and that Saudi Arabia prevented the FBI from being able to establish that fact clearly by refusing to cooperate with its investigation at all, while Prince Bandar whispered in Louis Freeh's ear that it was the Iranians' Saudi Hezbollah allies who were responsible. G. Porter, "Exclusive Part 1: Al Qaeda Excluded from the Suspects List," Inter Press Service (June 22, 2009).
22 Even though other accounts suggest he might have known. "Explanation of Ahmad Montazeri about the Transfer of Explosives at the Haj of 1987," *BBC Persian* (October 6, 2018). https://www.bbc.com/persian/iran-45771398.
23 R. Northonn-Taylor, "Rushdie Death Edict 'Hinged on Jurisprudence'," *The Guardian* (April 20, 1995).
24 S. MacDonogh, ed., *The Rushdie Letters: Freedom to Speak, Freedom to Write* (Lincoln: University of Nebraska, 1993), p. 157.
25 "Rafsanjani Memoirs from 1 Feb 1997," *Nameh News* (February 2, 2019). https://bit.ly/2DX2c9v.
26 "Russia Supplies $500m in Weapons," *Middle East Economic Digest* (March 4, 1996).
27 "Keep Your Mercenaries Out of Chechnya, Russia Tells Five Muslim Countries," Agence France-Presse (January 4, 1995).
28 "Who Was after Making the Hashemi Government a Permanent One?," SNN Student News Network (July 16, 2015). https://snn.ir/fa/news/425943/چه-کسانی-بدنبال-مادام-العمر-کردن-دولت-هاشمی-بودند.
29 B. M. Weitzman, ed., *Middle East Contemporary Survey Volume Xix*, vol. 6 (Nashville: Westview, 1995), p. 285.
30 "The Fifth Majlis, Start of Reform and Internal Fights," *BBC Persian* (February 24, 2016). https://www.bbc.com/persian/iran/2016/02/160214_ir94_5th_majlis.
31 "We All Disobeyed the Koran and Made Excuses," *Nameh News* (January 14, 2019). https://bit.ly/32q9Jaa.
32 H. Esfandiary, *Reconstructed Lives: Women and Iran's Islamic Revolution* (Washington, DC: Woodrow Wilson Center Press, 1997).
33 "Effat, Faezeh and Akbar Hashemi: The Place of Women in Politics," *BBC Persian* (January 16, 2016). https://www.bbc.com/persian/iran-features-38630050.
34 "Interview of Rafsanjani with Zan Magazine about the Role of Women in Parliament and in Society," Rafsanjani.ir (December 15, 1987). https://www.rafsanjani.ir/

مصاحبه-آقای-هاشمی-با-مجله-زن-روز-پیرامون-نقش-زن-در-جامعه-و-ضرورت-وجود-خانم-/records
ها-در-مجلس.

35 "Did Hashemi Vote for Khatami or Nateq Nouri in 1997?" *Eghtesadnews* (May 19, 2019). https://bit.ly/2DVCi60.
36 "I Asked Imam [Khomeini] to Put Us on Trial and Execute Us," *BBC Persian* (January 10, 2017). https://www.bbc.com/persian/iran-38568792.
37 Khamenei memoirs, pp. 320–8.
38 "Rafsanjani's Relations with Khamenei; the Love That Failed," Radio Farda (June 24, 2010). https://www.radiofarda.com/a/f4_Hashemi_khamenei_relation_cut_power_struggle/2081089.html.
39 "Why Did [Khamenei] Say No One Will Be Rafsanjani for Me?" *Mardm Salari* (May 9, 2013). https://www.mardomsalari.ir/
news/30489/چرا-رهبری-گفت-هیچ-کس-هاشمی-نمی-شود.
40 P. Weller, "The Salmon Rushdie Controversy, Religious Plurality, and Established Religion in England" (PhD Thesis, University of Leeds, 1996).
41 D. Pipes, "Salman Rushdie's Delusions, and Ours," *Commentary Magazine* (December 1998). https://www.commentarymagazine.com/articles/daniel-pipes/salman-rushdies-delusions-and-ours/.
42 A. Cowell, "Berlin Court Says Top Iran Leaders Ordered Killings," *New York Times* (April 11, 1997). https://www.nytimes.com/1997/04/11/world/berlin-court-says-top-iran-leaders-ordered-killings.html.
43 "Ali Falahian: The Plan Was for Rouhani to Become Rafsanjani's Intelligence Minister," Deutsche Welle (February 17, 2015). https://www.dw.com/
fa-ir/علی-فلاحیان-روحانی-قرار-بود-وزیر-اطلاعات-دولت-رفسنجانی-شود/a-18264682.

8 (1997–2005)—The Era of Reformist Hope: Rafsanjani under Fire; Khamenei Hits Back

1 "Hashemi as Told by the Leader of the Revolution," Document Center of Ayatollah Hashemi Rafsanjani, Rafsanjani.ir (May 27, 1997). https://rafsanjani.ir/
records/هاشمی-به-روایت-رهبر-معظم-انقلاب.
2 "Why Did Khatami Leave the Ershad?" *Sazandegi News* (January 11, 2019). http://sazandeginews.com/News/1305.
3 Muhammad Khatami, *Hope and Challenge, the Iranian President Speaks* (New York: Binghamton University, 1997), p. 17.
4 Ibid.
5 "A Closer Look at the Family Ties between Khamenei and Khatami," VOA (August 10, 2010). https://ne-np.facebook.com/voapersian/videos/871394693247676/.
6 E. Abrahamian, *A History of Modern Iran* (Cambridge: Cambridge University Press, 2008), pp. 186–8.
7 "Meeting of a Group of Youth with the Leader of the Revolution," Khamenei.ir (April 20, 2000). https://farsi.khamenei.ir/print-content?id=8716.
8 Interview with Sazegara.
9 A. Alfoneh, *Iran Unveiled: How the Revolutionary Guards Is Turning Theocracy into Military Dictatorship* (Washington, DC: AEI Press, 2013), p. 28.
10 "The 25 Years of the Ayatollah in Marble Palace," *Mashregh News* (January 22, 2020). https://www.mashreghnews.ir/news/1033921/زندگی-۲۵-ساله-آیت-الله-در-کاخ-مرمر.

11 E. Wastnidge, *Diplomacy and Reform in Iran: Foreign Policy Under Khatami* (London: I.B. Tauris, 2016).
12 M. Boroujerdi and K. Rahimkhani, *Post-revolutionary Iran: A Political Handbook* (Syracuse, NY: Syracuse University Press, 2018).
13 "They Said If Nateq Comes [to the Presidency], He Will Be Like the Taliban," *Alef* (May 10, 2017). http://old.alef.ir/vdcef78exjh8fpi.b9bj.html?470673.
14 Patrick Clawson, Michael Eisenstadt, Eliyahu Kanovsky, David Menashri, "Iran under Khatami: A Political, Economic, and Military Assessment," Washington Institute for Near East Policy (October 1998). https://www.washingtoninstitute.org/policy-analysis/view/iran-under-khatami-a-political-economic-and-military-assessment.
15 "President Khatami Addresses America," *New York Times* (January 8, 1998). https://www.nytimes.com/1998/01/08/opinion/president-khatami-addresses-america.html.
16 M. Kramer, "The Islamic Summit in Tehran: Beyond the Hype," Washington Institute for Near East Policy (December 9, 1997).
17 P. Younesipour, "Foreign Sports Coaches Are Fleeing Iran," *Iran Wire* (January 9, 2020). https://iranwire.com/en/features/6599.
18 "The Most Political Match in the History of the World Cup," Radio Farda (June 30, 2020). https://www.radiofarda.com/a/30682783.html.
19 K. Timmerman, "How Iran Does Business," *Wall Street Journal* (December 14, 1998).
20 S. Hunter, *Iran's Foreign Policy in the Post-Soviet Era: Resisting the New International Order* (United Kingdom: Praeger, 2010), p. 197.
21 D. Jehl, "Arrest of 13 Iranian Jews as Spies Divides Factions in Teheran," *New York Times* (June 18, 1999).
22 R. Collier, "Thirteen Prisoners in Iran: The Untold Story of a Negotiation That Worked," National Interest (December 11, 2013).
23 P. Yousefzadeh, "Hassan Rouhani: The Immoderate Moderate," Atlantic Council, (August 9, 2013).
24 F. Farzani, "The Feeble Crippled Authoritarian Strikes Again," *Iran Wire* (August 30, 2019).
25 M. Albright, *Madam Secretary: A Memoir* (New York: HarperCollins, 2003), p. 321.
26 M. Albright, *U.S.-Iran Relations* (Washington, DC: Asia Society) (March 17, 2000). https://asiasociety.org/us-iran-relations.
27 T. Friedman, "Waiting for Ayatollah Gorbachev," *New York Times* (September 8, 1996).
28 "How Khamenei and Khatami Looked at Each Other," Radio Zamaneh (April 29, 2013). https://www.radiozamaneh.com/66455.
29 M. Ayatollahi Tabaar, "Supreme Showdown in Tehran," *Foreign Policy* (February 4, 2013).
30 A. Ganji, "Can Iran Trust Russia?" National Interest (May 3, 2016).
31 "Taleban's Enemies Find Common Cause," Reuters (September 21, 2001).
32 J. Dobbins, "Negotiating with Iran: Reflections from Personal Experience," *Washington Quarterly*, 33(1) (2010): 149–62.
33 Crist, *The Twilight War*, p. 429.
34 Pollack, *The Persian Puzzle*, p. 352.
35 W. Arkin, "Secret Plan Outlines the Unthinkable," *Los Angeles Times* (March 10, 2002).

36. K. R. Al-Rodhan and A. H. Cordesman, *Iran's Weapons of Mass Destruction: The Real and Potential Threat* (Washington, DC: Center for Strategic and International Studies, 2006), p. 213.
37. "Timeline of nuclear diplomacy with Iran," Arms Control Association, https://www.armscontrol.org/factsheets/Timeline-of-Nuclear-Diplomacy-With-Iran.
38. J. Lewis, "NCRI Did Not Discover Natanz," Arms Control Wonk (October 28, 2006). See also M. Hibbs, "U.S. Briefed Suppliers Group in October on Suspected Iranian Enrichment Plant," *Nuclear Fuel*, 27(26) (December 23, 2002): 1.
39. "Iran's Nuclear Program Speeds Ahead," *Washington Post* (March 10, 2003).
40. H. Mousavian and S. Shahidsaless, *Iran and the United States* (London: Bloomsbury, 2014), p. 195.
41. "2003 Memo Says Iranian Leaders Backed Talks," *Washington Post* (February 14, 2007).
42. Mousavian and Shahidsaless, *Iran and the United States*, pp. 194–5.
43. "Kerry Claims That Iran Offered Bush a Nuclear Deal in 2003," *Washington Post* (December 9, 2013).
44. "U.S. Airlifts Disaster Aid into Iran," *CNN* (December 30, 2003).
45. E. Rakel, *Power, Islam, and Political Elite in Iran: A Study on the Iranian Political Elite from Khomeini to Ahmadinejad* (Netherlands: Brill, 2008), p. 121.
46. J. Cadiot, "Revolutionary Guards Fire Off Stiff Warning to Iran Reformers," Agence France-Presse (July 21, 2002). See also M. Mohammadi, *The Iranian Reform Movement: Civil and Constitutional Rights in Suspension* (Germany: Springer International, 2018).
47. The one figure mentioned to have been instrumental in allowing Ahmadinejad to be allowed to be appointed mayor was Nateq Nouri. See, for example, "Ahmadinejad's Posture toward Nateq Nouri Came at a Heavy Cost," ISNA (July 9, 2019). https://www.isna.ir/news/98041708509/رفتار-احمدی-نژاد-برای-ناطق-نوری-سنگین-تمام-شد.
48. "Accounts of Private Meetings between Khamenei and Rafsanjani during Ahmadinejad's Presidency," *BBC Persian* (January 17, 2017). https://www.bbc.com/persian/iran-features-38590538.

9 (2005–13)—The Election of Mahmoud Ahmadinejad

1. "Let Them Pass as Many Resolutions until They Run Out of Resolutions," *Asr Iran* (November 24, 2008). https://bit.ly/3hpfvNx.
2. "Ahmadi-Nejad Admits Sanctions Hurt Iran," *Financial Times* (October 2, 2012).
3. "What Slogans Did Presidents in the Islamic Republic Come with?" *BBC Persian* (April 20, 2017). https://www.bbc.com/persian/iran-features-39616020.
4. "From 2005, Ahmadinejad Began His Agenda by Destroying Hashemi," *Alef* (January 9, 2018). https://www.alef.ir/news/3961019136.html.
5. Alireza Kiani, "A Look at the Election Campaigns in the Presidential Race," Tavaana (2018), p. 74. https://tavaana.org/sites/default/files/نگاهی_به_تبلیغات_انتخاباتی_نامزدها.pdf.
6. Some accounts claim that Khamenei's office's initial choice was Baqer Qalibaf, who had been a friend of Mojtaba Khamenei since childhood, but the Guards convinced Khamenei's office to back Ahmadinejad instead.

7   "Ahmadinejad's Statements about Hashemi from 1993 to 2013," *Akharin News* (May 9, 2013). http://www.akharinnews.com/akharinkhabar/item/19742-نژاد-احمدی-اظهارات-92-تا-72-از-،هاشمی-مورد-در.html.
8   "A Total Employee: Son of Hashemi Rafsanjani Took Bribes from Us," Radio Farda (March 24, 2007). https://www.radiofarda.com/a/f2_Total_Rafsanjani/384434.html.
9   "[Ahmadinejad's] Ministry of Intelligence Would Not Permit Rafsanjani Meeting with the Public," *Nameh News* (December 15, 2017). https://bit.ly/2FxABMI.
10 "Seven Resignations in Less Than Six Years," ISNA (March 8, 2019). https://www.isna.ir/news/97121508157/۷-سال-۶-از-کمتر-در-استعفا.
11 "Ahmadinejad Said I Will Make Sure No One Can Govern This Country after Me," *Nameh News* (March 10, 2018). https://bit.ly/3httSAs.
12 "Ahmadinejad's Jewish Family," Radio RFE/RL (January 29, 2009). https://www.rferl.org/a/Were_Ahmadinejads_Ancestors_Jews_/1375318.html.
13 "Ahmadinejad Was Both Strange and a Fraud," *Khabar Online* (March 10, 2018). https://bit.ly/3hlAml2.
14 M. Boroujerdi, "Javad Zarif Returns—to a Foreign Ministry Still Out in the Cold," *Foreign Affairs* (March 6, 2019).
15 "Ahmadinejad Ignored Supreme Leader's Strategic Views," *Eghtesadnews* (March 18, 2018). https://bit.ly/2Zy9hoC.
16 "Kharazi: Ahmadinejad ignored advice coming from the Office of the Supreme Leader," *Jamaran* (March 18, 2018). https://bit.ly/3kqIPFF.
17 M. Ahmadinejad, "Address to the United Nations General Assembly" (September 14, 2005), United Nations Headquarters, New York.
18 "30 Years at the UN," *BBC Persian* (September 23, 2009). https://www.bbc.com/persian/iran/2009/09/090923_mg_iran_un_ahmadinejad_. See also "Did Hashemi Rafsanjani Go to New York?" Tasnim (September 27, 2016). https://bit.ly/2ZvuYp9.
19 N. Fathi, "Holocaust Deniers and Skeptics Gather in Iran," *New York Times* (December 11, 2006).
20 G. Bush and T. Blair, "Joint Press Conference on Global Diplomacy" (May 25, 2006), The White House, Washington, DC.
21 "Ahmadinejad at Columbia, Parries and Puzzles," *New York Times* (September 25, 2007).
22 "Ahmadinejad Cancels U.N. Trip amid Visa Spat," Reuters (March 23, 2007).
23 "Zarif: Ahmadinejad Firing Me Did Me the Biggest Favor in History," *Khabar Online* (December 6, 2015). https://bit.ly/2GXB0st.
24 "Zarif's Untold Tales about Ahmadinejad," *Eghtesad Online* (July 19, 2016). https://bit.ly/2ZwSJ0a.
25 A. Rahnema, *Superstition as Ideology in Iranian Politics: From Majlesi to Ahmadinejad* (Cambridge: Cambridge University Press, 2011), pp. 38–40.
26 J. Amuzegar, "Ahmadinejad's Legacy," *Middle East Policy Council*, 20(4) (2013). https://mepc.org/ahmadinejads-legacy.
27 Some of Rouhani's observations about nuclear negotiations with EU: H. Rouhani, "Beyond the Challenges Facing Iran and the IAEA Concerning the Nuclear Dossier," Speech to the Supreme Cultural Revolution Council (September 30, 2005). Available at: http://www.armscontrolwonk.com/files/2012/08/Rahbord.pdf.
28 "Ahmadinejad: World Leaders Expected Me to Manage World Affairs," Fararu (May 19, 2013). https://bit.ly/35zAwTM.
29 A. Ganji, "The Latter-Day Sultan: Power and Politics in Iran," *Foreign Affairs* (November/December 2008).

30 Capital Flight Alarming, Financial Tribune (June 13, 2018). See also H. Zobeiri, N. Akbarpour Roshan, and M. Shahrazi, "Capital Flight and Economic Growth in Iran," *International Economic Studies*, 45(2) (2015): 16.
31 R. Mostafavi, "Ahmadinejad Calls Sanctions Against Iran Pathetic," Reuters (July 3 2010).
32 "Concern Over Human Capital Flight," Financial Tribune (November 27, 2005). See also P. Azadi, M. Mirramezani, and M. Mesgaran, "Migration and Brain Drain from Iran," Stanford Iran (2040 Project). Working paper No. 9, April 2020.
33 "Accounts of Private Meetings between Khamenei and Rafsanjani during Ahmadinejad's Presidency," *BBC Persian* (January 17, 2017). https://www.bbc.com/persian/iran-features-38590538.
34 H. Rohani, "Beyond the Challenges Facing Iran and the IAEA Concerning the Nuclear Dossier," Speech to the Supreme Cultural Revolution Council (September 30, 2005).
35 "The Letter That Led to the Release of the British Sailors," *Asr Iran* (June 5, 2009). https://bit.ly/35xNlxO.
36 Mousavian and Shahidsaless, *Iran and the United States*, p. 210.
37 There were others arrested, including Ramin Jahanbegloo, Haleh Esfandiari, and Kian Tajbahsh. See N. Fathi, "Iran Puts Detained Scholars before TV," *New York Times* (July 17, 2007).
38 F. Arghanani Pirsalami, "Third Worldism and Ahmadinejad's Foreign Policy," *Iranian Review of Foreign Affairs*, 4(2) (Summer 2013): 81–109 (93).
39 A. Vatanka, "Iran's Awkward Diplomacy in Africa," National Interest (March 23, 2016).
40 J. Amuzegar, "Ahmadinejad's Legacy," *Middle East Policy Council*, 20(4) (2013).
41 A. Vatanka, "Iran Abroad," *Journal of Democracy*, 26(2) (April 2015): 61–70.
42 N. Habibi, *Economic Legacy of Mahmud Ahmadinejad* (Brandeis University: Crown Center for Middle East Studies, 2014).
43 "Ahmadinejad: 'Mottaki Was Not My Minister,'" *Shargh* (June 28, 2015). https://www.magiran.com/article/3182366.
44 "Political Climate Changes for Ahmadinejad," *Irish Times* (January 16, 2007). See also S. Maloney, *Iran's Political Economy since the Revolution* (Cambridge: Cambridge University Press, 2015).
45 "Accounts of private meetings between Khamenei and Rafsanjani during Ahmadinejad's presidency," *BBC Persian* (January 17, 2017).
46 "Ahmadinejad Said the Americans Had Attacked Baghdad to Prevent the Return of the Messiah," *Tabnak* (April 2, 2018). https://bit.ly/2ZBhUPn.
47 N. Fathi, "In Iran, Debate over an Article of Faith," *New York Times* (April 18, 2008).
48 T. Parsi, *Losing an Enemy: Obama, Iran, And the Triumph of diplomacy* (London: Yale University Press, 2017), p. 70.
49 "Dear Iranian Supreme Leader Ali Khamenei," Radio RFE/RL (November 7, 2014). https://www.rferl.org/a/persian-letters-iran-obama-khamenei-letters/26680116.html.
50 D. Ignatius, "The Omani 'Back Channel' to Iran and the Secrecy Surrounding the Nuclear Deal," *Washington Post* (June 7, 2016).
51 "The Controversial Statements of the [Presidential] Debate," *BBC Persian* (April 27, 2017). https://www.bbc.com/persian/iran-39735650.
52 "The Hashemis, the News-Making Family," *BBC Persian* (January 9, 2017). https://www.bbc.com/persian/iran-features-38554564.

53 A. Ganji, "Rafsanjani and Khamenei: The Ahmadinejad Years," Al Jazeera (September 25, 2013).
54 A. Khamenei, "Friday Prayers in Iran" (June 19, 2009), Tehran University, Tehran. https://www.c-span.org/video/?287161-1/ayatollah-khamenei-friday-prayers-iran.
55 G. Esfandiari, "All Eyes on Friday Prayers in Iran," Radio RFE/RL (July 16, 2009).
56 "Rafsanjani: Those Arrested in the Protests Need to Be Released," *BBC Persian* (June 17, 2009). https://www.bbc.com/persian/iran/2009/07/090717_ra_ rafsanjani_fridayprayer.
57 "A Letter for History That Is Worth Reading after 8 Years," Kaleme (June 11, 2017). https://www.kaleme.com/1396/03/21/klm-260484/?theme=fast.
58 G. Esfandiari, "Hard-Liners Attack Rafsanjani's Daughter, As He Faces Pressure," Radio RFE/RL (February 27, 2011).
59 S. Alavi, "Secret Speeches Suggest IRGC Rigged 2009 Election," *Iran Wire* (June 12, 2019). Also "The knife Cut the Hand: Ahmadinejad Complains about Revolutionary Guard Interference in Elections," Kaleme (April 3, 2017).
60 "Ahmadinejad and Mashaei Are after Neutralizing Rafsanjani," Deutsche Welle (February 20, 2011). https://www.dw.com/fa-ir/احمدی‌نژاد-و-مشایی-دنبال-حذف-رفسنجانی-هستند/a-6444866.
61 "Ahmadinejad's Trip to New York," *BBC Persian* (September 20, 2011). https://www.bbc.com/persian/iran/2011/09/110920_l33_ahmadinejad_un_newyork_trip_analysis.
62 A. Milani, "Is Ahmadinejad Islamic Enough for Iran," *Foreign Policy* (April 29, 2011).
63 "Ayatollah Khamenei Did Not Shout "Ya Ali at Birth,' " *Tabnak* (August 9, 2012). https://www.tabnak.ir/fa/news/264147/آیت-الله-خامنه-ای-هنگام-تولد-یا-علی-نگفت.
64 A. Ganji, "Meet Ahmadinejad's Chosen Successor," *Foreign Affairs* (April 30, 2013).
65 This was done through a "*hokm hokomati*" (ruling by dominion).
66 "Top Adviser Highlights Deadlock between Khamenei and Ahmadinejad," Radio Farda (March 30, 2018).
67 "Presidential or Parliamentary System?" *Javan Online* (January 7, 2019). https://bit.ly/2GP1f46.
68 "The Knife Cut the Hand: Ahmadinejad Complains about Revolutionary Guard Interference in Elections," Kaleme (April 3, 2017).

10 (2013–Present)—The Coming of President Hassan Rouhani

1 "Brother of Ayatollah Khamenei Calls Rafsanjani an American Agent," Radio Farda (May 4, 2013). https://www.radiofarda.com/a/f9_iranian_supreme_leader_brother_criticzed_hashemi_rafsanjani/24976469.html.
2 "Lawyer of Hashemi Family Claim Ahmadinejad Wanted to Eavesdrop on Him," *Nameh News* (January 8, 2018). https://bit.ly/2FtRYOy.
3 "Rafsanjani: Smells Like a Conspiracy," *BBC Persian* (January 26, 2010). https://www.bbc.com/persian/iran/2010/01/100126_l38_hashemi_yazdi.
4 M. Milani, "Why the Islamic Republic Disqualified One of Its Founding Fathers from Running for President," *The Atlantic* (June 7, 2013). https://www.theatlantic.com/international/archive/2013/06/why-the-islamic-republic-disqualified-one-of-its-founding-fathers-from-running-for-president/276671/. See also M. Tamadonfar,

Islamic Law and Governance in Contemporary Iran: Transcending Islam for Social, Economic, and Political Order (Washington, DC: Lexington Books, 2015), p. 256.

5 "Domestic and Foreign Reflections on Rafsanjani's Statements about Syria," Deutsche Welle (September 7, 2013). https://www.dw.com/fa-ir/سوریه-مورد-در-رفسنجانی-سخنان-خارجی-و-داخلی-بازتاب/a-17073040.

6 The nominee was Hamid Aboutalebi.

7 A. Vatanka, "Pulling the Strings: How Khamenei Will Prevent Reform in Iran," *Foreign Affairs* (November 25, 2015). https://www.foreignaffairs.com/articles/iran/2015-11-25/pulling-strings.

8 A. Detsch, "The Brain Trust Behind Iran's New President," *The Diplomat* (August 3, 2013). https://thediplomat.com/2013/08/the-brain-trust-behind-irans-new-president/.

9 S. Hunter, "Three New Trends in Iran's Politics," *Cairo Review of Global Affairs* (May 31, 2017). https://www.thecairoreview.com/tahrir-forum/three-new-trends-in-irans-politics/.

10 K. Ziabari, "Don't Fall for Mahmoud Ahmadinejad's Twitter Public Relations Campaign," Lobe Log (November 11, 2019). https://lobelog.com/dont-fall-for-mahmoud-ahmadinejads-twitter-public-relations-campaign/. For more see M. Warnaar, *Iranian Foreign Policy During Ahmadinejad: Ideology and Actions* (London: Palgrave Macmillan, 2013).

11 "Rouhani: After Barjam (JCPOA), Rafsanjani Told Me He Can Now Die in Peace," *Nameh News* (January 10, 2019). https://bit.ly/3hsz1ZB.

12 R. Brown, "Rouhani: The Republic's Repairman (2013–2021)," Iran Wire (May 20, 2017). See also S. Randjbar-Daemi, *The Quest for Authority in Iran: A History of the Presidency from Revolution to Rouhani* (London: I.B. Tauris, 2017), pp. 238–64.

13 "Rafsanjani: I Asked Imam [Khomeini] to Resolve the American Issue While He Lived." BBC Persian (April 3, 2012). https://www.bbc.com/persian/iran/2012/04/120403_l39_rafsanjani_iran-us_relations.

14 A. Ganji, "Rafsanjani and Khamenei: The Rouhani Element," Al Jazeera (September 27, 2013).

15 J. Ershadi, "Understanding Iran: Reading the Shahnameh in New York," *The Federalist* (December 18, 2013).

16 "Who Gave You Arms, Friday Prayers and Seda va Sima [National Television]?" Balatarin (February 3, 2016). https://www.balatarin.com/permlink/2016/2/3/4089431.

17 "I Told the Imam [Khomeini] to Put Us on Trial and Execute Us," BBC Persian (January 10, 2017). https://www.bbc.com/persian/iran-38568792.

18 "Faezeh Hashemi Rafsanjani in Exclusive Interview Says Iran Authorities Want to Silence Her," Euronews (October 2, 2018). https://per.euronews.com/2018/10/02/faezeh-hashemi-rafsanjani-in-exclusive-interview-says-iran-authorities-want-to-silence-her. See also "Rafsanjani's Daughter Says His 'Mysterious' Death Unresolved," Radio Farda (January 2, 2019). https://en.radiofarda.com/a/iran-rafsanjani-daughter-says-his-deat-unresolved/29688295.html.

19 "Fatemeh Hashemi: After My Father's Death They Quickly Emptied His Safe," *Nameh News* (October 5, 2017), https://bit.ly/3b2VCcr. Also: "Where Is the Will of Rafsanjani?" *Tabnak* (November 16, 2017). https://bit.ly/3iuViHz.

20 "Hashemi Family: 'A Will Exists; We Don't Know Where It Is'," BBC Persian (November 16, 2017).

21 "Faezeh Hashemi Reveals Five Family Members Are Banned from Travel," BBC Persian (September 23, 2017). https://www.bbc.com/persian/iran-42010411.

22 "Daughters of Hashemi Are Afraid of Historical Truths Coming to Light," *Tasnim* (August 4, 2016). https://www.tasnimnews.com/fa/news/1395/05/14/1148567/-دختران-هاشمی-رفسنجانی-از-افشای-کدام-واقعیت-تاریخی-واهمه-دارند-تصاویر-و-سند.

23 "The Last Speech of Rafsanjani about the Oppression of Amir Kabir," YouTube (January 8, 2017). https://www.youtube.com/watch?v=PKVveIuy1Zk.

24 "Hashemi Rafsanjani and Amir Kabir," Tribune Zamaneh (April 20, 2017). https://www.tribunezamaneh.com/archives/120292.

25 "Why Did Khamenei Have to Adjust His 'Armed to Act' Order?" Deutsche Welle (June 26, 2017). https://www.dw.com/fa-ir/چرا-فرمان-آتش-به-اختیار-تعدیل-شد/a-39421873.

26 M. Ataie, "Iran Supports Assad (But Not at Any Cost)," *Foreign Policy* (November 9, 2011).

27 A. Vatanka, "Iran's Islamic State Problem Is Not Going Away," *Foreign Policy* (June 19, 2017).

28 "Patrick Kennedy's Ties to Iranian Exile Groups Becomes Campaign Issue in South Jersey," *Politico* (June 10, 2020). https://www.politico.com/states/new-jersey/story/2020/06/10/patrick-kennedys-ties-to-iranian-exile-group-becomes-campaign-issue-in-south-jersey-1292255.

29 "Rouhani Holds Some Resentment for Ayatollah Rafsanjani," *Farda News* (October 17, 2017). https://bit.ly/3mfN20l.

30 "Has Rouhani Changed?" Radio Farda (October 27, 2017). https://www.radiofarda.com/a/has-rouhai-changed/28818941.html.

31 "Rouhani: The Americans Asked to Meet Me for at Least 23 Times," Salameno (July 27, 2020). https://www.salameno.com/news/55160568/روحانی-23-بار-درخواست-ملاقات-از-آمریکایی-ها-دریافت-کردم.

Epilogue

1 Ayatollah Ali Khamenei, p. 123.
2 A. Vatanka, "Iran's IRGC Has Long Kept Khamenei in Power," *Foreign Policy* (October 29, 2019).
3 A. Khamenei, "Friday Prayer Sermon: Our Islamic Power Will Overcome the Superficial Grandeur of Material and Corrupt Powers" (January 17, 2020), https://english.khamenei.ir/news/7318/Our-Islamic-power-will-overcome-the-superficial-grandeur-of-material.

Select Bibliography

Abrahamian, E. (2008), *A History of Modern Iran*, Cambridge: Cambridge University Press.

Alfoneh, A. (2013), *Iran Unveiled: How the Revolutionary Guards Is Turning Theocracy into Military Dictatorship*, Washington, DC: AEI Press.

Arjomand, S. A. (1989), *The Turban for the Crown: The Islamic Revolution in Iran*, Oxford: Oxford University Press.

Bakhash, S. (1986), *The Reign of the Ayatollahs: Iran and the Islamic Revolution*, New York: Basic Books.

Baktiari, B. (1996), *Parliamentary Politics in Revolutionary Iran*, Gainesville: University Press of Florida.

Byrne, M. (2014), *Iran Contra: Reagan's Scandal and the Unchecked Abuse of Presidential Power*, Lawrence: University Press of Kansas.

Calvert, J. (2010), *Sayyid Qutb and the Origins of Radical Islamism*, New York: Columbia University Press.

Crist, D. (2013), *The Twilight War*, London: Penguin Books.

Esfandiary, H. (1997), *Reconstructed Lives: Women and Iran's Islamic Revolution*, Washington, DC: Woodrow Wilson Center Press.

Gheissari, A., and Vali Nasr (2009), *Democracy in Iran: History and the Quest for Liberty*, Oxford: Oxford University Press, p. 84.

Hovsepian-Bearce, Y. (2015), *The Political Ideology of Ayatollah Khamenei*, New York: Routledge.

Huyser, R. E. (1986), *Mission to Tehran*, New York: Harper and Row.

Maloney, S. (2015), *Iran's Political Economy since the Revolution*, Cambridge: Cambridge University Press.

Parsons, Anthony (1984), *The Pride and the Fall*, London: Jonathan Cape.

Pollack, K. (2005), *The Persian Puzzle: The Conflict between Iran and America*, New York: Random House.

Randjbar-Daemi, S. (2017), *The Quest for Authority in Iran: A History of the Presidency from Revolution to Rouhani*, London: I.B. Tauris.

Ranstorp, M. (1997), *Hizb'Allah in Lebanon: The Politics of the Western Hostage Crisis*, London: Palgrave.

Sick, G. (1991), *October Surprise*, London: I.B. Tauris.

Sullivan, W. H. (1981), *Mission to Iran*, New York: W. W. Norton.

Summitt, A. R. (2004), 'For a White Revolution: John F. Kennedy and the Shah of Iran', *Middle East Journal*, 58 (4): 560–75.

Wastnidge, E. (2016), *Diplomacy and Reform in Iran: Foreign Policy under Khatami*, London: I.B. Tauris.

Index

Abdullah, Crown Prince (of Saudi Arabia) 137
Aboutalebi, Hamid 176, 226
Abrams, Elliot 74
Afghanistan 74, 92, 113
   Soviet invasion of in 1979 37, 65
   Taliban 97, 104, 135, 139–42
   US invasion of in 2001 143–4, 147
Africa 90, 156, 168, 224
   Ahmadinejad overtures toward 162
African Union 162
Aghazadeh, Gholam Reza 110
Ahmadinejad, Mahmoud 27, 53, 148, 174–81, 188, 198, 200, 222–6
   anti-clerical 169–73
   foreign policy 154–65
   Khamenei's support for 152–4, 169
   looking to China, Russia 162–4
   Mayor of Tehran 149
   presidency 151–76
   relations with Rafsanjani 154–5, 167–9
   relations with Rouhani 158
Akhoundi, Abbas 187
Alavi, Mahmoud 193
Alavi school 15–6
Albania 190
Albright, Madeline 111
   speech at Asia Society 140–1
   urging Iran to look for normalization 135–6, 137
Algeria 2, 91, 135
   US-Iran talks in 27
Allah 10, 44, 49, 65, 82, 164, 169
Al-Maliki, Nouri 175
Al-Mughassil, Ahmed 110
Al-Nimr, Nimr 178
Al-Saud Faisal 56–7
Al-Saud Nayyef 110
Allen, Charlie xiv
Alpher, Yossi 3, 205
American Islam 152, 173

American Israel Public Affairs Committee (AIPAC) 192
Ames, Bob 26
Amir Kabir 103, 186
Anderson, Terry 93
Ansar-e Hezbollah 138
anti-Americanism xvi, 6, 11, 26, 36, 47, 85, 91, 102, 135, 179, 183, 202–3
Arab states xvii, 90, 137, 178, 180, 192
Arab World 41, 55, 90, 137, 189–90
   Arab Spring 168–9, 170, 180
Arabian Peninsula 78
Arafat, Yasser 39, 94, 143
Arak 146
Araqi, Mehdi (Haj) 2
Ardebili, Abdul-Karim Mousavi 17, 86
Armenia 96
Artesh (Regular Iranian army) 4, 39, 44, 52, 107
Asadi, Houshang 9
Ash-Shiraa 66, 70–1, 213
Asharq Al-Awsat 137
Asia Society 140
Assad, Bashar 142, 175, 181–2, 189
Assad, Hafez 58, 70, 90
Austria 186
Axis of Evil 143–4, 148, 153
Azari Qomi, Ahmad 84
Azerbaijan 9, 37, 96, 104
   Azerbaijani faction in Tehran 72
   Azerbaijani dissidents 37

B_Team 192
Baazar 50, 66
Badr Corp (of Shia Iraqis) 55, 148
Bahai 155
Bahoonar, Mohammad 17, 45–6
Bahramani, Ali 68–9
Bakhtiar, Shapour 95, 110
   as prime minister 3–5, 13, 15
Baku 104

Bam 147
Bani Sadr, Abol-Hassan 6, 14, 50, 153, 167
  in opposition to Khomeini 52, 56
  as president 34–46
Barzegar, Kayhan 177
Bayt (Household of Khamenei) 154
Bazargan, Mehdi 41, 51, 101
  as head of provisional government 13–14, 19, 22, 25–8, 33
Behesht-e Zahra (cemetery) Khomeini's speech 12
Beheshti, Mohammad 15, 17–20, 22–9, 33,4, 36, 38, 43–6
Beirut 26, 69, 71
Biden, Joe 202–3
Blair, Tony 161
Bloody November 2019 193
Blunt, Roy 190
Boeing 1, 45
  sales of aircraft 177, 187
Bolivia 142, 162
Bolton, John 191–2, 194
Bollinger, Lee 158
Bonn Declaration (on Afghanistan) 143
Bonyads (Charitable foundations) 88
Boroujerdi, Grand Ayatollah 8
Bosnia 95
Bosniaks 95
Bouazizi, Mohamed 168
Brazil 162
Britain 2, 3, 31, 45, 79, 91, 103, 110, 117, 138, 160–1
  arrest of British sailors by Iran 160
  role in 1953 coup in Iran 7
British Broadcasting Corporation (BBC) 82, 132
Brzezinski, Zbigniew 3, 27, 29
Burns, Nicholas 111
Bush George H. 42, 76, 95, 108–9, 182
  initial hopes for dialogue with Iran 91–2
Bush, George W. 141, 157, 161
  policy toward Iran 143–8

C-130 aircraft 147
Camp David agreement 58
Canadians 201
Carter, Jimmy 1, 3, 22, 165
  seize of US embassy in Tehran 25–8, 36–7, 42

Casablanca (Organization of Islamic Conference summit) 105
Casey, William 42, 65
Caspian Sea 23, 93, 97, 104
Castro, Fidel 143
Caucasus 96, 111
Center for Strategic Research (CSR) 177
Central Asia 96–7
Central Intelligence Agency (CIA) xiv, 3, 7, 28, 35, 37–8, 42–3, 52, 59, 65–7, 70, 72, 74, 84, 91, 145–6, 176, 193
Central Bank of Iran 35
Chamran, Mostafa 39
Chain Murders (of political dissidents) 199
Chavez, Hugo 142, 162
Chechnya 111
China 10, 58, 63, 83, 89–90, 111, 156, 162–3, 176, 181–2
  China model 100, 106
  Chinese Communist Party 100
Christian-Muslim relations 137
Christopher, Warren 103
Clinton, Bill 103, 108–9
  administration's policies on Iran 134–5, 138, 140, 141, 145
Clinton, Hillary 182
Clinton Foundation 182
CNN (Cable News Network) 134
Cold War 25, 30, 37, 58, 65, 91
  end of Cold War 99–101, 103, 105, 108, 109
Colombia University 157
Communists (Iranian) 6, 11, 28, 52, 65
Conoco 108, 177
constitution 5, 26, 30, 34, 39, 51, 73, 87, 112, 114–15, 131, 183, 200
  earliest post-1979 debates on 19–23
  1906 constitutional revolution 20, 155
  1989 constitution 49, 86
Contras (of Nicaragua) 69
Cornyn, John 190
Council of the Revolution 12–15, 17–24, 29–30, 33–4, 38, 88, 101
  creation of 5–6
Crist, David 69
Crocker, Ryan 144
Cuba 143

Index

Damad, Mohammad 7
Defense Council 54
Dehghan, Hossein 171
Delhi 109–10
Deir Ezzor 189
Democratic Party (of the United States) 109, 182, 190
Deng, Xiaoping 100
Diaspora, Iranian xv, xviii, 52, 101, 193
Doaei, Mahmoud 40
Dobbins, James 143
Dole, Elizabeth 147
Dr. Sapir (Jewish) Hospital 176
Dual Containment Policy (of Bill Clinton against Iran and Iraq) 108
Dubai 105
Duke, David 157
Dzhagaryan, Levan 182

"East and South" (foreign policy priority) 162
economic self-sufficiency 179
Egypt 1–2, 4, 36, 39, 135, 137, 154, 168
Eisenhower, Dwight 26
Ejei, Gholam-Hossein 170
El-Baradei, Mohammad 161
Emami, Saeed 136
Emigration from Iran xv, 63
Enqelab Eslami (Islamic Revolution) newspaper 38
Entezam, Abbas Amir 28
Ershad (Islamic center in Tehran) 20
Esfahan 18
Esfandiari, Haleh 161
European Community/European Union 42, 111, 117
Evin Prison 46
Expediency Council 118, 133, 142, 160, 164

F-4 fighter jets (Sold to Iran) 40, 64
F-14 fighter jets (Sold to Iran) 30, 64, 67
Fallahian, Ali 101, 105, 117
Farhang, Mansour 36
Farrokhzad, Forough 33
Faw Peninsula 75
Fedayeen Islam (Devotees of Islam) 16, 137
Flynn, Michael 185, 187
Foreign Direct Investment (FDI) 192
Forouhar, Dariush 136

Forward Defense (military doctrine) 201
Foundation of the Oppressed and Disabled (*See also* "Bonyads") 185
France 6, 13, 15, 21, 46, 62–3, 136–7, 163, 167, 176
  air France flight from Paris to Tehran 5
  assassination of Iranian exiles in 110
Friday Prayers 89, 183
Friedman, Thomas 140–1
Furqan (Islamist militant group) 28, 44

Gambia 162
Gast, Philip 25
Gazprom 135
German Red Army 2
Germany 8, 18, 42, 63, 117, 130, 144, 146, 176
  German trade with Iran 15, 111
Ghaddar, Fariborz 14–15
Ghodousi, Javad Karimi 193
Ghotbzadeh, Sadeq 5–6
Giuliani, Rudy 190
Glasnost 140
Gol Agha (magazine) 100
Goldstein, Baruch 104
Gorbachev, Mikhail 78, 91, 104, 140–1, 148
Graham, Katharine 4
Grand Bargain (Offer from Iran to US) 146–7, 153, 202
Greece 117
Green opposition movement
  Rafsanjani support for 173–4, 198, 200
  the rise of 165–8
Guardian Council xix, 112
  creation of 88–90
  Khamenei control of 164, 174, 184, 194
  opposition to 131, 148
Gulf States (of the Persian Gulf) xvii, 75, 97, 137–8, 178, 180, 182, 192
Gulf Cooperation Council (GCC) *See* Gulf States (of the Persian Gulf)

Habibi, Hassan 5, 34, 133
Hafez (poet) 10
Hakemiyat (ruling class in Islamic Republic) 115
Hamas 108, 179, 187
Hamburg
  Islamic Center 130

Hamdoon, Nizar 64
Hamshahri (newspaper) 114
Hashemi, Mehdi 71–2
Hashemi Rafsanjani, Akbar *See* Rafsanjani
Hekmatyar, Gulbuddin 144
"Heroic flexibility" (Stance of Khamenei) 180
Hezbollah (of Lebanon)
  Iranian support for 54–6, 108–9, 142, 146, 179, 181, 187, 200
  role in hostage-taking 69, 71, 95
Hidden Imam
  Ahmadinejad's stance on 158, 164, 169
Hofi, Yitzhak 4
Holocaust 156–7
House of Saud 57, 78
Houthis (of Yemen) 200
human rights 132, 137
Hussein, Saddam 2–3, 23, 52–4, 57, 58, 87, 90, 108, 148, 199
  clashing with Khomeini 39–41, 62
  invasion of Kuwait 94
  Iran-Iraq war 75–7, 79
Huyser, Robert E. 3–4

Imam Reza Shrine 188
International Atomic Energy Agency (IAEA) 156, 161
International Monetary Fund (IMF) 35, 163
India 90, 110
Indyk, Martin 108
Iran
  foreign relations in immediate post-revolution period 41–3
  Trump's "maximum pressure" campaign 187–94
Iran Air flight 655 75–6
Iran Ajr 77
Iran International (television) 190
Iraq
  Chemical attacks on Iran 76
  Invasion of Iran 40
  Khomeini incitement of Iraq Shia 39–40
Iran-Iraq War 77, 89
Iran Sanctions Act (ISA) 108
IRGC *See* Islamic Revolution Guards Corps
Islam xiv, xvi, xx, 10–11, 13, 16–17, 19–20, 22, 38, 41, 46, 51, 56, 78, 82–4, 94, 102, 104, 137, 140, 143, 152, 164, 169, 170, 173–4, 177
  Shia clergy 8, 12, 61–2, 64–5
Islamic Jihad 108
Islamic Republican Party (IRP) xv, 19, 45, 71, 73, 112
Islamic Revolution Guards Corps (IRGC) (Also referred to as Revolutionary Guards) xvii, 5, 19, 75, 34, 52, 69, 71, 75, 95, 100
  in conflict with US 148–9, 175–7, 183
  performance during Iran-Iraq war 79, 81–2
  as political players 139–41, 152–5, 160, 161–71, 188–91, 199–203
  as protectors of the political system xviii, 19, 23, 30–1, 38–9, 41, 86–8, 105–7, 112–13, 129–31, 143–4, 197
  relations with Bani Sadr 43–6
  support for Hezbollah 54–5, 58
Islamic State of Iraq and Syria (ISIS) 182, 189, 197
Israel xvii, 2, 10–11, 57, 64, 78, 93–5, 104–5, 108–9, 135, 138, 142, 156–7, 170, 174–6, 182, 192–4
  invasion of Lebanon 54–5,
  Karin a incident 144–6
  Khomeinists cut diplomatic relations with 39, 49, 58
  role in Iran Contra Affair 66–70

Jafari, Mohammad Ali 169, 178, 190
Jamaran (Khomeini's residence) 88
Japan 8, 58, 74, 91, 96
Jannati, Ahmad 95
Jerusalem xvii, 41, 55, 57, 64
  army of Jerusalem 58
Jews 11, 138
  American Jews 140
  Jewish Community Center in Buenos Aires 95
Johns Hopkins University 103
Jordan 39, 64
Jomhuri-ye Eslami (Islamic Republic) (Newspaper) 19

Karin A 145
Kangarloo, Mohsen 68–9
Karachi 56

Karbala 41
Karbaschi, Gholam-hossein 114, 131
Kargozaran-e Sazandegi (the Executives of the Construction) 112
Karroubi, Hassan 42
Karroubi, Mehdi 42, 152–3, 166, 168
Karzai, Hamid 144
Kashani, Abol-Qasem 26
Kashani, Mohammad Emami 174
Kasravi, Ahmad 16
Kayhan (newspaper) 39, 131, 176
Kennedy, John 8
KGB 11
Khalkhali, Sadeq 102
Khamenei, Ali 16–20, 22–6, 33–6, 38–40, 64, 79–80, 129–49, 151–5, 157–161, 163–71, 197–203
   childhood 9–10
   contentious relations with Rouhani 173–95
   first time meeting Rafsanjani 8
   interest in Russian literature 11
   Khamenei relations with Rafsanjani xiii–1, 8–13, 28–9, 31, 45–9, 49–59, 61–2
   speech at the UN 77–8
   succession to power 83–97
   views on the United States 68–70, 72–4, 99–118
Khamenei, Dadri 46
Khamenei, Hadi 94, 136
Khamenei, Mohammad 68
Khamenei, Mojtaba 87, 132, 152, 199
Khan, Reza (Reza Pahlavi) 3
Kharrazi, Kamal 89, 133–4, 136, 146, 155
Kharrazi, Sadeq 163
Khatam ol-Anbia (Seal of the Prophets) 79, 107
Khatami, Mohammad xix, 8, 152–7, 161–2, 165–6, 170, 173, 178, 181, 186, 191, 197, 200
   dialogue among civilizations 115, 132, 137–8
   election to presidency 114–16, 129–49
Khazali, Mehdi 155
Khobar Towers 109–10
Khoeiniha, Mohammad Mousavi 28, 41, 57
Khomeini, Ahmad 14, 28, 35, 44, 47, 61, 66, 76, 78
   cooperation with Rafsanjani 71–2, 74, 81–7
   death of 116
Khomeini, Hassan 184, 186
Khomeini, Ruhollah xv–xix
   flight from Paris to Tehran 5–7
   foreign policy concerns 54–9
   Iran-Iraq war 61–72, 75, 79
   return to Iran and seizing power 8–9, 11–31, 33–47, 49–52
   stance toward the Americans 28–33
Khorram-shahr
   liberation of 54
Kim Il-Sung 83
Kohl, Helmuth 117
Koubbeh Palace (In Cairo) 4
Ku Klux Klan 157
Kurdish dissidents 37, 95, 117
Kuwait 55, 56, 75
   invasion of by Iraq 94, 97

Lahouti, Hassan 46
Larijani, Ali 88, 158, 163
Larijani, Mohammad Ardeshir 61
Latin America 9, 162
Lebanon 39, 54–5, 58, 67, 74, 99, 108–9, 142, 181, 187, 200
   American hostages in 69–71, 92–3, 95
Lenin, Vladimir 6
liberals 107, 133
   falling out with Khomeinists 28–9, 41
Libya 90–1, 112, 134, 143
   as an ally of Khomeinists 58, 63
Limbert, John 29, 36

McCain, John 191
McMaster, H.R. 191
Madani, Ahmad (presidential candidate) 42
Madrid 42
Majles (parliament) 50, 56, 71, 75, 90, 164, 193, 200
   elections of 2000 141, 154
   ISIS attack on 189
   Rafsanjani control of 51, 73, 114
Mahsouli, Sadeq 153, 166
Makhbalbaf, Mohsen 137
Mansour, Hassan Ali (prime minister) 36, 95

Marble Palace (in Tehran) 133
Marashi, Effat (Rafsanjani's wife) 166
Marashi, Hossein 168
Marxism 10, 78
Mashaei, Esfandiar Rahim 170-1
Mashhad xx, 11, 15, 20, 100
  Khamenei's hometown 8-9
  role in the revolution 18
Mazari Sharif 141
McFarlane, Robert 74, 135
  visit to Tehran 67-72
Mecca 28, 57, 78
MEK *See* Mujahedeen-e Khalq
Mekhubad, Feyzollah 104
MI6 3
Meshkini, Ali 71-2, 164
Metrinko, Michael 24, 29
Ministry of Culture (of Iran) 89
Ministry of Foreign Affairs (of Iran) 177, 52, 140, 147, 157, 160, 176-7, 190
  purge of 55-6
Ministry of Intelligence (of Iran) 89, 105, 132, 136, 177
  Monitoring Rafsanjani 173
Moezzi, Behzad 45
Mofaz, Shaul 156
Mohajerani, Ataollah 112
Moinfar, Ali Akbar 31, 51
Montazeri, Hossein-Ali 36, 61-2
  as deputy supreme leader 26, 70-2
  removal from deputy supreme leadership 81-5, 131
Montazeri, Mohammad 70
Morales, Eva 142, 162
Morocco 135
Mosharekat *(Participation)* (reformist newspaper) 131
Mossad 3, 138, 146, 176, 193
Mossadeq, Mohammad 2
Mostafavi, Zahra 84
Motahari, Morteza 15
Motalefeh 106-7, 113
Mottaki, Manouchehr 163
Mousavian, Hossein 146, 161
Mousavi, Mir Hossein 56-8, 63, 66-8, 73, 83, 114
  as prime minister 50, 165
  relations with Khamenei 58, 73, 86, 74
Moussawi, Abbas 95

Mozambique 90
Mujahedeen-e Khalq (MEK) 23, 26, 44-6, 52, 145-6, 190
Mykonos (restaurant in Berlin) 95, 117

Najd 78
Najaf 9, 14, 18-19, 39, 151
Natanz 146, 193,
Nateq-Nouri, Ali Akbar 103, 112-15, 129, 170
National Council of Resistance 45
Neauphle-le-Château 1-2
New York 77, 89, 135, 138, 156-8, 191
Nicaragua 69, 142
Nigeria 162
North Africa 90, 168
North Korea 63, 83, 90, 112, 144, 180
North, Oliver 69, 74
Norouz (Persian New Year) 169, 179
Nouri, Abdullah 145

Obama, Barack 162, 165, 176, 179-80, 182-3, 191-2
Office for Islamic Liberation Movements (OILM) 62
Office of the Supreme Leader *See* Supreme Leader.
  See also Khamenei
Olumi, Mehdi 24
Oman 165
Operation Eagle Claw 37
Operation Praying Mantis 75
Operation Staunch 67
Ortega, Daniel 142

Pahlavi, Mohammad Reza *See* Shah of Iran
Pahlavi, Reza *See* Reza Khan
Pakistan 15, 39, 55, 90, 168
Palestinians 54, 58, 94, 104, 108, 144, 145
Palestinian Liberation Organization (PLO) 2, 39, 54, 94, 143
Parliament (*See also* Majles) xv, xvii, 12, 21, 34-5, 38-9, 41-4, 47, 49, 50, 73-4, 89, 94, 102-3, 107, 112-13, 133, 142, 148, 160, 164, 166, 178, 194
Parsons, Anthony 31
Payam-e Azadi (Message of Freedom) (reformist newspaper) 131
Peacock Throne 4

Index   237

Perestroika 140
Persia 169, 186
Petronas 135
Philippines 55
Phoenix missiles 67
Picco, Giandomenico 138
Plasco (building in Tehran) 185
PLO *See* Palestinian Liberation
    Organization
Poindexter, John 74
Pollock, Kenneth 144
Pompeo, Mike 191–2
Pope John Paul II 137
Powell, Colin 144
Precht, Henry 29
Prophet Mohammad 1, 9, 56, 79, 84, 91
Prussia 186
Putin, Vladimir 125, 142, 170

Qaddafi, Muammar 143
Qarabaghi, Abbas 4
Qatar 75
Qom xx, 6–9, 16, 23, 36, 62, 136, 151,
    173
Qomi Tabatabaei, Hassan 62
Qutb, Sayyid 10, 20–1

Rafiqdoost, Mohsen 58
Rafsanjani, Akbar Hashemi xii xx, 24, 28,
    31, 129, 137, 139, 149, 160–1, 171
    Arab World 137
    attitude and relations with leftists 23–4
    attitude towards Ahmadinejad 154–5
    attitude towards the Revolutionary
        Guards 75
    competition for power with Bani Sadr
        33–6, 38–9, 41–7
    considering to extend his
        presidency 112–13
    early plans for Montazeri to succeed
        Khomeini 61–4
    fallout with European states 116–18
    the Green movement 165–9
    initial power-sharing with
        Khamenei 86–97
    as key member of Council of
        Revolution 18–20
    Khamenei's camp first attempts to go
        after Rafsanjani 105–8

Khamenei warning against Rafsanjani
    becoming supreme leader 184–6
as Khomeini's disciple 7–11, 13–17
looking to change foreign policy course
    as president 99–104; 109–12
not going to the United Nations 156
relations with the reform
    movement 130–3
relations with and support for Hassan
    Rouhani 173–7, 180
rivalry with Khamenei in the early
    1980s 49–59
role in ending Iran-Iraq war 74–80
role in Khatami's 1997 presidential
    win 113–16
role in making Khamenei supreme
    leader 81–6
role in what became the Iran Contra
    Affair 64–72
Rouhani and Rafsanjani's old
    network 191
run for parliament in 2000 141–4
run for presidency in 2005 151–3
trip to the United States 21
visit to Moscow in 1989 92
Washington's stance 72–4
Rafsanjani, Faezeh 113, 168, 186
Rafsanjani, Fatemeh 185
Rafsanjani, Mehdi 105
Rafsanjani, Mohammad Hashemi
    21, 85, 88
Rahbar (*See also* Supreme Leader) 21
Raisi, Ebrahim 187–8
Rajai, Mohammad Ali 35, 38, 43, 45–6
Rasputin 171
Reagan, Ronald 43, 56, 161, 182,
    Efforts to normalize relations with Iran
        66–72, 74–7, 81, 108–9
Red Brigades 2
Refah school 13, 15,
Referendum 84, 193
    of March 1979 22
    of July 1989 86
Reporters without Borders xviii
Republican Party (of the United States) 42,
    92–3, 108, 177, 182
Revolutionary Court 102
Revolutionary Guards (Formal name
    Islamic Revolution Guards Corps,

IRGC) *See* Islamic Revolution
  Guards Corps
Reyshahri, Mohammad 71–2, 82
Rezai, Mohsen 38–9, 41, 52, 71, 79, 88, 107
Rice, Condoleezza 146
Riyadh 57, 78, 109–10, 137, 178, 189
Romania 90
Roosevelt, Franklin 1
Rouhani, Hassan 12, 43, 52, 94, 112
  attitude towards the Revolutionary
    Guards 75
  attitude towards the United States 93
  Iran Contra Affair 67
  as Khamenei's representative at the
    Supreme National Security Council
    102, 139
  presidency xviii, 173–95
  relations with Ahmadinejad 158, 161
  relations with Rafsanjani 199–202
Rubin, Robert 109
Rushdie, Salman 61, 79, 91, 110–11, 117,
  134, 138, 156

Saad Abad Palace xiii, 184
Sadat, Anwar 2, 37, 137
Sadr, Mohammad 159
Safavi, Navab 16, 206
Safavi, Yahya (Rahim) 39, 53, 132, 183
Sahabi, Ezatollah 21, 101
Saqafi, Khadijeh (Khomeini's wife) 151
Sarshar, Behrooz 39
Satanic Verses 79
Saudi Arabia 28, 47, 55–7, 109–10, 137,
  182, 189, 192
  attack on Saudi embassy in Tehran 177
  clashes with Iranian pilgrims 78
  Saudi Hezbollah 109
SAVAK (Shah era intelligence service)
  10–11, 15, 31
Sazegara, Mohsen 4–5, 16
Serbs 95
Shah of Iran (Mohammad Reza Pahlavi)
  xiii, xv, xx, 72, 82, 88, 90, 93, 95, 102,
  106–7, 139–40, 153, 162, 169
  fall from power 1–21, 23, 25, 26, 27, 29,
    30–1, 33–41, 44, 52–55, 64–5, 70, 77
  Shah's stance on Israel 104
Shamkhani, Ali 144, 185
Shargh (newspaper) 184

Shariati, Ali 20
Shariatmadari, Kazem 22–3, 25
Shevardnadze, Edward 91
Shiraz 138
Sick, Gary 36
Sistani, Ali 23
Special Clerical Court 145
Sobeh Emrooz (Dawn) 131
Soleimani, Qassem 53, 107, 139, 143,
  188–9, 201–2
Solidarity Committee of Iranian
  Workers 64
South Pars (natural gas field) 110
Soviet Union 10–11, 58, 62–3, 65, 78, 91–2,
  96, 132, 140, 142
  invasion of Afghanistan 37
Statoil 105
Stemple, John 29
Strategic Council on Foreign Relations
  (SCFR) 155
Sullivan, William 3, 25–6, 208
Sunni 10, 39, 57, 78
Sunni jihadists 189
Supreme Leader xiii, xiv, xvii, xviii, xix,
  10–11, 15, 24, 26, 28
  conception of 19–22, 30, 34, 38, 54,
    81–9, 132, 136, 149, 188, 198
  restricting the president 200
Supreme National Security Council
  (SNSC) 93–4, 102, 139, 142, 158, 185
Sweden
  Swedish military mission to Iran 63

T-72 (Soviet) tanks 67
Taeb, Hossein 105, 132
Taleghani, Mahmoud 22–6, 46
Taliban 97, 104, 129, 135, 141, 143–5,
  148, 183
Technocrats 53, 107–8
Tehran xi, xiii, xv
  City Council 114
  Khomeini's return to 5–21
  Khomeini's house 52
Teicher, Howard 67
Tilis, Thom 190
Tillerson, Rex 191
Total (of France) 105, 108, 135
TOW missiles 67
Trump, Donald 182–3, 185, 187

"maximum pressure" against Iran
    189–94, 201–2
Tudeh (communist) party 52, 65
Turkey 39, 55, 104, 162
Turkmenistan 96
Twelver Shia Islam 170

Uganda 162
United Arab Emirates (UAE) 192
United Nations 89, 99, 110, 134–6, 138,
    141, 156–7, 160, 169, 176, 182, 191
    mediation to end hostage-crisis 36
    Security Council 147, 159, 162
    UN resolution 598 75–8, 80
United States (USA) 3, 7, 40–2, 45–7, 50
    assessments about post-Khomeini
        era 66–71
    Disaster Diplomacy 93–4
    National Intelligence Estimate 162
    seize of US embassy in Tehran in 1979
        xviii, 17–18, 21, 24–30, 33–7
    stance on Mohammad Khatami 134–41
    stance on Iran after 9/11 143–8
    Strategic Command 14
USS Vincennes 75
USA*Engage 108

Vance, Cyrus 25
Velayat-e Faqīlī (*See also* Supreme
    Leader) 21
Velayati, Ali Akbar 50, 52, 55, 58, 103,
    117, 163
    as Khamenei's foreign policy
        envoy 133–4

Venezuela 142, 162
Vienna 156
Vinogradov, Vladimir M. 24
Voice of America (VOA) 135

Wahhabism 78
War on Terror 143–4, 147
Weinberger, Casper 74
Western imperialism 133
World Bank 106
World Cup (in football/soccer) 136

Xi, Jinping 125

Yazdi, Ebrahim 21, 43
    in Paris 5–7, 14, 16, 25–6
Yazdi, Mohammad 138
Yeltsin, Boris 111, 141
    "Yeltsin List" 132
Yugoslavia 90

Zan (magazine) 113
Zangeneh, Bijan 187
Zarif, Javad 52, 77, 143, 146
    firing of by Ahmadinejad 158
    as Rouhani's foreign minister 176,
        180, 189–9
Zayed, Mohammad Bin 192
Zionists 61, 132

15th Khordad Foundation 117
90 Signatories 101
@realDonaldTrump 192

www.ingramcontent.com/pod-product-compliance
Lightning Source LLC
Chambersburg PA
CBHW050137240426
43673CB00043B/1700